SO-AHA-660

AREA OF GREATEST
NAZI OCCUPATION

Ob River

S.   S.   R.

• Sverdlovsk

Kuznetsk Basin

Omsk •   Novosibirsk •

• Kuibyshev   • Magnitogorsk

Aral
Sea   Lake Balkhash

Alma Ata •

spian
Sea   • Tashkent

aku   • Samarkand

No-shah

• Teheran   FRANK STOCKMAN

IRAN

THESE ARE
THE RUSSIANS

BY
RICHARD E. LAUTERBACH

HARPER & BROTHERS PUBLISHERS

NEW YORK and LONDON

To those in both countries who, in the interests of peace and prosperity, are working for better understanding and closer co-operation between the peoples of the U.S.A. and the U.S.S.R.

ACKNOWLEDGMENTS

My thanks to the editors of *Time* and *Life* for permission to draw on material cabled to them from Moscow; to Marshal Stalin and Eric A. Johnston, president of the U. S. Chamber of Commerce, for the permission and the invitation (respectively) to accompany Mr. Johnston on his tour of the Urals, Siberia and Central Asia; and especially to Nina Alexeyevna Moustel, *Time* and *Life* assistant in Moscow, for her great contribution as translator, researcher, critic and friend.

This book represents only the opinions of the author.

Contents

These Are the Russians

BOOK I

People Are Capital

SHORTLY after Wendell Willkie returned from his trip to the Soviet Union, I cornered him at a meeting and told him that I was planning to go to Moscow as correspondent for *Time* and *Life*. We chatted a minute. Then he said firmly: "My advice to you is to get to know the people. Too many reporters know all about how the Moscow subway looks and nothing about the people who ride in it."

Whenever there were important decisions on where and how to spend my time, I tried to use Willkie's advice as a guidepost. The first such decision came in Teheran en route to Moscow in the fall of 1943. There was a choice between the quick one-day flight to the Soviet capital and the two- or three-week overland route via Baku and Stalingrad. If I could manage to squeeze myself on a plane I would reach Moscow in time to cover the Moscow conference. Against the headline magic of the big names involved— Molotov, Eden, Hull—I weighed the alternative: a chance to meet a lot of unimportant people, practice my Russian and see a vast area of the Soviet Union which I might never again be able to visit.

After waiting more than a week for special permission to go overland, I reported one cool November evening at the Teheran terminus of the Iran-Sov-Trans Company. This is the name of the Soviet organization which ships goods into Russia from Iran (Persia) via the Caspian Sea. The storehouse sheds were jampacked with boxes and crates of every size and shape—all American. I saw row after row of *toushonka* (a pork meat loaf) from the Dubuque Packing Company, oleomargarine from Indianapolis, applesauce from Virginia. Everything was so clearly marked in Russian it was impossible for people to be unaware of American aid along the line.

1

The workers in the shed were Iranians, but the foremen were Russian. The entire operation was under the supervision of a Red Army colonel. I had visited him earlier in the day to cut through the red tape of the Soviet consulate. The colonel, the first Red Army officer I'd met, heard me state my case, then asked me a few questions. When I answered them, he merely said, "It will be arranged." The young naval officer who was traveling with me to expedite a shipment of American Embassy supplies (mostly vodka) said, when we left the colonel's immaculate office, "Those Red Army guys are all right. You can deal with the military. But the others—whew!"

In the dark corners of the shed old women sat on crossed legs, shaving and shaping soft wooden blocks with rusty razor blades. Since cardboard was unobtainable, the blocks were being used for baggage labels.

As I stood watching the trucks being loaded, two young Red Army officers strolled into the shed. They saluted me. I offered them cigarettes.

The tall blond one said, "They are very strong. Thank you."

The dark one—he looked like a Georgian—said, "Thank you, but you must have one of ours in exchange." I don't particularly care for Russian *papyrossi,* but I took one. They were fascinated by my "Zippo" lighter.

"Does it always work?" asked the dark one.

"When there is fuel."

They laughed. "Just like your trucks," said the blond one, nodding toward the International backed up in the doorway.

The dark one asked, "Have you seen Errol Flynn in 'Santa Fe Trail'?"

I hadn't. He said, "He looks like our great Nevsky." I told him I had seen the motion picture about Nevsky (a thirteenth century Russian prince who defeated the Teutonic Knights when they invaded Russia), but I didn't know if he meant that Flynn resembled the actor who portrayed Nevsky or Nevsky himself. Perhaps my unsteady Russian was not strong enough at this point to get across the difference. Anyhow, this observation caused both Russians to laugh heartily.

When they had stopped laughing and smoked their cigarettes down to the last few millimeters, they asked where I was going.

"You had better take very warm clothes to Moscow," said the blond one, who was born in that area. For an answer I walked over to my bags and picked up my army trenchcoat. They examined it carefully, admiring the zipped-in lining. After discussing the coat in a whisper they told me it was very beautiful but I would freeze.

The trucks were ready, so I shook hands with everyone.

"See you in Berlin," I said to the blond lieutenant. He grinned and answered me, "No, better in Moscow." I climbed up beside my driver. The trucks in the convoy were all two-and-a-half ton American Internationals. There must have been fifty of them. At exactly 9 P.M., the commander of the convoy, a twenty-year-old junior lieutenant in a threadbare uniform, cried out, *"Po mashina!"* In perfect co-ordination the drivers started up the motors and drove out of the terminal on the road to No-Shah, a small port on the Caspian Sea.

We drove until midnight. My driver, who told me he was a veteran and had lost a finger at Kiev, did not seem very friendly. The road out of Teheran was fair and we made good time. At midnight the trucks suddenly pulled off the road into an open field. The convoy commander appeared and asked me whether I would prefer sleeping in the cabin of the truck or in a dispatcher's tent. Since my driver had already expressed a decided preference for the cabin, I accepted the tent offer. The American naval officer and myself were taken across the field to a large tent where our hosts shook hands and then pointed to the ground.

Before we got to sleep my companion asked a few questions in Russian. That made getting to sleep very difficult. The Russians wanted to talk about American equipment, the second front, and about the strategy of the battle for Kiev. We were too tired to make much sense in a strange language, and we finally managed a few hours' sleep on the cold, soft grass.

At five in the morning the convoy started off in low gear on the long haul up the mountains. Dust swirled so thickly over the road that our truck seemed to be cutting through waves of fog, rain and sleet. My driver was still pretty silent except when we would pull up on the side of the road for repair or to let a southbound convoy pass. Then a dozen or more drivers would gather around to ask questions. All of them wore Red Army uniforms, many of them had orders and medals denoting service on more active fronts. The most talkative driver was a huge, blue-eyed, red-bearded Ukrainian named Fillip, who had been a photo retoucher in Kiev before the war. But now he was more interested in discussing world affairs than the photographic business.

"Everyone in uniform is a statesman," he said philosophically. "We are none of us farmers or teachers. We are all in the same business, war. We have as much right to talk about world affairs as the next fellow. Is it so with you?"

I said I imagined every American soldier liked to feel he could chip in his two cents' worth on any topic as well as the big shots. "We have a very democratic army," I said, probably for the want of anything else to say. It was that way at first with Russian. You sometimes had to dismiss one or two better sentences until you hit one you could say. After awhile I was less self-conscious and said anything, even if I had to draw a picture to get the idea across.

Fillip took my remark about a "democratic army" as a hint that the Red Army was not. So he pointed around at the drivers and called off their nationalities—Tadzhik, Uzbek, Azerbaidzhanian, Kazakh, Georgian, Russian. "You see," he said with infinite patience, "in the Red Army we have all nations and races and we are all friends."

I said we had many different nationalities in our army, too.

"How many Japanese in America?" he asked unexpectedly.

I guessed a half million.

"How goes the fight over there?"

"Slow," I said. "The Japs are strong. They have a powerful Navy." I added, "Someday you will be in the war against them, yes?"

Fillip agreed. "But first Hitler," from all sides.

"Who is the big man in Japan?" he asked.

"Hirohito."

"And who is your President?" I never had a chance to reply. A half dozen of the others shouted, "Roosevelt." Fillip looked sheepish and said, "Of course."

Then another driver asked me if Churchill was the head of England. Fillip, anxious to retrieve his lost face as intellectual leader, said: "He is our friend, but not the ruler."

The Russian driver challenged him to prove it.

"There is the King, Gregory," said the Ukrainian, proudly.

"King George," said the American naval lieutenant.

"*Neechevo*," said the Ukrainian, "Georgi? Gregory? *Vse rovno*

. . . it's all the same." Fillip had a pair of shoulders like a Notre Dame tackle and he shrugged them magnificently.

The young convoy commander joined the group and led the conversation into a discussion of the Moscow conference.

"The important thing is—was it good or not good?" said the Ukrainian.

The convoy commander looked surprised. "Stalin said it was good." Everyone nodded in agreement. Then the commander took a deep breath of the mountain air and shouted "*Po mashina!*" and we returned to our trucks.

The sun was slowly rising over the snowcapped Elbrus Mountains. The colorings of the foliage and shrubs were like New England in the early fall but the contours of the landscape were more like that of Montana or Wyoming. As the incline became steeper, the trucks groaned into lowest gear and wheezed around corners unevenly. Each new hairpin turn would have been an ideal setting for the penultimate scene in "The Perils of Pauline." By the time we stopped for breakfast at nine we were pretty well shaken up.

In the small town where we ate, our foreign uniforms quickly attracted a gathering of local Red Army guards with fixed bayonets and a few townspeople. We were the first Americans they had ever seen. One pretty Red Army girl inquired if I was an American. When I assented, her eyes gleamed and she gave me a solid whack on the shoulder, saying, "Good. Are there more coming?"

"Just my friend," I said, indicating the navy man.

She was disappointed. "Only one? How can we win the war quick?" She walked away slowly, sighing, "Only one."

The enlisted men had their mess in one barn while we ate with the convoy commander and the local officers in another. All of us carried our own food in knapsacks. There was no local Red Cross or USO canteen. They brought us boiling water for our tea and broke us off half a loaf of black bread. The Russians were so interested in the cans of food we were opening that they scarcely ate. After many *pozhaluistas* they were persuaded to sample everything and found it good. A high-cheekboned senior lieutenant, stationed in the mountain town, told us he was an Uzbek from Samarkand.

"Before the Revolution I could not have been an officer." He indicated his epaulets with the three small gold stars. "Are there

many Uzbeks in America?" he wanted to know. I had never considered the subject, but I said, "No." Over cigarettes he became
quite voluble over the possibility of Turkey entering the war and
assured me of the success of the Moscow conference. Then there
was a silence while he looked at his cigarette which he was not
enjoying because it was American and had no paper holder on
the end so that his mouth was full of tobacco. Suddenly he inquired, "How old is Mr. Hull?" I guessed. He threw away the
cigarette and began rolling a new one with a small piece of
Pravda.

"After the war England, Russia and America will have everything," he said. "And China?" I asked. "And China, also," he
said with the unhesitating largess of a man who has more than
enough. I found this attitude on the Big Three prevalent with
most Russians. And half the time they would accept China, too,
if I mentioned it first.

After breakfast the men washed their equipment and marched
back to the trucks singing. Walking behind them I noticed that
nearly everyone had great gaping holes in the back of their
uniforms—holes worn through from the friction generated by
bounces and bumps. My driver explained that his own shirt was
almost new, but that after a week of driving over the road to
No-Shah it had worn out. He took off his hat and said, "See, I
am bald on the top from batting my head against the truck roof."

I made a note that if Bob Hope and Bing Crosby ever made
"The Road to No-Shah" they had better wrap Dorothy Lamour
in something cushier than a sarong. The road had been getting
gradually worse. I would have much preferred doing a mile-a-
minute over a vicious accordion-pleated road in the Southwest or
even over a Vermont dirt road after the first spring thaw. The
Red Army drivers were willing to gripe about the road to No-
Shah, but only up to a certain point. They knew it was a vital
lifeline bringing food and equipment to their comrades. My
driver said he would have driven it if the going had been twenty
times as rough. But, of course, it was a physical impossibility for
the going to be twenty times as rough. In fact, the road *was* a
physical impossibility, but the Russians had no time to stop and
fix it beyond hiring a few natives to throw some loose stones in
the worst pits.

The trucks began the steep descent toward the Caspian. My
truck was second in the convoy. On some of the turns I could

look back and see all fifty winding downward. When I dug out my pocket dictionary to look up the Russian word for tires, I began to get dizzy. But I asked my question and found out that the heavy duty American tires built for 100,000 miles and more, lasted only about 10,000 on the road to No-Shah.

On one bad turn a dozen Iranians could be seen near the bottom of the sharp slope combing through the rocks. "Two days ago a driver and truck went over here," said the driver. "Finished. *Kaput.*"

"You must be very good drivers," I said.

"There are no bad ones," he said. "They do not live long enough." He paused. "Me, I'd rather be back at the front."

"Why don't you go?"

He shrugged and held up the hand with only the four fingers. "This is my assignment."

Very late that afternoon, sore in every joint, muscle, bone and cartilage, we reached No-Shah. We shook hands with the convoy commander. As we walked away from him into the Iran-Sov-Trans office, he called after us quite seriously, "Tell them in America that they make very good trucks but they bounce too much!"

2.

At No-Shah we met little except frustration. Everything was wrong. We had no business coming to No-Shah. There were no ships from there to Baku. Where did the ships go? Makhachkala. All right, we would go there. No, your entry visa is stamped "Baku." Could it be changed? No, there wasn't any Soviet consul or vice-consul in No-Shah. We must return to Teheran.

The navy officer argued most of the night. He called upon the names of everyone from Roosevelt to Admiral King before the Soviet officials allowed us to take two trucks and go on to Pahlevi, where we could presumably obtain passage to Baku. In Pahlevi we waited several days for a steamer. There, too, everything was firmly unbusinesslike and vague. The officials of the Soviet steamship company didn't seem to know when the next steamer would arrive, if ever. Finally it did arrive. Then there was a long delay about putting us on board. The reason for that was revealed later: the cabins had to be washed out and cleaned up before any Americans could be allowed to sleep in them.

One day in Pahlevi we stopped at an old-fashioned photographer's booth to have a picture taken. The booth was like those at Coney Island, with a romantic Persian background created by a local surrealist. The cameraman crouched behind a big box and put a black cloth over his head and asked you to look at the birdie.

We had to wait. The photographer was taking a picture of a little boy in uniform. The boy stood there very straight and correct with a wonderful military bearing and calm dignity. The boy had even white teeth and a smooth unshaven skin. He kept on his military hat. He wore knee breeches and high black boots. He had several poses taken, and he didn't smile in any of them, although the Iranian photographer tried to make him relax just a little.

While his pictures were being developed, I asked the boy about his uniform. "It looks just like a regular Red Army uniform," I said, meaning to be nice.

He gave me a cold glance. He was not any more than four feet, ten inches tall. "I *am* a Red Army *man*," he said, pulling the blouse of his uniform down over his slight chest and tightening the leather belt around his waist.

He was deadly serious. I apologized for my mistake. He accepted the apology silently. The lieutenant and I had our picture taken outside of the shop instead of against the wild horse background. The boy remained, watching. After we were snapped, I suggested that he pose with us. Although the idea seemed to tempt him, he looked very dubious. "My friend is an American naval officer," I said, "and I am an American war correspondent."

The boy nodded. "Permit me to introduce myself," he tried to keep the pitch of his high voice well modulated and as a result he practically whispered. "My name is Georgi Andreyvich Brabich. I am from Moscow." We shook hands. He had a surprisingly large hand and a firm grip.

"We are going to Moscow."

His light blue-gray eyes widened. "You are?"

"Yes."

We had a picture taken. Georgi stood in the middle. Then we waited for the developing and printing.

"Two prints," I told the man.

"Please, three," said Georgi, "I must have one, if you do not mind."

We didn't. I asked Georgi if he would mind a few questions.

He shook his head and dug into his pocket. He pulled out a smitch of a newspaper and a palmful of tobacco and began rolling cigarettes. When he was finished he offered one to each of us. We thanked him and offered him a Camel. He would not accept ours unless we smoked his.

Georgi Andreyvich Brabich was fourteen years old. "I will be fifteen, though, in January." He had been in the Red Army for two and a half years.

"Isn't that exceptional—you're so young and so small?"

Georgi shook his head. There were many like him in the Red Army. He was a dispatch carrier attached to a headquarters command. He drove a jeep. He had participated in the entire Battle of Stalingrad. Georgi had been a Pioneer; he was taken into the Komsomols (Young Communist party) despite his youth; he fervently hoped he could become a full-fledged party member when he was older.

"I, too, am going to Moscow," Georgi said gravely. "I am waiting for my orders. I am going to a school for officer candidates."

Then we asked him about his family. He had three brothers, two sisters. His mother was dead. His father and all his brothers and sisters were in the Red Army. "The only one left at home is my old grandmother."

"Do you have a girl?"

Georgi almost smiled. "No. I will not even think of such things until I am older—and bigger." Georgi had been in the fifth grade of school when the war came. One by one his family volunteered. "I refused to stay home with the *babushka*. But they wouldn't take me. Only when Moscow was threatened. Then I ran away and hid in the woods and joined a group of militia training there." He paused. Then without a trace of boastfulness in his voice, Georgi added, "We saved Moscow."

We were sitting outside of the photographic shop in the hot sun. We took off our ties and jackets but Georgi said he was not allowed to do so. "I have thought much about America and Americans when fighting," he said. "Your jeeps are good. I think of you when it takes me over a bump or up a hill. At Stalingrad I saw many of your Airacobras. Your tanks are nice, too. But light. Couldn't you send us some heavier ones?"

I said I thought we were sending what the Soviet Supreme Command needed most and also what we could spare. The answer satisfied him completely.

"Have you fought?" he asked me suddenly. I felt very uncomfortable. "No. Although the convoy I came over on saw action in the Mediterranean."

"Are the Americans really fighting in Italy?"

"Of course."

Georgi nodded. "You will find that the Germans fight very strongly. The Rumanians are always afraid." Then he asked about the second front. "I think the war will be over very soon after the second front," he said.

"What do you want to do when the war is over? Go back to school? To civilian school?"

Georgi shook his head. "I shall stay in the Red Army. I would like very much to become an aviator. I do not care to return to grade school. What can interest me there now? Grammar doesn't help me drive a jeep."

"Are you religious?"

This time Georgi really smiled. "That's for the older ones," he replied.

"But are you religious—how do you feel about God?"

"I don't know."

"Have you ever been to church?" I used the Russian word *tserkov*. Georgi was puzzled. He looked bewildered, first at me and then at the naval lieutenant. It was the word. We kept repeating it, each time with slightly different accent and stress.

"*Tserkov* . . . *tserkov*," Georgia repeated it, too. "A place where you play? . . ." he half defined it, half asked it. We probed a bit. It was clear that the word held a playground rather than a religious connotation for him. He had played games in a churchyard in Moscow. We gave him the words, "religious building," and all was understood.

"No, I have never been," he said with finality.

"Aren't you curious to go, to see a ceremony there?"

"No. I would rather go to a movie."

Georgi glanced at his wrist watch. It was a big one, bigger than an Ingersoll dollar watch.

Georgi saluted us. "I must go." We shook hands.

"I hope you will come to see me in Moscow," I said. He thanked me. Then, reaching into the brown leather dispatch case which he carried on a strap slung over his shoulder, Georgi said, "Here is a picture of me after the Battle of Stalingrad. I want you to have it, please."

I accepted the gift. "Will you write your name on the back?" He did. Then he asked us to write our names on the back of the new picture card of the three of us. When it was quite dry he placed it in the breast pocket of his tunic.

"This I will show at the school in Moscow," said Georgi Andreyvich Brabich. He saluted again, clicked his heels as he executed an about-face, and marched down the street.

"I wish we could bring him to America," I said to my friend as we strolled back to the hotel. "You could never hate people like that."

3.

We didn't get much sleep on the trip to Baku. We were more interested in talking to our companions. The ship's captain was a highly intelligent fellow from up near Leningrad. He was disappointed that I wouldn't—or rather couldn't—play chess with him. After supper we sat around a large table in the small salon. In one corner of the room which served as the passenger's and officer's mess, was a loudspeaker. At various times during the day it was plugged in and the tinny sounds of the Moscow broadcast came forth. None of the ship's officers ever missed a military communiqué. The ship probably ran itself while they crowded around to hear the latest news from the fronts.

About midnight I was able to steer the conversation to religion. This was the subject of my first assignment for *Time*. The group sitting around the table drinking tea consisted of myself and the American naval officer, the ship's captain and an Azerbaidzhanian Jew, who were playing chess, a slightly intoxicated Red Army private, a young Soviet Air Corps lieutenant, and two women. One was the ship's waitress, a sturdy honey-colored blonde who kept trying to make us eat. The other was a Red Army captain, also blond, with gold teeth, two medals, a smart gray karacul fur hat, and a long skirt that reached well below her knees. She was very stern and very silent, always reading a copy of the *Medical Worker*. She was a doctor. One of her decorations was for her work in evacuating wounded at Stalingrad.

The Azerbaidzhanian, a fifty-five-year-old buyer for the Textile Trust, was most voluble. "I went to synagogue before the Revolution. I do not often go now. I can, if I wish. But only old *babushkas* go."

The Red Army private was convalescing from a serious wound.

He had once been a fireman on an American ship and knew some English. He kept grabbing the stump of his right arm and saying, "You son-of-a-bitch-Hitler," all together and fast. I called him "Jigger" because he couldn't sit still a minute. He said, "There is no time for church. There is religious freedom, yes. But for my part, you could abolish it. A waste of time, certainly."

The captain smoked his pipe, the girl doctor seemed completely absorbed in her reading. The Azerbaidzhanian went on. "Where is God? Do you stop and ask yourself this question, my young friend? What is God? For my part, God is in the mind. God is a faith in right living, in not killing and stealing. We have that faith, what more is needed?"

The captain nodded and said, "True." He then took his opponent's queen.

Jigger got up and limped around the room, muttering "You son-of-a-bitch-Hitler." He disappeared into his cabin, probably for a swallow of vodka, and then returned.

The Azerbaidzhanian continued. "Mostly for my wife's sake, I tried to bring up my children religiously. Synagogue is all right. But I have two daughters. My son is dead. At the front. Rostov region. One daughter is married to a tankist, the other to a railroad worker. The railroad worker is a party member. They all make fun of me when I go to synagogue. So I usually don't go. Other things are more important. Peace in the family. Economic security."

"Are you afraid to go?" asked the United States naval officer. "Will it hurt you in your business?" Another passenger came in and sat down. He was a Kharkov city official, middle-aged, well dressed, very tired.

"It's not a question of fear," said the Azerbaidzhranian. "I still go for the holidays."

The newcomer spoke up. His voice was flat and weary. I found out later that he had lost two sons at Sevastopol. "It's quite possible to go to church and still be a party member or a Komsomol." I looked around. Some of the others agreed. Jigger said, "A waste of time." He grinned at me and felt his stump. "You son-of-a-bitch-Hitler, right American?"

I asked the girl captain what she thought. "I am a different generation," she said slowly. "At the front there is only science and Stalin." Then she shut up and didn't say another word, but went right on reading her paper.

When she had spoken the aviator evidently felt that he could. "I have been more than two years at the front," he said, slowly. "I have been a Komsomol since 1939. There are no chaplains at the front. There is no thought or talk of religion there."

"What about at home, behind the lines? Do people think more about religion there?" I asked.

"There is no need, and when there is no need . . ." he shrugged. "The war absorbs everything, all energy, all thought. Maybe some old folks have time to think about religion. Everyone else is too busy. Religion is an empty shell."

I asked him if he thought you could be a Communist and still be religious. He looked at the Kharkov official and then at the girl captain. "I think no," he replied.

"I am not a Communist," said Jigger. "I think no, too." He tried to do a tap dance, gave up, swore, "Jesus Christ, son-of-a-bitch-Hitler damn."

I turned to the ship's captain. He smiled. "I have nothing to contribute. A person's free time is his own. If he wants to think about God that's all right as long as it doesn't interfere with his work. I, personally, find the subject of Arctic explorations much more fascinating. That's *my* hobby."

The waitress came in with another pot of tea. After she had filled our glasses, she filled one for herself and sat down. "I agree with this *tovarisch*," she said, indicating the Azerbaidzhanian. "The old world has no faith in its society so it has religion. We have faith in our new society. That's enough."

After that they changed the subject, politely but firmly.

4.

The train ride from Baku to Stalingrad lasted four days and nights. There were no dining cars on the train, no restaurants at the stations. We carried our own food supply, augmenting it by purchases at the open markets usually located near the station stops. The train porter chopped up sticks of wood and "made" boiling water twice a day for tea. That was the extent of wartime service on a regular Russian train, even though we were traveling de luxe, first class, *wagons-lits*, etc.

By the third day we were very tired of cold unadulterated Spam. But we could not afford to pay the market prices for roast chicken and other delicacies. The Russian officers and officials on our car had plenty of rubles, but neither of us had any to spare. Not when a small chicken sold for as much as 200 rubles (about $40). Monotony led to desperation and desperation led to initiative. We began trading. First we traded a nickel's worth of Necco candy wafers for six eggs (selling at 12 rubles, or $2.40 apiece). The Russians were dubious, but my naval companion kept saying over and over again, "Sweet . . . sweet . . . candy." The people were obviously starved for sweets. And they didn't need the rubles. Every peasant came to market with two bags: a small one for the produce he brought to sell, a large one for the rubles he was prepared to take home with him.

Emboldened by the Necco success, I tried to trade a huge five-pound can of Spam. We had eaten about one-third of it—and the bottom seemed meals away. The old peasant woman was very suspicious. She couldn't read the label. She hefted the can and handed it around among her friends. They agreed it was pretty weighty. I suggested that they try some. "American army meat," I said. "American army eats only this meat all the time. Very good. Very tasty. Please eat." The old lady mumbled, "What do you want for it?"

"Two chickens," I answered. Could a can of Spam really be worth $80?

She dug her fingers into the Spam and put them in her mouth. Then she passed the can on to a neighbor. "Taste it," she ordered. The friend did. "What is it?" he asked, "which animal?" "Swine," I said, "like your *Toushanka*." The man nodded.

The old woman made up her mind. She wrapped the cooked chickens in an aged *Pravda* and shoved the bundle at me. Then she said something which caused my Russian train mates to laugh. Later they translated it, with gestures. The old woman had muttered, philosophically, "It's a fine big can, anyhow." This wasn't such a joke, really. Any old unbroken bottle brought from twenty to forty rubles on the market, and in the stores it is impossible to purchase wine or vodka without first turning in an empty bottle. Who knows how much a fine big can might be worth, especially with all that fine American lettering?

5.

It was several hours before dawn and snowing when the train arrived at Stalingrad. The once imposing railroad station was a symbol of the whole city, a mute monument to Stalingrad's magnificent stubbornness. For months it had been mercilessly pounded by bombs, shells, bullets and grenades, yet its outer walls still stood. The walls are old, Stalingrad is old, too, although we think of it as new. It was founded in 1589 as Tsaritsyn—and ever since it has been important—the key to the rich Volga basin, the gateway to the Caucasus—the heart of Russia as St. Louis is the heart of the United States.

Even the through passengers had remained awake for Stalingrad. I set out to see the city with Vladimir Stepanovich Garbatov, a Red Army captain whom I had met on the train. He was small-boned, compact, clean-shaven, and not much more than thirty. A native of Stalingrad, he proudly wore the gold medal for the defense of the city. Garbatov was not a party member, I discovered, but in conversation his intense loyalty to Stalin was evident. This loyalty had many component parts: the complete devotion of a soldier to a commander who had risked his life with him; the simple love of a son for the father who had reared him; the uncritical admiration of a student for his favorite teacher.

We trudged through the snow over to the temporary wooden station, about two blocks from the tracks. The well-heated building was crowded with sleeping people surrounded by their children, their luggage, their household equipment and food. Most of them were waiting to get on trains that usually arrived already crowded. The unpainted walls were decorated with portraits of Soviet leaders and colorful posters. A typical one showed the Red Army in the foreground with bayonets fixed and tanks rolling; in the background, the shadowy figure of Suvorov, an eighteenth century Russian marshal, on horseback, sword held aloft, galloping into battle. The slogan, a quotation from Suvorov, was *Bei, Koli, Goni, Beri V Poloi.* ("Fight, thrust, pursue, capture!") The captain pointed to this poster, remarking, "Suvorov was a great leader and our Stalin is truly in his footsteps."

In the station I made another futile attempt to obtain a *propusk* ("permit") which would permit me to stay in Stalingrad for a few days. It was denied. Permission must come from Moscow. In Baku, they had said Stalingrad. In Teheran, they had said Baku. But the control "point" in the station agreed to let me go anywhere I wanted in the city with Captain Garbatov. That is, until the train pulled out—which might be in one or three hours.

The streets were dark. No electric lights. Only the reflection of locomotive headlights in the snow. There was no activity. Altogether a very eerie, unhappy feeling, like walking down the hall of a strange house and not knowing the location of the light switch. Everywhere monstrous conformations cast jagged shadows on the new-fallen snow. All the buildings, or rather parts of them still hanging in the air, were silhouetted against the murky sky. My eyes became more accustomed to the dark. If beauty were here, only a Bruno Mussolini could really enjoy it.

Down the dark streets off Lenin Square, the stark ribs of buildings seemed to huddle together in their nakedness. I had questioned Garbatov about religion on the ride from Baku, so it was natural that he led me to an ancient cathedral—or what remained of one. It was quiet, the kind of stillness that rings against your ears. The crunch of our feet on the snow seemed abnormally, indecently loud. We stood in silence. The interior of the cathedral was an altar of rubble, blanketed by the snow, watched over only by the sightless, shattered window frames, guarded only by the skeletal walls.

In a low, musical voice Captain Garbatov began to talk. He talked about the Stalingrad children's hospital which had been blown up, about the devastated Palace of Physical Culture, about the ravished homes and the crushed factories. He became almost lyrical describing Stalingrad's beautiful prewar boulevards, its modern white homes. Now, all was shambles. He spoke, too, of Stalingrad's parks and gardens and stores and theaters and restaurants, of the circus, and of moonlight on the peaceful Volga. I had never heard an American speak this way about his city. We talk that way of our mountains and streams and natural wonders. To the Russians, the everlasting miracle of their lives was the new bright and shiny city.

I cannot quote just what the captain said that moved me so much. He spoke slowly, mixing French and Russian so that I would understand. It wasn't necessary to know all the words; the cadences of his voice were descriptive enough.

We left the cathedral, and wandered through some more streets. Once or twice we were stopped, but there was no trouble. Everywhere I could see slogans, even in the bad half-light. Some were huge red banners strung up across streets, others were printed on bright posters, others just scribbled on the sides of walls. One slogan carried Lenin's name: TO MAKE VICTORY SURE THE PEOPLE MUST BE INOCULATED WITH CONTEMPT FOR DEATH! But the motto which was repeated again and again and again was DEATH TO THE GERMAN FASCISTS, or DEATH TO THE GERMAN FASCIST INVADERS!

I tried to obtain some information about reconstruction, especially housing. It was evident that many were still living in the underground shelters constructed during the siege. The captain said that by midwinter they hoped to have all families out of the huts and caves which lined the banks of the freezing Volga. Most of the new buildings which I could make out were just temporary wooden shacks. I passed one or two factories and they were in operation—but without roofs, without glass windows. "War leaves little time for niceties," said the captain. "We build now only those things essential for destroying the enemy." He said, "If you are interested in reconstruction, come back after the war. Stalingrad will be more beautiful than ever."

We had to check back at the station. But the train was not leaving for some time. "After an hour," said a conductor. That could mean anything. We set out again across the tracks. "We do not have time to see Pavlov's house," Garbatov said, "but I will show you something very remarkable, very historic." A half mile away, or perhaps further, he stopped in front of what looked like a tremendous pile of battered and broken bricks. "Here was a seven-, maybe eight-story building," the captain told me. "During the thick of the battle, the top five caved in and crashed. By some great good fortune, the Red Army men fighting on the bottom floor were not trapped. They went right on fighting off the Nazis. Among them was a Kirgiz named Urazaliyev. Right after the crash he solemnly reloaded his automatic rifle and remarked to his comrades, 'City tired, house tired, bricks tired, we not tired. . . . '" These words, said the captain, had caught on. Soldiers and citizens all over Stalingrad were soon repeating them, just as embattled Spaniards in Madrid shouting, *No pasaran!*"

It was getting lighter. Snow still fell as we walked briskly back toward the center of the city. The streets were beginning to be busier. People were coming from and going to work. The morning was cold. Civilians were bundled up warmly, not perhaps in the latest modes. Most of them were women. When we passed Red Army men, they went out of their way to salute us. Occasionally the captain would pause to chat. When he introduced me, the other officers would say something nice about American aid. Particularly they mentioned trucks, Airacobras and tanks. Then they would say something very simple and very moving about Stalingrad and how they felt about it and what the fight meant to them. These were impressive soldiers. They wore their mantle of destiny proudly.

Just in these brief conversations I had the feeling that the men of Stalingrad had a sense of history. A Soviet war correspondent expressed it better when he wrote, "Heroism has become part of the life, the style and manner of the (Stalingrad) division and its men."

Back near the tracks where we could keep an eye and an ear on the train, I was accosted by a bent, white-haired *babushka*. She asked me, in English, if I were an Englishman. She said she had learned to speak some English before the Revolution. This was a rare opportunity, and I immediately reached for my notebook. Her name was Nadya Gregorovna, she was almost sixty, and she had lived in Stalingrad all her life. Employed at the Dzerzhinsky Tractor Plant, she had worked and fought there right through the siege. "Every day on my feet eighteen and twenty hours," she said. Her husband, a miner, was killed in 1918 during the revolutionary fighting around Voroponov, near Stalingrad. "Then I was schoolteacher," she said. Her English was difficult to understand because she had no teeth. At least she sounded that way. I could not determine her present job category, but it was semiskilled work similar to that of a "sorter." Nadya Gregorovna earned 650 rubles a month, which is not very much in wartime Russia.

"What about absenteeism in the plant?" I asked. After I had explained what the word meant, she replied, "Very small sum. Almost none. This war is for our lives. There is no time to absent oneself."

"Supposing a worker *is* absent," I said. "What are the penalties, the punishments?" She answered, "Very few are absent. Punishment is hard. We workers vote it ourselves. If worker is one minute late, he loses one-half his bread ration for one month. If fifteen minutes late, he loses one-fourth of wages for one month. If absent full day without doctor's certificate. . . ." Nadya Gregorovna concluded with the familiar Russian shrug.

I pressed her for the answer. She looked at the captain, and spoke to him quickly in Russian. I don't know what she said or what he said, but she finally tried to put the words into English. "It is hard. It is justice. Sometimes worker is absent one day and no excuse, that worker sent to special detention camp. He must work there, too, only he not have everything." She would not elaborate. Before I could ask any more, she wanted to know about absenteeism in America. I gave her some vague figures. "That is much," she said. "What is your penalty?" My answers on that didn't satisfy her. She spat into the snow and said, "Either you fight not all together or you are foolish. Do not your workers know when they lose time they lose not only money but lives and battles?"

If one wished to be cynical you could say this was just an old woman re-mouthing *Pravda* editorials. If you think about Stalingrad and how the workers made both the Germans and time stand still, her remarks sound more like horse sense. I was thinking about Stalingrad. I felt cold and tired but not cynical.

"How many days a week do you work?" I knew as soon as the question was out of my mouth that it would be ridiculous to Nadya Gregorovna. But maybe not to people back home. "Every day," she said. I asked, "No rest days?" Her hard blue eyes glinted even in the morning's gray light. Pulling her shawl tightly under her chin, she replied with more fierceness than seemed possible for her age and size, "When we kill Hitler, then we will have day of rest!"

While I alternately scribbled in my notebook and pounded my hands together to keep circulation going, Captain Garbatov carried on the interview. He had been away from Stalingrad for a few months. He wanted to know all the changes. The old woman told him about the Cherkassovites. She was one. That meant, the captain explained later, that she spent two or three hours daily helping to rebuild the city—in addition to her job in the tractor plant. They spoke about inflation, only they didn't call it that. People had many rubles, but there were very few products to buy. There was enough food for the workers at the plant, but there were many grumblers.

Suddenly Nadya Gregorovna said to me, "What is your rank, gentleman?" It was the first time she had called me that.

The captain explained that I was a war correspondent. The train was making expectant noises, as if it might actually start. As we said good-by, Nadya Gregorovna grabbed my arm in a vise-like grip. "Write about our glorious Stalingrad," she cried. "Not what we have done but what we will do."

As the train slowly chugged out, passengers pressed their noses against the windows for a look at Stalingrad. *"Geroi gorod"* ("hero city"), they whispered. For hours we goggled at the disheveled landscape. No amount of fresh snow could hide the crater-pocked fields, the tank-trap gulleys, the broken trees. Near the town of Kourman we passed what is known as the world's greatest junk heap. "Trophies," said the captain. "German." As far as the eye could see were the littered remains of Nazi war materiel: cannons, light tanks, heavy tanks, Ferdinands, Tigers, mortars, weapon carriers, machine guns, airplane bodies, command cars, motorcycles, bulldozers, assorted vehicles of all shapes and sizes. We also passed dozens of dismantled Nazi locomotives, many of them overturned near the rail bed. For every locomotive there were a hundred boxcars. Some were marked *Deutsche Reichsbahn*. Others still bore the names of occupied countries, France, Belgium, Holland, Poland, Czechoslovakia. German prisoners who were helping to clear Stalingrad, helping to build road and tracks, helping to salvage some of their own junk, lived in these cars. In Moscow I chalked up the "trophy" figures for the Battle of Stalingrad. The Russians had captured 1,125 of these railway cars. Probably because of the different gauge they had not refitted them for moving freight. Altogether, at Stalingrad the Red Army booty included 750 planes, 1,550 tanks, 670 big guns, 1,462 mortars, 8,135 machine guns, 90,000 rifles, 61,102 automobiles and trucks, 7,369 motorcycles, 480 traction engines and transporters, 320 radio installations, three armored trains, and 235 dumps of arms, ammunition and supplies. I'd have gladly signed an affidavit that I had seen at least that number of every item from the train.

A few hours out of Stalingrad the train stopped again. We climbed down. Captain Garbatov cleared the snow off the wooden rail ties to show me where the Germans had moved the rails closer in order to make their narrower European gauge. Near by was another field of trophies. This time the view was better, and I could single out smaller items like sleds and helmets among the wreckage.

"After the war," said the captain, "no more of this." Back aboard the train it was cold. We kept on our coats. Captain Garbatov poured out two fistfuls of vodka. He handed one to me and then raised his own. "*Odin mir*," he toasted. After drinking, blinking and coughing, I inquired about the meaning of the toast. "*Odin mir*" can be translated either as "one peace" or "one world."

"*Neechevo*," he said, putting an arm around my shoulder. "Can there be one without the other?"

6.

After Stalingrad there was Moscow. Then trips to Kharkov, Smolensk, Leningrad, Odessa, Yalta, Sevastopol, Kalinin, the

Urals, Siberia, Central Asia and Poland. Russia was bursting with people like the truck drivers in Iran, like young Georgi Brabich, like Captain Garbatov, like the old lady in Stalingrad. Everywhere I traveled—in the empty liberated cities, in the booming industrial cities, at the front, behind the Urals, I sought satisfactory answers for the question: why did Russia win?

We had overlooked some vital factor in estimating the Russians and their system. Fortunately, the Germans had overlooked it, too. It wasn't anything very tangible. The Russians hadn't fooled us. We had fooled ourselves, or allowed ourselves to be fooled. We had bought a certain picture of Russia, hung it in our minds and never re-examined it. The picture portrayed the Soviet system as a giant impersonal machine stamping out brawny Ivans with lots of muscle and little brain. Reports and rumors, books and bombast confirmed the authority of this picture: Russian initiative had been throttled, squelched and liquidated along with freedom of speech and press.

When the Germans invaded the Soviet Union it was widely predicted by friend and foe that the Nazis would conquer the Russians in a few months even though we anticipated that the Russian people would be tough, hardy, self-sacrificing and brave, good soldiers and good workers. We attributed to them a plodding, oxlike quality which fitted our mental picture of the robot people molded by an iron dictatorship. Only the tremendous victories of the Red Army at the front and the industrial achievements of the Soviets in the rear made it apparent that the standard concept of the U.S.S.R. and its people had become an anachronism. It had not been expected that in a time of crisis the Russian, like the American or the Englishman, would be capable of demonstrating great versatility, great initiative. It was expected that he would be able to take orders and carry them out faithfully and unimaginatively; it was not expected that the Russian could act as an individual, that when responsibility devolved upon him he could assume it, that when a new situation confronted him he could solve it—and very well, too.

Once I realized what was wrong with our picture of the Russians, I began to understand that this contained the key to the explanation of why Russia won.

Last summer at a dance given in honor of Soviet fliers in Moscow I suddenly remembered how Russian youngsters had danced the foxtrot in 1935. Then all of them were learning; everyone did the same steps at the same time in the same way. They danced almost automatically. You could hear them counting to keep time. When American couples took the floor the Russians thought we were doing the wrong steps because we had individual styles.

But last summer it was very, very different. The young Russian couples no longer executed the same stilted steps. They all had highly individual styles—no two couples danced exactly alike.

I remarked on this change to a Soviet pilot.

"It is true," he said. "First, the group basis. Then individuality. The same is true in the sky. First, we must learn to work together, teamwork. Then each man can write his own name in the sky."

I explained that I thought this individuality was an important element of Soviet life which most foreigners had failed to recognize. The Russian flier agreed. "But other countries have individuality," he pointed out. "What we have is something that includes a certain amount of individuality but subordinates it to the common good. That is our great bond." He proceeded to tell me a story about Valery Chkalov, the Soviet ace who flew across the North Pole to the United States. Returning to Europe on the French liner "Normandie" from New York, Chkalov was asked by an American passenger, "How rich are you?"

"A hundred and seventy million," Chkalov replied.

"Dollars or rubles?" queried the American.

"Neither," answered the flier. "People. They are all working for me and I for them."

To many Americans this sounds like propaganda from *Pravda*. But a vast number of that 170,000,000 believe the same as Chkalov did.

In other conversations with Russians I tried to find out how the trend toward individual initiative had started. Some said it had always existed, that the Revolution had released a great torrent of creative energy. But many traced it back to a notable speech by Stalin. In an address to the graduating class of the Frunze Academy (the elite Red Army school which is roughly equivalent to West Point plus a General Staff college) in 1935, Stalin said:

> Comrades, we talk too much about leaders. We attribute almost all our achievements to them. That is wrong and false. I want to talk about people.
>
> Comrades, the old slogan "machines decide everything" reflects a period now past. It must be replaced by a new slogan—"People, personnel decide everything." Now is the time to realize

that of all the valuable capital which the world possesses the most valuable is people.

When Stalin uttered these words of wisdom, things did not change overnight. But they did have a profound and lasting effect. The speech was widely printed and read, studied and discussed. It resulted in a growing emphasis on people—on their collective and individual development. In the prewar years the Russians began to feel their own importance. The other nationalities began to understand their own importance. People developed more self-reliance.

This did not mean that anyone was allowed to hop up on a soapbox and challenge the party or the government. But in his own factory, the worker was consulted and asked for suggestions. If he made one and it proved helpful, the worker received a reward. In army units, the study of tactics and strategy was not confined to officers alone: each individual soldier had to understand the whole plan of a campaign as well as his own role. A great national thirst was aroused, a thirst for knowledge, a thirst for self-expression, for creative work.

In the Soviet Union today there are still plenty of automatons. In Moscow there are as many bureaucrats per foot of red tape as in Washington. And Russian bureaucrats are more infuriating than American because they are less experienced and less polite. But by now it is obvious that the Soviets could not have won their military victories if the Red Army had been riddled with bureaucrats or automatons.

One murky afternoon last spring I stood next to a young Soviet general on the heights overlooking the wreckage of Sevastopol. The Crimean campaign had just been brought to a highly successful conclusion. The docks along the Black Sea were still smoldering. The general folded his staff maps, shoved them into the pocket of his greatcoat, and chatted for a moment. "You know I was little more than a boy in the last war. I was called up toward the end. You know then we had no idea why we were fighting. We were cattle in a slaughterhouse. No different. If our superior officer was killed, our impulse was to break ranks and take safety. We didn't want to die. We didn't know why we had to die." The general paused. "You see the difference? You see why Sevastopol could hold out so long? The modern Red Army soldier and sailor has been taught to think and act. We know why we fight. If we must die, we know why that is necessary, too."

Foreign observers have had enough substantiating evidence of this Red Army spirit to realize that there is something more to it than mere slogans. But for a long time British and American officials did not have a chance to see how the Red Army actually operated in the field. In the spring of 1944 and especially after the opening of the second front, the Soviets did permit competent Allied observers to visit combat areas. During the Belorussian offensive last year which swept the Nazis out of Minsk, Vitebsk, Vilna and other key strongholds, General Burrows, head of the British Military Mission in Moscow, was taken right up to the late General Cherniakhovsky's field headquarters.

Burrows was subjected to a series of surprises. Cherniakhovsky had a very large army and a very small staff. He was quartered in a wooden peasant hut. There were no typewriters, filing cabinets or other such paraphernalia which usually encumber the staff headquarters of a modern army. When Burrows inquired how Cherniakhovsky kept in touch with his various units, the Soviet commander indicated that his chief of staff, a major general, rode around to visit them in his jeep.

Early one morning Burrows set out with the chief of staff on an inspection tour of the front. They rode in an American jeep driven by a sergeant. As they rode through the marshy, lake-filled countryside Burrows made a mental note that he would tell Cherniakhovsky about the Bailey bridge. This bridge is easily thrown together from a set of prefabricated steel girders and beams, and had considerably facilitated Allied advances in Italy. Burrows decided the Russians might be able to put them to good advantage.

En route to the front the jeep stopped at a river crossing. A long, ragged-looking line of infantry was fording the river. The Red Army general watched the operation for several minutes. Then he summoned the nearest regimental commander.

"I'd like you to have about thirty or forty men—your older men—drop out here. Soon there will be some heavier equipment coming up along this road." The general then gave instructions about the size and type of wooden bridge which he wanted constructed on the spot.

The regimental commander took it all in. Then he asked, "Where shall the men report when they have finished this task, Tovarishch General?"

The chief of staff recalled that he had just whizzed past a patch of woods about a kilometer back on the left. The men could build a temporary camp in those woods. "In about a week when the mechanized equipment begins coming through they can join Division N. Tell the commander that I said he was to 'adopt' these men. Later they may be able to rejoin your unit."

Saluting, the regimental commander left and began selecting his bridge builders. Burrows, who understands Russian, had listened incredulously to the entire transaction. Such a thing could not happen, he was sure, in the British or American armies. A dozen questions, objections and "buts" flooded his orderly, military mind. No arrangements had been made with the quartermaster. Where were the written orders? What about sanitation? Did the men have proper food? What was the tensile quality of the wood? Was the proposed bridge certified by the Engineers Corps?

About a week later General Burrows returned along the same route. Heavy equipment was rumbling across the river on a fine, well-made log bridge. In the intervening days Burrows had seen much of the fighting abilities of the Red Army men. But this bridge which had been put together by a pick-up crew with axes and local materials was more of an eye opener to him than anything else.

General Burrows' eyes twinkled when he told me about his front trip. He had decided not to mention the Bailey bridge to Cherniakhovsky, but he had been tempted to ask for some Russian woodsmen who could teach the Allies how to build bridges so expertly and so rapidly. "I have just finished doing up a report. I don't quite think that they will believe me back in London. I can't blame them, you know. Wouldn't have believed the thing possible myself if I hadn't seen it."

The incident of the log bridge is only one of tens which illustrate the "secret" of the Red Army. There are illustrations in the work of organized partisans, in the amazingly simple way Soviet troops are kept supplied, in the astounding amount of independence and freedom of action given to local front commanders, in the exploits of Soviet airmen, in the brilliant, fresh strategy of the General Staff.

There is a strong, resonant note of hope for civilization in the key to "why Russia won." In the most highly mechanized war of all time they were able to defeat the nation generally credited with having the most complete mastery over machines. And I am convinced they did it by recognizing in their own fashion that people—not machines—decide everything.

BOOK 2

Above the Chaos

THERE is a curiously apt Russian proverb: "Nothing is above
Moscow except the Kremlin and nothing is above the Kremlin
except heaven." Physically, the Kremlin's spires do not dominate
Moscow as Rockefeller Center towers over mid-Manhattan, but in
Moscow you feel the Kremlin's dominance, rather than actually
see it. There are, in fact, no looming, spectacular skyscrapers. Moscow, despite its ever-changing five million population, looks like
a city no bigger than Trenton, New Jersey, or Oklahoma City.
There is no main stem; department stores, theaters and shops
are scattered. Gorky Street, which pales under the correspondents'
cliché, "Moscow's Fifth Avenue," is lined with many ten- and
twelve-story edifices, some in themselves impressive. But the
streets are as wide as Salt Lake City's and the canyon effect which
rubber-stamps the twentieth century American metropolis is
entirely lacking.

Moscow's architecture is a strange mixture of Gothic, Byzantine
and eclectic modern buildings, a few of them bombed and now rebuilt in a style called "Russian Restoration." Its largest chain stores
are bookshops which dot important streets and corners like drug-
stores in Los Angeles. Next are public bathhouses where most of
Moscow's population keeps amazingly clean. On macadam and
many cobblestone streets little kiosks mushroom, some selling
flowers (artificial in winter), magazines, tobacco and newspapers.
On corners, old women with shawled heads shine boots, sell laces
and patch holes, while you wait. Billboards along the sidewalks
carry the latest copies of newspapers and splashily colored war
posters.

The streets are full of earnest, scurrying people from early
morning until 1 A.M. curfew. They are thinner and they laugh
less than I remembered. They jostle along the sidewalks, carrying

net *sumpkas* which look like oversize snoods. Moscovites walk impatiently, only to wait patiently as they line up for movies, subways, rationed goods, newspapers and especially trams and trolley-busses. Unlike New York, where subways carry the main burden, 60 per cent of Moscow travels to and from work on trolleys. Riding on one of these is as exasperating, colorful, odoriferous, suffocating and hazardous as it would be to shoehorn yourself into a Toonerville Trolley rocketing over a Coney Island roller coaster jammed with an Ebbets Field crowd full of Brooklyn Dodger fans.

In addition to trams, Moscow is cluttered with an intricate trolley-bus system. Busses splatter and spark on overhead cables and the connections often slip off. When it is wet you get a shock by touching the metal handrails. Muscovites are much amused when this happens to foreigners. They seem to be immune.

The splendiferous metro costs forty kopecks or five cents a ride as against the ten to twenty kopecks on surface transport. The metro is usually as crowded as New York's subway during rush hour. The first section of the first car is reserved for women with children, but the rest is every man for himself. The new stations opened during the war are ornamental rather than functional. An old New Yorker can't accustom himself to the metro's magnificence. It is almost as if the lobby of Grauman's Chinese Theatre in Hollywood had been sunk underground at Times Square, Manhattan, and filled with savage commuters scrounging, shoving, bruising.

There are, however, other forms of exercise and entertainment available in Moscow beside the daily subway workout. On Sundays you can lose your rubles at the Hippodrome's pari-mutuel trotting races as fast as you could lose dollars at Agua Caliente. In the Park of Culture and Rest an imposing exhibition of captured German war trophies has been playing to standees for months. A one-ring, three-elephant circus is much favored by soldiers on leave. Art galleries hum with appreciative comment. Concert halls are usually sold out, especially when there is a performance of Shostakovich's enormously popular *Seventh Symphony* or *Piano Quintette*. Tschaikowsky also continues to draw well without the help of Freddy Martin's modernizing.

It is a major civilian victory to acquire tickets for the Bolshoi or Stanislavsky Theatres where the best ballets and operas are presented in repertoire. First choice goes to Red Army men, then diplomats and military missions. The latter pick up some of their choicest secondhand military gossip promenading between acts at the Bolshoi Theatre where intermissions last as long as forty minutes. Theater-hungry Moscovites cluster around Sverdlov Square on which the Bolshoi fronts, anxiously requesting extra tickets. On an opening night the mob of ticket seekers is like the front of Madison Square Garden when Joe Louis fights.

Most popular in the current Bolshoi repertoire are Glinka's *Ivan Susanin*, the tale of a simple peasant who sacrifices his life leading astray Polish invaders in the early seventeenth century; Rimsky-Korsakov's spectacular *Prince Igor*; Tschaikowsky's *Eugen Onegin* and *Queen of Spades*. It is really true what they say about the Russian ballet: it has intense, wide popularity and it is breathtakingly wonderful. Muscovites quarrel over the relative merits of première ballerinas Ulanova, Lepeshinskaya, and Semonova as high school girls in Kansas or G.I.'s in Europe would argue over Betty Grable, Ginger Rogers and Dorothy Lamour. The Bolshoi has old standbys like Tschaikowsky's *Swan Lake*, *Nutcracker*, and *Sleeping Beauty*, as well as modern Soviet creations like *Don Quixote* and Prokofiev's forthcoming *Cinderella*.

The Stanislavsky Theatre produces modern Soviet operas like Dzerzinsky's *And Quiet Flows the Don* and *Soil Upturned* and Khrennikov's *Into the Storm*. Musical comedy and operettas also flourish. Russians love such traditional favorites as Kalman's *Sylvia* and *Countess Maritza*, now playing to packed houses.

Moscow's legitimate theaters, draft-protected like the opera and ballet, have repertoires which shame Broadway. You can see firstrate productions of Shaw's *Pygmalion*, Shakespeare's *Othello*, Sheridan's *School for Scandal*, Chekhov's *Three Sisters* or *The Cherry Orchard*, Rostand's *Cyrano de Bergerac*, as well as recent Soviet dramas and comedies. One of the leading theaters produced Lillian Hellman's *Watch on the Rhine* last winter and I saw an amusing stage version of the Hollywood movie, "It Happened One Night."

If the emphasis of ballets, musicals and operas is on escaping austere, war-weary existence, Soviet films are usually just the opposite. The realism in the film version of Wanda Wasilewska's *Rainbow* is more than most American audiences can take, and many United States state censors refuse to pass its scenes of Nazis torturing a pregnant woman in labor. Moscow has about thirty or forty movie houses and they are always crowded. On Sundays and other holidays, lines form at six in the morning for tickets.

Muscovites flock to American and British films which are carefully selected for their nonrelation to modern realities. They roared over an indifferent English comedy called "Let George Do It," which was retitled "George From Dinky Jazz." The biggest (1944) hit in Moscow was the technicolor "Thief of Bagdad."

American jazz is much better known and liked now than in 1935. Moscow has no dance halls or night clubs, but hotels, restaurants and ballrooms are now open at "commercial" prices and several good dance bands play there as well as at private parties and clubs. At Foreign Commissar Molotov's Red Army Day reception, an eight-piece band swung out with such tunes as "Sonny Boy" and "Alexander's Ragtime Band." The Moscow radio favors classical excerpts and military marches, but occasionally broadcasts programs of American popular songs. Not long ago I heard "This Is The Army, Mr. Jones," with Russian words, and "Don't Sit under the Apple Tree" was rapidly reaching the hit class. "Coming in on a Wing and a Prayer" was rendered in Russian as "Coming in on a Wing and a Good Machine." Average teen-agers want to know about the postwar world and jitterbugging in about the same proportion as in America. They pick up new steps amazingly fast. Zoya Fedorovna, the hefty but pretty blond movie star of "Girl from Leningrad" fame, said she had never fox-trotted, much less "d-gitterbudged," but after one dance she could have passed for an oversize Roseland hostess.

Dancing and entertainment are not, however, the main topics of Moscow's conversation. There everyone lives with a map. Each day's *Svodka* is followed with breathless anxiety and interest. Every family has many members, both male and female, serving in the Red Army, Navy or Air Force and a large proportion have already lost someone dear. Since the front is widespread and mobile, communications are haphazard at best; millions of sweethearts, sons and husbands have been unreported since the Wehrmacht rumbled into the Ukraine on June 22, 1941.

Moscow's papers are full of hero stories. Colonel Alexander Pokryshkin, who shot down fifty-nine Nazi planes, shares space with a worker in a boot factory who overproduced his norm of *valinki* (felt boots) in honor of the Teheran agreement, or a "Heroine Mother" who has raised twelve children. This is a hero-worshiping people. They feel it, know it and need it. In some ways, perhaps, it takes more of a certain type of heroism to live and work day and night behind the lines than at the front. For Moscow life is not all vodka and caviar, ballets and borscht. Moscow life is hard despite songs, salutes and the peoples' certainty of eventual triumph.

2.

It was one thing to see Moscow from the outside. But what about inside? Foreigners do not have many opportunities to visit Russian homes. We might if our headquarters were in Tashkent or Minsk or Irkutsk. But Moscow is official. Correspondents are official, whether we like it or not. Muscovites know that we deal at the diplomatic stores, that we are accredited to the Foreign Office, that we are always prying for information. They believe, too, that we are always closely watched and closely guarded.

Once I asked a young couple why they had never asked me or any of my journalist friends to their home.

"We have so little space," apologized the husband, who was a correspondent for one of the evening newspapers in Moscow.

"But I know that," I said. "I know, too, that you don't have a lot of food. Naturally I'd bring some. We do that in America, too, you know."

"Ivan," said his wife quietly, "let's be perfectly honest with our American friend. You are our friend now. We think you will be our friend always. But we do not know. There have been foreigners here, journalists, who have been very friendly. They have said nice things. They have seemed to understand our country and our people."

"And then," continued Ivan, with more bitterness in his voice than his wife had betrayed, "you go home and make a lot of money writing lies about the Soviet Union. That makes us feel very bad. Perhaps our government suspects that we gave you some of this misinformation. If you didn't make it up, you must have gotten it somewhere. Yes? Well, they may find out who were your friends."

They looked embarrassed. I told them I was their friend and that I didn't intend to write anything very different when I returned to the United States. "Except," I added, "what the censors cut out."

"It's not you personally," said Ivan. "We make it a rule."

"But you are talking to me now. I see you both at parties. I meet you at the theater. You could be giving me misinformation now."

They both looked a little alarmed. Ivan's wife said, "For ourselves it doesn't matter so much. But four other families live in our apartment."

Before the year was over I did visit some Moscow homes, but not as many as I would have liked. One day in the summer of 1944 Natasha Andreyevna Denisov asked me if I would like to spend a week end with her family at their *dacha*. Natasha is a plain, billowy-bosomed woman between thirty-five and forty-five. She worked as a subeditor for one of the foreign language publishing houses in Moscow. Her husband, an engineer, was a major in the Red Army. They had one child, a little eight-year-old boy named Petya.

Natasha called for me at the hotel, her arms loaded with packages. "They have no bread in the country. I have sprats and dried apricots and *kolbassa* ("baloney"). What are you bringing?"

"Red wine, chocolate for Petya, sardines—American cheese, and a can of peaches. What else do you need?"

"Well," said Natasha, laughing, "if you like much sugar in your tea and if you rich Americans can spare some, bring a cup of that, too."

When my knapsack was packed we took the subway to the Komsomolskaya metro station which is adjacent to the Kazan railroad terminal. In the depot we bought tickets, 30 rubles apiece ($1.50) and followed the crowd out onto one of the train platforms. A long suburban train was standing in the station, gradually filling up with week-enders. One left every half hour. The cars were old with worn straw-covered seats. But they were meticulously clean. Nearly everybody in the car carried large parcels of some kind, and many of them also had gardening implements. As in the case of the subways, there was a government decree that nobody could carry a fork, hoe, or shovel unless it was "wrapped up." Editorially a Moscow daily explained that "it was not cultured to carry a naked shovel in a public conveyance."

We had to stand. There were about a hundred and twenty-five to a hundred and fifty people in the car. Besides myself, I counted only ten other men. Six of these were in Red Army uniforms, two were teen-age boys and the others were old grandfathers. The train kept stopping every four or five minutes at small station platforms even before it pulled out of the Moscow city limits.

After an hour's ride we got off at Iliashkin, a suburb about twenty-five miles from Moscow. Broken boards made it precarious to walk along the wooden platform. There was only one store near the station. It had nothing in its windows except an old picture of Stalin kissing a Uzbek child. Natasha said the place had been more or less closed since the war.

"What do you mean, more or less?"

"Well, it has a roof, hasn't it? I suppose people still live there." In Russia, to paraphrase Gertrude Stein, a roof is a roof is a roof and not to be sneezed at.

There are no public or private conveyances in Iliashkin. Somebody may have had a bicycle, but I didn't see one. The dirt, or rather sandy loam, streets were grown over with weeds. You could tell they were streets not because there were any sidewalks, but because there were telephone poles at regular intervals and on both sides were small frame bungalows. All of them looked gray. It was impossible to tell what their color might have been in 1929 or 1939. There were a lot of varied shrubs around, including lilac bushes. Most of the trees were evergreens, interspersed with weeping willows.

We had to penetrate a large gang of small boys who were playing "partisan." They froze in their tracks when they saw me. As soon as I had passed with Natasha, my knapsack and her bundles, they began an animated discussion. The subject was my strange American khaki uniform.

"He's a parachutist," said one.

"No, a tankist."

"Maybe a spy?"

"I think he's a sapper."

A couple of them ran after me to look at my shoulder tabs.

"Hey, that's English."

"Go away," said Natasha, "he's a war correspondent."

Laughter. One boy cried, "I know. I know. He's no tankist. He's a *porter!*" That delighted and satisfied them.

We walked on. "I hope your dignity is not offended," said Natasha.

"No."

"You see in the Red Army, officers are not allowed to carry packages. I have been imposing on you."

"Not at all," I answered smugly. "In our democracy the women always manage to make the men carry things, too."

After a twenty-five minute walk we came to Natasha's *dacha.* It was a one-story frame house on about an acre of land with nice trees and shrubs. The grass had not been cut all summer. The front porch was covered with vines. I started for it, but Natasha explained that the owners of the house lived on that side. Her family had the back end.

"What about the kitchen?"

"You'll see."

With Natasha's husband away, her family consisted of her mother-in-law, Marya Dmitrevna, Petya, and her sister's daughter, Anna Sergeyevna. The old lady and Petya were there to greet us.

Actually all that the Denisovs had of the house was two rooms and a half interest in the kitchen. The "bathroom" was a small wooden outhouse behind the victory garden. There was a sink in the kitchen and some shelves and an old makeshift icebox and a wood stove. In the summertime the wood stove was not used. Marya Dmitrevna had a small fire going near the back porch and was making a vegetable soup which required her constant attention. Water was drawn from a well not very far away which served about five or six neighboring families.

About a half hour after we arrived Marya Dmitrevna and Petya set the table on the porch and we had dinner. It was about five thirty in the afternoon, a perfectly reasonable hour for a "midday" meal in Russia. Dinner consisted of black bread, some fresh radishes from the victory garden, soup thick with potatoes and other home-grown garden products and tea. I gave Petya the chocolate. Without being instructed to do so, he broke one bar in half and then divided that half into four pieces which he solemnly offered around the table. We all refused. Petya took one piece and then glanced at his mother.

"Put the rest away," Natasha said. "You'll want some tomorrow and after tomorrow."

When it got dark Petya went to bed by himself. Candles were lit on the porch. "The house is wired for electricity," said Natasha, "but the ration is so low we decided not to use any. The candle-light is nicer, isn't it?"

Marya Dmitrevna cleaned up the dishes and changed into a black dress with a high collar around her sagging, wrinkled throat. Her hair was a dirty white. Her hands were very long and thin and bony and scrupulously clean except there was good Russian earth under her nails. She wore a religious medallion on her chest and she had tiny gold earrings.

"Have you brought the papers, my dear?" she asked Natasha.

"In my bag. *Pravda* for every day."

"No *Vechernaya?*" (the "*Evening Moscow*").

"I'm sorry." Natasha was smoking. "The news is all the same, anyhow."

"Not true." Marya Dmitrevna had a high voice. "You know I like *Vechernaya*. It has 'help wanted' notices."

"Thinking about getting a job, Mamushka?"

Marya Dmitrevna sat down opposite me, ignoring her daughter-in-law. She asked me again about my nationality, where I was born, about my family, my background. I told her as best I could.

"*Parlez-vous français?*" she asked, suddenly.

"A little." We talked in French. I found it difficult. I kept mixing in Russian words. Finally, I said, "I'd rather talk Russian. I need the practice."

The old lady sighed. "I haven't talked French in years. Yours is, of course, very bad."

"I know, I'm sorry. I haven't used it in about ten years."

"That's no excuse," she said. "I haven't used it much in thirty years." I didn't answer. "Did you hear that, monsieur?"

"Yes."

She asked, "Have you been to Petrograd, monsieur?"

"Yes, it is very beautiful."

"It was very beautiful. The war . . ." her voice softened and trailed off. "How do you think the war is going?"

I made some answer.

"I always admired your General Pershing," she said. "Tell me, how is he?"

"All right, I think."

She went on with her questions. Natasha maintained an amused silence. Sometimes it was difficult to tell which war the old lady was talking about. Other times her mind was very clear and her questions were sharp and up-to-the-minute.

Natasha interrupted once to suggest we might play cards.

"Cards?" the old lady scoffed. "You can play cards in Moscow, Natalia Andreyevna. You are here little enough with your family. Less than two days a week. You can talk to your old mother. Tell me the news of Moscow."

"Moscow is hot and humid," said Natasha. "People are tired. This month there were no matches at the store and we lost our ration. There is some crab. Do you like crab? I thought to buy some. It's canned. Do we have any eggs for the morning?"

"No. It was impossible to find any. Did you bring sugar? And berries? Petya has been asking for berries."

They talked about household matters for a few minutes.

"Is Anna coming out? Or maybe she is too busy with all her meetings?" Marya Dmitrevna sniffled.

"Anna is nineteen, a student," Natasha explained to me in English. "She's an active Komsomolka." She turned to her mother-in-law. "I think she is coming sometime tomorrow. We are going to the river to swim if it is nice."

Marya Dmitrevna stood up. "Good night. God bless you, monsieur. Sleep well." She lit another candle and disappeared inside.

"Is she religious?" I asked.

Natasha shrugged. "So-so. Mostly it is a custom with her. She likes to cling to a few old mannerisms. Her family had friends who had been to court. The Tsar's court. She finds it hard to forget. Her husband was a professor."

"What happened to him?"

"He died," Natasha said. After a pause, she added, "She's seventy-six or seventy-seven."

At that moment Marya Dmitrevna reappeared. "Please excuse me, monsieur," she said. "I sometimes forget my manners. Natasha is so young and not very cultured as you probably can see. Would you like to eat? Tea, perhaps?"

The usually even-tempered Natasha sounded annoyed. "Go to bed, *Babushka!*" she ordered. "If my friend wanted anything he would ask. He is an American. Besides this is not the Grand Duke's villa. Go to bed."

The old woman went to bed.

I was given a comfortable bed in the smaller of the two rooms. The other three slept in the large room. The furnishings were spare. No especial period. Just old wooden chairs, a few couches, a rickety table, a few amateur paintings on the bare wooden walls.

Petya woke me up the next morning. "Come have breakfast," he invited.

There was a plate of grapes—a great luxury, some smoked fish, black bread and hot coffee which tasted more like oatmeal. We didn't go swimming that day; the sky was overcast and there was an on-and-off-again drizzle. After breakfast I played volleyball with Petya, helped draw some water from the hand-pumped artesian well, and took a walk with Petya and his mother in the bordering woods. A few houses up from the Denisovs' there were a couple of goats tethered to the front gate, and in the woods I saw a few undersized milk cows.

When we came back from the walk Marya Dmitrevna was cross. "It's time to start the fire, Petya," she said, "and there are no twigs for kindling."

I thought perhaps she was getting blind. Not three feet from her was a goodly pile of small branches. Petya began scouring around for wood.

"What's wrong with those?" I asked Natasha.

She said, "They belong to the family in front."

"Why not borrow some and then return them?"

She shrugged. "It doesn't work out. We leave each other's personal property strictly alone. That's the only way to live collectively. If we start to use their wood supply, they'll start to use something of ours. Of course, we're neighborly and if they need anything we give it to them. But it's better to leave well enough alone."

"You picked up that expression from an American."

"No, no, we have the same thing in Russian."

After dinner which consisted of soup, sprats (small fish like sardines), potatoes, bread and tea, I asked Natasha about basic rationing. She had a worker's card which entitled her to the highest rations; Petya and his grandmother had dependents' rations, the lowest; Anna, too, had a worker's ration—all students have them.

"Bread is the base of everything," said Natasha. "The ration is not bad. I am allowed what amounts to a bit more than a pound a day. Petya and *Mamushka* receive about half that much."

"You eat it three meals a day?"

"Naturally. I suppose we always will. It keeps us healthy. I'm sure it has all those vitamins I see in the stories in American journals."

"Meat?"

"On my ration I'm supposed to get five and a half pounds a month and. . . ."

"Did you say a month?"

"Yes. The dependents only have about a pound and a half a month. Fats, that includes butter and bacon—I get a pound and three-quarters a month, Petya less than half a pound. Sweets, sugar. My ration is a pound a month but some months I'm lucky if I can buy half a pound. Petya's ration is about a quarter of a pound. That's why he was so happy over the chocolate bar. That is just about as much as he has per month regularly."

"I had some letters from people at home complaining about the sirloin steak and Scotch whisky situation in the States," I told Natasha. "I'll send them these figures."

"Every correspondent says that," Natasha smiled. "But it does no good. Nobody in America is much interested in how little to eat someone else has."

"That's not so. There's always a campaign to feed others—even Russians."

"I suppose so," she said, "but I bet it doesn't stop people from thinking of their own stomachs first. The only way to make people understand those figures is to put them on that diet."

Natasha made 1,350 rubles a month at her job. Sometimes she earned another 500 or 1,000 rubles doing some extra translations. She had plenty of money. Her basic rationed foods were ridiculously cheap. Bread cost about a ruble per pound, butter and sugar a ruble and a half. Prices went really sky high in the commercial stores or the black market where people could buy above their ration—as much as they could afford. The commercial stores had been opened for two reasons: to drain off the surplus rubles, and to close down the unofficial black markets.

I had priced things at these stores. A pound of bread was fifty or sixty rubles, a pound of sugar about five hundred, a pound of butter almost as much. Based on such prices Natasha's monthly wage would amount to two pounds of sugar and a pound of butter!

Before nightfall Anna appeared with the latest newspapers. She was a ruddy-cheeked, chubby girl who looked older than nineteen despite the fact that she wore her brown hair in braids and her skirts fairly short. She was a very lively girl, full of bounce both physically and mentally. When we had discussed the military situation to her satisfaction, she asked me the usual questions about American movies.

"You should not judge the United States or our movies by the ones you see here," I said. After all, "Union Pacific," "Sante Fe Trail," "100 Men and a Girl," "Sun Valley Serenade," "Elephant Boy" and "The Thief of Bagdad" are not typical. "You must understand," I said, "that your government buys only what we call 'escapist' pictures. They do not show our standard of living or our way of life."

Natasha had been silent, mending a pair of Petya's pants. She spoke up. "Our government is perfectly right. You are making a silly argument, my friend. You forget I have seen many of your movies at your Embassy, movies we do not see publicly in Moscow."

"What about it?"

"Do movies I've seen with Joan Crawford and Hedy Lamarr and Bette Davis really show the American standard of living? Aren't they better dressed than a worker's wife in Pittsburgh?"

"Yes, I suppose so." Natasha had known Erskine Caldwell when he was in Moscow, and her ideas of the U.S.A. were highly colored by reading his *God's Little Acre* and *Tobacco Road.*

"I think our government is right, too," chimed in Anna, "even if the movies Natasha talks about do show America as it really is. That is not important. We know you have more nice comforts than we have now. But we are taught that morale is important in a fight, and our movies must be selected to help that morale."

"True," said Natasha.

"And what about 'North Star'?" I asked. "Have you seen that? Did you like it?"

"Wonderful, very wonderful," Anna said.

"All right," Natasha was much less enthusiastic. "We laughed at the Hollywood conception of a Ukrainian collective farm. So much whitewash and such pretty smocks. But the plot was fine."

"About the songs," said Anna, "I did not understand. Why when there are so many fine Ukrainian and Russian songs, why did they have to make up some new ones?"

I said I didn't know.

Early in the morning Natasha and I went back to Moscow. The ride was uneventful. But as we walked down the platform into the station we passed a big statue of Lenin. A one-legged Red Army man was standing beneath the statue with a bouquet of wildflowers in his hand. He looked very happy. And he was whistling the tune of "Don't Sit Under the Apple Tree—with Anyone Else but Me."

3.

Compared to the first two war winters, the last two have been what Russians call "orphan's winters"—warm enough so that the fuel shortage did not cause severe suffering. Moscow's citizens are warmly garbed, quite shabbily "smart" in what has been described aptly as all that's left, their Sunday best. Except for two

waves of wartime flu, their health has been good. Food is not yet
plentiful but it seems sufficient. Stocks of vegetables from last
summer's "allotment" (victory) gardens—including beets, potatoes,
cabbage and carrots—help fill out the fare. Rations of meat, fish,
cheese, eggs and butter are cheap and adequate when and if
the stores have them to sell. American canned goods, once jokingly
called "Roosevelt's smile" and "second front," appear frequently
at *gastronomes* and Moscow has learned to like Spam almost as
well as *toushonica*, which is specially prepared for Russian consumption.

While Moscow's food shops are better stocked now than in the
past three war years, the supply of other consumer goods is still
mighty slim. The most frequented stores are commission shops
where people have their old possessions appraised and resold. In
a tour of several large ones I saw for sale a pure ivory mahjong
set, a bronze bust of Napoleon, an elegant hand-embroidered
Chinese robe, a silver-plated Gillette razor, but no ikons and no
samovars. Hardest-to-get things in Moscow continue to be women's
sheer stockings, tobacco, soap, razor blades, hairpins. Even vodka
is strictly rationed.

If material things are closely rationed in Moscow, spiritual joys
aren't. Churches are now fuller than at any time since the Revolution and everything is sweetness and light between the Orthodox
hierarchy and the Kremlin. But the rank-and-file Muscovite is
more interested in war maps than in the Bible. They would
rather hear front dispatches broadcast from one of the loudspeakers which overhang most of Moscow's squares than a sermon;
would rather sing such popular songs as "Wait for Me," "Beloved
City," "Blue Handkerchief" at a warm factory social than raise
their voices in hallelujahs at a cold cathedral.

Reminiscing correspondents like to think of Moscow as "the
Paris of this war." They get that feeling from recognizing Polish,
Czech, Yugoslav and French uniforms on Moscow's streets. There
are probably more different kinds of uniforms in Cairo or London,
but in Moscow you get the impression that the different pieces in
Europe's jigsaw are floating around waiting for the Red Army to
glue them together again.

Moscow's citizens discuss Europe, its future and the fate of
small nations, the same as Americans do, but with more unanimity.
These, however, are side issues. The average Muscovite worries
mostly about the war, his family and food rationing. He is more

opinionated on world politics than the average New Yorker and in some ways is better informed. He scans Roosevelt and Churchill's speeches which are excerpted in *Pravda* and *Izvestia*. He was upset by the United States elections. He could not figure out why, if Roosevelt and Churchill are doing a good job of winning the war, they are not as permanent as Stalin. He knows about the effectiveness of the Allied military campaign in Europe, but will probably never figure out why it took so long to materialize. The foreign news page of his newspaper reports almost daily on the progress of the Pacific war, but the significance of naval warfare and strategy is hard for him to grasp.

Most things in Moscow have one ultimate reason for existence —to help win the war. The horses that run at the Hippodrome are not really race horses; the track is just a testing ground for various strains and breeds of cavalry horses, to find and develop the fastest and sturdiest. The newly opened *Bolshoi Mostorg*, a department store where all kinds of prewar luxuries (leftover stocks) can be purchased, is a weapon—a weapon against inflation. The goods are not rationed, but the prices are prohibitive and meant to drain off surplus rubles. The commercial food stores and restaurants are also weapons against inflation and the fact that they help morale is almost incidental.

The theater, the concert halls, the opera, the ballet, some movies—they may be nonpolitical in character. But even *Ivan Susanin* has a message of patriotism, and so has Prokofiev's new *Alexander Nevsky Cantata*. Artists make their contribution by going off to the front in brigades to entertain the troops. They sing or act or dance in tents, in trenches, in forests, in blockhouses. They have suffered many casualties. One theatrical unit toured the fronts for seven months without ever having an opportunity to change clothes.

Every new book published must be a bullet, *Krasnaya Zvezda,* the army newspaper declared, and every line in every newspaper must shoot. There are no comic strips in Russian papers, no gossip columns, no large display advertisements, no stock exchange quotations, no crime stories—except daily stories of the greatest crime on earth, the German atrocities. The Russian equivalent of Ernie Pyle is a fifty-two-year-old native of Kiev, shaggy-haired, breast-beating Ilya Ehrenburg. He knows the man in the Red Army; he writes of his hopes and fears and mostly of his hates. He writes about the world from Moscow like an angry Walter

Lippmann. He is the Russian conscience, the spirit stimulator. From the first day of the war until long past the last, Ehrenburg will write lashing words, beating up the flame of hatred against the enemy, singing the glories of the peasant heroes, jabbing angry bayonets into Allies when he thinks they fail to understand Russian ways and Russian needs.

There are other popular writers in Russian papers, good ones, too. But none of them symbolizes the crusading spirit that this war has aroused like Ehrenburg. Not all Russians think as he thinks; they do not always agree with him or follow him. But to a greater or less degree he expresses sentiments they are trying to express; the government wants them in print, the people want to read them in print.

When Andrei Zhdanov, secretary of the Leningrad party, was chief of propaganda he was fond of exhorting Soviet writers to remember Gorky's definition of the writer's function—to be "the engineer of the human soul." Soviet writers have become engineers. They have recognized the war as an all-out fight for survival, and they have sharpened their pens so fine that they cannot write soft, in-between words. In the Soviet press, in Soviet wartime books, the Russians are good and true and brave and they scorn death; the Germans are bad and lying and cruel with no appreciation for life. What is written is censored and any lines of doubt that may have crept in are stricken out. In the mind's eye of every Soviet censor is a blazing placard with Stalin's declaration: "The printed word is the sharpest and most powerful weapon of the Communist party."

The writers and editors and censors have done their jobs well. The engineers can be congratulated. The Soviet people have dedicated their souls to winning the war.

4.

I found great changes in Moscow in 1943 when I returned there after eight years. The greatest change was nothing you could see. It wasn't the streets full of Red Army men, the splashy war posters, the unfinished buildings, the bomb damage, or the hollow cheeks. The difference was a difference of spirit. In 1935 these Russians were outcasts battling for the existence of a new social and economic order which, by its revolutionary nature, had set them apart from the outside world.

Today they are not only battling for their own survival, they are struggling for the continued existence of that outside world, or part of it; they are fighting together with great nations that once frowned on them. They have done well, and they know it. They have killed millions of Germans. Before our invasion of Europe, they had killed a half-dozen Nazis for every Nazi we destroyed. The Russians know they have suffered far greater losses in property and life than the other Allies combined.

They feel these sacrifices and these achievements have given them a right to be respected, a right to be able to make certain decisions for themselves which insure that they will never be invaded again. You can discuss many things with Russians, but not things that affect their future security. When we talk of the "Baltic problem," of "What to do with Germany," or "Should Russia return Bessarabia and the Western Ukraine," we are talking of theories illustrated on maps. To the Soviet citizen these are no longer matters for discussion. They are hard facts of Soviet security. They do not see these problems as pieces of a map; instead they see flaming houses, starving children, smashed factories. They want no advice from us on these subjects any more than we want theirs on the independence of Texas.

The average person in Moscow envisions a postwar world dominated by the Soviet Union, Britain and the United States. He is more interested in the future of the United Nations than the Comintern. He does not know when the war will end, but says it can't come too soon. He is tired but full of fight and hope and a growing sense of his country's importance.

The Russians are proud of their leaders, but chiefly they are proud of their Red Army. By the end of 1944 it was fighting in nine foreign countries: Poland, Rumania, Bulgaria, Hungary, Germany, Finland, Yugoslavia, Norway and Czechoslovakia. Never in all Russian history had Russian armies advanced onto so many foreign soils, and the Russian people are tremendously moved by the prowess of "their own."

The salutes in Moscow which celebrate each major Red Army victory are eagerly awaited by the war-weary population. The announcement on the radio is preceded by the tinkling bars from the song, "My Country Vast and Broad." Then the stentorian voice of Yuri Levitan is heard reading Stalin's Order of the Day or *Prekaz*. About fifteen minutes later, usually at nine, ten or eleven at night, the skies of Moscow are lit with simultaneous multicolored showers of Roman candles and sparkling rockets co-ordinated with the firing of hundreds of cannons. The number of cannons and the number of salvos fired depends on the size of the victory.

On one night last summer there were five victory salutes. But of all the salutes, the one which caused the greatest emotional reaction was that which celebrated the Red Army's gaining its own borders—reaching the River Prut on the Rumanian frontier after three years of fighting the enemy on Russian soil. When the news was announced at meetings, in theaters and movie houses, people cheered, clapped, stamped their feet. Orchestras struck up the new national anthem, and the people sang:

Unbreakable Union of freeborn Republics,
Great Russia has welded forever to stand;
Created in struggle by will of the peoples,
United and mighty, our Soviet Land!

Sing to our Motherland, glory undying,
Bulwark of peoples in brotherhood strong!
Flag of the Soviets, peoples' flag flying,
Lead us from vict'ry to victory on!

Through tempests the sunrays of freedom have cheered us,
Along the new path where great Lenin did lead,
Be true to the people, thus Stalin has reared us,
Inspired us to labor and valorous deed!

I was in the audience at the Mossoviet Theatre that night. Stalin's aide, Colonel General Golikov, was sitting very near me. It could not have been news to him this reaching of the border. But he was so moved by the demonstration that he cried. He wasn't the only one.

That night I thought some more about why the Russians had won. I had a long list. I supposed that various friends of mine in America would select different reasons. The Jeffersonian Democrat might like "the people." A business executive, "organization." A military man, "superior generalship."

It was obviously impossible to find a catch-all answer. "The weather," "nationalism," "patriotism" were all parts of a complex whole. But of all the capsule comments, one seemed less glib, more honest than any other. I found it in a piece by the famous Russian writer and humorist, Eugene Petrov, who was killed at the front in 1943 while serving as a war correspondent. Petrov believed that the reason for the Soviet Union's strength and for its victory lies in the fact that "it rose above the chaos of the war, while at the same time subordinating itself to the war."

I was fascinated by Petrov's words. I kept asking Russians what they thought of them as an interpretation. They liked them. Then I would ask, "How can you best illustrate it?"

There were various suggestions. Some pointed to the theater and how it flourished with deferments even in wartime. Someone else mentioned nurseries and clinics, and someone else said that science was the best example.

Then I read about the Boikos in *Red Star*. I think their story is a good illustration of Petrov's words. Ivan and Alexandra Boiko were Ukrainians working in the Far Eastern town of Magadan. He was a truck driver, the best in the town. She was a secretary in a factory. When the war broke out Ivan tried to enlist, but Ivan was too valuable a driver for the management to release. So the Boikos worked in the rear. They worked overtime and made a lot of money. Ivan taught his wife how to drive a truck. She volunteered, too, but the factory refused to release her. They were both unhappy because the Germans were pillaging their native Ukraine. They had captured Kiev, where Alexandra was born and went to school.

Then the young couple read in a newspaper that Ferapont Golovaty, a Saratov beekeeper, had donated 100,000 rubles for the construction of an airplane and had written a letter to Marshal Stalin about it. So they sat down and wrote to Stalin. They said they had savings of 50,000 rubles. Could they please buy a tank and go to the front in it?

Almost six months passed before a reply came. In the meantime Ivan studied after work, learning all he could from books about tanks. He taught Alexandra what he knew about simple motors. One day a letter came, postmarked MOSKVA. Stalin thanked them, congratulated them and said, "Your request will be granted."

The year that followed the two spent in a tank school. Classroom work came hard to Ivan Boiko who had been brought up in an orphan's home and had started working before he completed school. But Alexandra helped him and they finished the tank course in the same class, she with a rating of "excellent" and he with "good."

Several months after this story appeared in *Red Star* I saw the Boikos mentioned in one of Stalin's Orders of the Day. Upon graduation they had been given their own tank with BOIKO painted on the turret. They were assigned to a line unit. Just before she was to go into her first attack the regimental commander, who still had some old-fashioned notions about the best place for women, summoned Alexandra to headquarters and ordered her to remain there. At the risk of a court-martial Alexandra slipped out into the night, begged a ride from a motorcyclist heading for the front, found her tank and her husband and did not leave them.

The family tank saw only a few days' action before it got into a difficult tangle with two Tiger tanks and a company of tommy-gunners near Dvinsk. For three hours the Boikos beat off the enemy. When reinforcements came up they found the Boiko tank dented with shell marks, its main gun and caterpillar treads out of commission. Alexandra had an arm wound and Ivan was hit in the leg.

The two Nazi Tigers never left the battlefield. All in all during their brief battle career the Boikos destroyed five tanks, two field pieces, several supply wagons and machine-gun nests.

The next thing I read was that the Boikos were being decorated for valor. Alexandra received the Order of the Patriotic War and Ivan got the Order of the Red Banner. When a lieutenant general handed her the decoration in the hospital, he asked, "Now tell me the truth, were you scared before the battle?"

Alexandra looked him in the eye and answered, "Yes, I was."

Late last summer Alexandra turned up in Moscow as a delegate to the Fourth Women's Anti-Fascist Meeting. She didn't appear very ferocious. She was twenty-six and looked younger, slight of build, with hair the color of ripe rye. Her eyes were frank and blue. When interviewed she kept saying that reporters frightened her more than Nazi tanks. Someone asked her what she thought of American tanks. She hesitated and shot a questioning look at a Foreign Office official.

"Go right ahead," he said.

Alexandra said American tanks were fine and she was very grateful for them, but she liked Soviet tanks much, much better.

Then Alexandra was asked about the postwar. What did she want to do? Did she plan to have children? Alexandra was suddenly very grave. "I am not thinking about what I'm going to do after the war," she said. "First we have to fight for victory. I don't think about anything else now."

BOOK 3

Death Will Be Afraid of Us

I. Leningrad

FOR generations there will be poems and stories and novels and plays about how the Russian people rose up and defended their cities. Shostakovich has already composed a magnificent symphony about the defense of his native Leningrad, a popular book has been published on the siege of Sevastopol, a good play was produced in Moscow about the fight for Stalingrad, and there have been fine short stories on the Odessa underground.

While no foreigner will ever be able to tell these stories the way the Russians can, nothing is going to stop some of us from trying. In this instance, Leningrad and Odessa have been singled out for several reasons. As I had visited these cities before the war, there was a good basis for picturing what had happened to them physically. During 1944 there were opportunities to gather clear and colorful information in both places just after the enemy had been driven away.

My first trip to Leningrad was in 1935, and I well remembered its wide prospects and graceful river bridges, its old palaces and its new workers' apartment houses. Early in February, 1944, within a month after the blockade had been broken, we were permitted to go to Leningrad. In June, I returned again for a few days and had a chance to check the information gathered previously. Inevitably too much time was spent touring ruined palaces and not enough time talking to the people. But even so, you couldn't help catching some of the epic drama which Leningrad had lived and which the newly liberated Leningrad was still living.

2.

The city was built by Peter the First in 1703. He planned his city on the swamps of the Baltic Sea and called it St. Petersburg. He envisioned this "window on the west" as a great metropolis, symbolic of Russia's emergence as a great European power. Peter never lived to see his dream realized.

This was Lenin's city, too. Here the first Soviet was established Here Lenin returned from exile and won the siege of Petersburg. He envisioned the city as an outpost of a new and Soviet Russia which would demonstrate the success of Communism through its industrial, political and cultural development. So much of Lenin's hopes and dreams were here, that the city was renamed for him. He, too, never lived to see his dreams realized.

Hitler wanted Leningrad. He wanted it so badly he could almost taste it. In November, 1941, at Munich he dangled his vision before the glazed eyes of the German people. "Leningrad will put its hands up," he shouted. "It will fall sooner or later. Nobody is going to free it. No one will be able to pass through the lines we have erected. Leningrad will die of starvation."

He will never live to see his dream realized, either.

In terms of cold-blooded military analysis, Hitler should have been right. But somehow through a miracle, Leningrad never did "put its hands up," never did fall to the Nazis despite twenty-nine months of siege and blockade. The "miracle" that saved Leningrad was a miracle wrought by its people and its leaders.

When the Germans struck on June 22, 1941, the Soviets knew that Leningrad, because of its vulnerable position, would be one of the first major Nazi objectives. Mobilization began immediately. Not just calling up classes for the Red Army, but total mobilization of the population for active defense of the city. By July 7, less than three weeks later, 110,000 Leningrad civilians had volunteered for the Peoples' Guards. They began drilling in their spare time, learning to shoot and to crawl and to get along with a minimum of sleep.

In two months the Germans cut across the Baltic states and closed in on Leningrad. The siege began on August 21, 1941. By that time a half million of Leningrad's three and a half million prewar population had put aside everything else and were out building fortifications. Some rode out to the suburbs and dug trenches. Others made tank traps. Housewives, workers, actors, office clerks, scientists, artists, writers, college students, built barricades. Before the Nazis' steel ring was finally closed that fall, tens of thousands of mothers and young children were evacuated, along with some factories and skilled workers.

In August the ceaseless pounding began. The first raid of bombers hit food storage warehouses. That night the streets ran with melted chocolate and the air was rich and sticky with the smell of burning sugar and wheat. Every day, Nazi Heinkels, Junkers, Stukas roared overhead. Every day, long-range shells lobbed into the large workers' sections, crashing through buildings, tearing up the sewage system, chewing up the roads, demolishing gardens and schools, churches and stores.

In August Marshal Voroshilov came to Leningrad. On August 21 he and Party Secretary Zhdanov and Mayor Peter Popkov wrote a "Leningrad in Peril" appeal which the radio carried to the front lines, into the nurseries, into the factories, along the Neva River.

They said, "*Tovarishchi*—. The enemy is attempting to penetrate into Leningrad. . . . This shall not be. . . . With our own hands we built the powerful factories and workshops of Leningrad and the remarkable buildings and gardens, and they will not fall into the hands of the German robbers. This will never be. . . ."

Prewar Leningrad had become some of the things that Peter and Lenin had dreamed. In Leningrad the people boasted of their 60 institutions of higher learning, 103 technical schools, 487 elementary and secondary schools, 21 stadiums, 89 hospitals, 240 nurseries, 42 cinemas, 25 theaters. Leningrad was proud of its culture and its industry. It had been the home of Moussorgsky, Tschaikowsky, Dostoevsky. It was the home of Russia's first steel blooming mill, its first dynamo. Here had been produced Russia's first tractor, its first locomotive.

The people thought of these achievements as they listened to the words of their leaders coming to them over the loudspeaker. They heard an answer to Hitler's claims. The leaders promised: "He will never set foot in our beautiful city. We will form new detachments of the national militia to help the Red Army. . . . We will choose for these new detachments the bravest and the most gallant comrades, the workers and the intellectuals. . . . A terrible danger is now hanging over Leningrad."

These figures tell the story of what Leningrad did to meet "the terrible danger." The people built 15,000 blockhouses and 250 miles of wall. They dug 300 miles of antitank ditches (three times the distance from New York to Philadelphia) and erected 20 miles of barricades in the streets and squares of their city.

In September the Germans pushed closer from the west and south. The Finns pressed down the Karelian isthmus, helping to shut the trap from the north and east. Rail lines to Moscow were severed. Highways were controlled by the enemy. The Nazis had air superiority, and only a few Soviet transport planes ran the blockade. A slow paralysis began setting in. The Leningrad Defense Committee, headed by Zhdanov, understood the seriousness of the situation. Food supplies were dangerously low as a result of Nazi bombing. There might be enough to last through the winter for the Red Army, but there would definitely be nothing for civilians.

They radioed the Supreme Command in Moscow. But the outlook for full-scale aid from outside was also dismal. The military picture was critical everywhere. The Nazis were trampling through the Ukraine. Rumanians were helping them. They had taken Odessa, which next to Leningrad is the country's second largest port. German U-boats patrolled the sea. The routes from Murmansk were blocked. Panzer divisions were racing for Moscow.

There was no food coming into Leningrad. And there were no new guns, either, no artillery, no planes, no replacements. There was no oil left to run the Baltic Navy fleet. Big guns were dismounted from the battleships, hauled ashore and remounted to defend the city. Leningrad had to make its own munitions, supply its ragged armies. The choice was simple, fight or die. Or both.

Even the weather that winter was grim, the grimmest in decades. Snows were heavier, temperatures lower. At least the snow could be used to put out incendiaries. Every day 300,000 Leningrad women of all ages cleaned the streets. They kept the city's 27,000 sewers open to lessen the chance of epidemics. These women never stopped working until they collapsed. They camouflaged guns. They manned antiaircraft batteries. They repaired burst water mains. They hacked holes through three feet of ice to draw water from the Neva. They collected firewood.

The able-bodied men worked from eighty to one hundred hours a week. Schools remained open for part of the day. Then the children went out with their teachers to clear away the bomb and shell damage, to draw water, to find twigs. They did their lessons in pencil. The ink froze in their desk wells.

The Leningrad Library, which claims to be the world's largest

with its nine million volumes, was the city's most popular gathering place. No one seemed to care for "escape" literature. Biggest
demands were for books about the historic sieges of other wars.
People wanted books on how to do things without machinery.
They studied primitive times. Scientists went there to study, too.
They learned how to make matches with very little sulphur. They
spent hours researching the food value in moss or in the leaves of
chestnut trees. Professor Moshansky concocted a vitamin drink
made of fresh pine and fir needles. The library never closed down.

By Christmas there wasn't a cat or dog left on the streets or anywhere else in Leningrad. It was a common sight to see people
suddenly keel over on the streets, either in a faint or in death.
Husky men sometimes stood stock-still and leaned against a
building, just to catch their strength.

A Leningrad poet wrote:

> We do not cry
> For it is truly said:
> Our tears are frozen dry,
> We have no tears to shed.

And all the time the city was pounded, day and night. The Nazis
used fifty-two infantry divisions, four motorized divisions, and four
tank divisions in an attempt to break into the city. The suburbs
were taken, one by one. More than a thousand Nazi and Finnish
planes buzzed overhead, dropping their bombs indiscriminately.
But there never was any thought of surrender, despite high losses.
Nine workers' divisions dug in at the front. Four of them were
wiped out. The others had better than 50 per cent casualties.

In December, when things were blackest, an expedient idea
saved Leningrad. By December 15 the streetcars had stopped running. There was no heat. The water did not run, either. There was
no electric power. There was no tea. And kerosene enough only
for war plants. But Zhdanov had organized the "Road of Life"—
a 50-mile long highway across Lake Ladoga. Work on it had begun
as soon as the lake froze. Engineers drove great wooden piles
through the ice to the lake's bed, thus strengthening the causeway.
By February it was working. First only a trickle. First supplies for
the Army. Along it went gasoline, ammunition, medical supplies,
flour, sugar, and American canned meat. This lake road was the
pinprick that frustrated the German-Finnish "airtight" plan to
starve out the city by squatting in their trenches.

The rest of the Soviet Union worked to get food to Leningrad. Gifts came from Central Asia and Siberia and even from Sevastopol, which itself was engaged in a life and death struggle. Partisan units behind the German lines raided Nazi supplies, seizing food and sending it across the lake to Leningrad. The "Road of Life" was a perilous one. Always within mortar range, nearly always

The Road of Life

under attack from bombers, it nevertheless stayed open as long as the ice held. Nature, too, defied the Nazis. The lake's surface refroze nightly despite bomb and shell holes. During the winter of 1941-1942 over 360,000 tons of freight went across to Leningrad.

January, 1942, the month before the Ladoga road opened, was perhaps the worst month. The death toll from starvation had mounted into staggering figures. Some said two million, others claimed only half a million. Probably a figure between seven hundred and fifty thousand and a million would not be exaggerated.

Droves of children hauled their aged grandparents to burial grounds in sleds. When a relative died, the family would hide the body in a closet until the stench became too strong—just to get the extra ration.

But there wasn't much of this, the people said. Everyone knew they had to pull together. When the telephones weren't working, young Komsomols called from house to house to find out if neighbors needed help. When the bread trucks did arrive at stores, there was no rioting. Everyone waited patiently. When the bread ration was cut from three slices to a slice and a half for nonworkers, it was accepted without protest. The Army on the Leningrad front even asked the high command to reduce its rations so that the civilians could have more. But the high command decided the soldiers were receiving just a bare minimum and would not agree. The soldiers' rations then were three and one-half slices of black bread a day.

Even when everything seemed to have stopped in January, the Kirov plant kept going. This was Leningrad's stout heart. The Germans pushed to within two and a half miles of the factory's gates. They dropped millions of leaflets urging that Leningrad, like Paris, be proclaimed an "open city." For an answer the weary workers held a meeting and wrote out a message to be sent to the Red Army troops. The message was: "We are with you. *Death will be afraid of us before we are afraid of death.*"

Spring finally brought warmth and hope. Little boys flew kites, decorated with hammer and sickles, over the German lines. In April when the ice began to melt on Lake Ladoga, the trucks kept going until some of them broke through the thin layer under their own weight. But in another month the lake was ready for shipping, and the Ladoga fleet kept the lifeline open. Now there was a two-way commerce. Munitions and food poured into Leningrad; new tanks and mortars; flour and sugar and tea. Out of Leningrad went the sick and wounded, the very young and the very feeble. Between May 24, 1942, and the end of the year, more than 900,000 civilians and more than a million tons of equipment were evacuated to the East, most of them beyond the Urals. All were shipped across the lake, which became for them the road *to* life.

On April 15 the first streetcars ran again. Thousands leaned against buildings and watched, raising their voices in feeble cheers. Nikolai Tikhinov, the Leningrad writer, said, "Streetcars, not swallows, brought spring to Leningrad this year." Red Army men and civilian fighters at the "front" were able to come "home" at night into the heart of the city. Then shortly before dawn, they crammed into a tram and rode to the outskirts to fight again.

From then on life slowly ebbed back into Leningrad. But rations were still low. Everything was stored up, awaiting the moment when the force inside the city was strong enough to smash the force outside.

3.

The major Red Army offensive from Leningrad began at 9:20 A.M. the morning of January 15, 1944. The last shells fell on the city on the eighteenth. I left Moscow on February 6 with a group of correspondents and arrived in Leningrad by train on February 8.

We were quartered in the Hotel Astoria, Leningrad's finest. It is located on St. Isaak's Square, opposite the Cathedral of St. Isaak. This is the city's largest cathedral, a handsome granite and marble-columned nineteenth century structure shaped like a cross. Ten of its imposing columns had been cracked by shells and a half dozen nicked. Leningraders called these nicks "German kisses." The cathedral's golden dome was blackened. As we drove to our hotel we noticed that the graceful spire of the Admiralty was also dark.

Opposite the hotel was the red-brown brick façade of the old German Embassy, converted into a hospital; further up the street was the Tsar's War Ministry; in the center of the square stood the boarded-up statue of Nicholas the First, famous for its presentation of a heroic-sized horse and dwarfed man.

The streets of Leningrad were not nearly as crowded as before the war. The population of three and one-half million had been pared by evacuation, starvation, recruitment and deaths to about half a million. But for all its pounding, the city looked much better than Stalingrad, Kharkov, Smolensk, Sevastopol or Odessa. It was shabby and unpainted, but clean.

The first day in Leningrad we visited the historic suburbs. The rape of Peterhof, Russia's "little Versailles," was described by Nikolai Baranov, chief architect of Leningrad. He was a small, almond-eyed, pink-cheeked fat man, with a double chin, turned-up nose, and light blue eyes. He was dressed like any fashionable European in a dark blue overcoat with a beaver collar, gray fedora and leather-trimmed *valinki*. He spoke with the emotional intensity of a Frenchman as he pointed out the barren cascades without fountains and statuary, denuded of its *pièce de résistance*, Samson. Baranov pointed to the hollow shell of the imperial palace which was designed by Leblond in 1720 and enlarged by Rastrelli in 1756. Baranov said the walls and grounds could and would be rehabilitated. But the interior was wrecked and the furnishings had been stolen by the Nazis. Walking away from Peterhof along the snowy, recently de-mined paths, a Russian officer remarked to me: "Why do they have to pick such beautiful places for fighting when there are such dull ones?"

On the road from Peterhof Palace past the cathedral, which was riddled by shells and incendiaries, there were still German signs reading, "*Vorsicht Minen!*" And Red Army sapper patrols were working along the fields, exploding them. Every so often Moscow's "war correspondents" would jump like startled fawns when a sudden loud report and a puff of black smoke near by signaled another de-mining.

Returning to Leningrad we stopped at Bezzabotny ("Carefree") Hill 15 miles from the city to inspect a German mobile 210-millimeter cannon, weighing 34,450 kilograms, and firing a shell of 118 kilograms with a muzzle velocity of 865 meters per second. This 1939 model Krupp gun, manufactured in 1942, was operated by 12 men. It has a 54-foot barrel and fires 150 shells every 24 hours. The Red Army uncovered 30 such guns in this area, all with 30 kilometers' range. The cannon on Bezzabotny Hill pointed straight at Peterhof Cathedral. When asked how the gun's barrel had been broken, lieutenant colonel of the Engineers Lev Barshai smiled and said: "Oh, we've counterartillery batteries which take care of these intruders."

Along snow-covered roads we passed many strange and wonderful things. Red Army construction troops were working on German-built fortifications, and flapping in the breeze above their heads were women's underwear, stockings and brassières, belonging to the Red Army girls who were busily swinging picks. A tractor was hauling behind it a new wooden house on skis, which was being dragged to the front for the artillerists to live in. "I think I'll get out and look at that," said one correspondent. "I wouldn't do that," said A.P.'s Henry Cassidy. "How could we cable your office and explain that their Moscow correspondent was run over at the front by a house?"

Riding back through the gathering dusk, the sun—the first we had seen of it in two months—was setting in a splash of color while a full Leningrad moon was already looming in the pale sky. Along the roads on the outskirts of the city husky, warmly dressed Red Army girls were breaking up barricades which still blocked many of the key corners. The road was still littered with burned, overturned, battered tramcars, which the Germans had captured in their swift advance on Leningrad in the fall of 1941. Big signboards were there, with the biggest word "*He*" in Russian—only it means "No" and not "he." The sign tells civilians what *not* to do with incendiaries. There were also many advertisements on solitary walls of ruined buildings, urging the purchase of Russian war bonds.

The next day, with members of the Red Army staff who participated in the battle, we visited Finnskoye Koirovo, which is a hill overlooking Leningrad from the south. It rises to a height of forty-nine meters above the plain, stretching to the front. This height blocked any advance from Leningrad and also was a strong point in the protection of Krasnoye Selo, which lies directly behind the hill. Lieutenant Colonel Grigori Romanovich Ketlerov, describing the action, said that the German fortifications here were in many ways stronger than the Siegfried or Maginot Lines. They were completely fortified against attacks from the rear and flanks, making a direct frontal attack necessary. They were also constructed in such a way that it was impossible to trap a large number of troops in one spot. The entire elevation was encircled by barbed wire six times and between these six barriers lay tank blocks, traps and entanglements. The depth of the wire was 150 meters. Approaches to the hill were heavily mined on both sides of the barbed wire, as well as by tank booby traps. A circular trench ran a kilometer around the hill's base, then another 150 meters upwards and connected with the first. There was a third row of trenches nearer the top. On the crest a half dozen concrete and galvanized iron pillboxes were sunk in the ground with all the comforts of home except running water, and not excepting the telephone. Beyond the crest there were blockhouses and dugouts for reserves. In the passages between the trenches there was space for four or five men. All the firing points were connected. Ketlerov refused to give exact figures but he admitted 25 per cent of the attackers had been lost trying to take this vital height. The Russians began on January 15 by laying down a terrific artillery barrage estimated at a half million shells. When the weather cleared around noon, the attack was supported by air bombing. The Nazis had a regiment defending the hill, plus forty to fifty tanks. Russian forces, crawl-ing up the plain toward the hill and through a small patch of fir trees to the left, were led by Major General Semonyak, decorated last year by the United States with the Distinguished Service Medal for the defense of Leningrad.

Asked how the Russians got through the mine fields, Ketlerov explained that the artillery barrage was so thick and heavy it literally plowed up the fields, de-mining them. But the Russians also used sappers, hand grenades and bombs.

We walked to a point four hundred meters away where the German command headquarters were well camouflaged with evergreen trees. This was a communication center also, with phones and maps. It was protected from the rear by two huge con-crete slabs overlooking the hill. Between the slabs room was left for a periscope with which the officers surveyed the surrounding territory. It could also be used as a well-screened fire point for a machine gun.

All around Finnskoye Koirovo loose cartridges were strewn like Good Humor sticks on Coney Island after a July Fourth week end. One correspondent picked up a regimental Nazi flag as a trophy, slightly annoying the Red Army officers who would have liked it. A woman correspondent daintily lifted a trophy which was hur-riedly grabbed away from her. It was an unexploded percussion cap for a mine.

Further on, around the station at Krasnoye Selo where the fighting for the town had been heaviest, there was a great collec-tion of German munitions, including the newest field guns, tanks, Mark IV's, V's, Ferdinands, Tigers, and a 220-millimeter French gun. A trophy expert explained that much of this material was usable, especially mortar shells. One thirsty correspondent nearly lost an arm trying to pry open a box marked, *James Hennessey 3-Star Cognac,* which contained machine-gun cartridges.

At Catherine the Great's palace, Gatchina, which she built for her lover Grigori Orloff in 1768, I found a box marked, *Cordon Rouge—Mumm's.* In it the Germans had packed vases for ship-ment to Berlin. This little rustic "retreat" had been a museum for the history of Russian arms when I'd been there in 1935. Now it was just a shambles. During the occupation the Germans used the first floor for a warehouse and the second floor for barracks and a brothel for the air officers. By the time the Nazis were routed out of the building it was well looted and burned, its beautiful English style formal garden left as bleak and unattractive as a vacant lot in Hoboken.

There was very little left of other famous suburbs which we visited. Pushkin, which was named in 1937 for the poet's centennial, had been formerly known as Detskoye Selo ("Children's Village") and before the Revolution as Tsarskoye Selo ("Tsar's Village"). Pushkin went to school and lived summers in this town and later described it in his verses. But its lovely palaces had all been mined and burned.

To the Russians, Peterhof, Gatchina and Pushkin are cherished monuments of Russia's history. Americans can best realize the Russian's emotions by imagining their own heartbreak if the Germans had razed Mount Vernon, Monticello and Alexandria.

4.

In his large, comfortable, well-lit office the next day, Chief Architect Baranov's blue eyes sparkled as he talked of plans for rebuilding Leningrad. On the wall of the office was a large portrait of Stalin and another of Sergei Kirov, former Leningrad party leader. In one corner there was a grandfather's clock and in another, a large bust of Lenin, behind which curled a scarlet banner. On the wall was a huge map of Leningrad, showing plans for improvements adopted in 1935. After discussing building projects, Baranov turned to Major Mikhailov, chief of Leningrad's air-raid precaution. Pointing to a huge white map, Mikhailov explained that red spots indicated artillery shell hits and black ones were for bombs. It hurt my eyes to look at the map which was a delirium of dots. The preponderance of red and black spots were in civilian areas in spite of the fact that the Germans, and Finns from the north, were close enough to the city to select their objectives with precision. Another map with red splotches for incendiaries looked like a face with a bad case of measles. Mikhailov said the enemy gave up on incendiaries after a few months because they were not effective, due to the well-organized Leningrad populace. But for twenty-nine months the city had been showered daily with 250 to 1,000 shells per day. Occasionally as many as 2,500 fell. In all, there were over 100,000 shell hits on structures. Of Leningrad's 15,000,000 square meters of dwelling space, 3,000,000 square meters "just disappeared."

Inspecting the usual tourist sites in Leningrad with Baranov, it

was difficult to imagine the pounding. Leningrad appeared relatively untouched. One reason for this illusion was that bomb
damage had been quickly cleared away. For the good of home
morale, artists had painted false canvas or plywood façades on
wrecked buildings. And in some cases reconstruction had actually
been carried out even during the siege. Pompous Kazan Cathedral,
built as a memorial of the War of 1812 (it had been an antireligious museum in 1935), was hit by a shell on the roof. Most of
the structure remained intact. Kids were skiing under its arches,
dodging in and out of its columns. In front of the entrance was a
huge unframed propaganda painting, showing a group of partisans
coming upon a dead mother and bleeding child in the snow.

The Hall of Emblems, lecture hall in the Ethnological Museum,
the largest in Europe, was wrecked by a ton bomb. Nearly all the
exhibits had been evacuated, but gazing through a gaping hole
to the back of the building I saw a green frieze depicting the
nationalities of the Soviet Union and a white bas-relief of Stalin
on a red background. Walking gingerly through the rubble of the
long, unlit, drafty corridors, I stopped to look at a dusty exhibit
of children's crayon drawings which were slowly curling up in
windowless cases.

Another historically interesting structure—the castle of Paul the
First—was also partially destroyed. Leningrad's most famous
buildings, the Hermitage and Winter Palace, which had been wonderful art museums, were now dingy and unpainted, peeling and
completely windowless. The Hermitage Hall of Emblems had been
hit by a shell on January 4, 1944. Up to May 1, 1943, over eighty
tons of broken glass had been removed from the Hermitage and
Winter Palace and the damage to the buildings estimated at a
billion rubles. We were shown through empty art museum rooms
in which empty frames stared down at us like empty eye sockets.
Our guide was a wispy-haired little woman in a beret, black stockings and shoes which had seen jollier days. She seemed to resent
any attempt to rush through an empress' boudoir to inspect a
shell-splint. The famed Rubens room, which had once been so warm
and friendly with rosy, soft-skinned nudes bulging large in gilt
frames, was now as coldly musty as an eighteenth century attic.

Smolny Institute and the near-by Smolny Cathedral were still
intact. Smolny was a former girls' seminary where Lenin directed
the October revolution. It was now party headquarters and the
nerve center of the defense of Leningrad. Near by, the yellow

Duma Building, where Kerensky sang his brief swan song, without encores, was also in good condition.

Other places hadn't been so fortunate. On Suvorov Prospect, until recently called Soviet Prospect, a hospital had been hit by a bomb and those patients not killed by its explosion were caught in the fire which followed. The Frunze and Kirov districts, where most of the newer modern workers' apartment houses were located, now were fine examples of the twentieth century Nazi art of devastation.

5.

When we returned to the Astoria, new Red Army recruits were drilling in St. Isaak's Square. From a room on the second floor facing the square, I heard them singing. A dumpy, smiling, middle-aged chambermaid entered to draw the blackout curtains. On her plain black dress she proudly wore the gold-gilt medal with the green ribbon for the defense of Leningrad. It had been awarded to the 300,000 residents who physically aided the defense in a military sense. My roommate, Chicago *Sun's* Edward Angly, who came to Russia because he had run from the Germans on four other fronts since 1939 and wanted a chance to chase them, grabbed the startled woman by the shoulders: "I don't *panamyoo* Russian," he said, "but I do understand this," touching the medal on her breast. The woman's eyes glistened and she grinned from ear to ear. Suddenly she blushed as Angly bowed formally and then proceeded to kiss her soundly on both cheeks in his best French manner. "That's for getting that," said Uncle Ed. "*Spasibo bolshoi*," murmured the confused but pleased maid. She turned and fled from the room.

That evening Anglo-American correspondents were guests at the clubhouse of Leningrad scientists. At nine we filed into a warm, pleasant paneled room, with nut-brown ceiling, green walls and heavy white brocade portieres over the windows. An official greeting was made by the editor of Leningrad *Pravda*, Nikolai Dmitrovich Shumilov, a short, blond man standing stiffly in a single-breasted dark blue suit. Behind him burned a roaring open peat fire and on the mantlepiece was a bronze statue of Dante. In this room there were not the usual huge pictures of Soviet leaders, but several pleasant landscapes and two large nineteenth century oils of gracious gentlewomen. However, off to one side was a bronze bust of Lenin as a young man.

Fingering his dark, horn-rimmed glasses, Shumilov welcomed us on behalf of Leningrad's journalists, scientists, artists and writers, many of whom were in the room to meet us. Leningrad's intellectuals looked like a similar group in New York or London or Paris, except the men were less soft and the women less sophisticated looking. Most wore the Leningrad defense medal and some had other Soviet decorations.

Paul Kobeko, a corresponding member of the Academy of Sciences, discussed some of the scientific advances made during the siege. "Among other things," he said smiling, "in our topsy-turvy chemistry we discovered how to take ether and produce spirits which are, after all, the vital elixir of life."

Professor Alexander Berigo, director of the radium department of the Leningrad Institute, a short, fat man about sixty, told of developing luminous apparatus for air navigation and night flying. He also touched briefly on his work of producing ionized air and his new findings on longevity which may rival those of Ukrainian Alexander Bogomolets.

Tall, stoop-shouldered Karl Eliasberg, dressed in a dark, double-breasted suit with white piqué piping on the vest, talked about the work of the intelligentsia during the blockade, illustrating the discussion with deeds of his orchestra. This symphony of sixty-five men of the Leningrad Radio Committee was the only musical organization not evacuated. It was composed mostly of "old men." They all participated in air-raid precaution work. For periods of twenty days, groups of fifty of these musicians would leave to go to the front and dig trenches and build barricades. On their return they would be replaced by others. This meant that two-thirds were always away, leaving about twenty-five musicians. It necessitated reorchestrations as they were kept busy day and night playing for broadcasts, theaters, concerts, cinemas, hospitals, shelters, and even at the front. Those remaining in the city sandbagged the building of the Radio Committee, dug for water, propped ceilings and put out incendiaries.

On October 28, 1941, they were scheduled to broadcast Tschaikowsky's *Fifth* to London at 11 P.M., although the Germans were raiding the city regularly at seven. That evening bombs burst around the building, blasting windows, showering plaster off the walls. The orchestra spent twenty-four hours in the building, trying simultaneously to rehearse and attend to ARP duties. An hour and a half before the concert they were repairing blackout curtains which had been ripped off, and the raid was still on. One oboe player suffered a head wound and a violinist had the flesh torn from his leg. Fifteen minutes before eleven they assembled, tuned up, and played the scheduled concert.

During February of 1942, the musicians were so weakened by lack of food that they were unable to lift their fingers to play. By spring the orchestra had lost forty-two men through starvation, shelling and bombing, and couldn't find new recruits as all possible substitutes had been evacuated. The Red Army front commander recognized the importance of keeping up morale in the besieged city and sent twenty-three soldier-musicians from the front to Leningrad to play in the Philharmonic.

In May they received the score of Shostakovich's *Seventh Symphony* by plane, but due to a lack of musicians, score paper and oboe reeds, they were unable to orchestrate and rehearse it. The first performance was not given until August 9, 1942. On that memorable evening in the great hall of the Philharmonic the weary defenders of Leningrad heard their own Dmitri's glorious tribute to his native city. As if sensing the inspirational value of the Leningrad symphony, the Germans, more than usually, slugged the city with bombs and shells during rehearsals and even during the premiere performance.

We next interviewed handsome, thirty-year-old Hero of the Soviet Union, Major Vassili Antonovich Matsietich who had been a fighter pilot for eleven years. This dark-haired son of the Ukraine, with a large nose, full mouth, heavy-set chin and pointed sideburns, wore five decorations on his well-pressed uniform. Matsietich was the leader of a fearless squadron of Leningrad fighters who first smacked German planes from the air by ramming them. He recalled the night of November 4, 1943, when his friend Lieutenant Servostianov, in a fight with a Heinkel-111 ran out of ammunition and sent his Yak crashing into the Nazi headfirst. He bailed out and one of the Germans managed to parachute down also. Floating down in the glare of Leningrad's searchlights, Servostianov lost his *valinki*. When he toppled over in the snow, he was not recognized by civilians who, said Matsietich, took him for a German and treated him in a "somewhat critical spirit" until he established his identity. The Nazi flier rolled himself up in his parachute and burrowed into a snowbank. He was pulled out by irate women who pounced on him and dragged him through the streets in an even more critical spirit.

German ackack, although heavily concentrated around Leningrad to protect their long-range guns, had not worried Matsietich and his night fighters. "Our law has become not to avoid searchlight and antiaircraft batteries, but to sail into them and punish them. This makes it easier for us in the long run." Germans had air superiority on the Leningrad front until the end of 1942 at which time, with the aid of Spitfires, Hurricanes, Airacobras and their own Yaks and Lags, the Soviets became the scourge of the airways. With no false modesty, Matsietich said he found the Soviet Yak the best fighter, although he liked the Bell Airacobra's equipment, its powerful guns and armor, but "it is not quite fast enough and not quite maneuverable enough." The Messerschmitt 109-G he named as the toughest German fighter. *"Vot,"* said Matsietich whenever he paused, "the Focke-Wulf 190 is an unsuccessful German plane." He described the role aviation played in smashing up the blockade of Leningrad, recounted German air raids over Leningrad numbering one hundred planes and modestly admitted that he had accounted for only six Nazi planes himself. Under pressure, he told how he and five Russian fighters had bested twenty-six Nazis one night although almost out of ammunition and petrol. Matsietich's plane had a hole in the tank, plus wing damage, but he managed to crash his adversary by a "psychic attack" which shattered the German's morale. He did not elaborate.

About eleven thirty, Leningrad *Pravda* Editor Shumilov said: "Let's go downstairs for a cup of tea." The banquet table was piled high with food, wines and vodka—a feast fit for a visiting chief of state, including chicken, roast beef, baked apples, port wine, Madeira, scallions, tomatoes, pickles, candies, potatoes, salads, champagne. Soon after we had sat down, up rose little Mr. Shumilov, proposing a toast in Russian which needed no translation, so accustomed were correspondents to hearing it—"To our fighting Allies and Roosevelt, Churchill and Stalin." That was only the beginning. Toasts followed each other more quickly than shots from machine guns. I was sitting next to a woman member of the *Pravda* staff, Maria Shoubalova, who made it her duty as hostess to enforce my drinking each toast Russian style, which meant starting with a full glass and ending with a dry glass. There were toasts to the hosts, guests, Leningrad, the Red Army, victory in '44, the common soldier, writers, journalists and the second front, Leningrad and London, and three separate toasts for Zhdanov. Matsietich toasted the American and British aviators who were pounding

Berlin. Then "Uncle" Ed Angly struggled to his feet and said, "The best American pilots are from Texas, and the best Russian pilots are from the Ukraine. And since Mr. Molotov has seen fit to establish separate *Narkomindels* (Foreign Offices), and since the Ukraine is the Texas of the Soviet Union, I propose a toast to the first exchange of Ministers between Texas and the Ukraine." This suggestion was greeted with joyous shouts by guests and hosts alike.

During the drinking one Russian woman writer remarked: "I write books for which they hang people." This caused some surprise until she added, with a mischievous gleam in her large brown eyes: "In Germany."

Before the twentieth toast could be downed we joggled off to try to focus bleary eyes on a movie showing how Leningrad was supplied during the blockade by the ice road over Lake Ladoga. It seemed a strange mixture of realism and fantasy. With difficulty we dragged ourselves and one or two fallen stars back to the hotel about 3 A.M.

6.

The next morning after a breakfast which consisted of sardines, tomatoes, chicken, potatoes, bread and butter, hamburgers, peas, carrots, eggs and tea, we rode out to Leningrad's historic Putilov, now called Kirov, Works. This was the outstanding industrial plant in Russia for a hundred and forty-two years. The director, Nikolai Dmitrovich Puzyrev, received us in a plain, temporary office. He wore a greenish-khaki uniform, Sam Browne belt, high boots. He has a high forehead, circled eyes and a hoarse voice. He was confronted by six telephones and two clocks, one of which worked. He answered questions quickly, decisively, informatively, his deep-set blue eyes flicking around the crowded room to note any reactions to his replies.

Puzyrev was born forty-one years ago in the town of Tula, near Moscow. "I had no property before the Revolution and neither did my parents," he said, smiling. He started school late in life, attending the Leningrad Polytechnic Institute and, at the same time, working at the Kirov Works. Puzyrev was anxious to make clear that it was not *necessary* for him to work, as the government paid students a sufficient stipend. But he believed that the best training was a balanced combination of theory with practice, "although it takes twice as much energy." He started work at the Kirov plant as a laborer, then became a lathe operator and finally assistant to the shop head, department head, and a year ago, became director.

Before the war the Kirov Works had the most highly skilled technicians and equipment in Russia, producing tractors, turbines, electrical equipment, metro work shields, cannons. All special or emergency orders for machinery were given only to the Kirov plant. In September, 1941, the majority of the 35,000 employees were evacuated to the Urals, but a few technicians stayed behind for maintenance and to aid the front. During the blockade the plant was only two and a half miles from the German front lines and subject to continuous shelling. Despite high casualties, they kept the plant in operation during the twenty-nine-month blockade.

There were times when things almost went to pieces. Only the invincible spirit of the Kirov workers made up for the hardships. For example, in September, 1943, a shell hit a foundry department where there were twelve girls working. Three were killed and nine wounded. The next day the other girls in the foundry organized a shock brigade to avenge the death of their comrades. They did this by working faster, and working overtime. Production, instead of slumping, increased 150 per cent.

At the war's start, 23,000 Kirov workers volunteered for front-line duty. They had to be convinced that they were more valuable behind the lines. Very few wanted to leave Leningrad when the evacuation orders came. The Kirov plant in the east is now the "greatest center" of the Soviet war industry. All through the blockade the rest of the Kirov workers worked and fought, putting in long hours of military training at the day's end. They were assigned to key defense posts if the enemy entered Leningrad. The factory was turned into a fortress with brick machine-gun nests, pillboxes. Over 5,000 shells hit the plant, but only 137 workers were killed on the premises and 1,000 wounded.

Puzyrev said that 67 per cent of the employees at the moment were women. They were doing all kinds of jobs, including the repair of diesel engines which they had never done before the war.

During January and February of 1942 the workers were so weak they couldn't do much. The black bread ration was down to 250 grams per day—little more than two thin slices—to which the factory could add only a plate of thin soup. To save strength, the workers slept in the plant on cots as Leningrad's transport was not working. During this period the trade union, which was almost 100 per cent organized in the shop, assisted by checking up on absentees, bringing them help at home when they were too sick or weak, transporting ailing workers to the plant on sleds so they could be nursed back to health, setting up local dispensaries, urging the stronger to forego food for the weaker. The union also participated actively in the formation of the military brigades which formed the Kirov Division. Very few of that division are living—except as memories.

Describing the period from mid-December until April of that awful winter, Puzyrev told Alexander Werth, "I don't want to exaggerate. I am an engineer, not a politician, but the courage, the guts our people showed in those fearful days was truly amazing. A very large number of our people died. So many died, and transport was so difficult, that we decided to have our own graveyard right here. We registered the deaths and buried the corpses. . . . Sometimes people came to me to say good-by. They wanted to come and say good-by because they knew they were going to die almost at once."

But nobody ever quit their jobs during the twenty-nine months. Nobody ever asked to be evacuated. When Puzyrev was finished we understood what the words "Kirov worker" meant in Leningrad. The people in the plant wore this name like a badge, like a Congressional Medal of Honor.

Abruptly Puzyrev brought his narrative up to date. Although they were short of labor and materials, they were busily putting the plant back in shape. There were about 5,000 workers, most of them young girls between seventeen and twenty-three. Employees were working ten hours a day—eight at regular pay and two additional for time and a half. Thereafter the overtime rates doubled. The workers paid for food but not for plant shelter. The average wage was about 685 rubles per month. Before the war a Stakhanovite could earn up to 3,000 rubles monthly on a piecework system, and now only as much as 2,000. Puzyrev, himself, made 3,000 rubles a month with a 6,000-ruble bonus if his "plan" was over-fulfilled.

Puzyrev said the maximum Leningrad apartment rent was 1 ruble, 32 kopecks per square meter of dwelling space *not* including halls, kitchen. Water, light and heat were free. The rent maximums were scaled according to salary groups.

Rising to escort us through the plant, Puzyrev said with a twinkle: "After the war I was counting on buying lots of new machinery from the Germans, but I don't think they'll have any to sell. So I'll have to get it from America and Britain." He put on a Lenin-like cap and heavy coat and led us through the snow around the five square kilometer plant.

"This tank factory suffered more than any other building," said Puzyrev. "Germans have a certain prejudice against Russian tanks." He pointed out the turbine plant where President Kalinin worked before the Revolution. "We were saving the lathe on which he worked, but it had to be evacuated." Most of the windows in the buildings were boarded up because glass is not available.

In the glowing foundry, women workers were pouring molten metal into molds for mines. The plant was operating on two ten-hour shifts. Puzyrev explained that during 1942 they had been forced to use wood for furnaces, but were now receiving coal from northwest Siberia. They were able to continue operations due to large reserves of ore piled up before the war which was just now running low. Despite limited facilities the plant showed a fifteen million ruble profit during 1943 which was only a fraction of the peacetime figure.

In the Diesel repair shop, banners and signs proclaimed these slogans, LIQUIDATE IDLE TIME and HE WHO BELIEVES HE LOVES HIS COUNTRY AND DOES NOT EXECUTE DEMANDS OF THE FRONT IS NOT A PATRIOT.

Inside the shop the correspondents split up and wandered around questioning various workers at will. Ilarion Zuyev, a fitter, was born in Gorunkovo near Smolensk. He said his sister was in an antiaircraft battery and had brought down a Nazi plane. His brother was distinguishing himself in the Red Army. He was more anxious to tell me about his family than to discuss himself. He was graduated from the Leningrad Trade School, now earned 1,000 rubles per month. His wife, who worked in the same plant, received 600 to 800 rubles. For their 20 square meter room they paid 16 rubles per month. Their surplus cash was being invested in war bonds.

Pretty, blond Tonia Muzenik, aged twenty, said she had a good reason to become first in the plant socialist competition. Her father, who worked at the Kirov plant, her mother and brother all died during the blockade. This pink-cheeked, healthy, blue-eyed young-ster with a tiptilted nose was dressed in a white sweater, ragged wool skirt, black cotton stockings, old low-heeled shoes and a fur hat. She had come to work at the Kirov plant straight from middle

school where the war had interrupted her ten-year course almost
at its completion. For her accomplishments in tank construction
she had been awarded the Excellence Badge by the Commissar of
the Tank Industry. As she talked, she cast her long lashes downward, biting her chapped lips. "After the war I hope to complete
my schooling and become a construction engineer." Tonia earned
800 to 900 rubles per month. She was unmarried "but not because
there haven't been offers—I want to do some hard work first."
Smiling, Tonia sent best wishes to women workers in America.
"Tell them we're doing all we can. Let them also and soon the
war will be won."

Another pretty girl, this one slim and dark, with a slash of lip-
stick and a pert red beret, asked me my native city. When I told
her New York she said she dreamed of going there after the war.
Her name was Lyda Alexeyvna and her parents had been killed
by a bomb during an air raid in 1943. She was a welder, a job
which she had learned right at the plant in the trade union's up-
grading school. "After the war I want to become a doctor and put
together some bits of humanity which Hitler smashed up." I asked
Lyda what she thought of America. She said: "I know America is
our friend—you sent us help all during our worst winter." Then
she said something about the Allied second front bringing men
back to Leningrad sooner. But, when I inquired if there was one
particular man, she wouldn't answer.

A ruddy-cheeked, chubby girl polishing a piece of steel tubing
turned out to be Ilarion Zuyev's wife, Ira. She had just been entering medical college when the Germans reached Leningrad's outskirts. "As soon as the war is over I will go to a medical school to
study for five years and realize my ambition to become a surgeon."
Then she added, "Even if a baby or two stops me for awhile." She
and Ilarion already had a four-year-old boy. Ira kept working while
she answered our questions, and then she wanted to know if she
could ask us something. "Why is it that in America women are
prohibited by law from becoming coal miners?" We had no ready
answer.

When we compared notes on the Kirov plant, it was incredible
how many girls wanted to study medicine. The last girl I interviewed, seventeen-year-old Anna Vasileyeva, said she wanted to
enter a medical school when the war was over, too. "I want to
become a pediatrician," she said. Anna was bubbling with questions about England and America. "Last night," she said, "I read

all about the California gold rush in 1849 and last week I read a translation of Dickens' *Pickwick Papers* and the week before that I read one of Jack London's novels." There was no need to ask if she liked them, you could tell she did by the enthusiasm in her voice.

In the plant, as elsewhere in Leningrad, there seemed to be little mourning. Nobody asked for any sympathy. There was no whining. I never heard any in Russia. These Leningrad people who had each lost so much lived with a deep hatred. It wasn't the kind of surface hatred that leaps to the tongue in hot four-letter words. Everyone was resolved that they would have a reckoning, not only with the Germans but with the "White Guard Finns."

On the way out of the plant I gave a piece of candy to a girl worker who was just returning from lunch—with the admonition to "make bigger and better mines." She blushed happily and raced off to tell her friends. In her excitement she dropped, with a resounding clank, an iron pail which she had been lugging.

Examining the gaping holes in the roofs of the buildings, smashed walls, yawning bomb craters, it was hard to imagine how the Kirov Works had been able to continue. "Damage was very bad," the director said, "but we've saved the water system and boilers which are vital and the rest can be repaired." After the war, he implied that equipment and workers which had been evacuated to the Urals would probably not be brought back "unless my government thinks otherwise."

7.

Before leaving Leningrad Friday night, the Anglo-American correspondents were received at Smolny Institute by "Mayor" Peter Popkov, president of the Leningrad Soviet since 1939. The son of a cabinetmaker, he is forty-one years old and was trained as a construction engineer. Popkov looked like any tall, broad-shouldered, friendly, smooth-shaven executive in a dark blue suit, white shirt and blue tie. He might have been the mayor of Detroit. His strong hands were scrubbed clean and his nails neatly pared. His black hair was smoothly pompadoured. On tables, which were covered with green billiard felt, were cigarettes, ash trays and matches for the convenience of the reporters. Popkov sat at a huge desk, glass-topped, under which was a snapshot of a young son. He smoked Russian cigarettes using a Zippo lighter presented to

him by a visiting United States general. Behind him was a large
multicolored map of Leningrad. Four other huge, well-detailed
maps were on the walls of the room, including a red-flagged map of
the fighting front.

Around the room were handsome portraits of Lenin, Stalin,
Kalinin, Molotov and Zhdanov. Popkov talked clearly and slowly,
his powerful hands locked together on the desk before him. He had
a pleasant habit of looking directly at the person who asked him a
question despite the fact that the person did not speak Russian.
His voice was almost emotionless as he told of Leningrad's hardships during the worst months of the blockade. He ridiculed the
claim abroad that two million had perished. "That figure multi-
plies the fact several times," he said. Nor would he give the present
Leningrad population "for military reasons." "It has been strictly
controlled since the start of the war when all who were not essential were evacuated, beginning with women, old people and
children," he stated. Many children sent to suburbs eighteen or
twenty miles northwest of Leningrad, had just recently been returned since the end of the blockade. The morale of the population was excellent, with theaters, concerts and movies open
throughout the siege. Telegrams and messages from the United
States and Britain helped the people fight on, making them realize
"they were not alone."

The heaviest air raid on Leningrad had been one of 500 tons.
Eighty per cent of the casualties were due to shelling and the first
shell was always the worst. On days of very heavy shelling there
were not more casualties because people stayed inside. About
15,000 were wounded during the twenty-nine-month struggle,
5,000 killed. "In spite of sufferings, Leningrad held out, went on
working, building fortifications." His eyes glistening, Popkov continued proudly: "I think no other city ever suffered like this."

He reviewed plans for a greater postwar Leningrad, then told
us: "During the blockade we received many gifts from workers
in England and America. We gave them to children. I want to say
a big Russian *spasibo* for these gifts in which we see symbols of the
unity of democratic peoples in smashing Hitler's gangsters."

Shaking hands with Popkov, I said, "I hope to see you in New
York or London after the war." He grinned and shook his head
saying: "Let's win the war first and then there's time to talk about
travel."

II. Odessa

Novaya Odessa is a sleepy little Ukrainian farm town nestled in a fertile valley along the eastern bank of the Southern Bug River. It's a pretty town with its rows of thin, young trees, its individually shaped white limestone, thatched-roof houses, its white walls and fences, its sloping hillsides. Before the war Novaya Odessa was a *rayon* ("county") center with a population of 14,000. Its sun-browned, hardy, blue-eyed peasants worked long hours tilling the rich, black Ukrainian soil, growing prize potatoes, buck-toothed corn and luscious gold-grained wheat. The big collective farm which brought them modern machines, a new schoolhouse, a library and occasionally touring theatricals, was called *Krasnaya Zvezda* ("Red Star"). Most families boasted of an acre or more of their very own which they cultivated behind their homes in the early dawn or late sunset. Many of the more industrious owned their own cows and chickens. Life was good. They talked of the day soon when there would be electric light and indoor plumbing and sound movies. Meanwhile, there was plenty to eat and the children were strong and happy. Life was good and there was a dream of a better life ahead.

For more than two years under German overlords this dream became a nightmare. When I visited the town last April, people still seemed slightly dazed at their deliverance. They clustered in small groups in front of their gates, blinking at the sunlight like cave dwellers. They waved at every Red Army truck which bumped along the streets, whirling up mid-April dust. Some were painting their walls, others still were ripping down German proclamations, others were transplanting wild flowers or chopping wood. Bare-legged children scampered self-consciously along the dirt side-walks dressed in odd garments made from leftover green-gray German field tunics.

"We were the fortunates ones," said Marina Koslenko, a thick-legged, buxom peasant woman. "Before they reached the Dnieper, the Germans had time to burn all the homes when retreating.

Here ours (Red Army) swept in so speedily, they ran for their lives. They left behind many things."

A thin, dirty-faced six-year-old girl edged along a stone wall staring at my strange uniform with wide-eyed suspicion. She froze, almost petrified, as I approached her. I dug deep into my trench-coat pocket for a piece of chocolate. I held it out in the palm of my hand. "It's sweet," I said. Her lips whitened and trembled. "Take it," I kept repeating. When I reached down to put it in her hand she fled without uttering a word.

In two minutes she reappeared, half hiding behind the full skirts of her brawny mother. "Aha," the mother exclaimed. "Are you Czech?"

"American," I said.

She smacked her forehead with her palm. "Oy, oy, my God!" She grabbed her daughter and pushed her toward me. She explained that when the Germans first came to Novaya Odessa, their lonely soldiers tried to befriend the children by giving them candy. So that the children wouldn't take it, they were told by their parents that it was poison. The mother knelt down and said something to the little girl which I couldn't understand. But I held out the candy again and after slight hesitation the child took it. Slowly she unwrapped the covering. She quickly bit into it—a big bite. Then, as if realizing her whole treasure was melting away in her hand, she began to suck it slowly like an ice-cream cone.

2.

After our beautifully piloted Douglas transport had settled onto the soft green grass of a hillside overlooking Novaya Odessa, we were met by Major General Alexander Semyonovich Rogov. His smile was warm and friendly. His handshake was firm. He was only five feet ten but looked taller in his high Cossack-style gray karacul fur *shapka* topped by an orange-red crown with yellow stripings. He must have weighed about one hundred eighty and he seemed roly-poly in his bulky woolen greatcoat. Army General (now Marshal) Malinovsky had assigned his deputy chief of staff as his personal representative—our guide through the southern Ukraine and Odessa. It was only about three in the afternoon and many correspondents were anxious to push on to Odessa, about one hundred miles to the south. "I think it is better to stay here tonight," Rogov advised, "but you must understand if everything is not as clean and comfortable as we would like it." While billets were arranged we stood chatting with our host. He was born in 1901 in Yaroslav Oblast (Province) near Moscow, called up by the tsarist army in his teens, and joined the Red Guards in 1919. He had since trained as a professional soldier, culminating in four years at the Frunze Academy. After graduating in 1936, he served as an infantry and staff officer specializing in political and intelligence work. While at Frunze he took two years of English.

Questioned about his class background, Rogov grinned and said, "Most of our generals were peasants or workers, of simple origin. But I've been working and studying since 1919, so you can't very well say I'm still a peasant." He accepted an American cigarette and leaned back against a willow tree. "This is a typical Ukrainian village. It was saved from destruction by the exceptionally quick advance of the Red Army." He pointed to the road, deeply rutted and looking like a plaster model of the Rocky Mountains. "It wasn't easy. It's too bad you came in such good weather. You could have seen what we had to pass." Someone asked him, "How is the road to Odessa?" His gold teeth and his blue eyes glinted in the afternoon sun as he laughed, "Very good—just like this." The general took off his greatcoat, fished out a handful of sunflower seeds, which he passed around. Cracking them with his teeth and spitting out the shells, he described his advance 1,700 kilometers westward from Stalingrad with only one setback. That was when the Germans temporarily retook Kharkov from Malinovsky. He praised the combined operations of Stalin's armies. "As far as Hitler is concerned," he said, "the First Ukrainian Army is a kick in the head, the Second is a kick in the back, and the Third is a finishing kick in the pants." He spoke slowly in English, using gestures to illustrate his meaning.

He detailed the route of the German Sixth "Army of Revenge" and the Eighth during the retreat. "We've taken so much equipment many of our Red Army artillery and motorized regiments are now exclusively outfitted with German equipment." He paused and added in English, "It is very good, too."

Then, waving his arm, he told us something of Novaya Odessa's fate—its population depleted by manpower raids for German industry, its cattle and fields ravaged. "Now they understand what the Germans are," he said. Asked whether or not the people had hanged any Germans, Rogov shook his head.

After several hours the general was tired of answering questions.

As the correspondents trudged off to their various limestone huts, Rogov called out, "When our soldiers talk to you they will have many questions—and you had better be prepared for the first and most important one."

At supper that night in a farmhouse General Rogov joked and fraternized with correspondents, traded toasts on Allied unity, talked about his chief, Malinovsky. Sitting at the table's head he was constantly interrupted by healthy Ukrainian girls handing him platters of food, saying "Tovarishch General please pass this." Toward the end of the meal Rogov leaned across to me and said, "I don't mind doing this job but I think I'll choose a different seat at breakfast."

3.

I spent the night with Victor Vitrenko and his family. Tall, broad-shouldered Vitrenko is chairman of the collective farm. He had been in the Red Army since the start of the war but when Novaya Odessa was retaken, he was demobilized and returned to his job running the collective. His wife, thirteen-year-old daughter, seven- and four-year-old sons lived through the German occupation.

This is the story they told:

When the Germans came they announced that they were saving the Ukrainians from Bolshevism. They broke up the collective farm. But orders soon came from divisional commanders that Germany needed as much food as possible and that peasants must be returned to the collective farm in order to achieve maximum production. "This," said Vitrenko, "shook up many old peasants nonsympathetic to Communism. They began to have doubts about their so-called German friends." While the German Army was advancing, most people were not badly mistreated. Schools opened as usual. "They had no textbooks of their own," said Mrs. Vitrenko, "so at first they allowed Soviet books until a battalion commander found out that they praised Lenin and Stalin." There were few Jews in Novaya Odessa. Now there are none. They were killed immediately. A dentist was killed because he hurt a Nazi lieutenant, pulling a wisdom tooth. A teacher was killed for holding secret classes in her house. The village priest sided with the Germans and lost much of his following. Many villagers became Baptists. At the beginning, 3,000 men were sent to Germany in labor battalions. Young children and the very old were forced to work long hours in the fields. Most of the populace hated the Germans more and more. A few young girls had their heads turned by cameras, fountain pens and silk stockings and lived with soldiers.

The winter of 1943-1944 when the Germans' retreat became a rout, oppressions were stepped up. They began wholesale butchery of livestock. During one roundup, the Vitrenkos saved their cow by hiding her in the kitchen. Many cows were kept in cellars for weeks at a time.

In early March, 150 able-bodied men, who were due to be sent to Germany, escaped into the near-by woods, carrying axes, scythes and knives, to await the coming of the Red Army and to help as partisans. They were betrayed by a local Russian policeman, brought back by force and machine-gunned in the market place. During this period quarrels between the Germans on the east bank of the Southern Bug and Rumanians on the west bank became more frequent. Visas and special *propusks* were required to cross the river. If watering horses strayed to the Rumanian side, they were kept by them. Often there was shooting back and forth. The night late in March when the Red Army entered everyone hid in cellars for fear of being taken or shot by the Germans. "When someone called down in Ukrainian, 'Is anybody there?' we were afraid to reply, thinking it was a sly trick. Only when the shooting died away and we heard sounds of singing in the streets, we dared to come up," said Mrs. Vitrenko.

About half of Novaya Odessa's population was left, mostly women, children and old men. But the Red Army's advance was so swift that German demolition squads had no chance to do their work thoroughly. Vitrenko estimated that only about one-third of Novaya Odessa's buildings were completely destroyed.

Before retiring, I asked Mrs. Vitrenko for some boiled water. She reappeared fifteen minutes later with a pitcher of sizzling hot milk. They took blankets from their own beds and brought them to their guests.

The low-ceilinged, whitewashed room in which I slept was barely furnished. In a corner stood a tall rubber plant. On the walls were old family pictures, some snapshots of children and a large recent portrait of Stalin in his marshal's uniform.

In the morning the family gathered to say good-by. We left them some white bread, sugar and chocolate. "We do not have enough workers," said Vitrenko, "but we'll fulfill our quota. The soil is bursting with life and energy—almost as if it knows that old friends have come back to care for it." After we had shaken hands, Vitrenko asked, "When do you think the war will be finished?" Nobody had a ready reply. "It will be over very soon," said Vitrenko, solemnly, answering his own question. "Don't you worry about it."

4.

At 9 A.M. we set out on a roundabout trip to Odessa—General Rogov leading in his mud-spattered green Studebaker, followed by correspondents with Red Army staff officers in the backs of two Chevrolet trucks. Not far from Novaya Odessa we crossed the Southern Bug on a pontoon ferry rowed by sweating Red Army men. Both banks were scattered with wrecked German equipment, including bullet-riddled landing barges. As the ferry touched the western shore the general, with a grandiose gesture of the arm, proclaimed with mock pomp, "This is Rumania," and then roared at his own words. The Rumanians ruled the area between the Bug and the Dniester which they named "Transniestria."

The hundred-mile trip was accomplished in thirteen hours over roadless plains, bridgeless gulleys, hillocks of dried mud, bomb craters of muck, past dead men and dead fields. But on the whole the general had been right—the southern Ukraine had not suffered like the northern—many houses were untouched, many a field cultivated. The Germans and Rumanians in their mad panic had not done a thorough job of destruction. "It's the new psychology," Rogov explained. "They go faster now they're so near home."

We slept that night in the windowless, heatless, cold-penetrated Bristol Hotel on Odessa's Pushkin Street. Next morning we were treated to an excellent breakfast prepared mainly from captured Nazi food supplies. When one correspondent turned up sleepy-eyed, fifteen minutes after breakfast had begun, Rogov chided him in English, "You are late. You can have no vodka." Then, in a minute, he added, "Okay, kid, I make special permission for you." Toward the end of the four-course breakfast he stood up and called out in English, "Eat much, friends. No dinner till six."

The general told me he slept only three hours, that he liked to have five but since Stalingrad he had rarely been able to achieve it. He talked about his mother and father in Leningrad, his wife and young son in Moscow. "There's no chance now for a vacation, no time even to write much."

After breakfast Rogov toured us around Odessa's defenses, ex-

plaining offensive and defensive strategy with the aid of a staff
map. At the suburb "New Arcadia" on the Black Sea shore, the
beach was protected by tank barriers and barbed wire with a few
light fieldpieces scattered in the hills. Pointing to them, Rogov
said, "Very difficult for second front, yes?" An Englishman replied
that the French coast was much more strongly fortified. For a moment Rogov's big-featured face lost its usual good-natured smile.
The look in his large blue eyes hardened perceptibly. "I do not
agree," he snapped.

That evening correspondents gathered in the freezing, candlelit
dining room of the hotel, bundled in coats, hats, and mufflers,
while General Rogov discussed the Rumanian and German armies.
He sat with one hand between the buttons of his greatcoat, the
other behind his back. "Like Napoleon," I teased him. Quickly
he withdrew his hand and wagged it at me. "Two times wrong,"
he said. "I'm only a major general and I'm on the winning side."

The Rumanians, Rogov claimed, were "gypsies, scroungers,
speculators. But the main thing is they don't want to fight because
they do not know what they are fighting for." In 1941 they were
tougher foes, due to early successes in Bessarabia and the southern
Ukraine and Crimea. Now they pinch kitchen utensils, lamps, and
even sheets off the wash line. He differentiated between the population's quality of hatred—the Germans are hated as deadly enemies, the Rumanians as petty gangsters. He envisioned a complete
state of chaos in Rumania with the Germans now taking open
control after secret preparations as in Odessa. This German occupation means "The Rumanians are less likely than ever to put up
a stiff fight against us." Then, "When your air force bombs Ploesti
and Bucharest it is of the utmost importance in demoralizing the
Rumanians." I replied, "Some Russian officials do not think so."
Rogov smiled at me benignly, "Then do it more often."

He rated Rumanian officers below most Europeans, but said they
are not comic opera buffoons as they were in the last war. The
main difference between them and the Germans is that the Rumanian is unpolitical. Rogov said he had interrogated many
Rumanians, including General Mazarini, and "Rumanian officers
know as much about politics as a pig does about oranges. War is a
continuation of politics. We know why we are fighting and what
for. The Rumanians are only told, 'Antonescu says so.' "

Of the Germans, he said that "Ninety per cent of the officers and
men no longer have any faith in victory." He said the German

front lines were now often held by infantry with the tanks and mobile guns behind. If the infantry retreats the tanks and guns begin firing at them. This happened north of Nikopol and south-west of Dniepropetrovsk, where the front lines were so close to-gether it was clearly seen by Red Army observers. Rogov joked, "There are cases when it is essential and it does have the desired effect on soldiers." The only new German "secret weapon" is their *Faust Patrone*—antitank rocket tube with an armor-piercing grenade not unlike the bazooka. "Total mobilization products are officers and soldiers either too young or too old." He said the same applies to troops kept in the west. About tactics: "Now instead of organizing the defense of small sectors they are doing it on a general continuous front." On aviation: "I hear people say the Allies have drawn away a large proportion of the German air force from the U.S.S.R. front. This is not quite accurate. The Germans have as many planes as in 1941—and 1942, but we have more and that's the difference." When he concluded some correspondents in-dicated they wanted to attend midnight mass. Rogov shrugged and said, "I'd rather spend the time sleeping."

The following afternoon we drove to Odessa's Slobodka suburb, where the Rumanians had forced the Jews into a ghetto before shooting them. There in the modern public bathhouse were quar-tered Rumanian, Czech, Polish, French, and German prisoners. It was a depot for sorting. The general directed that the prisoners be brought out on the sunny street for questioning. After a while neighboring families brought out chairs and the correspondents sat and enjoyed the spectacle. In the beginning Rogov ordered that all questions be put in Russian through him, but he soon changed his mind and allowed them to be asked directly. He only half lis-tened to testimony, idled his time poking into prisoners' pockets with great curiosity, removing a toothpaste tube, a pencil, a picture which he held up for inspection with a wink at the audience. He was somewhat surprised how moved Allied correspondents were while conversing with Frenchmen who had been forced into the German Army and then deserted in Russia. A handsome young man from Lorraine delivered a stirring little speech. When the Allies landed, he said, the French people would take up arms and fight with them. Then, gesturing toward his group, he concluded, "And we'd like to be there with them." When the applause died down Rogov interjected, "Good material for the second front."

As the Rumanians filed in and the French out, Rogov sat down and said, "A regular theater. Okay kid." While the Rumanians were cross-questioned, Rogov said, "Mostly they keep asking only one question when captured at the front—is Bucharest fallen yet?" He laughed heartily when one comic-looking Rumanian who, asked to give his record, announced straight-faced and proudly, "I am three years a deserter." Rogov whispered to some of us, "You see they don't even make good Nazis."

A minute later another Rumanian remarked that "Everyone loves the King. At least I heard that." As the bedraggled satellites shuffled away, Rogov stood up, saying, "Well, didn't I tell you the truth? They're just a bunch of Gypsies."

One evening General Rogov discussed the German field command. His discourse was incredibly well organized. His facts were marshaled like an experienced trial lawyer's. He spoke clearly, concisely, quoting whole passages of German statements and counterstatements without a hitch. He related how inner quarreling resulted in placing the blame for the Sixth Army's defeats on Lieutenant General Graf von Swering, commander of the Sixteenth Motorized Division and his subsequent court-martial. "There is no monolithic unity in the German command." Asked if the Russians had bickered during their retreat, he denied it, saying, "We were sure of victory coming sooner or later. The Germans know defeat is sure. Of course, when any army suffers a reverse you naturally look for the persons most responsible."

The general was asked how many German prisoners claimed to be Communists. "Only about 10 per cent," he said, "but you don't get even that many who admit they are members of the National Socialist party." When I inquired how many of that 10 per cent I believed, Rogov thought two minutes and replied, "None," then added, "Few people are such liars. They'll do anything to try to save themselves. They still believe the German propaganda that the Russians will murder them."

General Rogov blew on his hands, lit a cigarette, and shoved his free hand back in his greatcoat, Napoleon style. "German officers were once very arrogant," he mused. "They refused to talk at all. Now they tell you more than they actually know."

When the sixteen correspondents piled into the back of an open truck to ride to the airport, the general climbed up on the fender and shook hands with everyone. As the truck roared off, he waved his fur hat and yelled, "I want to see you in Bucharest."

5.

During the days I spent in Odessa, there had been ample opportunity to walk around the town, visit shops, chat with people on
the streets and in the market places. They showed no fear of us,
although once I was almost arrested because a policeman decided
my British battle dress might be a Rumanian uniform. Everyone
wanted to talk, to tell their experiences. They even came to our
hotel and asked for us. We were able to buy German and Rumanian newspapers, and somebody would translate. We wandered
into the opera houses, looked over the palaces and the catacombs.
The mayor gave us all the facts and figures which he had available.

Leaving Odessa I had the conviction that I had a good picture
of what had gone on there during the occupation. It was a tapestry,
woven together with threads supplied by all the people I had
questioned, all the things I had seen. The dominant pattern was
the same as Kiev, Kharkov, Smolensk, Rostov, perhaps Antwerp,
Prague, Brussels, Paris. The design was ruthless rule by proclama-
tion. But in Odessa under the Rumanians there was one striking
contrast in the pattern: a background colored by complete corruption.

This, then, is a re-creation of Odessa under the Axis, with the
main threads supplied by a Jewish dressmaker who had lived in
America, a priest who refused to be intimidated, a brilliant
Ukrainian chemical engineer and a two-fisted Russian Communist
who lived underground during the day and slit Rumanian throats
on the streets at night.

6.

Great tyrants have grandiose ambitions. Lesser tyrants have just
as grandiose ambitions. Such a little tyrant was Ion Antonescu.
He dreamed that Adolf Hitler's new world map would glitter
with the jewels of a brilliant Rumanian Empire. This little tyrant
dreamed that he would someday loom as large in Rumanian history as Hitler did in Germany's. For he, Antonescu, would place
around the throat of resurgent Rumania a fabulous necklace
carved from Red Russia's rich, black earth—in the fertile section
of southern Ukraine between the Dniester and the Southern Bug
rivers. And for the sparkling center stone of Rumania's new finery
Der Führer had handed over the busy, beautiful Black Sea port
of Odessa.

In the summer of 1941, Marshal Antonescu sent his troops eastward to build his dreams over the dead bodies of peaceful Soviet citizens. On October 16, 1941, at 4 p.m., Rumanian troops stomped into Odessa. Hitler telegraphed Antonescu his congratulations:

THE CONQUERING OF ODESSA IS THE CROWN OF GREAT RUMANIA. THE HELP GIVEN BY US TO THE RUMANIAN ARMY CONTRIBUTES TO THE FINAL VICTORY OF OUR TROOPS, UNITED BY IRON AND BLOOD.

But at its dizziest height Antonescu's dream was shaken. There were no cheering people along Odessa's wide streets to welcome his "liberating" army. During the bitter seventy-day siege, the Axis had lost a quarter million men killed and wounded. Odessa, once the Soviet Union's seventh largest metropolis with a population of over 700,000, had shrunk to less than 300,000. Its fine old European style and modern Soviet buildings were battered by 384 air raids. What had not been destroyed had been evacuated to the east. The factories, equipment and machines which made Odessa's industries a rich prize, were ripped from their moorings, and already rehabilitated beyond the Urals with more than half the population to work against the Axis.

All this did not please Antonescu, his commanders and his Gestapo advisers. Looting, shooting and hanging began immediately. In Bucharest, Antonescu was momentarily saddened by the news from Odessa. "Don't fret," said the German Ambassador. "When the Jews and Communists have been ground out, the others will co-operate." Antonescu shut his eyes and envisioned a magnificent Rumanian trading center rising on the ashes of industrial Odessa. After the German envoy had left, Antonescu signed an order for 50,000 placards bearing his portrait, to be sent to Odessa, and discussed changing the city's name to "Antonescu." He appointed as puppet ruler of the new empire called "Transniestria," tall, long-faced Georgi Alexeanu, former Bucharest University dean. Antonescu instructed him to speedily exterminate the Jews, crush the Communists and any other leaders of the people. Then he must Rumanianize Odessa.

But like all tyrants, great or little, Antonescu reckoned without the resiliency, resourcefulness and readiness of "conquered" people. Even death cannot crush people like Anna Margulies, Father Vassily, Anatole Loshenko, Dmitri Gaushin, who told me their stories.

Frail, silver-toothed, frowzy, long-nosed Anna Margulies had most to fear. She was a Jew. She had lived in Passaic, New Jersey, from 1906 to 1910 and spoke English. Her husband was dead, her elder son in the Red Army, the younger in the Red Navy. She helped support her aged mother and feeble father by working as a seamstress. When the Rumanians came, she stayed close to her cold, second-floor room near Pushkin Street. On October 23, all Jews were ordered to register. The grapevine in the apartment house told her that Pushkin Street was gallows-lined and from the gallows Jews hung, dangling in the cold winter winds from the Black Sea. On October 24, a patrol of the Rumanian Seguranza forced its way into her flat, swiped everything of value including her samovar and gold wedding ring. They left her sick father but dragged her mother to a concentration camp. Anna was temporarily saved by a certificate stating that she was a member of the Russian Orthodox Church.

The next day at dawn, Anna set off to find her mother. She walked and begged rides eighteen kilometers westward to the village of Dalnik. On the long trip she passed mounds of bodies, mostly young Jewish girls naked and apparently raped. Unable to locate her mother, she returned to Odessa. There were proclamations everywhere saying that the Rumanians would take a hundred hostages for every soldier killed, two hundred for every officer. An explosion had killed some local gendarmes. The gallows were still on the streets. New victims were on them. Tortured people were hanging in a semicircle facing each other, their bare, bruised feet just off the ground. Mayor Herman Pintia was running around commanding, "Lower, lower." From a distance it looked as if groups of people were standing along the street and squares talking to each other.

One night shortly thereafter, Anna's father tried to light a candle and when the match fluttered from his powerless fingers, his blanket was set afire. The Rumanian police blamed Anna, accusing her of sabotage. Without trial, she was thrown in a jail room with thirty women. Their captors rubberhosed them. Many were beaten because they refused to say they were members of the Communist party. The second night a gang of drink-sodden Rumanian soldiers entered the cell. "I am embarrassed to admit this to you, but I feel you should know," Anna Margulies said. "They raped all of us, irrespective of age."

During the next two months there was hunger and suffering and more mass rapes. The commandant nightly satisfied his physical appetite with two or three of the prettiest younger women. At the end of two months Anna was released. She returned home to find her father dead, learned that her mother had perished in a concentration camp, that most of her friends were dead or missing. Fifteen thousand Jews had been rounded up, herded behind barbed wire at Strelbische Field—a rifle range—saturated with benzene and kerosene, and set afire. Anna considered herself lucky to have been in prison.

On January 10, 1942, Mayor Herman Pintia ordered all Jews mobilized for the ghetto. "It was bitter cold that day. Most of the children were insufficiently clad and froze en route," Anna related. Eyewitnesses described how, for sport, the Rumanians forced hundreds of Jews onto a frozen lake and then dynamited it. Anna was saved by her daughter-in-law's family, who were Poles. Through friends, they arranged to sell her overcoat on the market for 200 marks and bought her a forged Russian passport from a Rumanian speculator. (German occupation marks were used exclusively. At first they exchanged ten marks for a thousand rubles, later twenty marks for a thousand.) Then, for over two years, Anna Margulies lived a sunless existence, creeping from cellar to cellar like a water rat, waiting for the day of revenge and liberation.

In the spring of 1942, Antonescu himself visited Odessa and was royally entertained by Governor Alexeanu who had installed himself in the Palace of Pioneers, the pre-revolutionary home of Count Vorontsov, an early governor of Odessa. Here, in this beautiful example of classical Empire architecture overlooking Odessa's harbor, Alexeanu told the little tyrant from Bucharest about his successes and about his failures—but mostly about his successes.

Alexeanu wanted to make Odessa like Bucharest. He induced colonists to come from Bessarabia and Rumania, promising to make them rich. Little wineshops and sidewalk cafés opened, selling fine French champagnes and Dutch cocoa. Rumanian restaurant proprietors introduced "lotto" and other mass gambling games. Rumanian officers imported silk stockings and pretty trinkets. Shares were sold in imaginary corporations. Uspenskaya Street was renamed Antonescu, and Karl Marx Oolitza became Adolf Hitler Strasse. The Ukrainian language was forbidden. University students were ordered to learn Rumanian within a year or face expulsion. After the fall of Stalingrad, Rumanians were less insistent on this dictum.

Alexeanu set up an opera and ballet company which presented

Russian favorites like *Eugen Onegin*, as well as *Tosca* and *Traviata*. They also produced a modern version of *Oliver Twist* to show the cruelty of the British. Singing popular Russian songs on the radio was encouraged—all except "Katusha," which was barred because of the havoc wrought by the Soviet rocket gun of that name.

Dozens of brothels sprang up and prostitution became a major industry. Alexeanu also tried to start other industries but failed, owing to lack of equipment and trained labor. He did manage to utilize the giant grain elevators. But German trade experts insisted on exportation, to Germany, of most of the wheat. Odessa's workers received only two hundred grams of bread daily.

7.

When Alexeanu took over the governorship of Odessa and Transniestria, he was assured that he would receive the full support of the religious in his area. This, according to Father Vassily, assistant professor of theology and sometime priest, was just another of Antonescu's dreams. Thin, esthetic, middle-aged, Father Vassily had been a middle school director under the Tsar. During the Soviet regime he taught school and in recent years also acted as priest of Odessa's Uspenskaya Cathedral. He had established contact with Patriarch Sergei in Moscow, and had hoped for official recognition. The Rumanians compelled him and other priests to submit to the dictates of Rumanian Patriarch Nikodem. From Bucharest came a Nikodem-appointed mission of twelve priests headed by Juliu Scriban, who organized the clerical administration of Transniestria. The mission grabbed all the best houses and seized all the best parishes from the Russian priests. While the Russian clergy led a "miserable existence," Nikodem's commission tried to collect "bad information" about them. Rumanian priests said that Father Vassily "drank, held orgies, sold bracelets and other notions on the market, and speculated."

Father Vassily, because he remained loyal to his fatherland, was not allowed to act openly as a priest, but managed it privately through bribery. The commission continually accepted money and goods from Russian priests in return for small country parishes. "In reality, they were clerical police," Father Vassily said, "whose aim was to discredit and wipe out the Russian clergy."

Father Vassily did not approve of Governor Alexeanu, whom he described as "very haughty, with brown hair and the kind of shape that women liked." Alexeanu gave many gay parties in the high, mirrored ballroom, appeared in society with women "not his wife." Nor did the Rumanian Army seem overly influenced by holy ways. Corruption ranged from the lowest private to the top commander. Officers stole from the men and the men stole from the people. Paid only one occupation mark monthly, soldiers begged, scrounged and speculated to pay for pleasures. Everything had a price— passports, parishes, commissions, life itself.

So openly shameful was the behavior of Scriban that Antonescu ordered Nikodem to replace him with Vissarion, Metropolitan of Bessarabia and Chernovit. "Vissarion was met at the station like a tsar," Father Vassily recalled. His entourage was richly outfitted. Troops paraded in the streets. Bands blared. Flags fluttered from the rooftops. Special masses were celebrated. Vissarion was installed in one of Odessa's finest homes.

But the pomp and music soon soured into pounce and mewing. The metropolitan and governor fought like cats. Autocratic Vissarion could not agree with autocratic Alexeanu. They could not and would not divide their spheres of influence. After several months of continuous back-scratching, Metropolitan Vissarion quietly slunk out of Odessa on a droshky, carrying one small, worn suitcase.

In February, 1944, Governor Alexeanu himself, departed. He had embezzled funds like everyone else but he had made the mistake of letting Antonescu find out about it. "Our money was spent, not for civil welfare," said Father Vassily, "but for nice legs and the budget wouldn't stand it." Much concerned, Antonescu hoped to tighten discipline and reaffirm Rumanian rule by appointing as military governor, General Potopianu, the Rumanian commander who captured Odessa. Uneasy Antonescu already had an inkling that German Gestapo agents were filtering into Odessa and gradually taking over. In February and March, this became quite evident to Odessans. There were frequent barroom fights between Nazis and Rumanians. The Germans treated their allies with scorn, called them "gypsies." German officers commandeered the best brothels, and refused to allow Rumanian officers to enter. Behind the increased German activity was the fear that the Rumanians would "pull a Badoglio." When Antonescu protested to his master Hitler, he was told that ideas of Bolshevism were spreading dangerously among Rumanian troops.

8.

And while the great tyrant and the little tyrant fought, while two Axis partners argued, and even while Alexeanu danced mazurkas on the waxed floors of his ballroom, the people waited and planned. Under the artificial whirlwind of music and merriment, a natural volcano was brewing under the very feet of the conquerors. A volcano brewing in the bowels of the earth, ready to erupt when the time became ripe.

Thousands of determined, unbeaten, patriotic Soviet citizens bided their time. Two such were Anatole Loshenko, tall, blue-eyed, thirty-five-year-old Ukrainian who had been a chemical engineer before the war, and short, tough, violent, forty-year-old Russian Communist Dmitri Gaushin who had worked for a mining engineer. They suffered in silence under the invader, holding odd jobs, their tongues and their anger. On October 19, 1941, some 25,000 Odessa citizens were burned en masse. On December 21, 1941, more than 50,000 more were massacred in a concentration camp. They saw the Rumanian "Trophy Commission" strip Odessa's libraries and laboratories of valuable books and equipment. Word was passed that 2,000 pianos had been shipped to Bucharest from Odessa. They saw thousands of their male friends deported to Rumania in the early months of occupation as "prisoners of war." Antonescu had to show people at home some tangible results of his military conquests. They tried to hear Soviet *svodkas* on the radio until all receivers were confiscated by the Seguranza, Rumanian secret police.

They gauged the rising tide of the people's hatred for the Rumanians. They hated them as peaceful people despise petty gangsters. Everything was corrupt, even the schools. Education was supposedly free but the *gendarmerie* made the parents pay. Everything the Rumanians touched was two-faced, including the currency. Average salaries at the start of occupation were 100 marks monthly and later rose to 200 and 300 marks. But prices went even higher. Butter was 90 marks per kilo, sugar 40; bread was cheap on the ration card but not always easy to find at 10 marks per kilo. Most families were unable to buy on the open market unless they sold their personal belongings. The Rumanians opened many shops where goods and foods were plentiful and inexpensive, but Russian or Ukrainian civilians rarely were given cards to buy at these special stores.

Nothing much was done about an organized resistance in Odessa until after the tremendous German debacle at Stalingrad. Retreating Wehrmacht divisions were razing towns and villages, slaughtering civilians and deporting able-bodied workers on a more serious scale than ever before. After January 1, 1943, resistance units started spontaneously throughout Odessa. First the family group was the nucleus, then the place of work. Loshenko became chief of staff for one of the main partisan groupings which was located in the Moldavanka area, a large workers' district. In privacy he was called "Comrade Major" and his code name was "Volgin." Gaushin became chief of night fighters and was nicknamed "Dneiprov."

On a giant map of Odessa they worked out logistics for their *Vtoraya Odessa* ("second Odessa") in the catacombs.

The catacombs are almost as old as Odessa itself. The city was settled 150 years ago on foundation layers of porous but sturdy limestone. For decades home builders sawed or hewed out huge blocks of limestone for walls and erected their homes over the quarries, which served as excellent cellars. Today these corridors wind around under the city for 125 miles, are 5 to 7 feet in height, descend as much as 200 feet below the surface, and have dozens of entrances and exits. During the last century, smugglers used the catacombs to bring in and hide their illegal loot. In the 1920's during the fighting against General Wrangel's White Army, Red partisans employed their knowledge of the catacombs to advantage. Two decades later, during the siege, the catacombs became air-raid shelters. When the Rumanians entered, some Jews, unable to leave the city with evacuees, immediately took refuge underground. By the end of 1943, *Vtoraya Odessa* was actively being prepared to act as a *vtoraya* ("second") *front* in the enemy's rear when the Red Army approached.

While the men under Loshenko did most of the planning, women and even children did much of the preparation. They hoarded food, made sausages and preserves, rolled bandages. Four young pioneers toured the length of the catacombs, charting passages, uncovering possible mines. One of them was killed carrying out this task.

In November, 1943, an incident occurred which stirred the populace. On November 7, the anniversary of the Revolution, a red flag appeared on the bell tower of the Uspenskaya Cathedral.

The flag had been put there by a youngster named Zhora. He tried to get to the top of the opera house, but he didn't succeed. Then at dawn on November 7 he climbed the bell tower. The tower was in scaffolds, so he had to shinny up the spire. From early morning people collected around the cathedral with their heads thrown back, watching the red flag flutter in the sun. A squad of Rumanian militia drove up on motorcycles, dismounted, and began firing at the flag. Soon it was bullet-riddled, but still it flew. Finally a Rumanian climbed up to the bell tower, ripped off the flag and threw it down.

When the crowd dispersed they were somehow a little more defiant, a little prouder, a little surer of their own unity and ultimate victory.

Many Odessans, lulled by easygoing Rumanian corruption, at first had refused to participate in any resistance movement. But increased Gestapo activity by the Germans began to change their minds. One atrocity especially helped to crystallize the desire to save themselves and fight if necessary. Carloads of little children arrived in Odessa from Nikolayev and other towns. White-lipped, whimpering little children, wrenched from mothers who were being sent to Germany in labor battalions. Little children who were unwilling blood donors. Many lost so much blood en route that they withered, whitened and died in Odessa. Lost little children with drawn faces and circled eyes, haunted Odessa's streets, dodging cuffs from soldiers, and begging passers-by, "Please, please adopt me. I won't eat much. You see, I've nowhere to go. They couldn't use my blood."

One hundred and sixty feet below ground, partisans studied tactics, learned to use guns, drilled and prepared for revenge. Loshenko divided his 2,000 actives into companies and platoons, and assigned them to separate "camps" in the catacombs. Several "halls" in the Moldavanka region were large enough to hold meetings of all the members. Elsewhere in the city 8,000 more were organized. The time was coming. The Germans were falling back. The Red Army was driving forward. Repressions grew. On March 24, 1944, the Germans brought in the new mayor—small, blond, fat, fortyish Ivan Betoushkov, who was a Russian traitor. He had been mayor of Stalino and other occupied cities, all of which were lost to the Red Army as soon as he became mayor. It was an omen, the people said.

Working with the Gestapo, Betoushkov tried to round up more men for labor battalions. Suddenly Odessa men began to disappear. Betoushkov was baffled, the Gestapo infuriated. Even house-to-house searches were fruitless.

Their men safely underground, Odessa wives worked harder than ever. They appeared daily in Prevosa Market near Cathedral Square, carrying large black bags instead of their usual net *sumpkas*. They threaded along the rows of wooden stalls, bargaining with the Rumanians, not for precious French champagne or other imported delicacies, but for armaments. Rifles cost 50 to 75 marks, pistols 150 to 200, tommy-guns with cartridges, 250. Standard issue Rumanian Army grenades could be inveigled for a loaf of bread. Eight- and nine-year-old kids became expert at swiping grenades from under Rumanian noses—like East Side kids pilfering apples in New York.

Vtoraya Odessa was not idle either. A hospital, a kitchen and staff headquarters were prepared. Party meetings were held regularly. Propaganda was written, printed and above-ground distribution planned. Arms were buried deep. Artesian wells were found and cleared. In the makeshift chemical laboratory, pretty, blond, blue-eyed girl scientist Simonova mixed "Molotov" cocktails, using old jam jars and fish tins. There were special playrooms for youngsters, a library of sorts, a "trophy" room, and even a jail.

When individual members of Rumanian or German patrols became suspicious, there was little they could do about their suspicions. All catacombs entrances were camouflaged and guarded by inconspicuous partisans who often lived in houses over the entrances. Women and children took regular turns as lookouts and spotters. Loshenko's policy was to allow anyone to enter the catacombs after disarming them. But not everyone was allowed to leave once they got in. One day a young girl gained admittance, claiming herself a parachutist dropped by the Red Army to instruct Odessa guerrillas that it was far too early for any kind of overt action. Gaushin plied her with wine and when she was tipsy, pried out the fact that her parents had been taken by the Gestapo. To save them she had agreed to contact the partisans with false directives. Loshenko ordered her interned in the "jail room" until the arrival of the Red Army.

Several times the police raided the catacombs but were unable to force entrance. Suspected "entrance" houses were burned down, but rarely were the actual passageways discovered. During the latter part of March, Gaushin's men began going out on active raids themselves. "Only 50 per cent of our men were armed," Gaushin stated. "Fifty per cent more and we could have taken the city." They had to be satisfied with executing surprise attacks on munitions dumps, terrorizing police patrols at night, and distributing leaflets which warned the oppressors and asked the rest of the populace for assistance. Every man of the underground's 10,000 was a hero. Guerrilla Mikhail Kuliev, thirty-two, claimed to have killed thirteen Germans. When some friends back in the catacombs seemed skeptical, he vanished on another midnight prowl, and turned up with twenty-four prisoners.

The sound of Red artillery far off and Red planes overhead was the signal for more powerful raids by the partisans. "Perhaps greater than anything else, we constituted a psychological threat. They didn't know how many we were, how well-armed or where we'd strike. They were always looking over their shoulders," Loshenko mused. "When they discovered some exits, they would guard them all day. But the Rumanians refused to stay there at night. I can't blame them," he added grimly.

During the last hectic week the partisans established contact with the Red Army by secret radio. They were assigned the task to save important buildings and port installations which the Germans would surely try to destroy before leaving. Three times the partisans cut the wires of time bombs placed in the historic opera house—it is still virtually intact today. They continually de-mined port piers. Here the Germans were more thorough, and managed to re-mine all but the first thirty piers which the partisans had saved.

Reinforcements and munitions kept dribbling in during early April. Several hundred Slovak deserters contacted the partisans and came over to them, bringing their tommy-guns and equipment.

Four French soldiers from Lorraine who had been discharged from the French Army and then called up by the Germans in 1943, were sent to Russia in a Rumanian artillery division. They deserted their company at Dalnik, where two Soviet girls who spoke some French, hid them. When retreating Nazis crowded into the village, the Frenchmen struck out for Odessa on a roundabout route to avoid patrols of *Soldaten Klau* ("soldier thieves") who were arresting strays. In Odessa they entered the first house with a smoking chimney, threw down their arms and announced they wanted to wait for the Red Army. The Ukrainians gave them food, drink, and a place to rest. Later that night, six partisans appeared, accepted their guns, and brought them into the catacombs for custody.

On April 8, the Germans who had by now supplanted the Rumanians everywhere, announced on the radio and over loud-speakers, "Anyone on the streets after 3 P.M. will be shot on sight. Stay home. Leave your doors open. Keep your windows closed." This order drove more people into the catacombs. They feared they would be burned alive. Actually, the order meant that the Germans were afraid of grenades from windows and wanted the doors open to duck in during possible street fighting.

On the afternoon of April 9, while the Red Army infantry had already broken into the western suburbs, German radio cars screeched through Odessa's deserted streets, blasting forth this proud and empty threat: "Warning. We are not leaving for good. We shall return in three months. We will take full vengeance on those who co-operate with Bolsheviks." Then they began their wholesale demolitions—firing warehouses, blowing up the power station and water supply. Loshenko and his men saved the telephone center by a shrewd maneuver. They flooded the place with smoke bombs so that the Germans thought the building was already on fire and failed to burn it.

Rumanian ships under the bombardment of Soviet guns and planes tried to evacuate troops. As a final insult to their Rumanian "allies," the Germans shoved their way into the boats first, trampling on the bewildered Rumanians, pushing many into the bay in the mad scramble for safety. Thus after two and a half years, Antonescu's dream of an empire was drowned. The Red Army entered Odessa at 6 A.M. on April 10. Eighty thousand civilians had been killed during the occupation and one-quarter of the city wrecked. Anna Margulies came out into the sunlight and wept tears of joy. Father Vassily prayed in his church, composed telegrams of thanks to Marshal Stalin and Patriarch Sergei. Loshenko and Gaushin turned over their prisoners and information to the Red Army, and kept their resistance bands mobilized for the immediate tasks of de-mining the city, and restoring order. The victorious Red Army brought news of the Soviet advance into Rumania itself. The people laughed, ripped down Rumanian signs and burned pictures of Antonescu.

9.

When I left Odessa exactly one week after its recapture, docks and warehouses were still smoldering. But already, willing citizens were busy rebuilding a new Odessa. Already the Red Army was many miles southwest. They had thwarted the lesser tyrant and his ambitions. Soon they would come to final grips with the great one, his master.

BOOK 4

Fame Is Just a Footnote

═══════

I. Joseph Stalin

═══════

THERE is no nation in the world where the people have as much faith in their leaders as in the Soviet Union. And there are no people in the world who know less about their leaders than the Soviet people. I said as much to an editor of a Moscow newspaper one day and he disagreed, violently. "The first part about faith is true," he said, "but the second part is not. We know all we need to know. Our leaders have proved themselves by their words and deeds or they would not be leaders. We do not have leaders because they are good-looking or speak well on the radio or have nice backgrounds." He then gave me, in English, a little lecture on history. I did not have a chance to write it down until later, but I remember that he wound up with something like this: "Yes, our leaders are party members. The party is the vanguard of the people, but also part of the people. In the last analysis, in our victory over the enemy, in victory during the fight for a better life, it is the people who make the ultimate decision. They write our history. Fame is just a footnote."

The editor then called my attention to some remarks by Stalin on leadership. Addressing the Central Committee of the party in March, 1937, Stalin said:

We leaders see things, events, and people from one side only: I would say from above. Our field of vision, consequently, is more or less limited. The mass of people, on the contrary, see things, events, and people from another side; I would say, from below. Their field of vision, consequently, is also in a certain degree limited. To receive a correct solution to the question these two experiences must be united. Only in such a case will leadership be correct. This is what it means not only to teach the masses, but to learn from them.

How correct Soviet leaders have been can be judged chiefly by the results. In a nation which believes it has always been at war, there is no room for failures. If and when leaders prove to be unsuccessful, they are cold-bloodedly removed. But they are not always treated as ruthlessly as we were once led to believe. Marshal Budënny, for example, was a terrible failure in the early months of the war. He was removed and replaced by Timoshenko, just as Timoshenko was later replaced by Zhukov when he seemed unable to cope with German tactics. Budënny is no longer in an active command, but he sits as a member of the Presidium of the Supreme Soviet, the highest government body in the U.S.S.R. And Timoshenko has recently made a "comeback," after a temporary period of eclipse in which he trained reserves behind the front. Even some of the political prisoners taken into custody during the 1937 trials were given important war jobs, although they did not receive complete personal liberty.

But the public character, the public face of Soviet leaders is all one color. There is still little room in the Soviet Union for shadings. A man is either all white or all black. The Russians greatly admired the late Wendell Willkie, for example. But the minute he wrote an article suggesting that the question of the Baltic States was still a subject for "discussion," he was classed as an enemy and attacked as such.

The Soviets talk a good deal about "party democracy," but it is not the kind of party democracy which we know in the United States. In Russia men who are defeated on an issue within the party must accept their defeat and work wholeheartedly with the majority. The only alternative open to them if they wish to continue their opposition is to conspire in an underground fashion. Then if they are ever discovered, they become enemies of the state.

Perhaps when the perpetual state of crisis, which in a sense has existed in the Soviet Union since its inception, is over, there will be more room for opposition views. Not on any basic concepts, because Soviet democracy will not admit that democracy means freedom to act against the common good. And the Soviet state, according to the Russians, *is* for the common good, and is the common good.

2.

The only time that Soviet leaders publicly take on more than one dimension, especially for foreigners, is when they relax and take on the vodka bottle at a banquet or reception. On such occasions they tackle their fun with the same vigor as they do their jobs. After a few hours of good-natured toasts they become as friendly as a college classmate who is starting out in the insurance business. An official whom you haven't been able to see for ten months is likely to pin you in a corner and tell you what he thinks about the rest of the world—and he doesn't talk like a *Pravda* editorial either.

In February, 1944, I received an invitation to attend the reception celebrating the twenty-sixth anniversary of the Red Army. The invitation came from the Molotovs. It was engraved, and it specified "formal dress with orders." The party was held in the Spirodonivka Palace, where the Moscow Conference was staged. It is not in the Kremlin, but the building is just as well guarded. The NKVD men at the gates, however, didn't even look at my invitation or at my credentials. They know every foreigner in Moscow by sight. I often had the feeling they could tell me what I had for breakfast three weeks ago last Tuesday.

About eight-thirty the Molotovs began to receive in one of the large palace ballrooms. They stood under a glittering crystal chandelier and shook hands with everyone. The scene looked like the last act of Ziegfeld's "Rosalie." Wave after wave of bedecked diplomats, armchair generals and bathtub admirals from every civilized country in the world swept in—as well as Japan. The Japs arrived early in a protective wedge, their runt-sized correspondents flanked by a beefy general, their oh-so-dapper Ambassador overshadowed by a flashy admiral. They all kept smiling and I kept thinking of Mr. Moto. It was a terribly trite thought, but terribly right. The Japs huddled together in one corner, lonely tree stumps in a forest of people. The Bulgarian Minister said "Hello" to them, the Swedes nodded coolly. The Japs left early, long before the first drop of vodka was spilled. Nobody seemed to miss them.

For forty-five minutes the guests filed past, big and little. The loveliest was blond and Garbo-ish Madame Heglöff, graceful bride of the Swedish Chargé. The most resplendent was the Norwegian Ambassador who wore every shape, color and size medal, decoration and ribbon except an old Hoover button which he would have worn also—if he had had it. British Ambassador Sir Archibald Clark Kerr was ruddy, handsome and impeccable in tails. In sharp contrast United States Ambassador Averell Harriman looked like a nervous young curate at a national Episcopal convention. He seemed out of place in his too-long double-breasted business suit which he had tried to formalize with a stiff collar. But it only served to make him look uncomfortable.

The handshaking was followed by a few drinks and then by a concert. The guests crowded into another room and sat politely through songs by leading Russian singers, a harpist and a pianist. During the concert I wandered through the various rooms greeting old friends—mostly waiters recruited for the occasion from the Metropole Hotel. Out near the cloakroom I saw Shostakovich and his pretty blond wife. They were sitting stiffly on a wooden bench. He wore beautiful tails. He looked bored, like a young British left-wing poet. Someone said, "Say, he doesn't even look as if he *liked* music."

When the concert was over, Molotov led the dash for the food. There were ten dining rooms. In the center of each were tables laden with food and drink. *Zakuski,* ranging from sturgeon to roast beef and pressed duck, was so plentiful that when the hot dishes arrived hours later nobody was hungry except the waiters. They kept filling up plates and tucking them away behind the heavy silk portieres.

The buffet banquet was excellent and wound up in a blaze of crêpe suzettes, ice cream and purple champagne. Most of the guests helped themselves, but in a smaller back room there were tables. Here the Molotovs entertained Harriman and his lean daughter Kathy, radiant in a long Alice-blue gown, Czech Ambassador Firlinger and Ambassador Clark Kerr, Commissars Kaganovich and Mikoyan, Marshals Voroshilov and Budënny, and Alexander Korniechuk and his lanky wife, Wanda Wasilewska.

The toasting began early in both languages. The theme was Anglo-American-Soviet friendship with translations by British Major Birce and Stalin's interpreter, Pavlov. The only thing close to a political crisis occurred when General Berling joined the group for a drink. He is the tall, bald-headed, stern-looking soldier who commanded the Polish Army Corps in Russia. He drank Molotov's health. Molotov responded by toasting the Polish Army in the Soviet Union and a free, strong and independent Poland.

Following tradition, Berling stood and clicked his glass against the glasses held up by the other guests. But he carefully avoided those of Harriman and Clark-Kerr, whose governments were still backing the London Polish Government in Exile.

About midnight the guests began moving from room to room like fixers at a political convention. Molotov left Harriman and Clark-Kerr with Mikoyan, and the little Armenian was proposing toasts faster than Harriman could drink them. Clark-Kerr had learned his lesson at a party on November 7. He took two steps backwards every time Mikoyan fastened his bright eyes on Harriman's glass.

In another room I found the Shostakoviches trying the non-alcoholic ice cream. They said they were studying English and hoped to go to the United States after the war. Madame Shostakovich was making faster progress with her English than her husband. I asked her to dance. "Misha would get lost," she said, excusing herself. "He hates big parties like this." Misha was having his troubles with a jolly American army officer who wanted his signature on his short-snorter. The Shostakoviches both signed. Then the officer tackled Marshal Budënny, who was feeling no pain. Budënny stoutly refused to sign his name on Soviet currency with Lenin's picture. *"Nyet kulturni"* ("not cultured"), he kept repeating, shaking his Kaiser Wilhelm mustaches back and forth. But the American pulled out his wallet and shoved a fistful of other bills at the marshal. Budënny said he would not deface the currency of any sovereign nation. It was obviously a matter of protocol. Finally he agreed to scribble his name on a plain slip of white paper. Then they were buddies. The American and Budënny drank a toast.

"May the next one be in Berlin," said the American, who spoke Russian. *"Nyet, nyet!"* Budënny objected. He hoped the next one would be *much* sooner than that. It was.

In another ballroom an eight-piece jazz band swung out with such old favorites as "Alexander's Ragtime Band" and "Sonny Boy." The belle of the ball was definitely Olga Lepeshinskaya, the première ballerina of the Bolshoi Theatre. "Lepy" has a warm, gamin-like personality and Muscovites adore her. She had on an old flowered chiffon dress, but she could certainly dance even if she wasn't any bigger than Gracie Allen and not any prettier than Patsy Kelly. Besides neither Gracie nor Patsy is an active Komsomol.

Except for members of the supreme command and Leningrad party leader Zhdanov, the guests comprised a Soviet *Who's Who*. There was old Marshal Shaposhnikov, former Red Army chief of staff; Navy chief Admiral Kuznetsov; first vice-president of the Supreme Soviet Shvernik who wore a tired brown look and a tired brown business suit; small-eyed young Alexander Shcherbakov, his pillows of flesh bulging in a tight-fitting Red Army uniform—he was the general in charge of all army propaganda as well as general secretary of the Moscow Communist party; and Foreign Office vice-commissars Vishinsky, Litvinoff and Maisky. I joined a group of correspondents chatting with Korniechuk and his wife. The noted playwright, who was at the time also Foreign Commissar of the Ukrainian Republic, spoke charmingly about plans for rebuilding Kiev when asked about Polish-Ukrainian relations. But his angular wife, dressed in a long black silk skirt topped by a smart white lamé jacket, was more direct. She ripped into the Polish government in London, using words that sounded four-letterish even in Russian. Correspondents recalled a similar scene at the November 7 reception when General Golikov came up to Wasilewska and told her the news that General Berling was to be honored by the Order of Suvorov, first class. This is one of the highest Soviet awards which was later presented to General Eisenhower.

Wasilewska was anything but pleased by the news. Her pale thin cheeks flamed red, and her husky voice rose in anger. "You fools!" she cried. "You can't do this. Doesn't Stalin know what the name Suvorov means to the Poles? The very word is anathema to us. You can't do this, you can't commit this blunder." Golikov backed away, embarrassed. A few weeks later it was announced that Berling had been given the Order of Lenin. I had to check in a history book to find out that Suvorov had conquered the Poles and Warsaw and in doing so had not made many Polish friends back in 1794.

I walked back to the room where the principal characters had by now shifted from vodka to white champagne and then to purple champagne. Harriman, after many toasts, rested uneasily on the edge of a table, hemmed in by Mikoyan and his friends who still plied him with drinks. Earlier in the evening Molotov had espied Harriman trying to drink Narzan water instead of champagne or vodka. But now it was an endless succession of the real thing, and the Union Pacific's headlights were gradually dimming in the Russian fog.

At 2 A.M. the party was at its merriest. In the grand ballroom there was dancing and gaiety interspersed by songs from Koslovsky and Baturin, two popular vocalists. Vishinsky had obviously given up secret diplomacy for the evening, and was bent on having a good time and seeing to it that everyone else did, too. He was wearing one of the new dark blue formal Foreign Office uniforms, and on it his Order of Lenin. Journalist Ilya Ehrenburg had cornered Ivan Maisky, former Ambassador to the Court of St. James's, and was yelling about Soviet diplomacy and power politics. Ehrenburg's hair was as wild as Maisky's face was calm. The latter listened and that was all Ehrenburg needed. Earlier in the evening I had surprised Ehrenburg by confronting him with the abrupt demand, "Well, what about the second front?" This disconcerted him. But only for a minute. It was his own favorite way of beginning a diatribe. Scornfully Ehrenburg said, "At first we hoped for the second front. Then we prayed. Then we were anxious. Then we were eager. Then we were sad. Now it is only funny."

A group of us gathered around Railroad Commissar Kaganovich. He is a big, burly man with a very black mustache and very large features. He had absorbed quite a bit of vodka and he was not mincing any words. "We ought to run this war like I run my railroads," he said. "We work all the time, all together. There are three eight-hour shifts working day and night. We work under bombs, under shells, under all conditions. We never stop. But how are we running this war? Only *one* full-time shift. The Red Army is working its shift. But the British and Americans are only working part time."

We tried to explain the North African strategy and the Italian campaign. Kaganovich came back with a jumble of figures about the amount of Allied troops and equipment in England and other nonactive bases. "What you need are *pile-drivers!*" he kept repeating, hammering with his huge fist against the wall. "Pile-drivers. They get things done. We can't beat the Nazis with only one shift working. What you need are *pile-drivers!*" He protested as his brother led him away. He got into his coat and his fur hat still shouting back at us about pile-drivers.

In still another room Budënny and Voroshilov were alternating toasts while their aides stood anxiously around wondering how and when and if they could break it up. Voroshilov, his face beet-red, toasted the Russian wife of an American correspondent. "To the prettiest girl in the room!" he said. When he started to make his way around a table toward her a few junior officers moved in. Budënny quickly retreated and escaped. He had obviously learned a lesson from the Germans after his beating at Kiev.

At three in the morning the party was starting to break up. Waiters were counting the silverware. The orchestra was still playing, and Vishinsky was executing a beautiful Viennese waltz. Budënny had his arms around two cavalry officers and they were singing the chorus of an old Cossack song. Ehrenburg was still haranguing Maisky.

Many of the guests remained until the curfew was lifted at 6 A.M. I staggered home on foot with several other correspondents. On the way we were stopped by a patrol and asked for our night passes. Some of us had them, but we didn't show them. Instead we answered, "We've been calling on the Molotovs." There was no softening of the policeman's hard look. One of the engraved invitations was shoved into his hand. He tried to read it in the gray early morning fog, but he couldn't make it out. He walked across to the nearest traffic light and switched it to yellow so he could see. His expression and then his manner changed very quickly.

He came back, handed us the engraved invitation, saluted, begged our pardon and wished us a pleasant sleep.

In the morning one of the Russian secretaries of the Associated Press asked me how I had liked the reception.

"It was fine," I said, holding my head, "but Stalin wasn't there."

She looked amazed. "How could he be there?" she demanded. "Don't you know he *works* at night?"

3.

On December 21, 1944, Joseph Stalin was sixty-five years old. In the Union of Soviet Socialist Republics his birthdays have not been publicly celebrated, or even noted in the press, since his sixtieth in 1939. The Russians realize that Stalin is not getting any younger. But they almost never discuss the possibility of his death. Once, while having a late supper at the home of a young partisan in Moscow, I broached the subject by asking, "Who will succeed Stalin?"

The reaction of this family, which had what we would call a "middle-class" background, is an interesting indication of the attitudes of different generations. The mother, a disillusioned actress in her early forties, replied in a tone of contempt, "He's a Georgian. *He* will *never* die. They live forever."

The aged, toothless grandmother, intensely religious and nationalistic, quickly crossed herself and mumbled, "May God will it!" Her grandson, a partisan recuperating from a serious shoulder wound, glared at his mother and then said, matter-of-factly, "I suppose the man, Stalin, may have to die someday. But Stalin, the ideal, is ours now forever."

There are still anti-Stalinists in Russia, but they are no longer either potent or vocal. The majority of the anti-Kremlin leadership was exposed and exterminated during the prewar treason trials. The remnants are powerless and tongue-tied chiefly because nobody wants to listen to them. Three and a half years of what Stalin termed "the Great Patriotic War" has effectively united, as never before, most of the Soviet peoples behind the present dictatorship.

Today Stalin is still feared and hated by a minority. He is feared as the head of any machine is feared, whether it be Mayor Hague or Henry Ford or General de Gaulle. He is hated by those with long memories who have never accepted the Soviet system. But today there is much more than this residue of fear and hate. There is almost universal respect, often bordering on veneration.

The reasons are the obvious ones: Stalin's military successes as Supreme Commander in Chief; the expanding membership of the party and the Young Communists as more and more peasants join up through the Army; Stalin's relatively new role as Premier, and with it his status as an international statesman; the feeling of pride in the man who represents powerful, victorious Russia to the leaders and peoples of the world, in the man who can meet and talk on more than even terms with foreign generals, prime ministers, kings and businessmen; and finally, the washing away of the Orthodox Church's antagonism.

Americans may smirk when they read that the Patriarch Alexei of the Russian church recently addressed Stalin as "Our dear supreme leader whom God has sent us." But Russians do not find this tribute a cause for mirth, not even the Russian Communists who are still nonbelievers. Tens of millions of devout worshipers are convinced, as is the Patriarch, that the motherland has always been saved from destruction throughout the ages by the emergence of a potent and sage leader who is able to unite the masses and vanquish the foe.

The first time I saw Stalin I sensed this feeling which Russians have about their leader as the symbol of the Soviet power and as the savior of Russia. Last winter the first wartime session of the Supreme Soviet was held in the great hall of the Kremlin Palace. The delegates chatted noisily and read newspapers. Then, without fanfare, the members of the presidium began to walk onto the dais. First came the less important officials. They were warmly applauded. They joined the clapping as more imposing and familiar figures such as Molotov, Voroshilov, Kalinin and Mikoyan entered and took their places. They, too, started to clap. All remained standing. Finally Stalin emerged from a wing and unobtrusively took a position in the last row of seats. The applause, which had been gradually mounting, became thunderous. Looking unconcerned, Stalin applauded as intently as any of the others despite the fact that every eye in the room was fastened on him, including those of the other leaders on the dais. It was Stalin's way of interpreting the tribute—not for Stalin, the Premier or Marshal, but for Stalin, symbol of Soviet power.

The way things are arranged in the Soviet Union, there is no conflict in the public mind between the symbol and the man. If we thought of Roosevelt as a symbol, we would be slightly confused by having one of his sons turn up at the Stork Club or reading a newspaper attack on his wife or hearing that he allegedly cussed in an election booth. There is almost nothing that the Russian public learns about Stalin, the man, which does not jibe with Stalin, the ideal. It is not that people fear to talk about Stalin. It's that when they do talk, their stories usually picture Stalin, the man, as a kind of oracle crossed with an inspirational man of action who speaks rarely but always with decision, clarity and justice.

Dozens of Soviet anecdotes about Stalin and the present war lend color to this picture. In the perilous days of 1941, Marshal Budënny was retreating before the rapidly advancing Wehrmacht. While trying to cross the Dnieper near the great Dnieperstroi dam, he received a phone call from Moscow. It was Stalin. "Are most of the troops across the river?" asked Stalin. "Yes," said Budënny, "but. . . ." Stalin cut in. "All right. Blow up the dam."

On November 25 of that year the Germans' last offensive against Moscow was close to its objective. Advance units of Guderian's tank forces had penetrated Moscow's outskirts. That night General, now Marshal, Rokossovsky was fighting a losing battle on the road northwest of the capital. The phone rang in his dugout. Amid the roar of cannonfire he heard a calm voice. "*Govorit Stalin* . . . Stalin speaking. What's the situation?" Rokossovsky explained it to him in detail. Then the quiet voice of Stalin said, "Hold even stronger. We will help you. That's all." Soon after that powerful reserves which had been training in the woods behind Moscow were rushed up. The German offensive was checked and then smashed.

After the successful conclusion of the Battle of Moscow, Ilya Ehrenburg wrote this tribute to Stalin. It sounds like a paid "puff," but I am convinced it is indicative of the way most Russians think about Stalin:

In those days [wrote Ehrenburg, referring to the Moscow battle], we once again realized the humane strength of Stalin. He had not been thinking of the conquest of foreign countries. He had been thinking of a new world. He gave himself up to the construction of factories, to the utilization of the Arctic, to the question of canals, to turning wilderness into gardens, to schools, and the education of man. But not for a moment did he forget the danger which threatened our country. He watched the evil bustle of Germany, and when the German fanatics fell upon us, Stalin bent over the maps of the General Staff. Just as before he knew the number of tractors, the quality of this or that constructor, so now he commenced to calculate how many antitank guns were needed for this and that army. Englishmen and Americans who visited Moscow were amazed by his knowledge of military affairs. Russia was obliged to don a military greatcoat, and Stalin, who had worn such a coat for years, felt quite at home. He brought to the defense of Moscow, to the preparation of the offensive, his clearness of thought and his profound tranquillity. He said, "We shall not surrender Moscow." We did not surrender Moscow. He said, "We shall beat the Germans." And we have begun to beat the Germans.

In the latest official biography of Stalin, he is credited with achievements covering not only tractors, canals, schools, but even "the editing of Rules for Collective Farmers." He is also continually referred to as the "author" of the 1936 Constitution. Sergei Kirov, the Leningrad party leader who was assassinated in 1934 by the anti-Stalinists frankly admitted that "It is not easy to grasp the figure of Stalin in all its gigantic proportions." In fact, he said, "there has been no major development in our labors, no innovation, slogan or trend of policy of any importance of which Comrade Stalin was not the author."

The amazing thing is that the parade of world's greats who have trooped through Stalin's office in the past few years have reported very little that would detract from this glowing estimate of Stalin's capacities. That Stalin would have to perform six miracles at once does not worry the Russians, as long as the things are done. And everything they read tells them that Stalin did it.

How? First there is the legend of Stalin's wonderful storehouse of knowledge, both classical and practical, which is staggering. His speeches and his conversations are often studded with allusions to Greek mythology, to Aristotle, Plato, Hegel, Nietzsche and the Bible as well as Marx, Engels and Lenin. He is familiar with all the great Slav writers, and supposedly knows more about Shakespeare, Dickens and Fenimore Cooper than an Oxford dean. In a talk with Lion Feuchtwanger, the exiled writer, he revealed an astounding intimacy with modern fiction writers. Like Roosevelt and Churchill, Stalin has talented assistants helping him with his speeches, digesting foreign publications for him, and probably polishing his *bons mots*, but the Russians do not know this and if they did they would probably not admit it into the conscious mind.

On the practical side, Stalin's knowledge of politics, men, machines and even foreign industrial capacities is said to be incalculable. Last summer he argued with Eric Johnston, president of the U. S. Chamber of Commerce, about America's top prewar production of automobiles. Johnston persuaded Stalin to accept his estimate. But later Johnston found out that he had been wrong and Stalin right. Johnston willingly admitted that "Stalin knows American production figures better than 90 per cent of American businessmen. He has them at his finger tips."

Perhaps one secret of "doing six things at once" is that Stalin never does them that way. He has the knack of pushing everything aside, however briefly, and concentrating on a new problem until it is solved. The Russians have heard stories about this incredible power of concentration. They will tell you that when Sergei Ilyushin was constructing his famous Stormovik plane, Stalin cleared all other work from his desk until he mastered the details of this ship. Then he made an important suggestion which simplified the construction and considerably reduced the building time.

Russians say that when Chkalov proposed his transpolar trip to America, Stalin was consulted on the type of plane. When Papanin prepared his North Pole expedition, Stalin became an expert on Arctic meteorology and personally directed the efforts to rescue the group stranded on an ice floe. When Moscow's water system was being revised, Stalin plunged into the study of maps, blueprints and costs. By analyzing the defects in the proposed schemes, he saved the state millions of rubles. When Moscow's subway was under construction, Stalin went on an inspection tour. He came out of the tunnel furious. Many of the best Soviet technical engineers were working on the subway, but no provision had been made to train new personnel simultaneously. Stalin ordered that everyone performing a skilled job on the "metro" must be held responsible for training a substitute—without slowing down his daily output.

On the rare occasions when Stalin doesn't get his own way, he evidently can accept the verdict with good grace. Last summer he had a series of conferences with plane designers on increasing the range of Soviet airships. Sergei Lavochkin, designer of the LAGG fighter, reported in *Pravda* that he listened to Stalin's ideas for some time and then told the Marshal that he could not increase the range of the LAGG. "You don't want to accept my changes for your plane?" asked Stalin. Lavochkin replied, "I can't, Comrade Stalin." Stalin turned his back and consulted with other engineers for a few minutes. Then he turned to Lavochkin again and asked, "Now, what can I do with him? He doesn't want to. So we'll drop the matter there." The new model of the LAGG does *not* incorporate Stalin's ideas, and nothing dire has happened to Lavochkin.

In military matters Stalin also has displayed an inexhaustible fund of information. In conversation with foreigners he has spoken precisely about the Pacific theater of war as well as the European. He knows the exact dates when Hong Kong, Singapore, Rangoon, Bataan, Corregidor and other Allied fortresses fell, the size of the forces involved and, in each case, the reasons for the defeat. Some of this is due to good intelligence work, but even that must be studied and absorbed. On occasion Stalin has demonstrated some familiarity with United States military campaigns from Valley Forge to Vicksburg and St. Mihiel.

In 1942 he told an American general that "Timoshenko is my George Washington." He smiled and added a vivid description of how Washington saved the American Revolution by his retreat from Philadelphia. "It is a simple military fact," Stalin said, "that a nation is never defeated as long as its armies are held intact." For this reason he refused to be discouraged about German advances into the Caucasus. Continuing his discourse, Stalin said, "Zhukov is my George B. McClellan. Like McClellan he always wants more men, more cannon, more guns. Also more planes. He never has enough. But," and Stalin paused, "Zhukov has never lost a battle."

4.

As Ehrenburg says, the Russian people have a profound respect for Stalin as a military student and leader. This stems from Soviet history books which emphasize Stalin's role in the Revolution and civil war. In his book, Marshal Voroshilov gives Stalin complete credit as organizer and builder of the Red Army. The favorite incident of all Soviet historians is how Stalin saved Tsaritsyn (now Stalingrad). When Denikin's White Army approached the Volga city in June, 1918, Lenin sent Stalin there as commissar general of food supplies for the area. At a critical moment Stalin took command of the revolutionary military council and of the Tsaritsyn front. First, he purged the Red Army ranks of incompetents and disloyal elements. Then, he personally went to the front and planned the strategy, although he had had no previous military training. Denikin drove him back and captured the city in June, 1919. But before the year ended Stalin had regrouped his forces and pushed back into Tsaritsyn. Legend says he did this by cutting off further retreat for his ragged army. He dispatched all available boats up the Volga, leaving himself and his men with only one alternative: victory or death. They survived, as Stalin and Russia have always survived when the chips were down.

After that victory Lenin used Stalin as a trouble-shooter on various fronts. Wherever morale was bad and the Whites were winning, Stalin was sent off to reorganize the Army. It was he who instituted "political commissars" in the units, without whom Lenin said "there would have been no Red Army."

Stalin has also built up a considerable reputation, both at home and abroad, as an infallible military prognosticator. While his record as a prophet has certainly been better than that of the late Leon Trotsky* or of the current Major George Fielding Eliot, he

---

* Trotsky predicted after the outbreak of European hostilities in 1939 that "The Moscow oligarchy, in any case, will not survive the war, by which it is so thoroughly frightened."

is not infallible. On November 7, 1941, he stood atop Lenin's tomb in Red Square and assured the people that "the enemy is not so strong as some frightened little intellectuals imagine. The devil is not so terrible as he is painted. Another few months, another half year, perhaps another brief year, and Hitler Germany is bound to burst beneath the weight of its crimes." A "brief" year later and the Germans were at Stalingrad.

Such aberrations in Stalin's judgment do not seem to distort the popular image of him as a symbol. The so-called "deification" process cannot be handicapped by minor mistakes as long as the war is won. And there are no opposition newspapers to remind people of the November 7, 1941, speech. Nor are there any papers which ever poke into Stalin's private life. The Soviet press never goes in for "personality" articles about Russian leaders. While I was working in Moscow I soon discovered that government officials and censors believed it was none of my business what time Stalin went to bed or whether Marshal Zhukov's children went to school. The fact is that the average Russian knows far less about Stalin, personally, than the average American.

The average Muscovite has seen Stalin a half dozen times during his public appearances on Red Square for holidays. They have seen his picture in the newspapers, his portraits in every public building and office, his statue in every park. Over the years they have sensed a change in these portraits. First the face was the face of a youthful, bold revolutionist. Then of the simply dressed party leader. Then of the mature, wisdom-filled statesman. And more recently, with gray in his hair, the powerful soldier. The people can tell you Stalin's age, that he is quite short (five feet, five inches), that his shoulders are not very broad but that his uniform makes them look that way; that his head and mustache are large, and that he has a sallow, pocked complexion. They would not know that his lower teeth are rotten or that his uppers are black and brown. They know he smokes a pipe, but not that he prefers Edgeworth tobacco.

In the privacy of their homes, some Russians call Stalin, with tongue-in-check, "Father." More often they refer to him simply as "Stalin," without any of his titles. His mother called him "Soso," his revolutionary friends used "Koba," one of his party pseudonyms. The fact that many Americans talk about Marshal Stalin as "Uncle Joe" was mentioned for the first time in the Soviet press last winter in a dispatch from Iran to *War and*

The Working Class. Russians were more surprised than offended. "Do so many Americans feel on such casual terms with Stalin?" a Soviet journalist asked me.

Most Russians know that Stalin has been married twice, and some recall that he has three children. They know very little more than that about his actual family life. Prewar gossip, mostly foreign, linked his name to two prominent Russian women, Marina Rascova, the long-distance flier, and Semonova, the blond ballerina. The real wives and children have never received publicity. The kind of facts that people know are that Stalin has been jailed eight times, exiled to Siberia seven times, escaped six times; that his parents were poor Georgian peasants (his father became a cobbler in Tiflis); that he was an only son and was educated for the priesthood. They will tell you that while Lenin and Trotsky lived abroad and planned and plotted the Revolution, Stalin stayed at home and lived the Revolution in every detail from printing newspapers to committing acts of sabotage. They say he is a modest man, but there are no signs that he discourages the rabbit-like reproduction of big and little monuments in his name. Legion are the things in Stalin's name; great parks, great factories, great railroads and at least five great cities (Stalingrad, Stalinabad, Stalino, Stalinsk and Stalinagorsk). Each musical season includes the première of some new oratorio like Khachaturian's "Ode to Stalin." Soviet poets are constantly trying to get him down on paper in the measured pentameter of a hundred and twenty-five different languages. Last summer in the midst of the Red Army offensive, *Pravda* devoted one of its four pages to a poem from a North Caucasian in praise of Stalin. The verse offerings vary in quality, but these lines by a Kazakh admirer are typical of the sentiments expressed in them all:

> He is the strength of the poor
> He took into himself the tears of the ages,
> He took into himself the joy of the ages,
> He took into himself the wisdom of the ages,
> He took into himself the strength of the ages,
> He, like the morning, stands over the world.

Less eloquent Russians, too, like to lift their voices in praise of Stalin. The Red Army men as they rush over the top to face Nazi bullets yell *"Za Stalina!"* ("for Stalin!") . Militia women, marching through Moscow's streets every night on their way to the bath-house, sing about Stalin with towels slung over their broad shoulders. Audiences at the Moscow Art Theatre break into noisy raptures when "Stalin" appears on the stage in "Kremlin Chimes," a play in which Trotsky, Lenin, Stalin and others are portrayed as characters.

The average Muscovite knows that Stalin lives in the Kremlin, which is not a building but a high (fifty foot) walled fortress containing about forty buildings including palaces, churches, museums, barracks, gardens, meeting halls and offices. Stalin prefers to sleep at his *dacha*, which is a forty-minute drive from the Kremlin. This house once belonged to a millionaire gold mine owner. It stands near the Moscow River and is surrounded by a red-brick wall and NKVD sentries. Stalin's nearest neighbor is his friend and fellow-Georgian, Lorenti Beria, chief of the NKVD or internal police.

Behind the gray walls of the Kremlin and the red walls of the *dacha*, Stalin's activities are a mystery to the average Russian. All they see or hear about are the results of these activities, and this seems to satisfy them. Stalin rises about eleven in the morning and after a light snack is driven in his big, black, bulletproof Zis to Red Army staff headquarters. He sits up front with the driver (a Red Army captain) except when the car is crowded. Then he takes one of the folding jump seats. This latter custom is followed by so many Soviet big shots that Russians call these seats *politburos.* He spends a few hours studying reports radioed from the various fronts, and then goes to his own office in the Kremlin. This large room, with its familiar portraits of Marx, Engels, Lenin and Stalin has had some recent additions to its *décor*. When Stalin became a marshal in 1943, paintings of Alexander Nevsky, a fourteenth century prince and saint, and tsarist field marshals Suvorov and Kutuzov were added. Last October United States Ambassador Harriman presented Stalin with a bust of Franklin Delano Roosevelt.

Stalin keeps a staff of secretaries busy dictating orders and making out reports. About three or four in the afternoon he lunches at his desk, often alone. Except for an occasional glass of cold tea, this lasts him until ten or eleven at night when he has supper in his Kremlin apartment. This meal takes from one to three hours, and over it he discusses party, governmental and military problems with members of the *politburo* or the General Staff or both. Stalin eats heartily and drinks moderately, although at large state banquets he has been known to down as many as thirty *stakanchiki* of vodka without any apparent effects except increased jollity.

A favorite Russian tale about Stalin's apartment goes like this. For years he has had only a three-room suite on the second floor of an old building. It is furnished with barest simplicity. One day Stalin's *dvornik* decided the setup wasn't *kulturni* enough for such an important personage. While Stalin was away at the front for a few days, the old man persuaded the official in the next apartment to surrender his three adjoining rooms and add them to Stalin's flat. The old furnishings were replaced with treasures from a tsarist museum. When Stalin returned he demanded sharply, "What's all this? Where's my furniture? And why so many rooms? Don't you know there's a housing shortage in Moscow?" He promptly ordered everything restored to its former status.

No members of Stalin's immediate family have lived with him in the Kremlin for years. Russians, while not uninterested, know almost nothing about Stalin's kin. His first wife, the mother of his eldest son, Jacob, died in 1917 of pneumonia. In 1919, at the home of his locksmith friend, Sergei Alliluiev (which means Hallelujah), Stalin met Sergei's lovely seventeen-year-old daughter, Nadya. They fell in love and were happily married despite the difference in their ages. They had two children, Vassily and Svetlana. Nadya died on November 8, 1932. Although the Trotskyists spread rumors that she had been poisoned, she died of peritonitis. Despite pains from an appendicitis attack, she did not want to disturb her husband and tell him. By the time an appendectomy was performed, it was too late. Nadya was buried in the cemetery of the Convent of the New Virgins in Moscow. This convent is now the theological school of the Russian Orthodox Church.

The oldest son, Jacob, who has always used his father's family name, Djugashvili, was backward in school. After a period at a technical institute he became an engineer's assistant. Supposedly not in his father's favor, Jacob was working in the Soviet east when the war broke out. He volunteered in the Red Army. In July, 1941, the Germans claimed they had captured him. On August 16 of that year he was cited in *Red Star* for his gallantry during the fighting around Vitebsk and Smolensk when he "stood by his post until his last shell was fired." He held the rank of lieutenant in the artillery at that time. He has not been referred to since, and official Soviet sources have never admitted his capture by the Germans. The Nazis have attempted to utilize him for propaganda purposes, but, according to the underground reports, Jacob has remained loyal to father and fatherland. While the tall, dark Jacob is said to look like his mother, his half-brother Vassily resembles his father. At twenty-five, Vassily has much of his father's onetime swagger and bounce. He is small and handsome with a swarthy complexion, black hair and a long nose. At school he was considered fairly bright, but headstrong and vain. He was always getting into fights which were suddenly broken up when a plainclothes guard appeared and whispered his identity. His father had insisted that Vassily learn some English, but Vassily was more interested in mechanical things. Much to his father's satisfaction he decided to become an airman.

Before the war Vassily had a reputation as a ladies' man and a heavy drinker, but now he is married to a pretty Russian girl and has two small children. In 1941 he was graduated from a fighter pilots' school near Kuibyshev as a lieutenant. In 1942 he won the Order of the Red Banner for heroism. Since then he has fought on most of the major fronts without any special privileges. His record and that of his fellow fliers has been so good that his outfit has been named a special "Guards" regiment. During last summer's offensive Vassily, now a colonel, commanded a fighter squadron which distinguished itself continually in the Belorussian campaign. Several times Vassily was cited in Stalin's Order of the Day, but no official communiqué has mentioned the newsworthy fact that he is the Marshal's son.

The youngest Stalin offspring, Svetlana, is more diligent than her brothers. Her father's favorite, she is the only one of the children ever to appear in public with Stalin. She is a close friend of Molotov's daughter, an active member of the Komsomols and a good linguist. Recently she was married. After passing extremely stiff competitive examinations, she was admitted to the new International Relations school at the First Moscow University last fall. When she enrolled, next to the space left for "Father's Trade" on the printed application, Svetlana wrote: "Professional revolutionary."

Although it has never been officially verified (or denied), Stalin is said to be married for the third time. His wife is Rosa, younger sister of Lazar Kaganovich, the builder of the Moscow subway and now Commissar of Railroads. Rosa has never been seen in public with Stalin. She spends most of her time at the *dacha*. Stalin is devoted to her, and telephones her every night at midnight from his office. He rarely finishes work until three or four in the morning. But since he has averaged not more than five hours' sleep a day since the war's start, he still manages to spend a few hours with Rosa in the early mornings before retiring.

Stalin is not fond of children the way a good politician should be, probably because he has never had time for such a luxury. Occasionally he sends a car for his favorite niece and nephew, children of his second wife's sister. When he thinks of it, he gives them lavish presents. He prefers their company to that of his grandchildren, who are too young for reason.

5.

Stalin's closest friends and associates these days are Viacheslav Molotov, Anastas Mikoyan, Klimenti Voroshilov, Georgi Malenkov, Andrei Andreyev, Georgi Zhukov, Fillip Golikov and Alexander Shcherbakov. Golikov has been Stalin's personal aide-de-camp in his role as Supreme Commander in Chief. He is forty-five, egg-bald, stocky, a graduate of Frunze Academy with a first-hand knowledge of Russia's allies. In the summer of 1941 he was sent to the United States and England for military staff talks and conferences on supplies. After his return he commanded a Red Army "front" until 1943.

Molotov and Mikoyan are closely consulted on their specialties, foreign relations and foreign trade. Voroshilov, who now has more political than military significance, is a very close personal friend. Shcherbakov is secretary of the Moscow party and currently chief of propaganda. Zhukov is considered the real "brains" of the General Staff, aside from Stalin, and has the title of Deputy Supreme Commander in Chief. He is the personal link between Stalin and the armies at the front. Malenkov, forty-four, is Stalin's former private secretary. He and Andreyev, forty-nine, are two of the three alternates whom Stalin has trained in his role as general secretary of the party. The third alternate is chubby, handsome Andrei Zhdanov, forty-five, former Secretary of the Leningrad party, president of the Russian Republic, and a colonel general in the Red Army. It was he who concluded the armistice with Finland last fall and as chairman of the Allied

Control Commission he is now responsible for making sure that the terms are satisfactorily carried out. Of the three alternates, Zhdanov is the heir apparent. If any one man should succeed to Stalin's military-governmental-party leadership, Zhdanov would be the man.

Zhdanov is already the most inaccessible man in the Soviet Union. During his visit last summer, Eric Johnston was granted every request which he made except one. That one was permission to interview or meet Zhdanov in Leningrad. The technical excuse was, "Zhdanov is at the front." The same reason was given when I visited Leningrad in February, 1944. One reason for this inaccessibility is that Zhdanov now holds Kirov's position, and Kirov was assassinated in 1934 because the wrong man got into his office at the wrong time. The NKVD is taking no chances with Zhdanov.

When Kirov passed out of the picture, people in Leningrad swore that nobody could ever take his place in their affections. But to hear them talk in praise of the new party leader, one would not suspect that they could have revered Kirov more. His picture hangs everywhere in Leningrad next to Stalin's. Zhdanov is stocky like Stalin, with a swarthy, handsome face set off with a Stalin-type mustache. He is a priest's son (Russian Orthodox priests are allowed to marry), extremely well educated, studious, retiring, energetic. He fought in World War I as a noncommissioned officer. When the revolt began rumbling in the ranks, Zhdanov helped to break up the tsarist army by fiery, demagogic speeches. He is still considered one of the most brilliant and forceful speakers among the Soviet leaders. I saw and heard him at a session of the Russian congress, and was struck by the physical similarity between him and Stalin—even to their platform technique and poise.

Zhdanov's first important position was that of party secretary in the industrial town of Gorky. His record there was so excellent (high party enrollments, fulfillment of industrial plans, etc.) that he was chosen in 1934 to assume Kirov's post in Leningrad, considered one of the most ticklish jobs in the Soviet Union because of Leningrad's "personality"—its Europeanized culture, its long intellectual traditions, its feeling of being just a bit above the rest of Russia. Before the Finnish war it was rumored that Leningrad would become the capital of the Russian Republic—and that rumor has again been revived on good authority.

In 1934 Zhdanov was also elected to the party's all-powerful *politburo*, and named by Stalin as an alternate secretary of the party. Since then he has climbed rapidly up the various rungs of the Soviet ladder. In 1937 he was elected to the Supreme Soviet. In 1938 he became head of the Foreign Affairs Committee of the lower house of the Soviet parliament, and at a full session of the Russian Republic's congress he was elected President of that republic (a position analogous to that which Kalinin holds in the U.S.S.R.).

Once a man becomes a secretary of the Communist party in the Soviet Union, there doesn't seem to be any limit to the number of jobs which he can or must do. In 1939 Zhdanov became chairman of the (party) Central Committee's subcommittee on propaganda and agitation, a post which he held until 1940 when it was taken over by Alexander Shcherbakov. Zhdanov had to resign because he was appointed chief of the joint foreign affairs commission of both houses of the Supreme Soviet. In this post he was called by a British statesman "the architect of Russian foreign policy, while Molotov is only the builder."

When things went poorly for the Red Army during the Finnish war, there were stories that Zhdanov's star was sinking. But any such ideas have subsequently been dispelled. He is still very much a top member of Stalin's inner cabinet. In group photographs of the leaders, he and Stalin are often shown laughing and joking together. And in the present war, no political leader with the exception of Stalin, himself, has gained more military *kudos*. When the Germans attacked Leningrad in 1941, Zhdanov became head of the Leningrad Military Council with the rank of major general and has been generally credited with organizing and directing the successful defense of the city. In January, 1945, he was relieved of his post as Leningrad party secretary so that he could devote more time to his duties as head of the Allied Control Commission in Finland and as Stalin's No. 1 alternate in running the entire party.

If Stalin should die before the war's conclusion, the reins would not be taken over by Zhdanov but by the State Defense Committee which includes (aside from Stalin) Vice-Chairman Molotov, Army General Nikolai Bulganin (who replaced Voroshilov in November, 1944), Mikoyan, Malenkov, Beria, Kaganovich and Nikolai Vosnesensky. Then after the war, unless Zhdanov assumes the entire burden, the Stalin part might be divided up among three lesser actors—Zhukov (military), Molotov (governmental) and Zhdanov (party).

Once world peace is secured, it is considered probable that Stalin will retire as Premier in favor of Molotov and keep only one job, that of party secretary. Although his health is good he is feeling the strain of running the world's biggest and strongest army, the biggest country and the strongest single party. Often now the words "If I live . . ." creep into his conversations. When Stalin goes into two-thirds retirement, the likeliest candidate for Molotov's post as Foreign Commissar is Andrei Vishinsky, the smooth-skinned, smooth-talking lawyer who rose to fame as chief state prosecutor during the treason trials. He is now a First Vice-Commissar of Foreign Affairs, and one of the shewdest men in the Soviet hierarchy. Nikolai Shvernik, former head of Soviet trade unions, is being groomed to assume more and more of Mikhail Kalinin's duties as chairman or president of the Supreme Soviet and its presidium.

Although Zhdanov is a brilliant, strong and respected leader, it is difficult to imagine an individual ever again holding sway over the Soviet Union's 180,000,000 people. Joseph Stalin has done it for almost twenty years, but in that period of time there have been great strides in education, in self-respect, in breeding new leaders. It is perhaps the ultimate tribute to Stalin that so many Soviet citizens like their state, despite the fact that the likes, dislikes, theories and ambitions of one man can dominate it.

At sixty-five, Stalin is a man who knows what he wants and can get it. The man who succeeded Molotov as general secretary of the party in 1923 and then took over the same man's job as Premier in 1941, has come a long way from the Tiflis theological seminary where he first struggled against tsarist power. Today he has that power, although it is employed to pile up riches for the people and not for himself. Stalin wants for nothing, but he is not a rich man. He does not collect jewels or paintings or gold.

But his influence and prestige is so overpowering that his merest whim becomes an edict, although Stalin often may not mean that it should be. His household and his office are run quietly and efficiently, taking into account his pet likes and dislikes. He likes chess, skittles, movies and piano music. In his youth he liked to ride and shoot, but he hasn't done that for years. Stalin's artistic tastes are simple, almost conventional. When he listens to music he prefers folk songs or the great classics of

Russian opera like Glinka's *Ivan Susanin* or Borodin's *Prince Igor*. When his second wife was alive he also liked to hear *Aïda*, which was one of her special favorites.

For a man as busy as he is, Stalin manages to put his fingers into an incredible number of Moscow's intellectual pies. When he expresses displeasure with some creative work, however, it does not necessarily mean that the offending artist is "liquidated" or even shoved into convenient obscurity. Stalin walked out on Shostakovich's operatic attempt, *Lady MacBeth from Mtsensk*, because the music was too difficult and unmelodious—and besides he didn't care for the story. The Soviet press gave the young composer a severe critical laceration, but he has managed to survive Stalin's displeasure and to write even better music.

One of the most popular young Soviet writers is Konstantin Simonov. Before the war he courted an actress by writing passionate verses to her. Some of them were printed in the newspapers and magazines. All Russia followed the romance breathlessly. The verses were collected and published together with many more intimate ones. When a publisher asked Stalin for his opinion of the poetry, Stalin scoffed: "That's the kind of book which should have been printed in *two* copies. One for him and one for her. That's all." The book was hurriedly withdrawn from the bookstalls. But nothing dire happened to Simonov except that he married the girl and became better known as a correspondent and playwright than as a poet.

Stalin reads a lot, although he hasn't as much time for it as before the war. He has a habit of telephoning people in the middle of the night to express his opinion on their books. When Ilya Ehrenburg was writing *The Fall of Paris*, he had troubles with the Foreign Office censors who were reading his copy as fast as he finished it. The first half of the novel had been sent to Stalin by the author, more as a gesture than anything else. A few days later Stalin called Ehrenburg at the Moskva Hotel and said he liked the book but he sure hoped "you will bear down harder on the Germans in the second half." Ehrenburg agreed and mentioned, in passing, that he was having censorship difficulties. Stalin made no comment, but the rest of *The Fall of Paris* passed the censors without a single word being changed. Ehrenburg received the Stalin Prize for this book.

One night a woman named Anna Antonovskaya who had just written *The Great Mouravi*, a historical novel about Georgia, was surprised to receive a call from the Kremlin. Stalin came on the phone and, after praising the book, proceeded to give the author some pointers on Georgian history which she had omitted.

On several occasions Stalin's intervention has saved literary works from obscurity. When a play called "The Days of the Turbins" was attacked by *Izvestia's* critic as "counterrevolutionary," the conservative Moscow Art Theatre withdrew it although the play was very popular with audiences. The plot concerned a middle-class Kiev family during the civil war. Two of the characters most active in the fight against the Bolsheviks were portrayed in a favorable light. When Stalin heard the play had been withdrawn, he phoned the theater's director. He said it was a fine, stimulating play and that he had enjoyed it. Back went the play on the theater's schedule—where it still is.

A war story, "March-April," by Vadim Kozhevnikov had been turned down by the cinema committee as too flimsy for a screen play. But when the word spread around that Stalin had read the story and had personally congratulated the author, the committee changed its mind immediately. The movie version of "March-April" was showing on Moscow's screen last spring and an impartial observer might agree with the film committee's original decision.

Stalin himself is the world's best-selling author. His *Leninism* has been printed in every language, and the sales within the U.S.S.R. alone are close to three million copies. Shortly after the war, his booklet *On the Great Patriotic War of the Soviet Union* was published. Within a few days five and a half million copies were bought. It is now in a fourth printing totaling fifteen million copies.

Although his literary style is textbook dry, Stalin has a nice, unpredictable sense of humor. Very few of his witticisms reach the Russian public. But an old Bolshevik whom I met in Moscow recalled that Stalin always has had a humorous quirk. He worked with Stalin during the early days of the Revolution and he told me that if I ever wrote anything about Stalin, I must surely put this in it: "When our nerves were bad, when we lacked sleep and food, when things looked very black indeed, Stalin was always completely cool, like an icicle. Often in times of the severest stress he would suddenly say something very funny which relieved the tension. We all of us thought that Stalin was crude, even a crude joker. Trotsky was the witty one. A trifle unbalanced, perhaps. Well, when the crisis was over, we realized that Stalin's joke had been a deliberate psychological hypodermic. After awhile we came to appreciate him."

The world first heard about Stalin's crisp, edged retorts as a result of the long interview which he granted H. G. Wells many years ago. When asked if he was going to change the world, Stalin replied: "Not very much." He concluded the lengthy talk with Wells by saying, rather wistfully, "Much more could have been done had we Bolsheviks been cleverer."

When the present Finnish Premier, Paasikivi, visited Moscow in 1939 on a mission to learn Russia's terms for a peaceful settlement with Finland, he was gravely agitated after Stalin had named the conditions. Said Paasikivi, with a worried frown, "If we brought back to Helsinki such terms as these, there would be no crowds in the streets to sing and cheer for us as there were when we left to come to Moscow." Stalin, prowling the room like a great dane, stopped in his tracks and snapped back, "Don't worry about that—Molotov, Zhdanov and I will come to sing and cheer for you."

Several years ago a Moscow correspondent wrote to Stalin asking about the rumors that he was dying or about to undergo a serious operation. Back came a note from Stalin: "I know from reports of the foreign press that I long ago abandoned this sinful world and moved into the other world. As one cannot doubt such foreign press dispatches unless he wants to be expelled from the list of civilized people, I request you to believe them and don't disturb me in the calm of the other world."

Foreign correspondents have been bothering Stalin with letters ever since. Although Stalin has talked to no reporters since he gave an off-the-record interview in 1941, he has met and talked to many times more British and Americans during the war years than he did in his previous sixty-two years. Foreign correspondents fill his special mailbox at the Kremlin with a weekly deluge of letters. Once in awhile Stalin will use one of these letters as an excuse for clarifying some important point of Soviet policy.

Correspondents now get their stories about Stalin by interviewing his constant stream of important visitors. Last August the London Press sent a delegation to Moscow headed by Premier Mikolajczyk. One of the group was Professor Grabski, the man who drew up the Treaty of Riga which Stalin has many times denounced. During the discussions at the Kremlin, Grabski moved over and sat next to Stalin. He began pounding the table and shouting about Poland's claims to Vilna and Lwow. Stalin said very little, and some of the delegation felt that old Grabski had queered the act with his violence. But when they left Stalin shook Grabski's hand and said with a broad grin, "You know, you're a very good propagandist. I enjoyed it."

Stalin speaks and reads no other languages but Georgian and Russian, although he understands many of the Soviet Union's offshoot languages including Ukrainian. In 1934 he began to learn English. But he soon gave it up, deciding he was too old. "And besides," he supposedly told a friend, "I can understand the Mickey Mouse movies without English." He does know a few words, and on one occasion he surprised some British and American guests after a Kremlin banquet by saying in English, "The lavatory is on the left, friends."

Immediately after the Teheran conference two stories began making the rounds in Moscow. The first anecdote is about the three great men riding in a car. They found the road blocked by an obstinate bull. Churchill said, "I will get out and clear the way." He argued with the bull, then gave up. Next Roosevelt attempted to budge the animal, and he, too, failed. Finally Stalin, who had been smoking his pipe in amused silence, hopped out of the car and approached the stubborn bull. Almost instantly the bull reared up and fled, leaving the road clear. When Stalin resumed his seat in the automobile, the others asked him how he did it. "Very simple," said Stalin. "I merely whispered in the bull's ear, 'Come with me to a collective farm.'"

The second story reflected Russian impatience over the "second front." The Shah of Persia made a gift of an eleven-year-old girl to Churchill. Roosevelt was shocked by this oriental custom, but Stalin quieted him down. "But it's infamous," Roosevelt argued, "The girl hasn't even reached the age of puberty." To this Stalin replied, "Never mind. By the time Churchill makes up his mind to do anything, she will have long since matured."

Although Stalin's public utterances are very formal and consciously full of slogans, they do have flashes of the human touch. Once during a nationwide radio address, he paused to drink a glass of water. When he had finished—and the sounds of his drinking were audible over the air—he said, "Excuse me, comrades. I have eaten too much herring for breakfast."

At a party congress Stalin dealt critically with Soviet officials who are "honest and loyal" but also "incompetent as executives, incapable of organizing anything." He emphasized his point by repeating the following dialogue:

Stalin: How are you getting on with the sowing?
Executive: With the sowing, Comrade Stalin? We have mobilized ourselves.
Stalin: Well, and what then?
Executive: We have put the question.
Stalin: And what next?
Executive: There is a turn, Comrade Stalin, soon there will be a turn.
Stalin: But still?
Executive: We can say there is an indication of some progress.
Stalin: But for all that, how are you getting on with the sowing?
Executive: So far, Comrade Stalin, we have made no headway with the sowing.

6.

The Soviet Union is often called "the world's greatest bureaucracy," but foreign diplomats say that Stalin has consistently battled against red tape and bungling. He makes such quick decisions himself that he cannot understand why others act so slowly. He has little sympathy with stupidity in any form. Recently someone tried to excuse an official for making a garbled report on the grounds that he was an illiterate because his parents had been simple peasants. Stalin said, "That is no excuse. Our enemies do not wait to ask about our parents."

For years Stalin has impressed upon government and party leaders the necessity of studying American methods, not only in industry but in office routine. Long before the war, admiration for the United States was one of Stalin's strong traits. Years ago he characterized the essence of Leninism as a "combination of Russian revolutionary zeal with the practical American spirit." During the war this admiration for America has grown tremendously among all sections of the people.

Incidentally, during his talk with Eric Johnston, Stalin not only gave him a statement on how much American aid had meant to Russia, but he put it in a much stronger way. It did not sound much like Stalin, the tough, hardheaded businessman. Stalin said, "I suppose you'll have a bad depression in your country after the war." Johnston replied, "Many people feel so." Stalin snapped back, "How much will we have to buy to keep *all* your people employed?" Johnston parried, "That depends on whether it's a big or little depression." Stalin: "Well, how many people approximately will be out of work?" Johnston: "I don't know." Stalin: "I think you ought to start getting those figures together so we'll know how much we'll have to buy from you to keep all your people employed." Surprised, Johnston asked, "Why do you want to do this?" Stalin answered, "Because you did us a big favor and we want to do one for you."

While Stalin is not afraid of making such sweeping pledges, his colleagues very often are. There may be plenty of reasons for distrust, but that doesn't change the fact that the famous Russian "secretiveness" does persist even in very high places. The old, and some of the new Bolsheviks still put the wrong emphasis on an old maxim of Stalin's: "A reasonable amount of distrust is a good basis for collective work." During Churchill's Moscow visit last fall, there was an important military session at the Kremlin. Stalin sat in as an observer while Voroshilov, Vassilevsky, and other Red Army marshals conferred with Sir Alan Brooke and Sir Hastings Ismay. For half a day the British military men sought to obtain certain information from the Russians. After endless haranguing and pleading they got about 50 per cent of the data which they were seeking.

Stalin remained silent during the wrangling. Finally, with a gesture of impatience, he got up and said, *"Yah skazhyu"* ("I will tell"). Ignoring Voroshilov's complete stupefaction, Stalin spent a full hour on his feet telling the British everything they wanted to know with the most complete detail.

Another trait of Stalin's, a stubborn one, is his intense hatred of Russia's backwardness. He has hated Russia's backwardness more than he has hated world capitalism, and this fact has saved Russia—and perhaps world capitalism. This hatred drove him to push through the collective farm movement, to build up the Urals, to promote the Stakhanovite movement for all it was worth, to make peace with Hitler for enough time to build and plan and build for the war he knew was coming. Always Stalin has wanted his country to get over its easygoing ways. He kept reminding the people that "to slacken the tempo means to fall behind. And the backward are always beaten. The history of old Russia is the history of defeats, due to backwardness. She was beaten by the Mongol Khans. She was beaten by the Turkish Beys. She was beaten by the Swedish feudal lords. She was beaten by the Polish-Lithuanian squires. She was beaten by the Anglo-French capitalists. She was beaten by the Japanese warlords. All beat her for her backwardness, for military backwardness, for cultural backwardness, for governmental backwardness, for industrial backwardness, for agricultural backwardness."

When he lashed home this thesis, he would conclude by warning that the attitude of the outside world to the Soviet Union would be: "You are backward, you are weak, so you are wrong. Hence you can be beaten and enslaved. You are powerful, so you are right, hence we must look out for you."

Such nationalistic pleas caused foreigners to compare his dictatorship to that of Adolf Hitler. When Stalin read such comparisons in the American press during the Nazi-Soviet pact, he was furious. He told a British diplomat, "Russia has no intention whatsoever of expanding into Central or Western Europe. . . . Those who think I would ever embark on the adventurous path of conquest blatantly underestimate my sense of realities. People who make analogies between Hitler and myself show they know nothing about politics."

Many people who know things about politics are now saying that Stalin is too old to worry about the workers of the world. Stalin is certainly not interested in plotting and carrying through a world revolution. He wants peace. At sixty-five he believes that he can make his greatest contribution to the workers of the world by establishing socialism in one country, by raising the economic level of the masses in Russia to new highs, by setting up the Soviet Union as the shining example for others to follow—*if they wish to follow.*

It is not inconceivable that Stalin will be satisfied to go down in history as Lenin's successor, as the man who helped drive Russia out of her backwardness, as the man who solved the national minority problems, as the only ruler of Russia who ever defeated his nation's enemies in the West and in the East.

He will, I think, die happy knowing that he has lived to see the fulfillment of this poem which he wrote about his country when he was only sixteen:

> *Know that the one who fell like ashes to the ground,*
> *Who long ago became enslaved,*
> *Will rise more high than these great crags*
> *Winged with brilliant hope.*

II. Marshal Georgi Zhukov

On the blue-green hill called Khamardaba, nestled among the Mongolian steppes, was a thick-walled blockhouse deeply settled in the ground. Inside, a group of Soviet war correspondents were relaxing around an old iron stove. Into this informal gathering strode a thick-set, barrel-chested man with a large round head. The correspondents greeted him respectfully as "Tovarishch General." Tovarishch General had just come from his early morning *banya* and his full cheeks were pink and glowing. His mood was extraordinarily good. As he dressed he chatted with the correspondents. Suddenly two Red Army scouts rushed breathlessly into the room. With heavy apprehension they reported the Japanese massing large units, obviously preparatory to striking a potent counterattack. The correspondents braced themselves, expecting a galvanized Tovarishch General and curt, clear orders. But the general received the news with ironclad calmness. Drawing on his military blouse he coolly informed the scouts that such a counterattack was entirely impossible, that the Japs were in no position to deliver an effective offensive blow.

His words changed the atmosphere in the blockhouse immediately. The scouts wondered how they could have been deceived by their own eyes and the correspondents wondered how they could have been deceived by their own ears. Everyone felt completely secure. Tovarishch General had spoken and he was never wrong.

That was Marshal Georgi Konstantinovich Zhukov in the late summer of 1939, just a few days before the forces under his command wiped out the Japanese Sixth Army at Khalkin-Gol. Since that first great test of the modern Red Army, Zhukov has become the Soviet Union's Horatius at the bridge. Today he holds a position in Red Army leadership more than comparable to that of Eisenhower in the Anglo-American military firmament. As Deputy Commander-in-Chief and a First Vice Commissar for Defense, he is second only to Marshal Stalin as the Soviet Union's military guiding genius. Zhukov is twice a hero of the Soviet Union, proud wearer of the Orders of Lenin and Suvorov, victor over the Japs, successful defender of Moscow, Stalingrad and Leningrad—the first general of World War II who not only stopped the Nazi Wehrmacht but smashed it.

Unlike some of the older Red Army commanders, Zhukov is not an officer product of tsarist military training. He has been in the Red Army since it first was organized and is the perfect example of what it can produce. Son of simple peasant folk, Zhukov was born in Strelkova, a small village in central Russia, in 1894. He was an average student but a hard worker. He left school at an early age and became apprenticed to a furrier. In 1914, at the age of twenty, he was mobilized into the rapidly expanding tsarist army as a private. Young Zhukov saw active service against the Germans until 1918 when he was sent home because of ill health. When he recovered, Zhukov made a decision for which all the civilized world may be grateful—he decided the fur trade was too dull an occupation for a full-blooded, ambitious, intelligent Russian, and left home for Moscow, the city of his dreams. There he joined the cavalry division of the famous Red Guards. In the capital a whole new world of ideas blossomed for Zhukov. He had heard vague rumblings of unrest while at the front, but not until Moscow did his political sentiments begin to jell. Swept up in one of the great movements of history, young Zhukov joined the Communist party in March of 1919.

When civil war exploded throughout Russia, Zhukov fought on many fronts against former companions among the tsarist troops. At this period his military knowledge and his valor were not conspicuously more nor less than that demonstrated by thousands of other Red Guardists who became the dynamic nucleus for the Red Army. Before the conclusion of the anti-White campaign, Zhukov was wounded. When he regained his strength and hastened back to the front, he was decorated with the Order of the Red Banner and made a noncommissioned officer. While serving in the Far Eastern campaign against Admiral Kolchak's troops, Zhukov's growing talents as a military leader were discovered by Mikhail Frunze, foremost Soviet expert on military affairs and founder of the Frunze Military Academy which became the Soviet Union's West Point.

The Reds finally emerged victorious against the interventionists, and Zhukov was chosen to go to Frunze Academy to study military science and tactics. After graduation he was commissioned as commander of a regiment, then given a brigade. Succeeding in these assignments, he eventually became commander of the Fourth Cavalry Division which, during the civil war, had been the finest unit of Budënny's First Cavalry Army. Many of the Red Army's most famous generals once served in this First Army or other cavalry forces. For a time during the civil war, Marshal Timoshenko commanded the Sixth Cavalry Division; Gorodovikov, who was colonel general and inspector general of all cavalry, once was head of the Fourth Division; General Josef Apansenko, former commander of the Far Eastern armies of the Soviet Union until his death in action on the western front in 1943, also commanded the Sixth Cavalry. Other civil war cavalrymen are General Yeremenko, who was active on the Stalingrad front under Zhukov, and Army General Ivan Turenev, who recently was on the Transcaucasian front.

Like Budënny and Gorodovikov, Zhukov remained in the cavalry for a long period, learning much wisdom, history and military tactics from them. He rose to the rank of assistant inspector general of cavalry while Budënny was inspector general.

During this period in the early thirty's, Zhukov was unknown in the Soviet Union except in military circles. Foreigners never remember hearing his name. He lived quietly in Moscow with his young wife, intent on rearing a family. He had few intimate friends and spent his free time studying Marxist literature, writing tactical studies, and learning foreign languages. For a brief spell he was an instructor at Frunze Academy. He went to Germany to attend lectures given by the German General Staff in the pre-Hitler period for Russian and Chinese officers. In 1936 Stalin and Voroshilov selected him to go to Spain as the Soviet Union's chief military observer. With Zhukov went the first shipment of Soviet tanks sent to aid the Spanish government against Franco and his well-equipped Nazi and Fascist allies. This was Zhukov's first opportunity to test Red Army theories on tank warfare in actual battle. A few years later he was able to apply the lessons learned in Spain

2.

In July, 1939, the Japanese made an unprovoked attack on the Mongolian Republic and sent picked troops streaming across its border along Bain Tazagan mountains. The Soviet Union, which stood by its mutual aid pact with the Mongolian government, rushed Zhukov with a number of tank divisions under his command to repel the Japanese invaders. For the first time in Red Army history employing massed tanks and armored cars as an independent striking force, Zhukov surrounded and destroyed the Sixth Japanese Army—giving the lie to the Japanese myth that the Sons of Heaven never lost a war. The Soviet press hailed this victory as the "Bain Tazagan slaughter."

The remnants of the Japanese armies retreated across the Khalka River into Manchukuo, confident that Zhukov's "Panzer Division" couldn't pursue them across the shallow, mud-bottomed river. Then one cold August night Japanese sentries were startled by the rumble of tanks beyond the river. The commander refused to worry even then, believing that the overzealous Zhukov would meet his own Waterloo by bogging down in the muddy bottom. But as they have done many times since, Zhukov and his forces performed the impossible. They crossed the river, smashed through unprepared Jap outposts and then methodically proceeded to crack the enemy's chief defense points. The enemy fled in panic.

Only after the truce did the Japs discover that wily Zhukov had ordered engineers to work nights strengthening the river bottom to enable it to support the weight of the tanks.

At the time this victory was significant because it should have given the Western powers a line on the Red Army's potential, not withstanding later failures against the Finns. It still has a certain significance today because the army which beat the Japs, the Far Eastern Red Banner Army, has been kept pretty well intact by the Soviet Supreme Command and it is now the nucleus of the large force which faces the Japanese near Manchuria.

When Zhukov returned to Moscow after this campaign he was personally congratulated by Stalin and awarded the title of Hero of the Soviet Union and the rank of army commander. During the period of the Finnish war he did General Staff work under Timoshenko, never taking an active field command. Soon after the conclusion of the Finnish campaign, tsarist ranks were restored in the Army and Zhukov became an army general, next highest to marshal which was a purely honorary title.

In May, 1940, Zhukov was a key figure in the first of several Red Army shakeups. Timoshenko became Defense Commissar that spring, and Zhukov was appointed to the vital post of commander of the Kiev Military District. Timoshenko jumped him over dozens of other older and more famous generals who had ancient and honorable records as officers during the Revolution.

During his stay in Kiev, Zhukov demonstrated a remarkable ability for administrative work. He spent much of his energy drawing up plans for Red Army reform based on the experience gained in the Japanese and Finnish campaigns. Here for the first time he emerged not only as a military executive but as a political leader. His directives were those of a man with complete confidence in himself, and the knowledge that his superiors had given him carte blanche. Ukrainian party leaders looked to him for leadership, and he gave it. Speaking before a special party conference of the Kiev Military District, Zhukov declared that the year 1940 marked an important turning point in Red Army training. He warned the party people that military successes do not come through discussions, but through carefully thought out, persistent and strenuous work by the Red Army commanders as well as the political workers. Although the post of political commissar in the Red Army was not finally abolished until months after World War II, this audacious speech of Zhukov's was the first important public attack on this system.

Zhukov further astonished his party audience by charging that the Red Army's higher and senior command had failed constructively to assist in training the younger officers who were willing but needed to be coached on the intricacies of military tactics. The older officers, said Zhukov, were bad teachers. He specifically urged a closer study of the military history and traditions of the Russian Army and the Russian people. Like Suvorov, he stressed the necessity for instilling discipline and hatred of the enemy. He closed this eye-opening report with the warning that the Red Army found itself in a complicated international situation which might change at any moment, and cautioned against a possible "trick."

Since this was at the time of the Nazi-Soviet pact, his audience understood that the "trick" referred to possible German duplicity. Zhukov's friends say that he never trusted the Nazis even during the pact. Although grudgingly recognizing the political necessity for gaining time, he always privately anticipated the war with Germany.

3.

On June 28, 1940, Zhukov commanded the Soviet troops which moved into Bessarabia and northern Bukovina. He set up his headquarters at Chernovitz and later that summer he was elected

as a delegate to the Supreme Soviet of the U.S.S.R. as representative of this district. By winter the "complicated international
situation" which Zhukov had foreseen grew more complex. It
became increasingly apparent that the Red Army had to be prepared for the worst. It had to be prepared to meet a modern war
machine, and the Russian commander who understood this kind
of fighting best was Zhukov. He was brought to Moscow and
named chief of the General Staff directly under Stalin. Zhukov
immediately speeded up the reorganization of the army apparatus
which had been begun by Stalin and Timoshenko. He weeded
out incompetent officers in a manner which reminded observers
of Stalin at Tsaritsyn. He inveighed against bureaucracy, did his
best to channelize the functions of agitators so that they did not
in any way interfere with the purely military command.

On February 23, 1941, commemorating the twenty-third anniversary of the Red Army, Zhukov wrote the leading article in
Pravda and discussed the Red Army's progress. "Personnel, armaments, military thought—these are the three cardinal principles
for an army," he wrote, and added that the Red Army was now
speedily enveloping these principles. Recalling Khalkin-Gol,
Zhukov wrote that Soviet troops had undergone "a serious and
prolonged trial here." He pointed out that the fighting had
occurred at long distances from Soviet bases and rail lines but
nevertheless the Red Army had overcome all difficulties because
"they were able to bring the power of their Socialist technique
into play and apply it according to all the rules of modern warfare." Just how an army fights with socialist technique Zhukov
never made clear. But a United States Army officer stationed in
Moscow remembered Lincoln's remark on Grant's drinking and
said he thought other armies might use more of it—if it didn't
involve accepting Communism.

Turning to the Finnish campaign, Zhukov claimed it had been
an "acid test" and declared that the cracking of the Mannerheim
Line "is the only instance to date of a breach being driven through
modern permanent fortifications." Then characteristically, he
switched abruptly from praise to criticism. "But we would not be
Bolsheviks if we allowed the glamor of victory to blind us to
shortcomings that have been revealed in the training of our men.
These shortcomings were the result of conventionalism and routine
that had pervaded methods of training. They manifested themselves in the first period of the war and naturally had a negative

effect on operations." Later he claimed that on the Karelian Isthmus the "idea of training troops under conditions approximating as closely as possible actual conditions of modern warfare first was conceived and put into effect," and explained the collapse of the French Army on purely military terms as due to "insufficient training and complete unfamiliarity with equipment."

Zhukov evaluated 1940 as a year of readjustment in Red Army training. "In 1940 the principle of a one-man command took firm root, ranks of generals were introduced, rights and authority of the commander extended, and Soviet military discipline raised to a higher level."

The new army that Zhukov was hammering into shape was far different from Von Bulow's rapt dream of a Communist fighting force. The Red Army was no great big happy family of comrades who held meetings before making a military decision. In the months before the war it was welded into a strongly disciplined organization. Infraction of a command or regulation was severely punished. And in over three and one-half years of war, these trends have been intensified. Discipline and regulations in the Red Army today are more strict than in tsarist days. Officers and men cannot appear in public places in unpressed uniforms; their boots must be polished, their faces must be shaved and their hair combed. On the coldest days along Moscow's Gorky Street you will never see a Red Army man with the collar of his greatcoat turned up—it's against regulations. Nor will you see a Red Army man hanging on the outside step of an overcrowded streetcar or bus—it's against regulations. No officer or enlisted man can remain seated in a streetcar or subway while a man of higher rank stands, without his superior's permission—it's against regulations.

These are small and seemingly trivial outward examples of inner discipline in the Red Army, but it is symptomatic of intrinsic character changes. But with all this new tautness, in spite of sharpening differences between command, soldier and officers, the Red Army never forgets to pay attention to the individual man. It has been traditional in Russian armies since the time of Peter the First and Suvorov that the first duty of an officer is the comfort of each and every one of his men. Suvorov believed in developing the resourcefulness of all his men in order to increase their ability to make the right decisions in battle. He attached tremendous significance to proper relationships between officers and men and never regretted it. Zhukov, following in

Suvorov's footsteps, stressed the importance of officer-private mutual confidence and respect, but saw to it that outward discipline was tightened.

In February, 1941, Zhukov was elected an alternate member of the Central Committee of the Communist party and appointed Vice-Commissar of Defense. Four months later, when the Nazis pulled the "trick" which Zhukov had repeatedly warned against, he was in Moscow working with the newly formed State Defense Committee of which Stalin was chairman. Zhukov was sorely needed as a field commander and Stalin called upon old Marshal Boris Shaposhnikov to take over the desk duties as chief of staff.

4.

During the first months of war, Voroshilov commanded the northern front, Timoshenko the central front and Budënny the southern. By October the Germans had battered their way past Maloyaroslavets to within fifty miles of Moscow. On the twenty-first of that month, Stalin's decree establishing a state of siege in Moscow was front-paged in the papers and Muscovites learned that Timoshenko had been transferred to the southwest and that "It is declared that the defense of the capital, on lines that stand 100 to 120 kilometers west of Moscow, is entrusted to the Commander of the Western Front Army, General G. K. Zhukov."

The Red Army, which had been falling back for strategic reasons, found it difficult to check the backward momentum in the face of repeated German thrusts. Late in October, Zhukov's tired armies were reinforced with four divisions of Moscow volunteers who were poorly equipped and hurriedly trained. Despite heavy losses, Zhukov issued an impassioned "Hold or die" order on October 27, which had much to do with saving Moscow. "Not a step back!" he ordered his men. "Halt the Fascists! Don't let them reach Moscow. Every man must fight like ten! Cowards and panicmongers must be destroyed ruthlessly as traitors to the fatherland." His military directives specifically instructed the men to cease avoiding Nazi tanks, "but to hunt and destroy them."

The retreat slowed. Zhukov gained time to concentrate powerful reserves brought from Siberia in woods north, west and south of Moscow. During November he deliberately sucked the Wehrmacht into his trap. On December 6, Zhukov began his offensive which split off the point of the Nazi spearhead. The siege of Moscow was broken, and with it the myth of German military invincibility. By the end of January the Soviet offensive was still grinding ahead through the snows. Zhukov and the Red Army had made a lying braggart out of Hitler. Boldly the Führer had proclaimed in October, when the Wehrmacht was ripping through Smolensk at a faster clip than Napoleon, that the Germans would parade in Red Square on November 7, the Soviet Union's Fourth of July. There was a parade on Red Square on that November 7, 1941, but it was a parade of Red Army reserves on their way to join Zhukov's valiant army, the reserves which helped turn back the full fury of 50 German divisions, including 13 tank divisions and 700 planes. Once more Hitler bellowed: "Moscow must be finished off at any price," but evidently Hitler couldn't pay Zhukov's price, for his answer to the Nazi threats was made in the prophetic words of Alexander Nevsky, "Go, and say to all, whosoever comes against us with the sword shall perish by the sword. Such is the law of the Russian land, and such it will always be!"

Although Muscovites called Zhukov *spasitel* ("savior"), he was the first to attribute his success to the guidance of Stalin and to the unconquerable fighting qualities of his men. In a rare press interview on January 25, 1942, Zhukov outlined the reasons for the German shambles at Moscow: "Here they found real war, but they were not ready for it," he said. "They were used to easy victories. This deprived them of flexibility on one hand, of tenacity on the other. For them war was merely maneuvers. They have neither cavalry nor skiers, while their tanks cannot pass over the snow." Zhukov spread out a large map of the Moscow area and traced the action which "wore the Germans down." As he talked he sparkled with sarcasm and occasional flashes of wit. This stocky, strong, bull-like man was relaxing for the first hour in months. "The stubborn resistance Germans offer in towns and villages has a simple explanation—they are afraid of giving up warm houses for frozen fields. However, symptoms of demoralization are in evidence. German soldiers began surrendering despite threats of their officers. This is only the beginning.

"The Germans' plan was thoroughly worked out. They meant to deliver main blows on the two flanks, especially the northern. They concentrated at the approaches to Moscow some 3,000 tanks.

"That the Germans failed to prepare properly for a winter

campaign can be attributed only to their ignorance of Russia and the Russian people.

"Early in December, when the Germans announced the imminent fall of Moscow, it was clear that their offensive had petered out. They were capable of merely local actions. We retreated, preserving our materiel. Our tenacity in retreat determined the course of future developments. We had to gain time. It was not we who made haste. The day came and we launched a counterassault." Pointing with his thick, stubby forefinger at a colored wall map, Zhukov's bright, beady eyes glistened as he showed where the German high command, to conceal a fatal blunder, ordered a quick retreat of sixty-two miles. But after that the Wehrmacht kept falling back. "And now German generals find it hard to explain away their retreat," Zhukov said.

Zhukov indicated that Russian guerrillas in the rear of the Germans at Moscow constantly harassed German supply and up until then, the Nazis did not know how to cope with such attacks. These partisan raids, Zhukov said, were like an angry dog snapping at a tiger insistently enough so that the tiger never had a chance to eat his prey.

5.

The year 1942 was one of cumulative successes for Zhukov and the Red Army. When the Germans had been forced back on the central front, Zhukov was placed in charge of the defense of Stalingrad where the Germans were threatening to force the Volga and capture the city. Again he replaced Timoshenko. Under Zhukov, representing general headquarters of the Supreme Command at Stalingrad, was chief marshal of artillery, big, beefy Nikolai Voronov, then colonel general. For field commanders, Zhukov gathered together a group of men who have since proved to be among the most brilliant commanders of the Red Army: Tall, efficient, popular Rokossovsky, short, squat, dark "Lightning" Vatutin, Golikov, Tolbukhin, Popov, Malinovsky, Rodimtsev, and Chuikov, whose name is often confused with that of Zhukov by foreigners. All these men have achieved more imposing stature in the campaigns that followed the victory at Stalingrad, and all of them owe something to training in tactics learned in that epic battle on the Stalingrad front from Zhukov.

Even before Voronov and Rokossovsky sent their ultimatum to Nazi General von Paulus on January 8, 1943, the position of the German Sixth Army was helpless. Together with remnants of the Fourth Tank Army, it had been surrounded in a solid steel ring since November 23. The last hopes of being saved by Field Marshal von Mannstein with reinforcements from the southwest were crushed. Mannstein, recalled from another front by Hitler's panicky orders, attempted to drive two wedges into the ring, one from lower Chira and another, main drive, from Kotelnikovo to the north. The German command, within the Soviet encirclement, formed special shock units of picked troops from among twenty-two divisions available, and posted them in the southwest sector near Karpovka for the purpose of striking southward the minute Mannstein's reinforcements came within ten miles. Their function, as diagnosed by Zhukov, was to break the ring and rout the Soviet forces. But Hitler underestimated the strength of the Red Army. Fresh Soviet troops under Malinovsky were sent by Zhukov to intercept Mannstein. This maneuver was perfectly executed and Mannstein's armored units were smashed at Kotelnikovo and his whipped infantry limped back toward Rostov.

When news of the ultimatum to Paulus reached Moscow there was great surprise that Zhukov's name was not attached to the document. Foreign observers started the usual false rumors that his star was in eclipse. Nothing could have been further from the truth. Stalin, realizing that the Germans were gambling everything at Stalingrad, decided it was time to hit them elsewhere—where they least expected it. After a brief visit to Moscow to consult with Stalin and Voroshilov and to see his family, Zhukov made the dangerous flight to the Leningrad front. While the country was still reverberating with cheers over the epoch-making victory at Stalingrad, Zhukov was co-ordinating operations of the Leningrad and Valkhov fronts and succeeded in breaching the blockade of Leningrad.

On January 20, 1943, he was made marshal of the Soviet Union, the first field commander of this war to be so recognized. In an *Izvestia* editorial entitled, "Skill of Red Army Leaders," the names of the new marshals were announced and Zhukov's led all the rest. For the first time officially he was acclaimed as the "highly talented and brave leader" who carried out Stalin's plans for smashing the Germans at Moscow, Stalingrad and Leningrad.

Zhukov's name is rarely in the papers except when he is decorated. The average Soviet citizen (or even a fairly well-informed one on military matters) knows far less about Zhukov than about Stalin.

Little emphasis is placed on the work of individual commanders, except that Stalin's Orders of the Day are addressed to them when their armies have won a significant victory. That is why the *Izvestia* editorial on Zhukov was the strongest official tribute paid any general, except Stalin, during the war.

Like other Russian military men, Zhukov and his family are carefully guarded from the public eye. He lives on the upper floor of a two-story house in Arbat Square, one of Moscow's better residential areas, about five minutes' walk from the Kremlin. He has a gracious, dark wife who is taller than he, and three children: a daughter thirteen, and two sons, twelve and nine. They attend public school near their home. The twelve-year-old boy, who looks like his father, is nicknamed "Zhuk" by his classmates, but he doesn't like it. In Russian, "Zhuk" means "beetle."

Although he has had almost no time for such pleasures since the war, Zhukov is a talented performer on both the piano and accordion. On rare occasions during the Japanese campaign he would spend a few hours in the dusk of evening making music with the accordion. His favorite composers are Tschaikowsky, Glinka, and Moussorgsky, but most of his accordion selections are old folk songs which he learned back in Strelkova as a furrier's apprentice. He speaks a smattering of Spanish and German but is very fluent in French. Before the war he subscribed to most of the leading French periodicals.

The Zhukov apartment is small, but compared with Moscow residences, it is extremely comfortable. In the living room Mrs. Zhukov still displays the swords, helmets, remnants of enemy tunics and other trophies which the marshal has been collecting in his more than twenty years of warring. In a closet she has packed away some of Zhukov's "civilian" clothes—tough worsteds which he bought in Germany. He liked to put them on in the spring when he motored to the lake country north of Moscow for fishing. For the last few years his only "hobby" has been the study of great military tacticians. He is considered an authority on the wars of Hannibal and his friends often tease him about it. His library is full of books on military subjects, including Clausewitz.

Mrs. Zhukov is a plain, pleasant woman who is busy bringing up her children. She spends her spare time working on the Moscow District women's committee for helping families of Red Army men. She rarely hears from her husband, as his whereabouts are always a complete military secret and in the Soviet Union, complete means complete, and no exceptions are made for love or money. She follows the campaigns closely on a big, colored wall map of the Soviet Union and reads infrequently about her husband's successes in the *Red Star*. She can be sure that wherever something big in the way of an offensive is brewing, her Georgi will be near by.

As the wife of a leading Soviet citizen, Mrs. Zhukov is entitled to certain special privileges. She can buy clothing on a special floor of a special department store reserved for the families of top military personnel. And she receives a special discount on all her purchases. At a *gastronome* similar to the ones maintained for foreign diplomats, she is allowed a pretty good ration of caviar, wines, vodka, Soviet champagne and especially "mishka" chocolate candies which her children love.

Only in terms of these privileges can Marshal Zhukov's salary be computed or compared. The salaries of the Red Army's upper crust are not public domain, but no matter how much they are paid there isn't much they can do with the money unless their wives are given some place to spend it. Even during the war, however, the wives of generals and marshals do not receive any more privileges than that accorded high-ranking artists like composer Dmitri Shostakovich, novelist Alexei Tolstoy, correspondent Ilya Ehrenburg, ballerina Olga Lepeshinskaya or scientist Alexander Bogomolets.

When Zhukov is home there is a car at the family's disposal, driven by a Red Army man, but usually the family prefers to pay their forty kopeks and ride in the metro like other Muscovites. On his rare visits to Moscow, Zhukov likes to attend military and diplomatic parties where he is known as an intelligent, somewhat didactic conversationalist. But at the front he follows a Spartan regime. He is extremely tough, both physically and mentally. While stationed at Kiev he made it a practice to gallop twenty miles on his favorite black Caucasian charger before breakfast. He invariably worked a trying, twelve-hour day without lunch. When he felt the need for more exercise or a change from military routine and paper work, he would fence with his aides, one after another, until they were all exhausted. Since he insists on this rigid, back-breaking regime for himself, he considers it only fair to demand as much from his men. Stern disciplinarian though he is, Zhukov nevertheless respects a Russian military tradition, antedating the Red Army, of solicitude for the individual soldier. Instances of Zhukov's personal relationship with the men under his command are few but illuminating. Some years before the war when Zhukov was stationed in White Russia, he gave permission to a cavalry regiment to arrange a party for a junior officer who was getting married on a certain day. On the morning of that day Zhukov learned Marshal Budënny was arriving for an inspection tour. Shortly before the wedding he ordered the prospective bridegroom to the station to head a welcoming guard of honor. Foreseeing an all-day job, the young man groaned but marched off like a good soldier to his post. At the moment Budënny's train drew in, Zhukov appeared at the station and whispered in the junior officer's ear, "Sorry to be late, I just stopped by your wedding party and everyone was having a marvelous time." With a dig in the ribs he dismissed the impatient bridegroom and told him to have fun. Zhukov then strode forward in his place to welcome the visiting marshal.

In appearance and manner Zhukov is a military man from his apperceptive eyes to his polished boots. When he gives orders or discusses strategy he speaks directly, sharply and precisely in a calm, low voice. His full strong face is so dominated by his willfulness that few men readily object to his proposals. In upholding his views he can be extremely stubborn, but on occasions when he is outvoted by other members of the Supreme Command he executes their plans as precisely and solicitously as he would his own proposals.

During all of 1943 Zhukov's name appeared in the Soviet papers only once, and that was on July 28 when he was awarded the Order of Suvorov, First Class—for co-ordinating successful campaigns along the entire western front. With Marshals Stalin, Voroshilov and Vassilevsky, he participated in planning the Red Army summer offensive which swept the Germans out of Kursk, Orel, Belgorod, Kharkov, Smolensk and Kiev, and sent them bleeding and stumbling across the Dnieper, frantically clutching at every stream, hillock and rock as a possible "winter defense line." When Generals Konev, Vatutin and Malinovsky led the triumphant Red Army into twice-liberated Kharkov a great victory celebration was held in Dzerzhinsky Square amid its shattered skyscrapers. Zhukov sat on the platform at this "Bolshoi Prazdnik" as a representative of the Supreme Command.

No marshal or general in military history has ever had an

assignment exactly like Zhukov's in scope or character. Since the
Battle of Moscow, he has shuttled back and forth between the
Kremlin and field headquarters of the Supreme Command, up
and down the Red Army's long offensive line from the Baltic to
the Black Sea. He travels by plane and train, and often in an
American command car. Despite the importance of his desk work,
Zhukov is primarily a man of action who longs for the smell of
battle smoke. For the Deputy Supreme Commander in Chief of
the Red Army, he takes tremendous risks in order to observe
troops under actual enemy fire. Since the Red Army changed
over to a completely offensive fighting force, Zhukov has been
emphasizing at staff meetings and at the front conferences with
his field commanders that the rolling back of the invaders from the
motherland is no longer sufficient. The Red Army, he said, must
find ways and means to plan an *offense in depth* so that the
enemy's retreat can be cut off, its personnel and equipment destroyed completely or captured.

Early in 1944, Zhukov flew to Belaya and Serkov to co-ordinate
personally the strategy of General (now Marshal) Ivan Konev's
Second Ukrainian Army, and General Nikolai Vatutin's First
Ukrainian Army. As a result of the plan carefully mapped out in
advance by Zhukov, the Nazis under General Stemmerman were
surrounded in the Korsun-Shevchenkov area of the Dneiper
bend. On February 8, Zhukov sent Stemmerman an ultimatum
asking for surrender "to avoid unnecessary bloodshed." Although
some German generals saw the wisdom of accepting this ultimatum, they were overruled by Hitler's orders. When repeated German thrusts to wedge a break-through were beaten back with the
same tactic Zhukov used at Stalingrad, 11,000 Nazis finally threw
down their arms and up their hands, leaving 52,000 dead on the
snow-covered battlefield, including General Stemmerman.

Shortly after pulling the string on this "sack," General Vatutin was gravely injured by a mine explosion. He died on the
operating table a few weeks later. Rather than entrust this important sector to a less experienced commander, Stalin allowed
Zhukov to remain in active command of the First Ukrainian
Front, thus utilizing his chief assistant's intimate knowledge of
the campaign, plus his knowledge of this area of the Ukraine.
Foreign military observers in Moscow raised their eyebrows and
said, "Zhukov's taking a great chance. What a triumph for Mannstein if he could stop Russia's greatest professional soldier! What

a blow to Russian morale." Zhukov quickly answered skeptics with a brilliant break-through west of Shepatovka. He had not lost his touch. With one fell swoop he achieved one of the primary objectives of the entire Soviet winter campaign—cutting the Odessa-Lwow rail line, which was the last major east-to-west trackage remaining for the Germans, the last means of extricating by rail the hundreds of thousands of German troops remaining in the Dnieper bend and the Crimea, and the last means of supplying them without using the long, out-of-the-way route through Rumania and the Black Sea.

Everything was against Zhukov's success. One of the earliest spring thaws in history set in. His troops were up to their knees in greasy, slimy mud. The caterpillar treads on his tanks spun in the gooey earth, churning up flying bits of batter. Communications were impossible. Roads were morasses and fields were impassable seas of bog. But time was all-important. Zhukov knew the Germans must not be allowed to supply or rescue their trapped troops. He had preached this lesson to other commanders. Now he had to carry out the orders himself. March 4 was the date. Overhead conditions made extensive air operations unfeasible. Zhukov gave the command and his artillery opened up. For forty minutes the Ukrainian earth trembled and rumbled as never before. Then, rolling up his staff maps and giving final instructions to his deputies, Zhukov got in a U-2 plane and went to see the attack for himself. His tanks slipped forward through the mud, striking in many directions simultaneously over the 158 kilometer front.

The troops at the First Ukrainian Front were inspired by Zhukov's presence, and in two days' bitter fighting they smashed four German tank and eight infantry divisions.

6.

A month later, Zhukov caught the Germans in another trap, this time around Skala. He drove them back to the borders of the Soviet Union, followed them into Rumania. In the early part of the summer the Red armies, after their terrific advances during the winter and spring, paused for regrouping and bringing up of supplies. Stalin reshuffled the army commands, bringing Zhukov back to headquarters again as a co-ordinator. For his achievement at the front, the Supreme Soviet awarded him the Order of Victory, an incredibly magnificent bauble of diamonds, rubies and platinum, with an estimated value of more than $100,000.

During the summer offensive, Zhukov's work was greatly increased. As the pressure of international affairs, treaties, postwar plans and trade took more and more of Stalin's time and energy, the bulk of the military strategy fell on Zhukov. Working closely with Vassilevsky, Air Marshal Novikov and Artillery Chief Marshal Voronov, he planned the Belorussian offensive. He also contributed to the inter-staff communications with the British and Americans regarding a joint plan of action so that the Allied blows against Germany could be co-ordinated and timed to achieve maximum effectiveness.

By winter of 1944-1945 the job of co-ordinating the various Red Army fronts became more complex than ever. Rokossovsky pressed on Warsaw. Tolbukhin was in Bulgaria, Malinovsky swept through Rumania and into Hungary, Cherniakhovsky crossed into East Prussia, while other forces pursued the Germans into Czechoslovakia, Finland, Norway, and Yugoslavia. Zhukov, in August, had called in Timoshenko to co-ordinate the strategy in Bessarabia and Rumania. Bulganin was sent to Poland, for the same purpose. However, the entry of the Red Army into foreign countries posed new problems not only in co-ordination, supply, and communications, but in morale and in politics. Zhukov left most of these new headaches to other members of the Supreme Command, including the able Vassilevsky, chief of the General Staff, Scherbakov, in charge of propaganda and morale, and others.

Zhukov became increasingly concerned with the grand plan for ending the war, for wiping out the German armies as quickly as possible. He stuck to his belief that such a plan must be fluid and flexible, that it could not be completely envisaged at a table in the Kremlin. Hence while he studies and evaluates field reports carefully, he habitually insists on getting to the front to see the troops in action, to see how back-room strategy compares with battlefield tactics. One reason why Lord Beaverbrook's remark that "Communism under Stalin has produced the best generals of the war" comes so close to the truth, is that these generals have been trained never to forget the common denominator. Zhukov had defined war as "a science, a series of mathematical problems to be solved through proper integration and co-ordination of men and weapons in time and space." But he has also said, time and time again, that it is the common denominator that counts: the simple soldier carrying the gun who shoots the bullet and stops the bullet.

If Marshal Zhukov has any one bugaboo, which he harps on over and over it is that theory cannot be divorced from practice.

The country supplies us with the material [Zhukov once wrote]. It also supplies us with men capable of mastering this material in the shortest possible time. The young man entering the Red Army today is a young man of a new type. Life and work in socialist society have not only prepared him to assimilate Soviet Army discipline, but have also fitted him for efficient performance of his duties in the army. In our industrial country, not only the workers, but also the collective farmers, too, grew up among machinery, became acquainted with machinery in their work. That is why they are quickly able to master the technical end of their military studies which is such an essential part of military science. Soviet young men enter the army with faith in the power of machinery, mechanisms and weapons . . . the principle of "teaching the armed forces only what is done in actual warfare, and only how it is done in actual warfare" rejects the blind assimilation of outmoded principles of doing things in a set way, although in war they are done otherwise.

Thus, Zhukov and the Supreme Command and officers and the whole Red Army continually learn by experience and reapply these lessons. Long years of "Bolshevik examination," party and government planning have taught these leaders the value of self-criticisms. In the hour of the Russians' gravest peril this training is standing them in good stead. When Stalin demands that officers follow "the best traditions of the Russian Army," he means they must adopt the best, whether it be Bolshevik or tsarist. At Stalin's suggestion Zhukov had a pamphlet of Suvorovisms printed and sent to Red Army leaders. To Tolbukhin, Rokossovsky, Vassilevsky, Malinovsky, Cherniakovsky and Konev, he commended these words of Suvorov: "Regardless of what happens to me, the soldier is dearer than myself. . . . I neither sleep nor rest so that my Army may have sleep and rest."

7.

By the beginning of 1945 Zhukov's plans for the climactic offensive against Berlin were ready. London and Washington had been duly notified. Even the Germans foresaw something of the size and scope of the coming drive. The Russians had over two hundred divisions ready to roll. They had moved their supply bases hundreds of miles closer to the battlelines.

On January 12 when the blood-soaked Polish soil quaked like a bog under the terrific barrage of Red artillery, Zhukov had again left the warm comfort of his desk job for active duty in the field. The thinker became the man of action. Zhukov was to enjoy the pleasure, seldom experienced by staff officers, of translating his own strategical concepts into tactical reality. In the execution of the great winter offensive he had assigned himself the most critical and most difficult sector of the entire four-hundred-mile front from East Prussia to the Carpathians. Zhukov assumed the command of the First White Russian Army which had been stalled along the banks of the Vistula facing Warsaw since the summer of 1944.

This army group, formerly commanded by Rokossovsky, had been rested and refitted. Under Zhukov when the signal to attack sounded were approximately 750,000 men led by 51 generals. The troops plunged forward yelling *"Dayosh Berlin!"* ("Give us Berlin!"). They struck across two Vistula bridgeheads. Expecting a frontal assault, the Germans began to pull out of Warsaw. Wily as ever, Zhukov outfoxed the enemy. He dispatched his mechanized forces around Warsaw's flanks, closed in on the city from the rear. All up and down the broad front the Red Army attacked from different directions. The retreating Germans were amazed to find Russians already dug in behind them. In six days Warsaw was Zhukov's prize; and, more importantly from a military viewpoint, large segments of the Nazi garrison were caught and annihilated.

Zhukov's avalanche did not slow up with the fall of the ruined Polish capital. By-passing strong points and leaving them for rear echelons to mop up, the marshal hurled his armored spearheads and motorized infantry across more than three hundred miles of swamps and woodlands in the first three weeks of his campaign. The speed with which Zhukov's forces advanced (fifteen to twenty miles a day) was faster than even the Wehrmacht's blitzkrieg at its dizziest pace.

While Roosevelt, Churchill and Stalin were sealing the doom of Hitler's Reich at Yalta in the Crimea, Zhukov was applying the brunt of the force needed to back up the Big Three's declarations. By February 12, one month after his offensive opened, he had pushed from the Vistula to the Oder and across the Oder almost to the gates of Berlin. Frantically the Nazi radio bleated, "Nothing in five years of war is comparable to Zhukov's offensive."

For once, the Allied world was prepared to believe the Nazis. They were prepared to believe, too, that Georgi Zhukov had established himself more clearly than ever as the greatest general of World War II. His record of military achievement from Moscow to Berlin was without parallel in the annals of modern warfare.

8.

Georgi Zhukov is a good Bolshevik. He does not believe in God. But he does believe in history, in progress, in decency. For these things, for his home, his wife, his children and for Russia, he fought an unbeatable kind of war. And with him have been fighting 15,000,000 front line soldiers and behind him, almost 200,000,000 more home-front fighters.

Much has been written about Russians, like Zhukov, but nobody has characterized them as well as Alexei Tolstoy, most famous modern Russian novelist, who some months before his death in February, 1945, said of his people:

> We have many failings, as we ourselves know, but we have also one great virtue: We recognize our own failings and do not consider them virtues. We want to outlive them and, perhaps, turn many of them, dialectically, into virtues. The Russian people want to grow and progress. The Russian is a restless person. The self-satisfaction and calmness of being settled for centuries in one place are qualities of the German burgher, but not of the Russian. When the weight of the Tsarist Empire pressed so heavily on him that it was difficult to breathe, he either traveled to the ends of the earth or rose up in bloody revolution. An expansive nature—this is no definition of the Russian. He is inexhaustible and fathomless, a man of unlimited possibilities. I am sure that we ourselves do not know much about the Russian. The war has exposed and developed the strength of the Russian which will continue to grow.

And that is the story of Georgi Konstantinovich Zhukov, son of a humble peasant. "In the time of civilization's crisis," a Russian soldier told me, "Zhukov rose up like David to smite the German Goliath."

III. Marshal Alexander Novikov

The air was heavy with the sweet scent of apple blossoms. The date: July, 1944. At an observation post near the front lines, broad-shouldered Marshal Ivan Konev briefed his commanders. He summarized German positions and forces, stressing complete Russian air superiority. This time, word went around, "We will smack them on the head with planes and whang them in the back with artillery."

At a signal the infantry crept forward and seized the first German defense lines. Then suddenly the bright, early morning sun was blotted out by waves of Stormoviks. First they selected enemy batteries. Then some fanned out to riddle the enemy's communication lines. Then when the Germans attempted to bring up armored reserves, a task force of Stormoviks skimmed along at apple-blossom height and finished them off before they ever went into action. Konev was using Stormoviks for everything—attacking tanks and Ferdinands, setting trucks on fire, shelling permanent gun emplacements and dugouts, mowing down German infantry with fire from cannon and machine guns.

Nazi Field Marshal Model frantically bellowed to his Supreme Command for more planes, more Messerschmitts, Focke-Wulfs, anything to clear the air of the Russians' "flying tanks." It was the same cry which Field Marshal Busch had raised for two previous weeks during the Soviet's great Belorussian offensive.

These distress cries came as sweet music to the ears of the Soviet Supreme Command, who, grouped together at field headquarters, recognized the mighty role of Soviet aviation in the summer's terrific drive—a drive which recaptured 70,000 square miles in the month between June 22 and July 22. The Luftwaffe's helplessness in the face of the increased tempo of Russian air attacks was especially good news to short, stocky, clean-cut Alexander Novikov, the Soviet Union's chief marshal of aviation.

For Novikov the building up of the Soviet air force had been a long uphill fight against odds which would have discouraged a

less determined, a less capable executive. Even during the Finnish
war the Soviet aviation industry was largely devoted to peacetime
pursuits—commercial aviation and particularly air freight transport, which was perhaps more highly developed in the U.S.S.R.
than in any other nation. The Russians' only mass-produced plane
until 1939 was the slow, outmoded biplane, Udva, relic of the last
war. In 1940 when Stalin, during the "breathing spell" obtained
through the German-Soviet pact, began overhauling the Red Army,
aviation was not overlooked. Russian plane designers, including
the three most brilliant—Lavochkin, Ilyushin and Yakovlev—were
summoned to the Kremlin for conference attended by Stalin,
Timoshenko, Voroshilov, and the famous Soviet fliers Gromov,
Baidukov and Vassily Molokov, who at that time was head of the
Soviet Union's civil aviation board.

Little known at the conference table was Novikov, a curly-
headed former infantry officer who had just recently become an
air force commander with the rank of major general. His sponsor
was bald, sober-faced Timoshenko, who affectionately called him
"Shurik." During the talks Stalin was impressed by Novikov. He
spoke up on almost every subject under discussion and his main
thesis appealed to Stalin's realism: the Soviet Union did not have
the resources to build a highly diversified series of planes. What it
needed most were all-weather, all-height, easy-to-handle, easy-to-
build fighters. Next it needed a versatile attack bomber which
could be directed against blitz warfare. That meeting secured for
Novikov a bright and shining position in the country's aviation
firmament. In the months that followed Shurik became an adviser
to Aviation Commissar A. I. Skakhurin, and he often visited Lavochkin, Yakovlev and Ilyushin at their studios and factories.

During the winter of 1940 and the spring of 1941 Novikov served
on the committee of air officers which overhauled the curriculum
of pilot training schools; they saw to it that existing training fields
and schools were enlarged and new ones set up, not only in the
Ukraine but as far east as Novosibirsk.

When Göring's Luftwaffe buzzed and bombed over the Ukraine
on June 22, 1941, the Red Air Force was an "unknown" quantity
—even to the Germans. While it wasn't as strong as the Soviet
Supreme Command would have liked, it was by no means the
ineffective fighting force which tipsters like Lindbergh had led
outsiders to believe. Numerically it couldn't compare with the
Luftwaffe in the first year or more. But the groundwork had been

laid in the years before the war and laid extremely soundly. For example, during its maneuvers in 1935 the Red Air Force astounded the world by carrying out mass parachute jumping for the first time. In 1936 the Soviet Union joined the International Air Federation. By 1940 Soviet citizens held 62 of the 168 international aviation records on the federation's books. Where the German observers and the Lindberghs failed as prophets was in paying too much attention to the paint job and not enough to the motor. Hidden away beneath the shoddy veneer was a vast potential which couldn't be checked despite the setbacks and heartaches of the war's early months.

The German blitz through the Ukraine and northward toward Moscow and Leningrad would have throttled the Red Air Force in its infancy if farsighted preparations had not been made. Plants producing light metals and high-grade steels needed by the aircraft industry lay in the path of the German invaders. They had to be quickly evacuated to the east and set up in new homes. New skilled workers had to be found and trained, old ones moved with their factories.

During this period Stalin gave personal attention to the critical problems of the aviation industry. With the State Defense Committee he approved Novikov's plans for making the Yak the primary fighter for mass production. In the summer of 1941 the Yak-1 (one cannon, two machine guns) flew bravely out to tangle with the fast-moving Messerschmitts and Focke-Wulfs. It was not quite on a par with them. Also coming slowly from Soviet factories were the Mig-3, a high-ceilinged fighter which the Russians claim was later copied by the Nazis in their Messerschmitt 109-G, the Lagg-3 fighter, Il-2 Stormovik, and the Pe-2, which is a two-seater dive-bomber.

While the defense committee wrestled with the problem of priorities and plant evacuation, General Novikov (now titular head of the air arm) tried everything within his power to minimize the initial advantages of the Luftwaffe. Everywhere there were desperate demands for fighters to protect the civilian population as well as the retreating armies and supply lines against German bombing and strafing. It was more than difficult—it was impossible to meet all these demands. Production had been temporarily cut down due to evacuations and the inevitable loss of some plants and workers. Although the exact figures were never released for all fronts, some idea of how the Luftwaffe quantitatively outstripped

Novikov's men is derived from the battle for Leningrad. When the Germans attacked Leningrad in 1942 the best Novikov could spare from the central front was 594 planes, not all of them first line. Against Leningrad the Germans hurled a minimum of 1,500 and probably as many as 2,000 aircraft.

The appearance of fleets of Udvas (U-2) during the Battle of Stalingrad has been second-guessed by military commentators as a "master stroke of genius." Novikov would be the first to admit this "master stroke" was dictated by necessity. The Udvas, which the Germans once scornfully called "sewing machines" proved so effective that they won the nickname of "standing death." How these squadrons of Udvas were scooped up from airports throughout the Soviet Union and rushed to Stalingrad with supplies badly needed by the Red armies, and then were thrown into the breach as bombers, is one of the most amazing stories of this war. It underscores the keynote of Novikov's air force—improvisation.

2.

Toward the end of 1942 and the beginning of 1943 the Soviets began catching up with the Germans in the air. Defects in early planes were corrected and new models came winging out of the east, where evacuated factories stepped up their output. Through Iran and across Alaska Lend-Lease Airacobras and Bostons began arriving. In this connection it is interesting to note Novikov's "improvisation" again. While the Soviets greatly admire the Airacobra and have employed it successfully as a fighter, they began to have greater need for fast bombers on a larger scale as the tide turned last year. Quickly they converted the Airacobras into light bombers.

The reason that Novikov had selected the Airacobra—at a time when our experts considered it already outmoded—was that it had a tricycle landing gear which made it easy to set down on almost any kind of a field. It had a few too many fussy gadgets for Novikov's fliers, but the unnecessary ones were ripped out when the red paint was splashed over the U. S. white star insignia.

American fliers who have inspected Russian planes have not been impressed, at least not at first glance. But they have looked at them from American standards, and not through the eyes of a Russian production board confronted with stringent shortages both in materiel and personnel. Guided by these shortages and by tactical requirements, Russian plane designers had to compromise between plywood and metal construction. As a result they were forced to turn out lightweight planes, stripped of conveniences, even of self-starters. They used a plastic, bonded plywood made of birch and pine split into very thin boards, then covered with resins and subjected to pressure.

When it came to firepower, they had to make the most of what they had, too. They discarded wing guns to save weight and because they were not found to be as accurate as others. They placed fewer guns in the fuselage, too. The newer model Yaks have one gun poking through the hub of the propeller, one or two through the prop.

What the Yak lacks in firepower and armor, the Il-2 Stormovik has. To the casual observer it seems a clumsy, heavy, almost foolish plane. It is heavy and somewhat clumsy, but it is far from foolish. The Il-2, designed by Ilyushin, is a low-winged monoplane with an in-line liquid-cooled engine. The fuselage from the prop to a point well behind the observer and gunner is solid armor plate. The bulletproof glass which covers the pilot's cabin is made of a shatter-proof substance developed in Leningrad and called "Stalinite." The Stormovik's fuselage is very unconventional. The armor plating is not patched or hung as it is on other planes. The armor plating *is* the fuselage—and even the engine is welded to it. Thus the plane is not vulnerable to small-arms fire from the ground. The Stormovik packs a terrific wallop itself. It is heavily armed with cannon, machine guns, bombs and rocket-firing equipment. In action its target is selected by observation posts pushed out ahead of the advance. Then the pilot is guided by radio instructions.

3.

Alexander Alexandrovich Novikov, the man who has piloted the Red Air Force through the dark days into the present limelight, was born in 1902 in a small central Russian village. Today he is not only one of the most successful wartime leaders but one of the most popular. Five years ago unknown nationally, his portrait now hangs prominently in airports from Kharkov to Alma Ata. But the public rarely sees his name in newspapers. A news agency which keeps a "personality" file on Soviet generals reveals just this much on Novikov as gleaned from a regular reading of the daily press: November, 1941, promoted to lieutenant general; Summer, 1942, included as air commander in new seven-man Supreme Command; January, 1943, promoted to colonel-general; January, 1943, received Order of Suvorov, first class; March, 1943, promoted to marshal of aviation, the first Russian ever to receive that rank; January, 1944, promoted to chief marshal of aviation. Like all Soviet leaders Novikov's private life is his own. There have never been any interviews with him published in the Soviet press and he has never had a press conference. He prefers to have the publicity go to his famed aces—Pokryshkin, Pokrishev, Gulayev, Rechkalov, Lavrinenkov, Lugensky, Kamazin, the Glinka brothers, Molodchy and others.

When in Moscow Novikov lives in a small, well-furnished apartment not far from the Smolensk metro station. He has a pretty blond wife but no children. He is five feet, eight inches tall, weighs 160 pounds, has gray eyes, dark, curly hair, and a quick, friendly smile. He is always promising his wife that he will take her to the latest musical comedy or operetta but usually staff work keeps him at his Bolshaya Peregovskaya Street office until three or four in the morning. Like most Soviet officials his day rarely starts before noon, except when he is at the front. In the early afternoon he confers with his deputy for operations, tall, gold-toothed Colonel General Alexei Nikitin, who has the face of a philosopher and the handshake of a truck driver. Sometime during the day he may be called to the Kremlin for a conference with Red Army chief of staff Vassilevsky, Zhukov or Stalin himself.

Novikov has surrounded himself with a strong, able staff, small but efficient and hard-working. Highest ranker is Chief Marshal A. S. Golovanov, who plans large-scale tactical offensives with the General Staff. Chief of liaison with the Allied forces is Marshal Khudiakov who represented Novikov at the Crimean conference in February, 1945. Chief of air technical forces, Colonel General A. K. Repin, had to be spared for another assignment—head of the Soviet Military Mission to the United States. The air force ordnance chief is Major General Nikolai Stepanov. Other essential men on Novikov's staff are Lieutenant General Dmitri Grendal, who specializes in air intelligence, and Major General Feodorov, who is chief of the air force hydrometeorological service.

As his staff grew during the early days of the war, Novikov found it difficult to accustom himself to adjutants following him about, and jokes went around his headquarters that he kept falling over them. Although he has an unusually large number of medals and orders he wears them only on state occasions, preferring to use ribbons. His uniforms are invariably tailored impeccably, but close observation shows tiny holes where decorations have been screwed into the cloth.

In the late thirties, when Novikov switched over to the air force, he became a bomber pilot and still can handle any ship in his force. Occasionally while visiting an airdrome, he will give in to a whim and surprise his companions by stepping into an Udva, an Airacobra, or a late-model Tupolev two-engine bomber and quickly taking off. He never offers any explanation except, "I just felt like trying it out."

During prewar emphasis on learning parachute-jumping, Novikov himself became expert at it. But he has not been allowed to try it since the start of the war. He spends a few spare hours each week studying English. Despite the irregularity of his lessons he is making good progress, although he refuses to speak it. During a reception at Spaso House last June for General Ira Eaker, a United States Embassy secretary who was acting as translator for Novikov and Eaker couldn't find the correct expression. Much to his amazement Novikov helped him out of his quandary by supplying the exact English.

Previously Eaker had been received by Novikov and spent more than an hour discussing air tactics and plans. On this and other occasions Novikov impressed American observers with his keen knowledge of Allied plane types and performance records, as well as plant production figures. He talked frankly and intelligently regarding his own air force, its problems, successes, and limitations, in a pleasant baritone voice with a "Moscow accent." Eaker and the marshal's other guests sat around a large oblong conference table at the head of which was Novikov's desk. On the walls of the simply furnished office were the usual pictures of Stalin, Lenin, Molotov, Voroshilov and Timoshenko. On Novikov's desk was a wooden plane model presented to him by the workers of the Chkalov plant in Novosibirsk. Under the glass top of his desk is a picture of his wife, and a clipping from an aviation journal with a penciled mark around these words: "The Slavs will never understand air warfare. That is a brave man's weapon; it is the German method of fighting." The words, of course, are Hitler's; the pencil mark, Novikov's.

After conferring with his guests, Novikov invited them into a small anteroom for *chai*, which literally means "tea." In most cases it turns out to be vodka, wine, caviar and other *zakuski*, if not a full twelve-course meal. Novikov prefers vodka without water. He usually fills himself a good-sized tumbler and drinks it bottoms up. But he is not a heavy drinker by Russian standards.

During the past year Novikov has been in Moscow only rarely, and never for more than a few days at a time. With Zhukov or some other member of the Supreme Command, he makes trips to the front to check over preparations for offensives and to improvise solutions for the growing problem of supply for his expanding air force. In June he personally conferred with Rokossovsky's air chief, General Sergei Rudenko just before the opening of the Belorussian offensive which pushed the Germans back to East Prussia. He wanted badly to go up and have a look at German soil for himself, but Stalin has ordered him to stay on the ground in combat areas.

Through Marshal Khudiakov and General Nikitin, Novikov maintains close contact with Allied air officers. Where and when possible our bombers have aided the Red Army's advances through the Balkans and into the heart of Germany by blowing up Nazi supply lines and dumps. For even though the Red Air Force has been getting bigger, it does not have any super-bombers like our B-17's or B-29's. It remains strictly "tactical."

When Major General John Deane, chief of the U. S. Military Mission in Moscow, reopened the subject of obtaining Ukrainian bases for shuttle-bombing, Novikov interested himself in the proposition. The idea had been broached earlier in the war, but it was one of those things that the Russians put off until after the Teheran conference. Once they agreed to let us in, things went fast. The bases were built with Russian labor in a miraculously short time. On several occasions Novikov checked over the plans for the bases and for supplying them, and offered constructive assistance to American officials. Before the first operation went through, Novikov flew south to inspect the bases personally. According to Deane, the marshal made several changes for the better as a result of his observations. At the Crimean conference in Yalta, President Roosevelt presented to Marshal Stalin a decoration (Legion of Merit, commander rank) for Novikov "in recognition of distinguished services" rendered in connection with the establishment of the American shuttle-bombing bases.

The success of these shuttle-bombings was a revelation to the Red Air Force. On the first day when the Fifteenth United States Air Force flew in from Italy, the Russians watched open-mouthed as the great Forts landed as gracefully as swans. They were even more amazed when they were permitted to inspect the planes at close range with no restraints and no "guided tours"—unless requested. They were even allowed to look through the Norden bombsight.

Not long afterward, the Germans paid a visit to this United States base and gave it a terrific pasting. There was a good deal of hard feeling over this, because the protection of the field had been left up to the Russians. When it was all over and the pieces of wrecked Forts were being scraped off the field, none questioned the bravery of the Russians. The question which many Americans did raise was, "Where was the Soviet fighter protection?" The answer: For all intents and purposes, it just wasn't.

In discussing this fiasco with Russians, I first met apologies and then logic. The logic, according to the Russians, is this: Even in 1944 the Red Air Force had only a limited number of fighters and a limited number of skilled pilots. They were strung out loosely along a 1,400-mile battle line. They dropped back in depth where supply lines had to be protected. They were over some key cities where war production had been resumed. But just on the rule of using what they had where it was needed most, our bases were given slim protection. The bases were miles behind the front, and no one figured the Germans would risk a large bomber force to attack it. But the Germans did, and no amount of Russian logic would convince U. S. pilots and correspondents that our side hadn't been let down.

The results of our shuttle-bombings were as unbelievable to members of the Red Air Force as the "tinseled grandeur" of capitalist Bucharest was to members of the Red Army when they captured that Rumanian city. Last summer at the Architects' Club in Moscow the United States Embassy arranged an exhibit picturing the results of American precision bombing over enemy targets. I talked to some young officers on Novikov's staff there. They were wide-eyed with amazement at the amount of devastation and at the extreme accuracy obtained by our high-level mass bombing.

I asked one of General Nikitin's assistants who was at this exhibit why the Soviets had never gone in for strategical bombing. He said that the experience of the German blitz over England in 1940 had convinced Novikov and other leaders that such bombing produced major results only if carried on in mass and over a

lengthy period of time. "We could not build up our fighter and
bomber production and at the same time develop such long-range
bombers," said the air officer. "We had to have tactical strength.
So we had to let the other go." He did, of course, remind me that
long-range bombing was quite within the scope of Soviet airmen,
and mentioned that Alexander Molodchy, twice Hero of the
Soviet Union, had bombed Berlin before the Americans. "You
know," he said, "Molodchy reported seeing two rings of ackack
fire around Berlin—a gunfire ring directed by Göring and an
inkwell ring directed by Goebbels." He thought that was pretty
funny.

During the summer of 1944 I had a chance to meet quite a few
Soviet fliers and to ask them questions about their air force. One
night, however, at the Red Flyers' Club, a handsome white stone
building out on the Leningrad Chaussée in Moscow, I became
embroiled in a discussion of a different nature and had a lot of
questions thrown at me. I went to the club with an American
captain who speaks excellent Russian, having studied in Moscow
for several years. We both wore U. S. Army Officers' uniforms, and
during an intermission in the dancing, found ourselves surrounded
by young pilots.

They asked us how we liked the music. I said it was fine.

"The band here," said one flier, indicating the bandstand, "is
better than the band in there." He nodded toward the restaurant.
I agreed.

"What are the best bands in America today?" another demanded.

The captain, who was not very interested in such subjects, faded
away, leaving me to answer the eager crowd of questioners with
my limited vocabulary.

"Oh, Tommy Dorsey, Glenn Miller, Benny Goodman, Sammy
Kaye. . . ." I began reeling off every name I could remember.

A redheaded lieutenant wearing the Order of the Red Star and
several ribbons grabbed my arm excitedly. "What about Duke
Ellington and Count Basie and Fats Waller?"

"Fats Waller is dead," someone in the crowd said unexpectedly.
This was news to me, and since I had never seen it mentioned in
the Soviet press I couldn't figure out how he knew. While I looked
around frantically for my friend, the redhead and one of the
musicians from the band started an argument. They were trying
to settle on the "order" of "best" bands in America. Benny Goodman, they agreed, was No. 1. Duke Ellington was No. 2. Artie

Shaw was No. 3. But when it came to fourth place they argued violently. Everyone in the crowd seemed to be taking sides. The redhead kept yelling "Bunny Berigan!" and the musician kept yelling, "Charlie Barnet!" I am frank to admit that I know very little about either of them to this day.

Finally they appealed to me to settle the argument. I sided with the musician, just to be on the safe side. "Barnet, of course," I said like an oracle. That seemed to settle it with nearly everyone except the redhead. He glared at his opponent, then at me, and stomped off, saying very decisively, "Bunny Berigan, *on moy bog*!" ("he's my god!") .

The musician, who played the saxophone, wanted to show his appreciation. He took my arm and led me to a quiet corner. He put his hand on his back pocket and drew out a frayed leather wallet. He opened it and gently pulled out a picture. It was like one of those small pasteboard pictures which small boys collect. And not unlike the kind you get "for free" when you are weighed. It was a picture of Benny Goodman, with Goodman's autograph. Not really, but his signature was printed. The saxophonist showed me this, his eyes gleaming as though it were his best girl. I told him it was very nice and he put it away.

"Who is playing saxophone now in Count Basie's band?" he asked. I made him repeat the question. "Who is playing saxophone now in Count Basie's band?" he said.

I had to tell him I didn't know. His mouth dropped open.

"But you *are* an American, aren't you?" He looked at my uniform suspiciously.

"Yes."

"Where do you live?"

"New York," I replied.

Again disbelief in his dark eyes. "But then you *must* know," he said a bit testily. I assured him I didn't and quickly asked him what he thought about swing. Since there is no letter "w" in Russian, they call it "sving."

"Ah, sving," he said, and his eyes lit up again, almost friendly. "I love to play it like Artie Shaw. But, unfortunately," he said, with a deprecating movement of his hand, indicating the crowded dance floor, "it is too sophisticated for these children." He could not have been more than twenty, himself. But I had him on the defensive, so I fired another question.

"What about boogie-voogie?"

He sighed. "Boogie-voogie is not yet for the masses." At that moment he was called to the bandstand and the dance music resumed. During the remainder of the evening I found plenty of young officers who wanted to talk about jazz, or even about American planes. But when I asked them any questions about Marshal Novikov, they didn't know any more about him than I had known about Bunny Berigan or who plays saxophone in Count Basie's band.

But every flier whom I questioned at this club, or anywhere else in the Soviet Union, had a definite answer about his own peacetime future. They were staying in aviation. Some of them meant it in terms of the Army, but most of them expected to become civil aviation pilots.

"If before the war we had the greatest airlines" a colonel told me at the bar, "after the war it will be even greater. I cannot say if Marshal Novikov will run it, and I cannot say if there are plans. Well, perhaps. You see, we had such great plans years before the war for airlines. I worked for Molokov, I know." He gulped his cognac. "You come back here after the war on a Soviet plane." I walked back to the dance floor and he yelled, "Bring Eric Johnston with you!"

4.

The success of the Red Air Force, while largely attributable to Novikov, has its roots in the correctness of early Soviet thinking about the role of military aviation. An article written on this subject for the Military Encyclopedia in 1932 states that—

The role played by aviation in cooperation with other arms, both in maneuvers and in battle, continues to grow. By carrying on air reconnaissance for cavalry units and mechanized formations, aviation lends flexibility to their maneuvers. It defends them from enemy aviation. Attached to mechanized formations, stormer and bomber planes greatly increase their effectiveness in independent operations. The appearance of armored storming planes and the growth of their armaments create favorable conditions for their cooperation with infantry and tanks in the battle. Moreover, aviation will undoubtedly become a potent weapon of antitank defense. It will attack enemy tanks in the areas of their concentration and will control the artillery fire directed against them. . . .

These principles, formulated thirteen years ago, are still the basis for operations of the tactical Red Air Force. They were tested during the Spanish war. The Germans tested their ideas, too, in Spain and decided that the dive-bomber was the deadliest attack weapon. But the Russians never accepted this idea. Their experience taught them the need for a stormer plane with plenty of armor, one that could take a tremendous amount of antiaircraft fire and still survive. Ilyushin absorbed this experience and built his Il-2 Stormovik.

The war in Spain also demonstrated that Russian fighter planes were obsolete, and that an air force had to be incredibly large and powerful to successfully perform a great many tasks. Wisely, Novikov in World War II refrained from making the same mistake as the Luftwaffe did. The Germans spread themselves too much in Russia. Besides tactically supporting the Wehrmacht, they bombed border cities and other targets as far east as Moscow and Gorky. They attacked the industrial rear. They went after sprawling Russian supply lines. They tried to do so much in the opening months of the war that their losses were very heavy; according to Soviet figures the Germans lost 7,000 planes in the first two months.

From the very first day of the war, Novikov not only limited the types of planes to be produced, he also restricted the tasks which his air force could and would undertake. Chiefly, they were to give air protection to the front and the *main* bases; to inflict maximum loss on greatest concentrations of the enemy's air fleet, and to defend against their attacks; to attempt dispersal where possible of enemy reserves near the front; when sufficient materiel became available, to back up the Red Army's offensives.

But for the first year and a half it was difficult to do even this much. The German attack on June 22 almost did to the Red Air Force what the Jap attack on December 7 did to our Pacific Navy. Airdromes and aviation plants were primary Nazi targets. The fields were left a shambles, and thousands of planes never got off the ground while Nazi Heinkels blasted them.

The year 1941 was the year in which the Red Air Force was gradually shifting over to new plane models. They had been put on the production lines late in 1940 and began emerging in the first half of 1941. But at the moment of the Nazi attack, most of the air force had obsolescent planes. Considering this series of initial setbacks, and not forgetting the necessity of evacuating plants, the comeback which Novikov managed is magnificent.

Summarizing the air war last June 22, the Soviet Information

Bureau stated that the Germans had lost 60,000 planes in three years as against Russian losses of 31,000.

5.

It was early in 1943 that Novikov's forces began to have superiority over the Germans. In the two years since then, this superiority has been on the increase. The Germans began to complain about the unexpected power of the "Bolshevik vultures" during the spring of 1944 in the Crimean campaign when the trapped Nazis attempted to fly additional planes, equipment and men from Rumania to the Crimea. I flew over most of the broad, flat Crimean battlefield myself and saw some of it from a bouncing jeep at much closer range. Even an untrained observer could tell that the Luftwaffe had taken a terrible beating on the peninsula: the landscape was littered with every type of German plane from Stuka dive-bombers to heavy Junker transports.

Even today, with Soviet plants turning out better than 35,000 planes a year, Novikov's air arm is small and select as compared to our own or Britain's. The Red Air Force has never been a mass air force. The Russians, although confronted with four-fifths of the Luftwaffe until the invasion of North Africa, never had to fight an air war. Not in the sense that the war over western Europe was an air war during 1943 and most of 1944. It is true that the Russians have been able to rely more and more upon their aviation in scoring break-throughs, but even their mighty summer offensives of 1944 did not feature air power on a major multi-thousand plane scale.

During 1944 Zhukov and Novikov used a concentrated fleet of Stormoviks, protected by Yaks, to start things rolling. One week this fleet would turn up in Belorussia. A few weeks later, after that offensive had been successfully begun, the fleet would be pulled out and sent to the Ukraine or the Balkans or Poland where it would perform the same job.

Soviet airmen are expendable. There is no age limit for pilots— they range from nineteen to forty and older. Most pilots are in their thirties, averaging eight and ten years older than U. S. fliers. Trained men and women are now pouring out of Novikov's thirty-two higher aviation schools, but still Russian fliers put in long, grueling hours. They think nothing of flying as many as six sorties in a day, or of spending ten to twelve hours aloft during a twenty-four-hour period.

As in our country, the fliers are the big heroes. Often the military papers are joined by *Pravda* and *Izvestia* in reminding people that the foot soldier is the basic hero, that the artillerymen are incomparable, that the partisans are peerless, that the sappers are most intrepid. But everyone loves a flier. In the Soviet Union, this affection is nothing new. Speaking at the first session of the Supreme Soviet in Moscow, Stalin said: "I must confess that I love fliers. If I knew that any one of the fliers is offended, my heart simply aches. We must steadfastly support our fliers."

BOOK 5

Stalin's Falcon

FOR the past two years the leading United Nations' ace in the air war against the Axis has been a stern-faced, chestnut-haired Siberian peasant. His current acknowledged total of Nazi planes shot down—by himself—is 59, although unconfirmed reports from the front have put his score as high as 75. He has won a majority of his air battles flying an American Airacobra. His name is Alexander Ivanovich Pokryshkin. In the hearts and minds and histories of the Russian people he has already taken his place alongside Dmitri Donskoi, Alexander Nevsky, Suvorov, Kutuzov, Chapayev, Budënny and other gallant defenders of the fatherland. Already they speak of him in the stilted slogan language of yesterday's *Pravda* and tomorrow's textbook. To the Russians he is already three times life-size and all of him one dimensional: *strong*. That is his greatness and theirs, too.

On August 20, 1944, the U.S.S.R. celebrated its annual Aviation Day. In Moscow at four in the afternoon waves of Soviet planes zoomed low over the Kremlin and hundreds of cannons roared in a tribute to the Red Air Force. Stalin issued a special Order of the Day. In the awards published on this date Guards Colonel Alexander "Sasha" Pokryshkin became the first in the history of the U.S.S.R. to win the title "Hero of the Soviet Union" for the third time. While Pokryshkin's exploits had been the subject for many newspaper articles during the war, the Soviet press on Aviation Day devoted more space to the personal life, training, deeds and ambitions of the three-time Hero than has been accorded any individual since the war's start. A Foreign Office official agreed that no man, with the exception of Lenin, had received such personal publicity during the entire existence of the Soviet press.

Since almost nothing is ever printed concerning generals and marshals, and even less about ranking members of the party or the government, the significance of this organized build-up for one solitary air hero is difficult to understand without a close examination not only of Pokryshkin's record and background but of what he symbolizes in the present Soviet struggle.

Men like Stalin, Molotov and Voroshilov won their fame and their leadership during the earliest days of the Revolution. The next age group, men like Zhukov, Vassilevsky, Novikov and Konev were tempered during the civil wars, sharpened for leadership by years of Soviet education and had already achieved some standing before June 22, 1941.

But Pokryshkin typifies the Russian hero-leader who has emerged completely as a result of the Great Patriotic War. On June 22, 1941 he was just another farm boy in his late twenties who could fly a plane. When Stalin was burning bridges at Tsaritsyn, Sasha was learning how to skip down Lyskov Street in the Siberian frontier town of Novonikolaevsk (now Novosibirsk). When Zhukov was battling with White Guards, Sasha was trudging barefooted to school. While Konev was living the Revolution in the Far East, Pokryshkin was hearing it as a child hears a wild West story—in tales about Chapayev, in the books of Nikolai Ostrovsky. While Vassilevsky, Novikov and others as students in the Frunze Academy were learning Napoleon's mistakes at Smolensk, Pokryshkin was getting fair marks in middle school and fitting himself for a technical career. When Hitler seized power, the old Bolsheviks weighed its eventual political and military implications for Russia. Pokryshkin, struggling to understand the complicated business of making farm machinery, was aware of little except his home, his family, his job and his yearning to fly an airplane.

2.

On August 21, 1944, the good citizens of Novosibirsk came to pay homage to the mother of Guards Colonel Alexander Pokryshkin. They walked down the calm, narrow street—too narrow to permit the passage of automobiles—until they came to the old timber hut which was numbered 43A. There were brown shutters and potato bushes and acacias in bloom just the same as there had been in 1914, the year Alexander was born. All day long on August 21 people dropped in, neighbors, city officials, party leaders, military men. Among them were Mikhail Kulagin, general secretary of the Novosibirsk Province party, and tall, bald Mayor

Vladimir Khaionovsky. Everyone embraced the hero's mother, Aksinya Stepanova.

"How wonderful such a tiny woman could give birth to such a great hero," whispered one visitor, gazing at the white-haired old peasant woman with her gnarled hands and wrinkled little animated face. She wore a printed house dress, with the traditional peasant scarf tied around her head.

Everyone tried to tell her about her "Sashinka." But she had heard the news on the radio. They brought her copies of the local newspaper. A local artist came to make a pencil sketch of the spry fifty-nine-year-old mother of the hero sitting in her living room against a background of her son's portraits.

"These pictures on the wall," she said, "were given to me by the city soviet and by the collective of the plant where Sasha worked."

The reporters came, too. Aksinya Stepanova was glad to talk. "Just a usual family," she told them. "A family's a family. My husband was a stonemason. Now it is already ten years since he is dead. May God rest his soul. I had seven children. Six sons and one daughter. I can't complain. They were good children, nice children, respectful. Sasha was the next to the oldest. Before him was Vassinka. Scarlet fever entered our house. I saved all the children except Vassinka. Fate was not for Vassinka to live."

The old lady paused and offered her guests some vodka and *zakuski*. They filled their glasses and drank to the three-time Hero. She continued, "About Sasha now, what can I say? You know. He's not only a hero. All the people consider him to be the foremost hero, the first hero. Well, two years after Sasha I gave birth to Alexei. Now he's in the Far East, a senior sergeant. He's also a good military man. Next was Peter. He served in the Army. He was the first who met the Fascists at the border. I've heard nothing about him since." The old lady paused and rubbed her fingers as if they hurt. "Is he alive, my drop of blood?"

Nobody answered her. Her gray-blue eyes filled with tears. At that moment a young man entered in the uniform of a *Kursant*, an air cadet. He looked like Sasha. The mother brightened. There was life in her voice again as she introduced him. "And here's my younger one, Valentine. He doesn't live at home either. He came to visit us for several days. He keeps telling me, 'Mamushka, I'll finish studying and soon fly over to join my brother at the front. We'll beat the Fascists together.' You see what they're like, my boys, they grow up a little and fly away."

The reporters scribbled and then drank another toast. Aksinya Stepanova went through the roster of her family. The very youngest, Vitally, was just thirteen and in the sixth grade. The daughter, Marya, was married to a man who was at the front. She had two children of her own. And so it went.

They had no trouble bringing her back to the subject of Sasha, her favorite. Aksinya Stepanova rambled through her mental scrapbook, "He was born near the Kamenka River. Then the town was not large. From our little house the town grew. In his early childhood he was like all children, funny and affectionate. Of course, we were not rich. We worked from dawn to dark. We lacked many things. Those years were difficult. You know yourself how it was. When Sasha was a little older we moved to Kolltsov Street. He was at school already. A sudden seriousness appeared prematurely, an exceptional fondness for books. He had a friend also named Sasha. They used to take a lot of books and hide themselves. The boys of their age on Kolltsov Street didn't like this behavior. They even called them nicknames. 'Engineers' they called them. This other Sasha, too."

The old lady stopped and greeted some new guests. When they had joined her in a toast to the three-time Hero, she resumed, "Every day he became more fond of mechanical things. He kept wanting to build things. From the very first they were planes, all kinds. The whole house was full of them. At that period Sasha, my Sashinka, was a silent, serious boy but he'd leave his favorite work to help me in the household. From the middle school he went to a plant factory school. When he graduated he helped to build the plant and then worked in it. Then aviation school, now this."

She excused herself and went quickly into the other room for a minute and reappeared with a fine heavy cloth coat trimmed with black Persian lamb. "Sasha sent this to me from Moscow. He is always sending me things. The coat, dress material, letters, money."

A reporter interrupted Aksinya Stepanova to ask, "Have you any message to send to Alexander Ivanovich? We will be glad to send it on the wireless."

The old lady dug in the bosom of her pretty new house dress and pulled out a crumpled sheet. She handed it to Valentine. "You can read my writing, Valya, read it." Seriously Valentine accepted the note and the responsibility. He read, too loudly, as if delivering a speech:

My dear Sasha:
I embrace you, my dear falcon. I thank you for all the happiness you have given me and all the people. Now at home is your younger brother, Valentine, who will very soon finish fliers school and fight with you at the front. Today I thank the one who raised you, educated you and gave you an eagle's wings, great Stalin.

Everyone applauded including the old lady. They drank a toast *za Stalina* and then left after asking for the health of Pokryshkin's wife, Marya Kuzminishna.

3.

On August 21, 1944, the wife of the hero, who was expecting a baby, their first, met the reporters. She was young, twenty-two, not very big as Russian women are built, with even features and dark-gray eyes. Her hair was done in a modern, upswept coiffure. In her thin, pretty hands she firmly held a copy of the Novosibirsk paper. Tenderly she kissed it. She was wearing a blue cotton dress, maternity style, and on it was pinned the Order of the Patriotic War, a reward for her excellent service as a nurse. She has been on many fronts, usually attached to flight units. Once when Pokryshkin was sick she treated him and they fell in love. When he recovered, their romantic rendezvous under German shell fire soon gave way to long periods of separation and worry. So they were married and she became permanently attached to his unit.

Marya Kuzminishna is now living in a beautiful pine-gladed rest home in a suburb of Novosibirsk. She has a private room. On her walls, too, are pictures of Alexander Pokryshkin. On the night table next to her bed is a thin volume of Konstantin Simonov's love poems. She is very fond of them, especially, "Wait for Me," a poem which every Russian girl who loves a man at the front knows by heart. Sometimes she looks at her husband's picture and murmurs the lines:

> *Wait when from far off at last*
> *No letters come to you.*
> *Wait when all others have ceased*
> *To wait, who waited too.*

But today she is happy and not sad, and she feels that her husband is close to her. The reporters stand and ask her questions. She has a soft, quiet voice. When her face is calm she seems almost as solemn as Alexander, but when she smiles or talks her face becomes animated and attractive.

"When Pokryshkin flies," she recalls, "I shut my eyes from fear. Oh, God, it's frightening. On whatever flight he is, I can always recognize his plane even if there are ten. He has a step of his own. All the fliers recognize his air walk, it's not me alone."

Someone said she must not worry any more, that Pokryshkin only commands now and doesn't fly. Marya Kuzminishna clenches her fist and her quiet voice rises slightly with emotion. "In the first place," she answers, "it can't be that Pokryshkin would not fly. And in the second place where do the shot-down planes come from? It cannot be that an uncle shoots them down for him?"

The consoling reporter is embarrassed. Marya Kuzminishna says she is afraid that she and Sasha are coming in for too much fuss. "Sasha hates that and so do I."

Another reporter asks for her last letter from Pokryshkin. Quickly Marya Kuzminishna goes to the night table and brings it out. It has just recently come from the front—from Rumania. She reads a part of it aloud:

My boys work very well. Sometimes I, too, remember the past and go up together with them. It's true the enemy is not so numerous as before but we succeed in catching something from time to time.

Then another letter:

Recently we fought a little with the Germans and they finished more than 100 Fritzes. I had personally no meeting with the *bombori*. But I followed the Khudujeh (Messerschmitts) a little. They escaped so it's obvious they had no great desire to fight.

Before they left, the reporters asked if she had any message to send her husband. She beamed. "I have sent one." They asked to see it. She showed them a copy. It read:

My darling:
I am overwhelmed with joy at your new award. Proud of you and waiting for you with victory.

Marya

4·

On August 27, a week after Aviation Day, a group of fliers at an advanced Soviet base near the banks of the Vistula are having a celebration to honor their comrade, Colonel Alexander Pokryshkin. There are the usual speeches. His friend Major Rechkalov, twice Hero of the Soviet Union and credited with fifty-three Nazi planes, talks about his adventures with Pokryshkin. Another officer speaks in behalf of the regimental staff and wishes the colonel new successes. Telegrams are read from prominent Soviet leaders. There is one from Marshal Konev and one from Novikov. Finally the shy, hesitant Pokryshkin gets up to speak. He is not very tall, but his figure is strongly built. His whole appearance gives that feeling of great internal strength, concentration and balance which always distinguishes those who are used to looking death straight in the eye. He tells of his gratitude to great Stalin for the care and attention which he gives to Soviet fliers. He pledges to go on destroying the enemy to the very end. "I will not be satisfied with 100," he declares solemnly, sitting down amid the cheers of his friends. . . .

When Alexander was a boy on Lyskov Street he dreamed of becoming a pilot. When he wasn't helping his mother to run the tiny three-room house or looking after his younger brothers, he would sit and read aviation magazines and make paper models of the latest planes. In the summer he would hang around the civil airport watching the skies for the passenger planes which flew over Novosibirsk on their way to Central Asia and Vladivostok. Novosibirsk was even then a thriving boom town with its mushrooming wooden houses, its wooden planked sidewalks, its new railroad marshaling yards and the factories that were being built as part of Stalin's Five-Year Plan.

He finished school and immediately received a job at Sibcombine, a new Novosibirsk plant making machine tools for agricultural equipment. But he had long ago decided that he must become a great pilot, like Valery Chkalov, his hero. He recalls, "Chkalov's wings eclipsed everything else in the world for me." And so he applied for aviation school and was accepted. But his joy was short-lived. When he arrived at the school he discovered that it was for aviation mechanics. The thought that he could not fly depressed him terribly. The chief of the school seemed to understand the young Siberian's brooding mood.

"Is it necessary for you to become a Chkalov?" he asked.

"*Absoliutno!*" ("absolutely"). Pokryshkin answered very morosely.

The chief sighed, "All of you want to fly. Who will fix the motors?" So Pokryshkin was left in the technical school. Looking back on it now, he is glad to have had that training. "I must confess it was useful. I studied the performance of the airplane in every detail. Twice a year I applied to flying school, but since I was considered 'not bad' as a mechanic I was not allowed to go."

When he graduated from the technical school Pokryshkin began working at an airdrome. He never gave up the idea of flying and stored away all the wisdom of the fliers whom he met at the field. On his free days he managed to fly, and eventually made a few solos in a U-2, the ancient Russian biplane. Eventually, says Pokryshkin, he had to "resort to cunning." It was 1937, the year that Chkalov flew across the Pole to the United States. This flight stirred Pokryshkin as no other event in his young life. He asked for a two-week leave to visit his family. "But instead of going to Novosibirsk I went straight to Krasnodar, made a beeline for the aero-club and persuaded them to take me on for exactly two weeks. I had some difficulty in overriding their objections but I finally won my point. Two weeks later I passed the test. The head of the club said it was the first time anyone had received the flying certificate in two weeks. He didn't know, of course, about my contraband flights while working as a mechanic."

The instructor at Krasnodar remembers Pokryshkin very well. "He made brilliant, firm landings. I told him at the time, 'You feel the earth very well.'" With his certificate, several fields were open to Pokryshkin. He talked it over with his friends. "Everyone had to define his place in the future war," he said. "Our ideas about the war were vague, but one thing was certain—the need for a destroyer pilot."

He went home briefly to Novosibirsk. Then, enrolled in the Red Air Force, he was sent to school at Kacha. He arrived at the base even before his papers were ready. At Kacha, Pokryshkin learned discipline. In his eagerness to impress his superiors he made a flashy landing, but when he was dressed down for this performance he never repeated the mistake. His confidence in his own ability continued to grow. He was so patient, so sure of himself, that the school asked him to become an instructor. But Pokryshkin had other ideas. In his spare time he was reading and rereading everything he could find by his hero, Chkalov, and by the French ace, René Fonck. He strove for individuality because Chkalov had written, "Would I be the same as others, I would not fly as I do."

"And these words," Pokryshkin says, "fitted me. A good fighter must be cocksure and vain, assured that he will be the conqueror." He liked Fonck's articles which were printed in *Red Star* even though he realized air battles of the World War were in "a baby state." Pokryshkin began about that time to keep an album of his flights with comments about his own emotions and the behavior of his machine. He wrote down these words of Fonck's and underlined them: "The fighter who cannot abstract himself from danger in the air as on earth can only have several victories and sooner or later he will be shot down."

Pokryshkin was so absorbed in his air world during this period that he gave almost no attention to political events, either within the Soviet Union or outside. Because of his aloofness and obvious indifference little or no attempt was made to recruit him for the Komsomols or the party. He usually preferred to play chess, listen to music or study books on aviation rather than attend the lectures and classes arranged by active members of the party's propaganda unit at the school. He had arrived at the school with technical insignia on his sleeve, and because of that peculiar fraternity feeling which exists among pilots of all nations, he was rather looked down upon as a "foreign bird." If Pokryshkin minded this, he never said so.

In 1939 he graduated from the school in Kacha and was sent off to join a Red Air Force regiment. Here he suffered another serious disappointment. On his arrival he was assigned to duty as a scouter, a reconnaissance pilot and not a fighter. Again he accepted his fate, but again he resolved to become a fighter. He went over his marks at Kacha, decided that his weakest point was firing. So for months, long after other pilots had left the field for other pleasures, Pokryshkin practiced on targets, first stationary and then moving.

For his friends he selected three of the best fighter pilots in the regiment, Pankratov, Mironov and Sokolov. He admired Sokolov most of all. "He was calm and cool, the same on earth as in the air. He was brisk. He was successful because he showed in battles a larger stock of reflexes than the enemy," Pokryshkin says, and then admits frankly, "I began to train myself in Sokolov's pattern."

5.

When the Germans attacked, Pokryshkin was stationed in
Bessarabia, near the river Prut. He recalls the first day of war. "A
large group of German planes attacked the airdrome where our
unit was located. The Germans resorted to cunning. In order to
distract our fighters from the airdrome they sent forward one
spotter. He tried to draw off our fighters. Simultaneously German
bombers flew toward the base. But our fighters shot down the
spotter and went after the bombers. The Germans lost ten aircraft."

But it wasn't always like that. The Germans had superior equipment and superior numbers at first. Their pilots were trained by
actual combat in Holland, Belgium, France—and Spain. Day after
day Pokryshkin was in the air, watching the Wehrmacht roll forward almost unchecked. He remembers to this day the "thick,
honeyish smell of the grass that summer of 1941," the crowds of
people fleeing east, the walls of Kiev crumbling under Nazi shell
fire, the gardens of Poltava pockmarked, the steppe airdrome of
Slobozhanshina. He was beginning to develop then "an absinthe
bitterness" in his heart.

He recalls how "during the first days of the war, German aviation
acted insolently. The German fliers were convinced that the Soviet
aviation could be handled without much effort. But very soon the
Germans had to realize how badly they had miscalculated. . . ."

In the winter of 1941 Pokryshkin was still a scouter. He thought
it the dullest job in aviation. Only later he realized how valuable
a part of his training these months as a scouter had been. Even
then he was making a reputation for never failing in an assignment. He went up in mist, rain, snow and low ceilings. He trained
his mind with the enemy's every trick. He learned how to evaluate
what he saw, how to turn the eye's pictures into words. He made
out reports on the tanks of Von Kleist which he spied on their
way to Matveyev Kurgan, on the cavalry of the Rumanians massing behind the river Mius, on the long columns of German trucks
bumping along the highway to Rostov, on the never-ending chain
of Nazi barges moving on the once quiet Don. Pokryshkin's reports
were the basis for the work of Soviet bombers, trying to slow down
the German advance, trying to punch holes in the flow of supplies.

Early in 1942 Pokryshkin took the next step toward his goal.
His shooting had improved to such an extent that he was given

a Stormovik. But his first fight was as a scouter, flying a striped Yak. Here is how Pokryshkin tells about it, speaking slowly, thinking out every word thoroughly: "I was one of a pair who had the task of discovering the enemy's crossing place on the Dniester. In the area of the target we met five 'Messers.' I was seized by an irresistible impulse to attack the Nazis, but did not risk violating my orders. I was on reconnaissance. However, the Germans pursued us and forced us into battle. My plane was pierced full of holes and I hardly reached the airdrome. In this fight, though an inexperienced fighter, I managed to shoot down one plane. I pondered over my baptism of fire and came to the conclusion that German aces were not so terrible and could be shot down."

When Pokryshkin was asked to analyze his emotions at the moment of greatest danger, he merely replied, "I have no right for death."

In the Stormovik he came close to death often. Once, when attacking a German motorized column, he had to sweep low over it three times to accomplish his objective. An antiaircraft shell pierced his motor. The plane, afire, began spiraling downward. The Germans rushed toward the spot. With incredible coolness Pokryshkin managed to land the burning plane "on its stomach" in enemy territory. He wriggled clear of the fuselage and crawled into the bushes before the Nazis arrived. Hiding there until night, he made his way to the front lines where he joined a Red Army Ranger battalion.

The captain of the battalion welcomed him. They were about to go into action. "You fought in the sky," said the captain, "try on earth. Not being accustomed to it, maybe it will be bad. Then stand in the second row and acclimatize yourself."

Pokryshkin shook his head. "It's not nice for me, a flier, in the second row. I am always at the forefront. Thus is my business."

A writer for *Pravda,* describing Pokryshkin's account of himself as a foot soldier, wrote simply: ". . . And was at the front and led the battle in an infantry line and was victorious." When the battle was over, the captain died in Pokryshkin's arms. He whispered his last words, ". . . Fought well, flier, fought well. A falcon bravery you have. Here, take my papers. If you'll happen to be in Poltava, tell that, here . . . you see."

"I see," said Pokryshkin, "I'll take revenge, believe me."

Scenes like this kept building up Pokryshkin's desire for personal

revenge against the Fascists. Like any Red Army man he has seen
so many firsthand examples of Nazi brutality that no printed words
were necessary to ignite his hatred. Pokryshkin says when he is flying he remembers many things—the martyred face of a woman
hanging from a tree in a Bessarabian village with her child pinned
to her breast by a German bayonet; a ditch near Melitopol piled
high with dead civilians; and Krasnodar. He had won his wings
at the aero-club in Krasnodar. He had fought the Nazis over
Krasnodar, and in the summer of 1943 he went back there to hear
the Nazi killers put on trial. When he looked into the cruel faces
of the *"Sonderbanditen"* and "group executioners" he recalled the
long rows of gallows which he had seen in the towns and villages
of the Kuban. He sat stolidly through the hearings.

"You are as if a member of the jury," his comrades told him,
teasingly.

"It's true," Pokryshkin admitted. "We are all judges. All of us,
and we must remember this always."

But still he did not have the living, quick-tempered hatred of
those fliers who came from western parts of the Soviet Union.
Novosibirsk was safe from Nazi rape, pillage and slavery. Until
one morning his best friend, Sokolov, failed to come back from a
flight, Pokryshkin had never lost anyone near and dear to him.
The loss of Sokolov made him cooler, more deadly than ever.

Even so, Sasha didn't much relish his work during 1942 as a
dive-bomber. He was no slaughterer. Clogged roads and neighing
cavalry were not targets for a true airman. He longed to meet
the Fritzes plane to plane, wing to wing, to prove to himself and
to the world that a simple Siberian, a Slav, could outfight a Teuton.

Finally in the spring of 1943 things changed. The buds that
formed that spring were somehow bigger, and the grass that
sprouted was stronger. Stalingrad had been the storm of blood
which soaked the Soviet soil with new strength and life and singing determination and confidence. Sasha became a captain and
after a short leave was sent to a fighter pilots' school. For three
weeks he trained in a new plane, the P-39 Bell Airacobra, our
medium altitude interceptor-fighter. He learned to love its stout
37-mm. cannon, its super-quick pickup. He found it was more dur-
able than the Yak, and faster, too. Like all Russian pilots, he
stripped off the belly tanks and took out the wing guns. Sasha
called the plane, "Cobrushka," or dear little Cobra.

By the spring of 1943 the Red Air Force was really ready for the first time to assert its superiority. By now it had good equipment, as good as the Germans'. Its pilots were more seasoned. Pokryshkin was sent as a member of a team to the Kuban Air Command, renowned for its intrepid aces. Here he attained his manhood, his goal. In a few short weeks he became the terror of the skies. In every sortie he left his mark in the sky and his hot lead in a Nazi plane. As soon as his Cobra hurtled out of the clouds, the German radio shrieked a frantic warning: *"Achtung! Achtung! Pokryshkin's in the air!"*

This was the busiest, most hectic time of his life, and it was also the happiest. He was averaging better than a Nazi plane per week when he became ill and was forced to go to the base hospital. Even that was fortunate, for here he met a wonderful Ukrainian girl, his nurse, Marya. She was young and blond and very feminine. While Pokryshkin would sit in silence for long hours, Marya would chat cheerfully about her home near Kharkov, about her life on the collective farm, about how she had volunteered as a medical "sister."

His illness was soon over and forgotten, but Pokryshkin never forgot his Mariusa. He devoted as much of his free time to her as possible, but that wasn't much. When he wasn't in the air fighting Nazis, he was in his quarters developing new theories of combat, working out new methods of attack and defense. He would argue for hours with his friends, great Soviet airmen like the Glinka brothers, Rechkalov, Fadeyev, Kudrya, Kardanov over the kind of tactics to be used against each type of enemy plane.

The silent Siberian became the most voluble of the lot. When he talked about air fighting he was no longer phlegmatic; the words tumbled out, and he emphasized his points with his strong, mechanics' hands. Each air battle is a problem to be solved as it develops, Pokryshkin repeats, and on its own merits. A flier, he says, must constantly perfect his tactical skill and if he employs old methods and moves they must be used in combinations appropriate to the occasion. These combinations are unending and are all based on three fundamental principles: maneuver, speed and fire. He does not believe that because of their increased speed new planes have limited maneuverability in action, nor that old stand-bys like the figure eight and the ascending and horizontal barrel turn are now outlived. He believes any figure will do in fighting, providing fliers are equal to it.

Pokryshkin himself is given credit by Soviet airmen for introducing the "falcon attack." He describes it in terms of how a falcon, when attacking his prey "flies straight toward the victim, head-on, then suddenly shoots upwards, swings right and drops down to strike from the side." According to Pokryshkin the enemy is thrown off balance, and in his surprise does not have time to defend himself.

I am not an aviator, and I cannot judge the originality or the practicality of Pokryshkin's theories—except by results. But Soviet experts take them most seriously, and his words are printed in aviation newspapers and discussed at length by important military commentators. Colonel Nikolai Denisov, aviation editor of *Red Star*, pays high tribute to Pokryshkin as an air theorist. Interpreting the ace's methods, Denisov has written that Pokryshkin's skill "often surpasses all accepted conceptions of flying. Sharpness and irregularity of execution are the constituent elements. For instance, he can go over from one sharp banking turn to another not by going through the accepted figure but by instantaneously spinning around, up and behind; and in order to shake off an enemy plane clinging to his tail, he can effect an irregular barrel turn."

In May, 1943, with a record of twenty Nazi planes shot down, Captain Pokryshkin became a Hero of the Soviet Union for the first time. He earned a short leave and flew to Moscow. It was his first visit and an exciting one, even though he was unable to bring Marya with him. He spent the night at the great new Moscow Hotel, and then in the morning walked across the Kamenny Bridge to the Kremlin. There he waited in the impressive reception hall of the Council of People's Commissars while other heroes were decorated. Pokryshkin already wore on his gray-green dress uniform the prized Order of Lenin as well as three orders of the Red Banner. When his name was called he walked forward and received his first gold star, emblematic of the Hero of the Soviet Union. He shook hands with white-haired, stooped President Mikhail Kalinin. Then the old man kissed him fervently on both cheeks and wished him Godspeed.

Outside the Kremlin he had his picture taken. A reporter inquired, "To what do you attribute your success?" Slowly and with dignity the airman replied, "I was thus educated by my country."

Before he left Moscow the next day Pokryshkin had another honor. Called to the central headquarters of the Red Air Force, Marshal Novikov pinned on the young Siberian's chest the United

States Distinguished Service Medal with a citation from President Roosevelt.

That night he went to the opera to hear Offenbach's *La Belle Hélène* and in the morning he flew back to his regiment. Shortly afterwards he received a letter from Novosibirsk describing how his mother and youngest brother, Victor, had been guests of honor at the local theater the night he had been in Moscow. Before the play the mayor had made a speech about Pokryshkin and announced that the night shift at Sibcombine, his old factory, had pledged to increase their output in the flier's honor.

"Then," the letter ran, "they shouted for your mother. I suppose she had never spoken in public before in her life but she came up on the stage with that white Orenburg shawl which you sent her over her shoulders and a bunch of red roses in her trembling hand. And it may interest you to know she said you had always been a good boy and done your duty methodically, but that she wished you would get married soon."

Before the summer was over Pokryshkin fulfilled his mother's wish. He and Marya were married, and she was allowed to come and live with her husband at the air base. Marriage did not tame Pokryshkin's ferociousness in the air. There was no stopping him. By the end of August he was promoted to a major, credited with thirty-two planes shot down and at least a dozen more knocked out with the help of his unit. And on August 24 he was awarded his second gold star—a two-time Hero of the Soviet Union, a double honor then held by only fifteen others in the U.S.S.R.

During this summer Pokryshkin had one of his most exciting battles, but he has never been able to describe it in detail. He just says he was attacking a bunch of Junkers-87's when eight Messerschmitts suddenly swooped down from the clouds. "That was a close shave. My plane was a mess when I got back to the airdrome. It was fairly riddled with bullets and the motor had been hit." Then he pauses and apologizes because this doesn't sound exciting. "But it was darned interesting for me. It gave me a good lesson to keep my wits about me in battle and never let myself be carried away by the excitement of the chase." Asked about the outcome of the fight, he adds, "Oh, we shot down some planes and chased the rest of the Fritzes away. I got two myself."

Americans who find it hard to believe the impressive "shot-down" figures scored by Soviet aces probably are not familiar with the

Russian system of "destroyer teams." When a fighter pilot like Pokryshkin distinguishes himself in formation combat by his daring, his technique and his markmanship, he is given a team of his own. This team usually consists of two wing planes and one tail who, while fighting themselves, are nevertheless instructed to guard the ace and lead him to the target. Pokryshkin's team was composed of three youngsters who would follow him through burning oil and back. Their names are Junior Lieutenant Zherdev, Lieutenant Sukhov and Junior Lieutenant Golubev.

Pokryshkin tells them, "Don't hurry. Don't throw yourselves at the enemy immediately. Size up the situation first. Above all, behave reasonably, comrades. Don't be reckless. Your life belongs not only to yourself, but to the country. Remember that, always."

But Pokryshkin himself does not always remember that, and the men love him for his fearlessness even when they fear for him. Time after time he has gone after the enemy despite overwhelming odds, and always he picks the toughest assignment for himself. Here, in his typical laconic style, is Pokryshkin's report on one such battle:

Flying with two wing flyers in the region of our operations I met 24 Junkers bombers. Their fighters were lagging behind. From behind the clouds I suddenly attacked the first formation of eight and shot down the lead plane at once. The Germans were confused. Hastily dropping their bombs they rushed for the clouds and attempted to turn tail. Ordering the two wing flyers to pursue them, I alone attacked the second formation. The panic of the enemy increased. The second formation of Germans turned tail. I started to pursue one of the planes and suddenly noticed that the third German formation was beginning to drop bombs on our troops. Another moment and they would open target bombing. I turned against them and furiously attacked them. They did not show much firmness and after I machinegunned and set on fire one bomber, they dispersed in different directions. I chased after them and shot down another U-88.

Thus ended an airbattle in which three Soviet aircraft held the upper hand over the enemy who had eight times more planes.

Pokryshkin did not include in his brief report the fact that he had to repeat his order twice before his wing fliers would leave him when he sent them after the fleeing Junkers.

6.

In October, 1943, Pokryshkin wrote to his mother:

My dear relatives.
    Pray do not be offended that I write so rarely. We are having a hot time now. I sent you a cutting from a newspaper which mentions me briefly. It is written there that I have shot down 37 airplanes. That was before. Now the count is up to 44. In the future I propose to increase this amount.
    My greetings to all my relatives.

His mother replied with the news that Valentine, an air cadet, was most anxious to join up with his famous brother's unit. Pokryshkin wrote back that Valya could start thinking about belonging to his regiment "when he showed his mettle."

By the fall of 1943 people everywhere in the Soviet Union were becoming interested in Pokryshkin, watching his total of victims climb as Americans might watch Joe Di Maggio's batting average. The nation was becoming conscious of the new power and effectiveness of its air force. To them Pokryshkin's career was a symbol of this fresh growing force. Many of his fans were much disturbed by the following incident. The noted Soviet plane designer and builder, Yakovlev, received a Stalin award in the winter of 1943 for his work in aviation. He publicly announced that he would use the 150,000 rubles to construct a new model plane for the finest fighter pilot in the U.S.S.R. Air force officials almost immediately named Pokryshkin. But this proved an embarrassing selection. While Pokryshkin had flown a Yak (named after designer Yakovlev) in his early days as a scouter, he had since insisted on an American Airacobra. Although the ace was never consulted, the plane designer was feeling slightly miffed—and besides Alexander Ivanovich might refuse to fly the new Yak. So signals were reversed and the plane was presented to Major Peter A. Pokrishev, an Odessa-born twice Hero of the Soviet Union who had distinguished himself by shooting down more than a score of planes in the Leningrad area.

But Pokryshkin had already captured the No. 1 spot in the hearts of Soviet workers and fliers, too. Letters arrived for him merely addressed "Our greatest ace," or more explicitly to "Twice Hero of the Soviet Union, Pokryshkin." There were letters from beginners who dreamed of becoming fighter pilots; from infantry and artillerymen; from workers and collective farmers thanking him and praising him and wishing him success. These messages disturbed Pokryshkin because he couldn't possibly begin to answer them. But Marya solved it for him. "Every time you shoot down a German," she said wisely, "you send them an answer."

In February, 1944, Pokryshkin earned a two weeks' leave and this time he brought Marya to Moscow with him. They stayed at the Central House of the Red Army and saw all the sights. They toured the subway stations and visited as many of the theaters as they could. Sasha sat for the famous portrait painter, Vassily Meshkov, and had his picture taken by Gregory Wehl, the noted photographer. He also spent long hours with Lavochkin, the plane designer, who promised to build him a new fighter which would incorporate all the best features of the Airacobra and yet be shiftier—and Soviet made. (Pokryshkin scored 48 of his 59 victories in the United States-built plane.)

In Moscow, Marya was stopped by a KP (Russian version of MP) and scolded for not saluting. Pokryshkin tried to explain that his wife was shy and that she hadn't meant any offense. While he was talking he opened his greatcoat and the KP caught sight of the two gold stars on Pokryshkin's chest. He hurriedly saluted and marched away.

Heroes of the Soviet Union have a long list of special privileges: they can ride on the subway or trams without paying, they get fifty per cent discounts at commercial restaurants and stores, and they do not have to stand in line for anything. One morning the Pokryshkins set out quite early to see "The Thief of Bagdad" which was running at most Moscow movie houses. There was already a long line and at Marya's insistence, Sasha walked right up to the box office. The civilians and military men told the major to get right back to the end of the line.

"But he's twice a Hero of the Soviet Union," exclaimed Marya.

"And I'm Peter the First," said a captain of Naval Engineers who was waiting patiently to buy a ticket.

Reluctantly Sasha opened his greatcoat again. They bought their tickets and went inside. Sasha was furious, one of the few instances when he has been really angry with Marya. He told her that his position was not to be used as a *propusk* ("pass"). "These people work just as hard as I do," he said. Marya never mentioned the subject again.

When they returned to the Central House of the Red Army

they found reporters waiting. Mostly they asked about Sasha's air battles, but his descriptions weren't very vivid. He tried to answer their questions in his slow, hesitant, thoughtful manner. He said he had been offered a job as instructor but that he did not intend to retire from active service until the fighting was over. After the war he expected to stay in the aviation industry, probably as a plane designer. His errors? Well, at first he used to open fire too soon fearing the enemy would elude him. Now he prefers to come in close and fire point-blank.

As to his character, well, he admits he has great tenacity, which might be described as "stubborn as a mule." Yes, he loves his work, but it isn't always easy. Sometimes he has made three flights in a single morning to beat off enemy attacks at the front. When asked what type of plane he liked, he replied cagily: "When I was young and foolish I used to get hit no matter what type of plane I happened to be flying. In those days I divided planes into good and bad. Nowadays I consider all planes equally good."

In the afternoon, leaving Marya behind to do some shopping, Pokryshkin walked around the streets of the capital in a short fur coat (a gift from the Foreign Trade Commissariat) and in fur-lined boots. Later he was driven to plane plants where he spoke briefly to the workers, telling them how much their labors meant to the men at the front. He even visited a Palace of Pioneers where a choral group, composed of youngsters under ten, sang "Beloved City" for him.

7.

Pokryshkin next appeared in action over the Crimea. Now a lieutenant colonel he commanded his own regiment. This regiment was being used as a special task force. It shifted from front to front as the occasion demanded. Pokryshkin had instituted a system of "free-hunting," in which pairs of planes went out together to see what they could bag. Pokryshkin paired up with Georgi Golubev who had been his "tail" ever since he had become a fighter pilot. Golubev was a twenty-two-year-old Siberian, very jolly, very witty. They had flown together in more than a hundred air battles, and Golubev had learned to understand his commander and friend from one word by radio or one movement of the plane in the air.

Golubev says, "The colonel flies like a bird. After his attacks there is almost nothing left for me to do." And he adds, "Boldness, courage and strict calculation based upon tremendous military experience, these are his outstanding features. And how he watches every detail! How he prepares his seat in the plane before battle! The colonel never fails to check whether the seat is comfortable, whether it should be raised or lowered. He always checks the position of the sights in relation to his eyes, adjusts the pedals just so."

Pokryshkin has grown in the last year, as a man, as a flier, as a leader. Despite his desire for active duty, his store of knowledge is so rich he devotes many hours to lecturing. He knows more about the political meaning of the war, too. This time when he is nominated as a party candidate, he does not refuse. Party members have always been leaders, as far back as he can remember. At the Sibcombine, at the aviation school, at the airdrome. Now he is proud and happy to enroll in the party of Kalinin, Stalin and Novikov.

But he rarely discusses politics or economics. Fighting is his business. When he relaxes he likes to talk about Siberia and its future, about its mines and factories and its windswept steppes. Other men talk about their homes. Somebody begins to sing a merry Cossack song. It's Dmitri Glinka, also twice the Hero of the Soviet Union. He and his brother Boris were born in Krivoi Rog, the great iron ore center. Dmitri has a good voice and he sings about the brave Cossack, Morozenko, who was as fearless as he was courageous.

When the song has died away, Pokryshkin says, "Look, Mitya, you have a Ukrainian song about the Cossack Baida. The one in which the Sultan offers him his freedom if he would shoot a pigeon with his bow and arrow. And he took his bow and arrow and shot the Sultan. Sing it. Such songs teach us much. Folk songs are good songs. Sing it."

And suddenly an alarm signal interrupts the songs and dreams. Pokryshkin is all seriousness again as the men race for their planes. He goes first to the control room. While the planes are warming up he briefs the men. The Nazis are trying to fly some of their staff officers out of Sevastopol to Rumania. No transport must be allowed through.

During nineteen days Pokryshkin's group burnt thirty German transports in the air. When the fighting for Sevastopol was over, he moved on to Jassy. In the fighting over Rumanian soil Pokryshkin's unit made an even more remarkable record. In three days of air combats (May 30, 31 and June 3) they shot down 175 enemy planes. The colonel, himself, did not fly on these days. Golubev was sick, and Pokryshkin would not fly without him.

"Yes, he's superstitious," his friends say. "He won't allow his picture to be taken before a flight—but any number afterwards."

After Jassy, the twenty men under his command move on to the fighting around Lwow. Pokryshkin's personal score has already reached 59, and everyone in the unit knows that he has been recommended for his third gold star. Marya has left them, gone to stay with Sasha's mother in Novosibirsk until her baby comes. Once Golubev asked Pokryshkin if he would call the child "Cobrushka," but the colonel didn't think this was very funny.

In the evenings now he is busy writing articles so that his flying wisdom can be shared by other units. In his writing there are sudden flashes of poetry. The hero has not become too toughened. If anything his emergence as a leader has quickened his appreciation of life. He is still pretty solemn, and he certainly isn't very introspective. But now he has a flair, a flair that comes to all men who know they are good in their line of work, whether it's Babe Ruth or Enrico Caruso. When he writes of Rechkalov taking off he says "the tall grass of the airfield seemed to bow to him in reverence," and when he describes the wind sweeping over the Ukrainian cornfields he says "they shuddered."

One of his articles takes up the question of what he does when he meets an adversary who is not an inferior pilot. In such cases after "feeling out" the enemy, Pokryshkin discards all accepted moves and improvises new ones. When engaging an experienced, excellent airman whose plan of action is difficult to fathom immediately, he repeats every maneuver the enemy makes, exactly duplicating every movement until he is able to catch the opponent in the slightest mistake—then he pounces.

He emphasizes that one must never shoot straight into the enemy's tail but at an angle thus exposing the maximum surface of the enemy craft to gunfire—including the most vulnerable spots. He believes that fliers are wrong who open up at long range, relying on watching the trail of tracer bullets instead of using sights. "The fighter pilot who does that," Pokryshkin writes, "is like the night watchman who lets the thieves know in advance that he is discovering them."

In an article for *Red Star*, Pokryshkin analyzes why some airmen fail. His answer: "They haven't absorbed into themselves the feel of a fighter. If they know the enemy, it is only on the surface. They're not sly or calculating enough and they act in a stereotyped manner. Sometimes such airmen have good individual preparation as pilots, but they cannot guess the enemy's aims, schemes and habits—and I will say even more—his psychology. It is clear such airmen cannot fight successfully."

"The culture of the airman," he concludes, "is knowing his own plane plus the enemy's techniques. And in flight, it's working not only with your steering wheel but with your head."

8.

On September 9, 1944, Colonel Pokryshkin walked again to the Kremlin. He went with a group of other Heroes of the Soviet Union. As they strode toward Red Square, many Muscovites recognized Pokryshkin and shouted his name warmly. Small boys tried to run in front of him to count the medals glistening on his chest. In the Kremlin, Pokryshkin received his third gold star from Nikolai Shvernik, first vice-president of the Presidium of the Supreme Soviet.

Once more the Soviet press lauded Pokryshkin. He was already being clothed in the magic mantle of a legendary character. Fighting since the war's beginning, they said, the Hero had never received a single wound. Editorial writers now skipped the fact that he had been shot down three times. They recalled his more than six hundred battles over Kiev, Poltava, Melitopol, the Donbas, Stavropol, the foothills of the Caucusus, the Kuban, Lwow—over the rivers Prut, Mius, Dnieper and Vistula.

In an editorial on "the manhood and heroism of Soviet warriors," *Pravda* wrote:

One of the wonderful qualities of a Soviet person is mutual help in battle. This characteristic has been passed on from generation to generation. "Die yourself, but save a comrade," said Suvorov. Samples of such friendship are seen daily—it is an iron law among our Soviet warriors. Illustrative of this is the first air battle of our thrice Hero of the Soviet Union, Alexander Pokryshkin. While scouting, Pokryshkin and his comrade met five German fighters. Our flyers were not very high and therefore at a disadvantage in an air battle. Pokryshkin decided not to attack, especially since a scouter is not supposed to fight. But his comrade, a young flyer, was not able to maneuver away and a Messerschmitt closed on his tail. Several seconds more and the young flyer would die. Alexander Pokryshkin, himself only a young air warrior, went to the rescue, attacked and shot down the German, saving his comrade in the most complicated conditions of struggle—when he, himself, had to take a great risk.

Meanwhile out in Novosibirsk the city soviet is building a shrine for the legend and his family. It is on the central street of the city, not far from the expensive new opera house. When I visited Novosibirsk last summer, the mayor apologized to me because Aksinya Stepanova and Marya Kuzminishna were out in the suburbs gathering potatoes from their victory garden.

"But you must come back to Novosibirsk again and see their new house," said the mayor hospitably. "It will be large, convenient, substantial with garden and grounds. After all, Alexander Ivanovich is one of our most prominent citizens. Is it right for his family, his mother, his wife and his child to live like simple peasants any more?"

A statue of Pokryshkin is being made ready in Novosibirsk, too. The decree on Heroes of the Soviet Union stipulates that every twice Hero must have a statue erected in his honor in the important square of his birthplace. And a three-time Hero is also entitled to have a bronze bust of himself placed in the Palace of the Soviets in Moscow.

Since the Palace of the Soviets is not yet built, and is, in fact, no more than a big excavation at present, Guards Colonel Alexander Ivanovich Pokryshkin will have to be satisfied with a bronze bust in the Kremlin.

Book 6

Land Beyond the Volga

DURING the early days of the fight for Stalingrad when the Germans were squeezing the Red Army back against the west bank of the Volga, a Komsomol wrote a letter to Stalin. He made a fervent pledge never to retreat across the Volga to the east bank. "For me there is no land beyond the Volga," he declared.

For foreign correspondents in Moscow there didn't seem to be any land beyond the Volga, either. My first and most urgent request when I arrived was for permission to go to the Urals, to Siberia or to Central Asia. Every correspondent received the same reply: "It is very difficult." When we pressed the question the reasons were vaguely "transport," "too many arrangements," or "the war." No correspondent had visited the great armament arsenal in the Urals since peacetime, none had been through the new Siberian factories, and none had fully toured Central Asia since the opening of the Trans-Sib railroad in 1930.

It was both tantalizing and paradoxical. There were obviously so many wonderfully "pro-Soviet" stories beyond the Volga. I wanted to meet the people who had given Russia its great hero, Pokryshkin, the people who had saved Stalingrad with their sturdy fighting men, the people who had made the defeat of Hitler inevitable. I had seen the vast devastated areas of the west, I knew the statistics. In the Ukraine-Donbas area there had been 18 per cent of Soviet heavy industry; it produced 60 per cent of the nation's pig iron, 50 per cent of its coal, 40 per cent of its aluminum, 20 per cent of its chemicals, 20 per cent of its machinery. And the Germans had captured all this. Yet the Soviets kept fighting, kept producing in even greater than peacetime quantities. Was it all done with mirrors?

If you kept your eyes and ears open in Moscow you could pick up some of the bare statistics; enough to make you want to see the land beyond the Volga more than ever. In the first two years of the war the aggregate power capacity of the Urals increased 80 per cent; the output of manganese went up ten times between 1940 and 1943 to make up for the loss of Nikopol to the Germans. These achievements were astounding; but how were the people who made them possible?

Then there was the story of the evacuation of 1941. I had nibbled at the edges of this story, talking to a few people who had returned from Siberia with amazing tales of hardships and triumphs. I met a Kharkov official while crossing the Caspian Sea who told me how more than 7,000 freight cars had been required to move the machinery and workers of the Kharkov tractor plant to a Urals town east of Kuibyshev. Altogether over *one million carloads* of equipment and materials had been shipped eastward during the evacuation. And over twenty million people. To anyone familiar with Russia's prewar railroad system, this seemed not only amazing but incredible. In 1941 France, for example, had proportionately to its size eighty times more rail trackage than the Soviet Union.

Yet the miracle of evacuation had taken place. It was pointless to doubt the facts and figures because the results proved them. Factories were dismantled, loaded on flatcars, shipped east—often under German bombing and shell fire. When many of these big western plants had been built, Soviet planners had made provisions for such a war emergency. Instead of being permanently emplaced on concrete foundations, machines were only bolted to bases so that they could be quickly removed. As each machine was strapped onto a car, its operators went right along with it. When the factory arrived at its new destination the skilled workers helped set it up and started to work immediately.

The records of these transplantings were the formula for Germany's defeat in Russia. The Voroshilov tractor plant shipped from Dniepropetrovsk late in September, 1941, was in production in the Urals on October 11; by December 1 of the same year it was exceeding its former output.

But I still didn't know—how were twenty million refugees housed? Fed? Who was doing the skilled work? What were living conditions like? How much support was coming from Central Asia? What was the wage scale? Why the big mystery?

Despite the magnitude and importance of these questions to

the rest of the world, the Soviet press department was unrelent-
ing in its "no can see" attitude toward foreign reporters. Some
of the "secrets" of the Urals had been shown to Donald Nelson,
Wendell Willkie and a few other sufficiently distinguished Americans. Therefore, when Eric Johnston arrived in Moscow last
summer, some of us glimpsed a faint hope. The smooth-talking,
dynamic president of the U. S. Chamber of Commerce had a
specific invitation to visit the Urals, Siberia and Central Asia
from Foreign Trade Commissar Mikoyan. Johnston is not only a
shrewd, enlightened businessman and a gregarious go-getter, but a
politician. He readily understood the power of the press in selling
the world on Russia as a future partner and customer. He agreed
to take a few correspondents with him, perhaps realizing that they
might also help to sell Eric Johnston. Which is all to his credit.

But our hope for the trip was short-lived. The press department of the Foreign Office said no. Harrison Salisbury of the
United Press, W. H. ("Bill") Lawrence of the New York *Times*
and Robert Magidoff of National Broadcasting Company, three
of the ablest correspondents in Moscow, went with me to argue
with Colonel General Apollon Petrov.* Mr. Petrov, whose military title is purely honorary, had been a professor of Chinese
history at Leningrad University. He had as much understanding
of the problems of American journalism as could be expected
from a professor of Chinese history at Leningrad or any other
university. His mind was made up even before we stated our case.
His face remained inscrutable. He retreated behind a Chinese
wall and defended himself by Russian canons of logic.

"There is no longer any question of transport," I argued. He
shrugged.

"It will help get postwar credits for your country," said Lawrence. He shrugged.

"The Narkomvneshtorg (Commissariat of Foreign Trade) has
invited us," said Magidoff. Petrov had an answer. "This is a
matter for the Narkomindel. You are accredited to us."

"Why, why, why?" we all shouted.

Finally Mr. Petrov said, "I cannot let you go. It would be too
big an advantage for you over the other correspondents. It would
be discrimination."

Salisbury, remembering some recent favors done for a rival
press association, wanted to know if the press department meant

* In April, 1945, he was appointed as Soviet Ambassador to China.

that it would not discriminate again in the future. "No," said Mr. Petrov, "it means no such thing."

Salisbury got quite mad. He has a wonderful way of becoming more and more calm, more and more soft-spoken when he is worked up. He said very gently, "Boys, I understand Mr. Petrov *perfectly*. He doesn't *want* Mr. Johnston to leave with an unfair picture of the Soviet Union and the way it treats the press. He wants Mr. Johnston to get a *balanced* picture, he wants him to see the *bad* along with the *good*."

Magidoff, who was translating, hesitated. Reluctantly he put the sarcasm into Russian. Mr. Petrov understood more than enough English to catch the gist of Salisbury's remarks. He waited for several minutes, tapping his fingers together. Then he said, coldly, as he rose to indicate the interview was over, "Let that remark be on Mr. Salisbury's conscience for the rest of his life."

Back at the Metropole, the other correspondents voluntarily signed a statement that they had no objection whatsoever to the four of us going with Johnston, and that they did not consider it discriminatory. They realized if we broke the ice, there might be other Urals trips in the future. We sent this petition over to Petrov. Time was running out. Johnston was scheduled to see Stalin about 9 that night and then leave at 4 or 5 A.M. for the Urals.

In the meantime, we also wrote a letter to Vishinsky, explaining the problem. All evening we called, first Vishinsky, then Petrov. Finally one of Vishinsky's secretaries said our answer would have to come from Petrov. It did. *"Nyet"* ("No"). It was still discrimination even if the other correspondents didn't have sense enough to realize it.

Our last hope was Stalin. We telephoned Johnston just before he stepped into an Embassy car to drive to the Kremlin. He promised to take up our case. At midnight we were waiting for him at Spaso House when he returned with Ambassador Harriman. We were going on the trip. Later Johnston told us how it had happened. He and Stalin were discussing the need for mutual understanding between our countries. Stalin agreed that Americans had to learn more about Russia and hoped that Johnston would tell them.

"But I am only one," said Johnston. He then made a little speech about the American correspondents in Moscow representing millions and millions of readers. "For example, Americans

would like to know more about your new industrial empire in
the Urals, but the correspondents have not been allowed to go
there. That's why I would like to ask permission to take four
correspondents with me to the Urals."

"*Poochymoo nyet?*" ("Why not?") Stalin replied.

Sometime much later that night Mr. Petrov telephoned to
say that he had "relented" and we could go.

So the next morning at the Moscow Central Airport there were
two Douglas passenger planes instead of one. Before we took off
there was a little farewell banquet. Toasts were drunk in wine,
vodka, champagne and cognac. Here we had a preview of Eric
Johnston's best Chamber of Commerce technique. He held his
glass aloft until he had the attention of everyone in the tiny waiting room. Then he intoned: "To one of the grandest men it has
ever been my pleasure to meet—Marshal Stalin." This was well
received by the Russian officials. They barely had time to swallow
their vodka and take a bite of black bread and caviar before
Johnston gave them his second toast: "In our country we would
call him a big businessman. In your country you call him Commissar of Foreign Trade—here's to Mr. Mikoyan."

About 6:30 A.M. that June morning we walked out to the two
DC-3's. The first was a super-deluxe plane. Its equipment for this
trip included two beds, a *maître d'hôtel*, a waiter, a blond
Russian translator named Lucy, a plainclothes secret service man
(also Russian) named Nick, a barrel of apples, a case of bottled
sparkling water, a half dozen cases of champagne, huge boxes of
cheese, meat and sandwiches and, we supposed, the usual crew
and some apparatus for measuring speed and altitude. This plane
was not for the working press. Into it climbed Johnston, his assistant
Joyce O'Hara, his Boswell, William L. White, the president of the
Russian Chamber of Trade M. V. Nesterov, a first secretary of the
United States Embassy who was also an economic expert, and the
Chief of Protocol of the Foreign Trade Commissariat, Vassily
Kirillov. Nesterov is a small, mild, gentle, blue-eyed man who
could have passed for the president of any United States Mid-
western bank. Kirillov is big, brawny and dour. He looked as if
he could have played football for the Colorado School of Mines—
and as a matter of fact, he once did.

The second plane was a bucket-seat job. But it, too, had certain
amenities. Besides Salisbury, Lawrence, Magidoff and myself, it
carried a crew, a censor, a waiter from the Hotel National, six

cases of champagne, bottled water, apples, assorted chocolates and enough miscellaneous equipment for setting up housekeeping. The censor was a mild enough young man named Nikolai Zemenkov who had been too briefly educated at Columbia. Zemenkov asserted himself exactly once on the whole trip. The first morning he routed us out of bed two hours too early. He never recovered from the upbraiding which we gave him.

"You must remember," said Lawrence savagely, "that *we* are on this trip as Marshal Stalin's special guests and *you* are only along because that Petrov sent you along to spoil it for us." Zemenkov was very docile thereafter. I even grew to like him, which is a terrible admission to make about any censor. I changed my mind when we returned to Moscow and he began hacking at my stories.

Our planes made the flight to Magnitogorsk in six hours. That city is eight hundred-odd miles east and slightly south of Moscow. We were met at the airport by our host, Gregory Nosov, director of the industrial combine which is Magnitogorsk. He was big and beefy like Kirillov, but much jollier. We climbed into slightly dilapidated cars of Soviet make and drove through the city.

Magnitogorsk was a keen disappointment esthetically. There just didn't seem to be any city at all in the accepted physical sense of the word. There were a lot of rutted dirt streets, along which were set down a series of dull, jerry-built stucco and wooden houses. Everything needed paint. The people on the streets needed new, bright clothes. The city had never been bombed, but there were shattered windowpanes everywhere.

The ride to our destination took a long time. I kept looking for the "center" of the city, but I never found it. The only center in Magnitogorsk is the guts—the steel mills. There is no business district, no theater district. The living area just sprawls and rambles. Once in awhile we would pass a big modern (architecturally) apartment house which looked old and worn.

The section where Director Nosov resided was surprising in a totally different way. Suddenly you left Nevada City of the wide-open mining days and found yourself in Tarrytown, Bronxville or some other upper-class New York suburb. Our convoy of cars rolled smoothly up a paved, three-laned, tree-lined avenue. On both sides of us were solid, prosperous, Tudor-style, two-story stucco houses surrounded by spacious grounds, well-groomed shrubs and stout iron fences. This is where the highly paid, highly skilled technicians and executives of Magnitogorsk lived.

Nosov's house was just like the others, maybe a bit more plushy. The furnishings were heavy and solid like Nosov himself, but not particularly attractive. As soon as we had washed we sat down to another banquet. Between courses we interviewed Director Nosov. The man had shaggy eyebrows, a galaxy of gold teeth, sandy hair and two Orders of Lenin. The son of a blacksmith, Nosov was a graduate of the Tomsk Technological Institute, one of the finest scientific universities in Siberia. At thirty-eight, he had a wife, three children, and a good job, His base salary was 3,500 rubles monthly but with bonuses for maintaining and exceeding planned production he usually earned closer to 10,000 rubles monthly. He had been director for five years.

And just in case any of us were doubting that he was worth that much in a socialist society, Nosov announced: "My plant now produces more steel than was made in all of tsarist Russia."

As early as 1930 Stalin had foreseen the need for building Magnitogorsk. He warned of the inherent danger in the Soviet Union's dependence on the Ukrainian coal and metallurgical base and urged the creation of a second such base, the Urals-Kuznetsk combine—a combination of Kuznetsk coking coal with the ores of the Urals. Iron and steel centers 1,200 miles apart were immediately established at both ends fed by a double traffic carrying Kuznetsk coal westward and Magnet Mountain iron ore eastward. This system is by no means as economically arranged as the Donbas or Gary, Indiana, where the coal supply is much closer.

Nosov readily admitted that the Magnitogorsk combine had lost money as recently as 1939. The plant now does a 1,200,000,000 ruble annual business. For 1944 Nosov anticipated a 50,000,000 ruble profit on the plant's capital investment of 2,000,000,000 rubles.

Between liberal helpings of shirred eggs and broiled trout, Nosov proudly pointed out that the Gary works had been begun in 1911 and finished in 1943. But Magnitogorsk, conceived in 1930, would be completed in 1948 despite the invasion of the Soviet Union. It will be, when finished, the largest metallurgical plant in the world. Now it has six blast furnaces (with a seventh being built), twenty open hearths, eight rolling mills, two blooming mills. Daily production figures, according to Nosov, are:

8,000 tons of coke, 8,000 tons of pig iron ingot, 7,500 tons of steel ingot.

After eating, we toured four of the six blast furnaces, dodging sprays of sparks and sweating like workers. In the open hearth department we saw the "men" with the best production records at their jobs. They looked like black dwarfs. Actually they were kids, fourteen to sixteen years, and undersized. Throughout the entire trip we were to be confronted with this fact: the bulk of the work was being done by youngsters and women. The kids, in particular, were doing a spectacular job. Nimble, adaptable, quick to pick up mechanical skills, they have proved to be very sensitive to Soviet production stimulants like socialist competition bonuses, medals and other awards. They strive for them with all the eagerness of an Indianapolis high school junior trying to win his letter in basketball. Many of these Russian boys— and girls—have a brief training period in a trade school. An American engineer who had been working in the Urals told me in Moscow how successful these teen-age Russian youngsters were with highly complicated machine tools. "Of course," he said, "a foreman will occasionally enter a shop and find it deserted. All the boys will be out pitching snowballs at each other. But on the whole they are amazingly conscientious." He also pointed out that the production records of these "youth front brigades" depends on the ability of the foremen and shop managers. They must often combine the qualities of scoutmasters, confessors, teachers, fathers and psychologists.

There are 45,000 workers in the Magnitogorsk steel plant. Of this number 45 per cent are women. The average age is thirty-two. Wages, including bonuses but without overtime, vary between 800 and 1,000 rubles monthly. In a combine of this size wages are negotiated directly between a union committee and Director Nosov, irrespective of the nationwide scale. If no agreement can be achieved, the negotiations are then taken up by the Central Committee of the trade union in Moscow which bargains directly with the Commissariat of Black Metallurgy. There have been no strikes in wartime Russia for the same reasons that there are none in the Red Army or, for that matter, in the United States Army.

Magnitogorsk is a tremendously impressive enterprise despite obvious hardships and limitations. In Pittsburgh or Gary, American laborers would refuse to work under similar conditions. Half the workers had no shoes. Magnitogorsk needs safety precautions, paint, better ventilation, sanitary and other conveniences, and a more scientific arrangement of equipment. But, say the Russians, there is no labor supply to waste on clean-up gangs; there is no time to stop for constructing anything but a new blast furnace; and as for toilets—some Russians still think they are a damned nuisance anyhow.

As he walked swiftly through the plant, hurdling a red-hot stream of molten lead, chatting with workers, Johnston stopped once to give us his opinion: "Not as neat as an American plant but they do the work." I asked Nosov about the accident rate. "Injuries are three-quarters of 1 per cent per year," he answered, "or 8 per 10,000 workers per month." That sounded very low to me.

At a shell factory which was part of the combine, Eric talked to a grimy-faced, barefooted girl worker: "I hope this one kills Hitler," Johnston said, tapping a shell. A little later he asked a fourteen-year-old girl polisher if any of her family had been killed in the war. She replied soberly, "My brother." Johnston said, "Tell her I am from America and we will give it to them (the Germans) and I hope the war will be over soon."

Besides shells, Magnitogorsk produces plane engines, wire, aluminum, machine tools and machinery. Every department works night and day with three shifts. Before the war there was a month's vacation with pay; now there is none. The plant was full of slogans about keeping on the job. The workers seemed tired. But when you talked to any of them, as I often did, you found them still fired with enthusiasm, ambition and hope. And they always knew why they were working so hard—"To beat the German Fascists"—"To build a greater Soviet Union"—"To make a lasting peace"—"To go back home to Leningrad and study medicine."

When we left the plant we drove out to the open-face mining operation at Magnet Mountain. En route we looked at other parts of the huge combine which covers an area of twenty-seven square miles. On the face of it, the fabulously rich mountain itself was also unimpressive: just a low-running ridge rising from the barren steppe, the color of a mangy orange alley cat. Director Nosov was very proud of this mountain; so proud, you felt that he almost believed he had made it with his own hands.

"The range has proven reserves of 300,000,000 tons of ore assaying 65 per cent iron plus 85,000,000 tons assaying 45 per cent iron," he told us. "At the present rate of mining your own great Mesabi Range in the state of Minnesota will be exhausted in per-haps five years while Magnet Mountain will be good for 500 years." Nosov beamed.

In the evening we went to the theater—the play was "Zo-lushka," a Russian version of Cinderella. At night Magnitogorsk looked very strange and different—the first Soviet city without a blackout. Electric power was cheap here and every shack seemed to have a 200-watt bulb burning in the window.

Johnston, White, O'Hara and party slept at Nosov's, but the correspondents spent the night at the Stalin Hotel, an early 1930 Bauhaus construction. About a half hour after we had retired a sleepy Russian opened the door and tried to get in bed. It took Lawrence, myself and two chambermaids to convince him that this room had been usurped by foreigners. As he left he mumbled something which I couldn't quite catch.

"What did he say?" asked Lawrence, who knows very little Russian.

"He said, 'Why in the hell don't you go back where you came from?' "

"Jesus Christ," said Lawrence, trying to turn on a narrow cot, "I sure as hell wish I could."

In the morning Johnston and Nosov began and ended break-fast by exchanging the usual compliments. But in the middle somewhere each man did a little boosting about his country's natural resources and production possibilities. Johnston kept dragging his interview with Stalin into the conversation to im-press the Russians and it usually did. "Marshal Stalin told me," said Eric, with an air of taking a select few into his and Stalin's confidence, "that you are going to have two more Five-Year Plans after the war to achieve an annual steel production of 60 million tons." The Soviet Union's top steel production in 1940-1941 was about twenty million tons. Loss of the Ukraine cut it down as low as 8 or 9 million tons. In 1944 it was up to twelve and in 1945 the Soviets hope to have it back as high as sixteen and a half million tons. Steel production in the United States at the 1944 peak was eighty-nine and a half million tons.

None of the Russians present seemed overly surprised by John-ston's announcement. They drank to Marshal Stalin whose name means "steel." Then Nosov said, "In spite of Allied help, most

of the steel for our war purposes comes from Soviet plants."
There was an uneasy second, but Eric was equal to it. He lifted
his glass and said, "One good thing Hitler has done in this war—
he has brought the Russian and American people together." After
several more drinks Johnston prevailed upon himself to sing
"Jenny," a song from the movie "Lady in the Dark." He sang it
very nicely, but when it was translated the Russians thought it
rather vulgar. The women left the room. After breakfast the rest
of us Americans, except O'Hara, Johnston's assistant, held a little
meeting and decided it was time that Johnston sang something
else besides "Jenny." We elected a delegate to break the news.

Magidoff and I had another cup of tea with Nosov and tried to
find out about the housing situation and the discrepancy between
the way the people lived in "boomtown" and in "Tarrytown."

Nosov didn't deny that conditions were bad. "The population
shot up from 160,000 to 240,000 during the war. Evacuees overcrowded us. We had no opportunity to build or repair dwellings.
Of course, the evacuees did much for us. They created new industries, they helped our cultural life. Now skilled workers are
being sent back to the Donbas, the Ukraine and Leningrad. But
evacuated plants and shops will stay here and we hope many
workers. Of course, we will have to offer them better conditions—
their own homes and gardens. In the two or three years after the
war we will build thousands of new, individual homes, streetcar
lines, better roads, new theaters, movies, clubs and restaurants."

We asked him if the new houses would be like his own. He
replied, "I am the director. I make more money than the average
worker, so I can afford a better house. But they will be good,
maybe not so big."

Then he went on to discuss food. After war production this is
usually the most serious problem in every Soviet city. Housing
shortages are serious, too, but except in extreme cold, people can
sleep anywhere in an emergency. They have to eat or they can't
work, and if they can't work the production suffers. In Magnitogorsk—and later we found the same thing true in Sverdlovsk,
Omsk, Novosibirsk and other cities—the shortage was partially
solved by a vast victory garden campaign. The main crop was
potatoes: 28,000 acres were planted and the yield was enough to
give almost 900 lbs. to every man, woman and child. The combine
itself had over 50,000 acres of farmland, jointly run for and by its
workers. "Our workers *privately* own," Nosov stressed the word

for capitalist ears, "6,400 cows, 7,300 goats and 800 pigs. The combine owns an additional 3,100 pigs."

It has always surprised me how Soviet officials can rattle off figures. They never refer to notes. Once I tried to cross up one of them by asking how many pianos there were in his town. He looked at me in complete surprise and apologized for not knowing. "We've been so busy," he explained. "Before there were 4,653 . . . but now? . . ." his voice trailed off.

2.

From Magnitogorsk we flew northeast for about an hour and a half to Sverdlovsk. The two hundred and fifty miles of terrain between these cities is like the northern part of Wisconsin—full of lakes and green woods and grazing cattle. Sverdlovsk was nothing like Magnitogorsk. It had the well-settled quality of an old city. When founded in 1721 it was called Ekaterinburg. By 1914 the population was only 75,000 but between world wars it had grown to half a million. Evacuations from the Ukraine and the Moscow region had swelled its wartime population to over a million. But when we were there last summer the population had shrunk to 750,000—a quarter of a million refugees having already returned to liberated territory.

We stayed in a big hotel across from the pre-revolutionary opera house on Sverdlovsk's main square. There were copies of late newspapers and magazines as well as cigarettes in our rooms. After washing and eating we got into very comfortable Zis cars and drove through the rain to Uralmash, Sverdlovsk's giant machine-building plant. The factory, founded only ten years ago, lacked all American-style modern conveniences. As we inspected different sections of the plant rain poured through the roof. Deep pools of water on the uneven dirt floors made us thankful for our G.I. boots.

Uralmash makes complete mobile artillery, tank parts, gun mounts and heavy machinery. Before the war its output was 30,000 tons of machine tools per year—including all the recent equipment for Magnitogorsk. Present production is seven times greater than in 1941 despite the fact that the workers appeared to be even younger than those at the steel mills.

We asked Boris Mazurukov, the director, about that. He is a big, thickset blond, about forty years old. He was born near Lenin-

grad of peasant parents. He attended the Leningrad Technical
Institute and worked his way up to become chief engineer of the
great Kirov plant which he left in 1939 to help reorganize Uralmash on a war footing. He had 30,000 employees. "Thirty-five
per cent are women," he said. "You must understand that less
than 20 per cent of all the workers are experienced or skilled.
We have here 20,000 young people. The average age in the whole
combine is only twenty-four."

Johnston handed out sticks of chewing gum and jotted down the
names of U. S. machines in the shops. He estimated that two-
thirds of the plant's equipment came from America; the rest was
German, British and Soviet. I stopped and read the plant bulletin
board. There were two news headlines on it. A big one proclaimed: RED ARMY TAKES ORSHA. Beneath it was this
smaller one: ALLIES CAPTURE CHERBOURG. I wondered if our war
plants considered the triumphs of the Russians newsworthy. I
mentioned this bulletin to the director. He said, "The second
front was a great production stimulant." That's a businessman
for you, I thought. "We overfulfilled our plan for the half year
on June 26," he said. "When will you be in Paris?"

"Before the Red Army is in Warsaw."

He laughed. "It doesn't make much difference, does it? As long
as we are winning, eh?"

At a luncheon in the director's dining room, we learned that
Uralmash had made a 100 per cent conversion to war products.
Now it was making some equipment for the factories of the
liberated areas, *i.e.*, steel castings for new turbines and blast
furnaces. Mazurukov and Lev Gonor, director of the combine's
artillery plant, were much interested in the problem of recon-
version. They kept asking about what kind of consumer items
our war plants made with their waste products. None of us knew
exactly. So they asked whether Johnston could arrange to send
an exhibit of U.S. consumer items to Sverdlovsk. Johnston said
he would have to consult his good friend Mr. Mikoyan which put
him in mind of a toast.

The official sitting on my right related how the workers of the
combine had volunteered to form a special Urals tank corps.
Others in the plant then pledged to produce over their plan to
equip the corps; the women made them clothing and supplied
food. The corps has been fighting with distinction at the front,
and the people at home have the satisfaction of knowing that

everything the men use has been contributed by Uralmash workers and their families. "Morale is excellent," the official concluded.

3.

The next day we flew five hundred miles east to Omsk. We had a big banquet in Sverdlovsk before we left, but the minute we stepped into our plane the waiter from the National put on his white jacket and began serving food and drink. He always seemed slightly insulted when we refused him. Sometimes to keep him happy Magidoff ate an apple, Zemenkov took a bottle of water, and we drank a little vodka. The waiter was a great guy; he thought of everything to make us comfortable except cleaning the tiny toilet in the tail of the plane. The Omsk airfield on which we landed was one of the largest and best equipped in the Soviet Union, with long concrete runways and up-to-date equipment for night flight operations. Around the edges of the field there were at least five hundred planes—Stormoviks, probably being shipped west. The airport was a modern, white stone building. From its many flagpoles flew the Soviet and American flags.

There was another banquet waiting for us in the airport dining room. A really grand and luxurious one, with some strange new fish dishes and huge red strawberries. We heard a new toast from Johnston. He was quite lyrical: "Leningrad is sophisticated, Moscow is official, but here in Siberia we Americans feel at home. Let's drink to home." Five minutes later he was on his feet again, comparing Siberia and Omsk to "God's country." This brought a retort from Konstantin Zadorozhni, director of the local tank factory. He jumped up and said he didn't think his products were "quite divine" and he would welcome Johnston's earthly criticism. This drew a laugh from the guests which included city and army officials, pilots, local newspaper reporters, and factory workers with the best production records.

At Zadorozhni's plant, Johnston found that he had run out of chewing gum. He made a gift and a speech to pretty, seventeen-year-old Valya Petrova who was busily welding a turret. "This is an American pencil," Johnston said. "Ask her if she has a sweetheart to write to." The girl replied, "Not yet." Johnston grinned, waved his hand and said to his translator, "Tell her I will be her sweetheart and she can write to me." The girl blushed and welded.

Everyone in the plant appeared to be working hard. Tanks

were certainly not rolling off the production line the way they do in the Hollywood movies. In fact the line was a bit hard to follow. The low rambling building was old and all chopped up into sections. Some of this was explained later by Zadorozhni. He was forty-seven years old, a carpenter's son from the Donbas region. Until 1941 he had been director of the famous Stalingrad Tractor Plant. Evacuated to Omsk with equipment and 3,000 workers, he did not have time to build a new plant. He and his men and machines had done the best they could in an old locomotive repair shop. In three months Zadorozhni had found and trained another 12,000 workers and was starting to turn out T-34 tanks. Most of the new workers were young and without previous experience. About 40 per cent of them were women.

"They are less efficient in heavy work," said Director Zadorozhni, "but for light, skilled jobs women have proved just as good or better than men."

The workers I saw in the tank plant were both very young and very dirty. Beyond that it was difficult to form much of an impression. They glanced up at us with sharp-eyed interest when we passed them, but they never left their jobs—not even for one of Eric's pencils. We all had the feeling that they were probably pretty unhappy and dissatisfied. In plant after plant one of us would complain, "Philip Murray or William Green would sure raise a stink about *these* conditions."

We were overtired from flying, eating and touring, and we didn't realize that the Russians often understood what they were up against better than we did. I never heard any of them complain.

Director Zadorozhni and the collective of the plant had prepared another banquet for us. We begged for a little time to work up an appetite and then used it to interview the mayor of Omsk, a white-haired, smooth-shaven man who looked a little bit like Edward Stettinius. His name was Kuzma Koshelev and he'd been mayor for two years. Before that he was director of the Institute for Automobile Highways. He was forty-four years old and came from a peasant family in Belorussia.

We asked Koshelev to explain how he had been elected. He told us there had been five candidates, all nominated by different trade unions. Two of the five were members of the Communist party. Koshelev, nominee of the Professional Workers Union, received the majority vote in direct, secret balloting. He received 28 per cent more votes than the other four candidates put together and was elected for a three-year term.

"And where did the other Communist finish?" I asked.

"He was the runner-up."

"How do you explain your election?"

Koshelev was at a loss for words. It was evidently pretty obvious to him, but he didn't know how to put it into speech. His answer came slowly. "Popularity . . . know the people in the town . . . the authority of the Communist party . . . the prestige of the party." He rubbed his soft white hands together. "Popularity? Well, I am a veteran of the civil war. I was an officer in the Red Army. I have two orders and one medal." He seemed uncomfortable praising himself. Zadorozhni helped him out. "The people know of his good work," he added.

"Do you have to be a Communist to be elected mayor?"

"No," said Koshelev quickly. "All of Omsk's mayors have been party members—since the Revolution. But in Omsk County 60 per cent of those elected to the governing council are nonparty people."

Someone wanted to know the number of party members in the Soviet Union. Neither Koshelev nor Zadorozhni could tell us. Finally we asked Mikhail Demedenko, deputy governor of the province, who was the highest ranking official present.

Demedenko said, "I do not know." When we looked skeptical, he added, "I am a Soviet state functionary, not a party functionary."

When we veered off the subject of politics, we found Mayor Koshelev more eager to talk. He began outlining the major problems of his city: (1) Fuel for the winter; this had to be hauled anywhere from 250 to 1,250 miles; (2) The housing shortage; the population had increased from 320,000 to 514,000 due to evacuations from Leningrad, Stalingrad, Rostov, the Ukraine. The refugees had been installed in temporary barracks, but they were now trying to put up some brick buildings in their spare time; the mayor hoped they would be completed before winter. Omsk had nine brick mills he would have us know, producing 86,000,000 bricks a year. (3) Water supply. At present, Omsk, due to the increased population, could furnish only 28 liters per person per day, while the city plan called for 44. The city council was still fretting over this headache.

We asked why the population of Omsk hadn't begun to shrink back to normal as had been the experience in Sverdlovsk and

Magnitogorsk. The mayor smiled, "It is reducing slowly. But per-haps people like Omsk. It's not so bad, is it? Then, too, Omsk is becoming a big center for retraining war cripples and invalids. Already 14,000 have been rehabilitated and placed in jobs. There are six large homes in Omsk carrying on this program and there will be more soon." After a pause, he added, "Another reason for our growth. Like other eastern cities we are adopting many thou-sands of war orphans. And many of them have adopted us." Ko-shelev, himself, had taken in two orphans.

After the banquet, Johnston was interviewed by a charming brown-eyed little girl who was the local Tass correspondent. She had no trouble making Johnston talk. He said a lot of things, in-cluding, "Your growth and development will only be limited by the courage, vision and determination of your people. From what I have seen here your people possess all three of these qualities."

That evening we were taken to a concert at the Omsk Park of Culture and Rest. Bill White and I slipped out during the first intermission to get a drink of water. We were accompanied by an NKVD captain in uniform. He was extremely friendly. After he had shown us where to get the water, we wanted to walk down to the open-air dance pavilion. At first I thought he might be coming along to see that we didn't talk to anybody, but it turned out that the officer had just the opposite idea. He ushered us past the ticket taker so that we didn't have to pay, and stood there on the edge of the dance floor beaming. "Whom would you like to dance with?" he asked. I told him I just wanted to look around first. It was hard to realize that these were the same tired, grimy-faced kids we had seen slaving away in the tank factory earlier. Their evening attire was not elegant, but it was clean. They were full of fun and energy, and having a marvelous time. On the wooden bandstand a Red Army musical training unit was playing, loudly.

Bill made his courtly Kansas bow in front of a bewildered little girl, and they were off dancing. I don't suppose he ever had so much fun at the Workers' Alliance in Emporia. The NKVD man was worried about me, and offered to bring over some girls. "Don't bother about me," I said. "I'm all right. Go dance yourself, if you want to." He didn't and finally I asked a delicate little *blondinka* to dance. She had been staring at my uniform with frank curiosity.

We danced in silence. Then I said, "I suppose you don't know who we are."

"I know," she said. "You came through our tank plant today. You walked right past me. You were writing in a little book."

I took another look at her. I would have bet that nothing so feminine and fragile had been in that factory. She continued, "You were with Gospodin Djonstone, yes?"

"Yes. What do you do in the plant?"

"I grease the turret treads. A dirty job."

"Do you like it?"

She laughed. "I would rather be back in art school in Leningrad."

"Will you be able to go back?"

She didn't answer immediately, but she seemed a trifle disturbed. I repeated the question, this time with gestures to make sure she understood my Russian. After a few minutes, she said, "It's pretty nice here in Omsk. Not bad at all."

When the number was over I complimented her on her dancing and she apologized for not being able to follow all my steps. I caught sight of the NKVD officer grinning approval at me. He nodded and yelled, "More."

The girl disappeared and I wondered if she had become frightened. When the next dance started I picked out a tall, dark girl who was wearing a very pretty blue dress with a lot of embroidery in different colors around the neck and cuffs. She was quite gay. Before we went out on the floor she introduced herself very formally, "My name is Tanya Sergeyevna." She waited. I told her mine. "You are British?" she asked. Then she caught sight of the "U.S." insignia on my uniform and quickly corrected herself, "Oh, no, American, of course."

While we danced she asked me how I liked Omsk, where I lived, what paper I worked for, and how did I learn Russian. My answers were fairly monosyllabic, but that did not cut down her barrage of questions. When we finished dancing she led me by the hand and presented me to a group of her friends. They all shook hands very formally and pronounced their names. "We saw you in the factory today," they said.

A minute or two later I found myself backed up against one of the trees which bordered the open-air pavilion, with a circle of twenty or more eager kids surrounding me.

"How big is a B-29?" they wanted to know. "What's its range?" The Soviet press had just carried news of one of the Tokyo raids. My vocabulary wasn't large enough to satisfy the specific questions which followed the more general ones. So I asked them questions. Where were they from? The results showed quite a cross-section— Leningrad, Kharkov, Rostov, Kiev, Odessa, Sevastopol and smaller towns and villages which would always be identified as "near the city of. . . ." I said that I had visited many of their home towns since they were liberated by the Red Army. This erupted a new set of questions.

"Tell me how Odessa looked?" asked one thin boy who wore a white Ukrainian blouse.

"Not so bad. Not like Stalingrad or Sevastopol. It's a pretty city."

"It's a very beautiful city," he said. "We had great culture. I, myself, was studying violin with one of the foremost professors in the world." Then he asked, "Was the Palace of Pioneers damaged? Tell me about the opera house." I tried to tell him as best I could. Then I asked them if they were going home after the war. There was some indecision, but the more vocal ones said Omsk was a nice place to live, and they thought they'd settle in Omsk. "If that's what the government decrees," they always added.

"What about your family?" I asked Tanya Sergeyevna, who was from the Donbas.

"All dead," she said.

The music started up. It sounded familiar. It was. I recognized a strange arrangement of "Am I Blue?"

"Come," I said, grabbing Tanya, "let's dance this one. I know that song. It's American."

"It's Russian," she said. We argued. It reminded me of a concert at Rostov one night in August, 1935. The announcer said that we would now hear a new Shostakovich composition. What followed was a musical hodgepodge but the recurring melody was definitely "Tea for Two." We Americans protested that we were hearing Youmans and not Shostakovich. The argument was never settled to our satisfaction. The Russians would only admit that perhaps Shostakovich had employed this tune "to burlesque the decadence of American music."

Here in Omsk everyone liked "Am I Blue?" almost as much as they enjoyed the No. 1 song on the Omsk Hit Parade that week. Tanya identified it—a teary kind of ballad called *Moi Malchik* ("My Little Boy"). The band repeated it about every fourth number.

After the *Am I Blue?* dance, the NKVD captain wanted to know if White and I were ready to go back to the concert. We told him it was fun and that we'd like to stay. I watched a few dances, and the captain asked me if there was something wrong with the music. "Do you find this hard to dance?" he inquired. I shook my head. "Perhaps you'd like them to play a tango for you and your friend?" I didn't know about Gaucho White, but I am no whirling dervish when it comes to Latin American rhythms. "Waltzes," I told the captain. "My friend and I are old galoshes." That is quite a joke in Russia, to call anyone an "old galosh." The captain laughed heartily. He stopped the band in the middle of a selection. There was a hurried shuffling of sheet music and then a Strauss waltz floated forth, not perhaps as Strauss would have liked to hear it, but a waltz, nonetheless.

I danced the waltz with one of Tanya's friends. Her name was Nina. This name is as popular in Russia as Mary or Jane in America. Nina worked at the factory, and she was curious about how it compared with factories in America. Factories are such an important and integral part of Soviet life that it never occurs to a Russian that all Americans are not necessarily very familiar with their own factories. My knowledge is limited, but I tried to tell her in terms which I had heard Eric Johnston employ.

"Your progress is wonderful," I said, because I knew the word for "wonderful" and not for "amazing." Then I made the point that working conditions were very bad as compared to America. "I understand it's wartime," I said in conclusion. Nina stopped abruptly right in the middle of one of my giddiest whirls. Fortunately she was a solid, heavy-set girl and she managed to hold onto me. She practically dragged me off the floor.

"What's the matter?" I demanded.

She led me over to a tall, sallow youth. She introduced me. "Georgi Ivanovich is a member of the union executive," she said. "You tell him what you told me." So I told Georgi Ivanovich.

Georgi nodded as I spoke. "What you say is true, my friend. We would like to have good light and air and shorter hours and a cleaner place to work. We were striving for goals like that before the war. Now they must temporarily be put aside. We must use what we have, and use it completely." He said a lot of other things, too, but I didn't get all the words. But what he finally said was familiar. So many Russians had said it to me. "Come back five years after the war. Maybe ten years. It will be different then. We will have the biggest and the cleanest and the most beautiful factories in the world. Even better than your Detroit."

He grinned, very pleased with using the name of an American industrial city.

"How do you know about Detroit?"

Georgi said, "I went to trade school in Voronezh. In our textbooks we learned about Detroit. The Ford plant is there, yes?"

The NKVD captain was afraid the concert would be over. He gathered us up very pleasantly and we walked back through the park to join the others. The benches were crowded with teen-age young people, acting as young people do on park benches in the moonlight anywhere.

"This is certainly different from Moscow," I said to Bill, indicating the NKVD captain.

"And how!" said Bill. "Tell him that it's been awfully nice and that we thank him for everything."

After my translation the captain said he was very glad that we were very glad. It didn't take the Russians long to find out which words I knew.

4.

Novosibirsk, the "Chicago" of the U.S.S.R., is almost four hundred miles due east of Omsk. It is now a great city, and in the postwar era it is certain to become an even greater one. Strategically and safely situated thousands of miles from the Soviet Union's west and east borders, Novosibirsk is an important rail and industrial center.

Lying on the Ob, the largest river in the Soviet Union and the third largest in the world, Novosibirsk is the junction point of two very vital Soviet railroads—the east-west Trans-Siberian which goes all the way to Vladivostok, and the north-south Turko-Siberian which runs down to Tashkent and other points in Central Asia. Before the war the area's main industries were timber, fishing, furs, and machines. Now it is also a leading center for the manufacture of munitions, radio, aircraft and optical products.

In 1925 when it was called Novonikolaevsk, the city had only a 100,000 population. Under the three Stalin Five-Year Plans the city rapidly expanded. By 1941 there were 450,000 inhabitants, and at the peak of the evacuation the number had increased to 800,000. Last summer the total was about 700,000.

Novosibirsk's leaders are tough, dynamic, efficient, accessible and friendly. They have a pioneering outlook similar to that of American westerners in the last century. They like big things and big challenges. They want to do things on a big scale. Fifteen years ago they began creating a new Novosibirsk. Today the results are both sound and attractive.

The central avenue of the new city is one of Russia's finest: double-laned, tree-lined Krasny Prospect. Along this boulevard have been constructed some of the better examples of Soviet architecture. The buildings are only five and six stories high, styled in an odd mixture of Russian traditional and modern. But they have worn well, which is more than can be said for the newer constructions in other Russian cities.

Krasny Prospect and the buildings which surround it are in sharp contrast to the old city. That section of Novosibirsk looks like nothing so much as a gigantic Hooverville—drab wooden shacks stuck on the sides of hills or growing in the valleys like weeds. People are still living in the old city. But, according to officials, if the war had not interrupted Novosibirsk's building program they would have been out of these "slums" by 1945.

Instead of new homes for the peasants who still tether their goats to the front doors of their dilapidated huts, Novosibirsk was forced to build still a third city. This helter-skelter melange of barracks and dugouts, of tents and trenches, of dormitories and lean-tos was born in the winter of 1941 when over 300,000 refugees flooded into booming Novosibirsk. Winters are freezing cold in this part of Siberia, and the shelter situation was extremely critical. The people of Novosibirsk reacted like the people of Leningrad. After their regular jobs the entire population grabbed every available spade, hammer, saw and ax and went to work. Supply centers were set up where citizens dumped their extra blankets, sheets, pots, pans, clothes, food, nails and logs.

In seventy-five days living space was built for 300,000. It doesn't look much like Beverly Hills; there are few comforts. "But," wrote a young girl to her mother in Moscow, "there are no bombs either and after all Yasha (her brother) has to live in a trench at the front. I have made wonderful new friends. There's the wonderful spirit of all of us sacrificing together."

While the housing problem was being met in the most expedient way by the people themselves, officials wrestled with the impossible task of feeding the almost doubled population. In the summer of 1941 only 5 per cent of the population had planted victory gardens. That made the months between autumn, 1941, and spring, 1942, the most trying period for Novosibirsk—as it was for nearly all of Russia. Surplus supplies and transport were tied up by the Army and little food was shipped in. There were short rations in Novosibirsk that grim winter, perhaps even starvation. But there were no epidemics, no breakdowns in morale.

In the spring everyone pitched in to make sure it didn't happen again. Factories and all other organizations were assigned portions of near-by collective farms and were made responsible for planting, farming and harvesting. Individuals were assigned additional plots along the local suburban railroad lines running out of the city. Late at night and early in the morning special trains transported citizens out to their gardens and back. When I visited Novosibirsk in July, 1944, the food problem was no longer serious: 75 per cent of the people had their own gardens.

Mayor Vladimir Khaionovsky told us about this fight to feed the city. They had sent 30,000 workers onto the farms for the 1942 summer season to insure building up an adequate winter reserve. In 1944 it was only necessary to send out 7,000. The situation had been eased not only by the success of the victory garden campaign, but by the arrival of new farm equipment and a government regulation that war plants could devote some time and space to producing spare farm machinery parts and to repairing tractors.

At the Novosibirsk airport we had been met by the mayor, the deputy governor of the province, Leonid Malinin, and the general secretary of the Novosibirsk party, Mikhail ("Mike") Kulagin. They drove us to a lovely white frame house set in a wooded glen overlooking the broad, swift-flowing Ob River. This was the official party *dacha*. It had been used to entertain many previous American visitors including Henry Wallace, who had been there just the previous month.

That evening, after banqueting and playing volleyball, we went for a houseboat ride on the Ob. This river flows 2,400 miles from its source in the Altai Mountains of Central Asia to its delta in the Arctic Ocean. Around Novosibirsk it is usually partly frozen from November through May. At points the Ob is so wide it looks like a large lake, and there are wooded islands in the middle creating a two-way channel.

To entertain us on the boat were two Red Army bands, a group of Cossack and Siberian dancers, and finally an exhibition of fireworks put on by "Mike" Kulagin who brought out a Very pistol and taught Eric Johnston how to shoot at the moon.

This Kulagin was quite a character, even in Siberia. He is short.

His sandy hair flecked with white on the sides is bushy, and is usually flopping over his bright green eyes. He squints often. His quick eyes are deep-set in his tough, red skin. Mike wears a business suit with built-up shoulders, and he swaggers around just like the James Cagney of the grapefruit-pushing gangster days. He laughs a lot and likes to slap people on the back—or, in the case of a pretty girl, on the backside. He is forty-four years old, but looks younger. He is bouncy on his feet, very restless, and his mind is as active as his body.

Kulagin told us that he was born on a farm near Moscow. He began working at fourteen. Later he studied to become an agronomist. During the civil war he served with the Cossacks, fighting against the White Guards "and it was a poor day when I didn't kill at least two White officers." He joined the party in 1928 and his first political post was as party secretary in the Belorussian village of Slutsk. His back-slapping gregariousness plus his core of hardness helped him reach the top very quickly. At an early age he became Vice-Premier of the Belorussian Republic, a position which he held until transferred to Novosibirsk in 1937. Mike is now first vice-chairman of the Council of Nationalities, one of the two houses in the Supreme Soviet. As such he is one of Russia's most important young leaders. He has been awarded the Order of Lenin and two Orders of the Red Banner for his achievements as an administrator. He wears only the ribbons in his lapel. Although his wife made no appearance during our stay in Novosibirsk, Mike is married and has a teen-age son who is studying to be a fighter pilot.

On our second day in Novosibirsk we had a closer look at the city. The show place is the new forty million ruble opera house where Henry Wallace startled the good people of Novosibirsk by making a speech in Russian. The building doesn't look especially ornate from the outside, but the interior is only slightly less fancy than the Paramount Theater in New York. The auditorium, begun in 1932, is now almost finished. Its *décor* is a riot of crystal chandeliers, red velvet drapes, Roman statuary and Victorian bric-a-brac. It has two thousand seats and a magnificent stage which is more than one hundred feet wide and one hundred feet deep.

"Now," said our guide, "you will see something that even Moscow does not have, not even the Bolshoi." He nodded to a mechanic. Presently we heard a whirring noise. An electrically controlled, motor-operated concrete safety curtain began to close

behind us. Half of it descended from the roof, half came up from
the stage like the gigantic jaws of a prehistoric monster.

"We couldn't get any asbestos because of the war," the guide
said, "so we built this. It weighs ninety tons. The fire can't get
past it. See how thick it is!"

As we turned to go, he asked, "Don't you want to see it open
and close again?"

We didn't, much to the disappointment of Zemenkov, the censor
from Moscow, who watched the whole operation with open-
mouthed fascination. We followed Johnston into a rehearsal room
where fifty girls were practicing vocal numbers. They sang "The
Chorus of Women" from Tschaikovsky's *Eugen Onegin* for Johnston, and he responded with a brief speech. "Not all the women of
Russia sing as well as you do, but I have found that all the women
of Russia go about their work with a song in their hearts," he
said. "The world owes a great debt of gratitude to the women of
Russia."

Novosibirsk also has a huge railroad terminal which was officially completed in 1942 but which functioned before the last
mural was painted back in the toughest days of the 1941 evacuation. Beyond the station are dozens of tracks, the largest marshaling yards I had yet seen in Russia. The terminal was very
busy, handling more than 10,000 transients daily. The giant
central waiting room, almost as large as Grand Central's, was a
vivid, heart-rending sight. It recalled old movie scenes of refugees
at Ellis Island. Dense masses of people were sprawled on the
benches, overflowing onto the stone floor. Families were sleeping
on mattresses, or rolled up in ragged blankets. Around them were
strewn their earthly possessions. They were awaiting transporta-
tion back to liberated areas. Some of them slept sitting up, propped
against a wall or a pillar. Children played quietly. Mothers were
breast-feeding hungry infants. Grandfathers waited in line for
boiling water before making tea. Others read copies of the local
paper.

It was an incredible picture, full of the immense suffering, patience and courage of the Russian people. It may sound like a
picture of disorder. But despite the pots, pans, black bread and
crutches, everything seemed in order once you blotted out the
anachronism of the super-modern station.

The authorities made no objection to our walking around the
station or to one's interviewing anybody. There was a special

waiting room for wounded troops, legless, armless men en route to rest homes, sanitariums, rehabilitation clinics and farms. I had never seen so many broken men gathered together in one place before. I couldn't get up my nerve to talk to them.

In the main room long lines of people were quietly waiting for tickets. I stopped and spoke to one bent old woman. She said she was seventy. She had been waiting for two weeks to buy a ticket.

"That's too bad," I said sympathetically. Quickly she replied, "It's not long to wait. I'm going back to my home near Mogilev. I've been waiting *two years* for that, young boy."

Later we went with Kulagin to the Chkalov plane factory. This was his baby, his pride and joy. The attractive grounds around the new brick buildings were full of Allied flags. The plant is modern in every detail, its floors concrete and clean, its walls well windowed and well ventilated, its interiors spacious and full of light; they would compare favorably with an American aircraft factory.

Although the conveyor belt system is not used throughout, parts of the plane do move toward final assembly. They were turning out 25 Yak-9's every twenty-four hours. The plant seemed so young and sunny, it felt more efficient even if it wasn't a production world-beater. There were bright banners and slogans everywhere hailing "The Soviet-Anglo-American fighting alliance."

The Yak had been manufactured here before the war, but the plant was enlarged many times with evacuated machinery. There were 35,000 workers in the plant, and they were cheerful, not badly dressed, and very youthful. They all had shoes. Most of them were girls. Everybody knew Mike. He greeted party workers by their first names, chatted with key people, smiled at the pretty girls, shouted words of encouragement to others. He paused alongside one buxom young girl who was testing propellers.

"Valya, when will you be eighteen? Or weren't you just eighteen?"

Valya said she had been eighteen for a month.

"Well," said Mike, grinning and slapping his knee, "what are you waiting for? Why don't you apply for the Komsomols?"

Valya said she was going to, real soon.

"Make it today," roared Mike. He chucked her under the chin and started off. Then he stopped, wheeled and kissed her on the forehead.

Not to be outdone, Johnston gave a girl a two-cent U. S. stamp. "Tell her that's so she will remember me," Eric said.

"Thank you very much, Mr. Johnston," said the girl in English.

There was a banquet in our honor at the Yak factory, and then we went to an optical plant, and there was a banquet there, too. No matter how much we protested, each new host felt it would be rude not to honor us in the traditional Russian manner—with food and drink. Optical Plant No. 69 had been evacuated from Moscow on November 16, 1941. Many of the skilled workers traveled the two thousand miles with the precision machinery. In Novosibirsk they set up shop in an old college building. And twenty-two days after their arrival binoculars, telescopes and lenses for Red Army guns were being shipped to the front.

In his office, the plant's director gave us an interview. He was Alexander Kotliar, aged thirty-six, and very handsome. Before the war he had 7,000 workers; now there were 15,000. About 70 per cent were women. He had brought 60 per cent of his Moscow workers with him; the others had volunteered to defend the city.

The average base pay in the plant is 850 rubles per month, but with premiums it runs as high as 1,000 to 1,100. There is an eleven-hour work day (three hours overtime) for all those over eighteen. The plant maintains its own institute and technicum for training young workers to take over skilled jobs.

"Optical Plant No. 69 will remain in Novosibirsk," Kotliar said in response to my question. "Already a small 'filial' factory has restarted in Moscow. That will be built up separately. The workers, too, will stay here."

"Same story with most plants," Kulagin observed.

"But supposing a husband returns to Moscow after the war and finds that his wife is in Siberia in Optical Plant No. 69?" I asked.

"The wife goes back to the husband in Moscow," said Kotliar.

Kulagin broke in again, "Of course, if the wife likes Siberia very much, she might order her husband to return here." He laughed.

At that moment a delegation of rosy-cheeked girls entered carrying large bouquets of flowers. The leader stepped forward and approached Johnston timidly. She greeted him and then began stammering so badly that Mike got up and took the flowers and gave them to Eric. He patted the girl and smiled at her. She found her voice. "Through you we would like to greet the American people and thank them for their great help during the war."

She shook hands with Johnston. Now she was sure of herself, completely. "We will get revenge for our brothers, fathers, friends . . ." she said. "Beautiful," I whispered to Mike. "Komsomol—and party candidate," he replied.

Eric coughed and winked at us. "We want you to help us beat Japan," he said. "Will you?"

The girl looked at Mike. He grinned and brushed the hair out of his eyes.

"Pravilno!" ("correct"), said the girl.

There were other delegations and other speeches as we went through the plant from department to department. Kotliar said that Plant 69 was the Russian counterpart of the German Zeiss firm. Most of its precision equipment was German-made. Before the war the Germans did finer work, but in recent months Kotliar felt sure that his factory had suppressed the Nazis. "We have captured their newest equipment. The quality of their workmanship has gone down, ours up."

Before we left the plant we were each presented with a pair of Red Army field glasses.

Late in the afternoon some of us went swimming in the Ob. We also had a chance to obtain more information about Novosibirsk from Malinin, the deputy governor. His province was an area about the size of Pennsylvania. It had been bigger, he told us, but the province grew so fast it was split in two.

"Three-quarters of our industrial workers are kids, sixteen, seventeen, some fifteen. They learn very fast, wonderfully fast. Our production is up 43 per cent for the first six months of 1944 over the whole year of 1943. How's that?"

"How's it done?" we asked.

"Rationalization of labor. Training. We give outstanding workers honors. We put their pictures on bulletin boards and in the paper. A courageous worker in the Yak plant gets as much publicity as a courageous soldier at the front. We also give them better pay for improved work. And you know about the special privileges for the best workers? Low-priced meals, first choice in buying consumer goods, reservations at health resorts."

Malinin asked how we liked Kulagin.

"He's terrific," was the consensus.

"He's wonderful," admitted Malinin. "Listen to this. We reduced production costs about 25 per cent at the Chkalov factory through workers' suggestions, replanning and other things. You know what Mike's idea was? Well, he suggested we take that saving and instead of giving it to the Aircraft Trust in Moscow we turn it back to the workers. How? We set up a special fund with that money which pays premiums to the best workers. How's that?"

We pointed out to him that similar stunts had been successful in capitalist plants.

"That's all right, too. Whatever gets production, that's Kulagin's motto."

Malinin said that his province was 70 per cent industrial. "We have to pay more attention to agriculture, though. Our plants are making some machinery for farms. Our railroads are so busy we can't rely on imports of food from other places." He then confirmed the fact that Novosibirsk's evacuated plants would not return. "The evacuees were good for us. Gave us new industry. We never had a radio industry before. Now it is our second biggest. Have you been to our theater? Have you heard our singers? Wonderful. From Leningrad. Well, no matter. Comrade Kulagin will have them all here for you tonight."

Malinin said Novosibirsk had a few postwar industrial plans, too. "We will make more consumer's goods. Shoes, clothes, pails, stoves, kitchen utensils. We need them. We'll have a big market for them right in Siberia."

Mike's farewell party for us was as lavish as a Kremlin banquet and twice as informal. It was served on plates bearing the coat of arms of a former grand duke. There was a nonstop floor show from the first toast to the last, a span of about seven or eight hours. Through it all the dominating figure was Mike; he called the courses, the songs, the girls, the toasts and the tunes. Most of the evening was gay and unrestrained. But at one point little Kulagin suddenly shifted from uproarious fun-making to stone-sober point making. The point he made in a little speech was this: Mr. Johnston was saying some very nice things about the Soviet Union while he was there; other people had done the same thing and then changed their minds when they left; he hoped that his friend, Mr. Johnston, would remain his friend and Russia's friend and not change his mind when he went home.

The singing stopped. The drinking stopped. The waitresses and waiters stood stock-still. Slowly Johnston rose to his feet and answered the challenge. He said what he had said at Mikoyan's first banquet: that the U. S. was individualist and the U.S.S.R. was collectivist and that the U. S. was going to become more individualistic; but if we didn't attempt to interfere with each other's forms of government, there was no reason why we couldn't be friends.

Mike accepted that and the merriment, which had been held in suspense, shattered all around us. Mike sang and danced with furious energy. He pranced around the room insisting that everyone have a fine time. He engaged in a drinking contest with one U. S. correspondent who introduced him to the "katusha." This potent cocktail, like the Soviet rocket gun for which it was named, is an anti-personnel weapon. The ingredients are half vodka, half champagne. Mike, although he never had sense enough to surrender, came off second best.

At breakfast later that same morning the mayor attempted to make a farewell address. It was about how the Germans had been Russia's friends and then betrayed them. Mike was nervous. First of all he said, *sotto voce,* "Farewells are not time for speeches." The mayor labored on. Mike sprang out of his chair and began pacing up and down behind the speaker. "A good speech is a short speech," said Mike, louder. The mayor droned on, mixing his metaphors and his nationalities. "Silence is golden," Mike was shouting by now. The mayor turned. He said three or four words more. Then Mike began clapping his hands. The other Russians applauded, too, and the mayor found himself sitting.

En route from Novosibirsk to Alma Ata, Johnston told us the following story. The night before we left, Kulagin had handed him an envelope. Johnston opened it. It was filled with about forty precious and semiprecious stones.

"They're very beautiful," Johnston said, "but I can't accept such a lavish gift."

"Nonsense," cried Mike, "they are nothing to me. I have all of Siberia's vast resources at my command. You are my friend."

Johnston tried to explain that he would have to pay a very heavy duty on the jewels when he returned to America. Wouldn't Kulagin take them back? He appreciated the thought and all that. Kulagin was adamant.

Several more arguments were advanced, but Kulagin did not retreat. A gift had been made, and he would not take it back.

Later that night there was a frantic conference between Johnston, O'Hara and Bill White. White was quite sure he couldn't accept any jewels. "How do I know what I'll write or say about these people when I get out of here?" he said. "A journalist can't take gifts." Finally it was White who thought up the idea which eventually solved the situation.

About ten minutes before we motored out to the airport, Johnston told Kulagin he would like to have a few last words with him "upstairs in private."

"Fine, very fine." Kulagin was obviously much pleased. "It is an old Russian custom. Before departures the closest and dearest ones always foregather for a little intimate talk. Before I left to fight in the civil war I had such a talk with my mother. Come on."

Upstairs Johnston asked, "Mike, what do you think about party discipline?"

The turn of the intimate conversation did not surprise Mike. He quoted Comrade Stalin on party discipline and indicated that he, too, considered it a necessary and a good thing.

"Well," said Eric, taking a deep breath, "you know I am a member of the Republican party?" Mike nodded. "As such I must make a full report to the leaders of my party when I return to America. I must abide by their rules and decisions." Mike's blue eyes were sober and the line of his mouth was thin and taut. "You see our party does not like its members to take such large gifts without its approval."

Mike grunted noncommittally.

Johnston plunged on. "I am a member of the Republican party. I like being a member of the Republican party. I want to remain a member of the Republican party. And so, Mr. Kulagin, because of party discipline, I must regretfully return these beautiful jewels to you with thanks."

Johnston held out the envelope. Quickly and silently Mike took the envelope and shoved it in his jacket pocket. They shook hands. "I understand perfectly," Mike said at last. "Mr. Johnston, I want you to know that we will keep these jewels in trust for you here in Novosibirsk. Someday you will come back and claim them. They will grow many, many times."

5.

Alma Ata, the capital of the Kazakh Republic, lies about eight hundred miles south and slightly west of Novosibirsk. Kazakhstan is one of the world's least known larger countries, covering an area a third the size of the United States. On the east it borders Sinkiang (western China). It stretches from the lower reaches of the Volga to the Altai Mountains and from the Siberian railway to the mountain of Tien-Shan. The geographical features of this vast country are varied: arid deserts in the lowlands surrounded by snowcapped mountains and glaciers; sun-scorched steppes on one hand and flourishing oases on the other.

Until the urgencies of war caused the Soviets to accelerate the change, a great part of Kazakhstan's land could not be cultivated. In the past few years millions of acres have been reclaimed for agriculture to compensate for the loss of tillable soil in Belorussia and the Ukraine.

Under the tsars, the natural resources of Kazakhstan remained almost untouched and uncharted. The Soviets are just beginning to tap its riches. Their discoveries have been staggering. The mountains and tablelands of Kazakhstan contain 100,000 million tons of coal, over 1,000 million tons of oil, plus tremendous deposits of lead, gold, zinc, copper, tin, nickel, mineral salts, chromites and phosphorites, iron and aluminum ores.

For centuries the Kazakh people have been nomads, wandering over the steppes and deserts with their cattle and domestic belongings. Until 1920 they were nearly all illiterate, only 2.3 per cent being able to read and write. Today this nomadic, primitive, illiterate existence has been changed. Education has spread throughout the country. There are eight thousand schools attended by more than a million children—sixty times the number that attended before the Revolution.

Under the tsars, not a single newspaper had been printed in the Kazakh language. A Kazakh written language was introduced by the Soviets. Today, the editor of the local paper in Alma Ata told me, there are 350 newspapers in the republic and 170 of them are in the Kazakh language. The Kazakhs, incidentally, make up 60 per cent of the republic's 6,146,000 population; the rest are Russians, Ukrainians, Kirghiz, Uzbeks, Kara-Kalpaks, Dungans and Uigurs.

Nothing that the Soviets have done in the last two decades has been more successful than their development of backward, national groups like the Kazakhs and Uzbeks. Instead of supressing their national desires, the Communists have encouraged them—within the framework of the Soviet Union. It has not only helped the native peoples to obtain a higher standard of living and a rebirth of their own culture, but it has paid dividends to the Russians

during the present war. In World War I the Tsar had to use force
to raise a handful of troops among his "colonials." There were
armed rebellions against even the smallest conscriptions.

In this war Kazakhs and Uzbeks, many volunteers, have distin-
guished themselves in the Red Army. Up to October 1, 1944, the
Soviet government had decorated 31,688 Kazakhs and 22,004
Uzbeks with orders and medals; 57 Kazakhs are Heroes of the
Soviet Union. Hundreds of thousands of them have fought for
Stalingrad, Moscow, Kiev, Kharkov and Sevastopol—not as a sub-
ject people but as a free people who feel a brotherhood with the
other nations in the Union.

Soviet investments in local agriculture and industry have proved
magnificently successful. Today Kazakhstan is one of the largest
stock-breeding sections of the U.S.S.R., the greatest center of nonferrous metal production, the third biggest coal-producing region.
Huge plants have been erected for the processing of lead, zinc,
nickel, tungsten, tin and other metals which have contributed
immeasurably to sustaining the Soviet war effort. The coal output,
concentrated mainly in Karaganda, is now 100 times greater than
it was before the Revolution. When the Germans took the Donbas, the famous Alexei Stakhanov evacuated to Karaganda with
thousands of miners. Their production record is breath-taking.
In 1942 the coal mined was 90,000 tons. By 1944 it was more than
16,000,000 tons.

Russian engineers have set up machine-building plants, big
electric power stations, and since 1941 a steel mill. The Soviets
have also constructed new cotton-ginning mills, meat-packing
plants, sugar refineries, tobacco factories, fisheries, tanneries, fruit
and vegetable canneries. New railroads and highways have been
laid to carry the ever-increasing produce to large consumer areas.

Alma Ata (which means "Father of Apples") is built on the
fertile slopes of the snowcapped Khungai Ala Tau mountains, a
branch of the Tien-Shan range. It is about a two-hour flight from
the capital of Sinkiang (western China), and much closer to
Chungking than to Moscow. In 1925 Alma Ata was a small trading
post with 40,000 inhabitants. The railroad line was extended to
the town in 1929, and then it began to expand and grow. By 1941
its population was 180,000. Due to the influx of refugees and evacuated plant personnel the population more than doubled during
the war. Last July it had 400,000 inhabitants.

Most of the bigger buildings in Alma Ata have been constructed since 1938. The city is spacious and cool-looking although the climate is hot. There is a good deal of greenery around, and most of the streets are well shaded by trees. The non-Russian citizens have high cheekbones, and the color of their skin ranges from a deep bronze to a delicate yellow. They are handsome, and some of the women are very beautiful. Racially the Kazakhs are Turkmenian-Mongols. By faith they are Mohammedan. But religion under the Soviet system has not flourished as well in Central Asia as cotton or the opera. I found the citizens of Alma Ata are extremely proud of the latter, and very quiet on the subject of the former.

I asked Mayor Peter Orekhov, a thirty-seven-year-old Russian, about this and he referred my question to one of the local Kazakh officials. He was an oriental type with thick horn-rimmed glasses named Amarov. "We are too much absorbed in the wonders of the machine age—what you call in England the Industrial Revolution," he said. "Perhaps when they have ceased to marvel at these earthly miracles the people will find a greater need for religion." He paused and then said, proudly: "*I* am a Communist." His tone closed the discussion. I later learned he was chief of the local Commissariat of the Internal Police.

We were quartered at a pleasant hostel near Alma Ata in the mountain foothills. Our Kazakh hosts were more relaxed than the Siberians. They gave us more time for the simple things of life such as sun bathing, changing our clothes, showering, sleeping and writing out our notes.

The Kazakhstan Institute of Agriculture maintains a network of eighteen experimental stations throughout the republic. We drove out to one of these farms, passing some very good-looking cornfields on the way. At the station we were treated to a two-hour lecture (with the aid of weather maps, charts and samples of local fruits) on the development of planned agriculture in Kazakhstan. The statistics I jotted down would fill a book. Here's a sample: apple production increased twenty-five times between 1914 and 1944 and grape acreage was up ten times. As a result of the latter fact, a champagne factory is being built in Alma Ata.

Then we went out and walked through the fields and orchards. The orchards are irrigated underground. The plum and apple trees are scientifically spaced and mixed to permit maximum growth. I am not a farmer, but I am told that the achievements of this farm deeply impressed Henry Wallace, who once was a farmer.

Questioning the director of the farm, we were able to get some firsthand figures on how the local farmers were making out. Soviet farmers are always referred to as peasants although many of them now know much more about scientific agriculture than most of the farmers I've met in Vermont or New Hampshire. The Russian "peasants" have been making out very well, financially, during the war years. While prices for their collectively sold crops are fixed, they get harvest bonuses in surplus produce which they are allowed to sell on the market. The farmers at this station in Alma Ata received only 300 rubles per month in wages—about one-third the average for a city worker. Actually they are better off when you figure in their share of the harvest yield and what they reap from good-sized gardens of their own.

Last year each farm worker at the station received, in addition to his wages, 884 lbs. of apples, 332 lbs. of plums, 1,547 lbs. of vegetables, including melons, tomatoes, pumpkins and beets. Since each worker also has a quarter-acre for planting his own corn or beans, he usually has a surplus which he can sell.

He may rent rooms cheaply or he can own a small private house on the farm. They all own chickens and as many as three cows. Horses are scarcer, and they are only owned on a communal basis by the farm.

The director receives a base wage of 1,700 rubles monthly (about half that of a factory manager). But at the end of the season his share of the surplus yield is twice that of the ordinary farm laborers.

6.

In 1941 when the Germans threatened Leningrad and Moscow, the biggest movie studios in Russia—Lenfilm and Mosfilm—were evacuated part and parcel to Alma Ata. There they pooled their equipment and talent to form Central United Film Studios. Not until the middle of 1944 did they return to their home studios.

The impetus which directors like Eisenstein and Ermler gave to the local film industry has been so tremendous that Alma Ata will remain one of the Soviet Union's great movie centers. The Moscow and Leningrad outfits have left some technicians behind to help. The new Kazakh industry has ambitious plans for 1945, including six feature pictures to be produced both in Kazakh and Russian. They will also make some shorts in the languages of other Central Asian republics.

During the evacuation the joint studios produced twenty-five films in Alma Ata. The most grandiose project was still uncompleted—three full-length features based on the life of Ivan the Terrible. While one of the supervisors was describing this mammoth production, the director himself strode in. Eisenstein was wearing a loud yellow polo shirt, black and white saddle shoes and a pair of gray pleated flannel slacks. He said, "Hello, howyah" to everyone as informally as if he had just come back from eating a quick hamburger at the Hollywood Brown Derby.

He waxed quite enthusiastic about "Ivan." "He has been misunderstood," Eisenstein explained. "Until late in life he was a very progressive influence. He had a farsighted foreign policy. Of course, there was an underlying pathology in his character throughout, but it didn't assert itself until his last years. In the beginning he was quite normal, see? My task was to show his real face and character." Then in his best Hollywood English, he went on to sketch the highlights of the misunderstood Tsar's life.

Eisenstein was leaving for Moscow the next day. He had just finished shooting his last scene at Alma Ata, and he took us upstairs to see the set. It was a gloomy, massive sixteenth century interior of Ivan's Gold Palace in the Kremlin. The room was barely furnished. All the ornaments were jeweled—not with paste jewels but with semiprecious stones. On the walls hung authentic ikons.

"I've already shot more than 140,000 feet just on the first two pictures," Eisenstein told me. "My God, what a cutting job I have to do!" He held his head and gave a bad imitation of Gregory Ratoff imitating a Russian director.

As we left he presented Johnston with one of the bejeweled papier-mâché goblets from the Gold Palace set.

The concert they arranged for us at the Alma Ata opera house was rivaled for its beauty and charm only by the one a few days later in Tashkent. The first act was a scene from a native Kazakh opera called The Silken Girl, sung in what sounded to untrained ears like high-pitched Chinese baby talk; the second act was a potpourri of local songs, colorful dances, ballet and choral numbers; the last act was a scene from Gounod's Faust, excellently sung in Russian. I sat in a box next to the editor of the Alma Ata Russian daily newspaper. He was talkative and brimming with facts on the "raising of the cultural level of Kazakhstan."

"There are now thirty-five theaters," he said. I encouraged him by writing this in my notebook. He went on, "There are two thousand public libraries, four thousand reading and recreation rooms. Think of that, in Kazakhstan! This was nothing before. Look at the faces of the people down there in the orchestra. How do they look to you? They are happy. This is their theater, their art."

I asked him how it happened that the mayor was a Russian. "There are many Russians here in Alma Ata. More Russians than Kazakhs. The Kazakhs are not city dwellers," he said. Later the Kazakh Premier told Johnston that before the Revolution only one per cent of his people had lived in towns. The editor continued, "Someday all the officials will be Kazakh. You know, of course, that the premier of Kazakhstan is a Kazakh. Also the general secretary of the party. Orekhov is a good administrator. He was once Mayor of Chkalov."

During the intermission we walked around the crowded lobby. The women were dressed in an odd mixture of Asiatic and European clothing. Many of the men wore clean pongee silk suits—without ties. Nearly everyone had on a fairly presentable pair of shoes, which more than anything else is Russia's superficial index of wealth and well-being.

7.

From Alma Ata we flew to Tashkent, 450 miles due west. Tashkent is the capital of Uzbekestan, a republic with one-seventh the amount of territory of neighboring Kazakhstan but with a slightly larger population—6,282,000. This ancient country on the frontier between the U.S.S.R. and Afghanistan is a pastureland for millions of head of cattle. But it is not cattle that makes Uzbekestan important, it is cotton.

Uzbekestan produces 63 per cent of the Soviet Union's cotton. The republic annually yields three times as much cotton as grown in all of tsarist Russia. When the Germans seized the large cotton plantations of the southern Ukraine, the Kuban, Stavropol and Stalingrad areas, Uzbekestan's cotton crop took on an added significance. In the war years it has almost singlehandedly supplied the Soviet Union's growing needs.

As in Kazakhstan, the amazing acceleration of agriculture has been due primarily to mechanization and a gigantic network of irrigation systems. Tractors by the ten thousands have replaced the primitive hoe and the Uzbeks have gradually learned to use the machinery placed at their disposal by the Soviet state. This slow training in the past twenty years has given them some slight background for machine work in factories. Throughout Central Asia the rural peasant population is becoming increasingly urban and industrialized. Watching them in Tashkent's modern factories you can't help applying Thomas Carlyle's famous line: "The staircase of history resounding to the noise of the wooden shoe of the peasant ascending."

But without farsighted, far-reaching, planned irrigation, none of this progress could have been made. For agriculture is Uzbekestan's economic base. And Uzbekestan is hot and dry in the summer—hotter than any part of the United States. The ground springs dry up and the sun-scorched land is uncultivable—unless there is water. To supply this water, sixty large irrigation canals have been excavated and five hundred mechanical pumping stations have been built during the twenty years of Soviet power in Uzbekestan. As a result millions of acres were made arable and Uzbekestan is thriving.

Tashkent is the heart of the new Uzbek Republic. It has broad macadam streets lined by tall poplars and willows, and many large parks. The city had 700,000 inhabitants in 1941, and more than a million during the height of the German invasion. Nearly all of the 2,000,000 evacuees who found haven in Uzbekestan funneled through Tashkent. Sixty per cent of these refugees settled in the cities, and 90 per cent of them have already returned to the west. The remainder are skilled workers who came to Uzbekestan with their plants. They are staying until they can train local residents to do their jobs.

The sudden unplanned influx of men and machines caused grave problems for the government of Uzbekestan. Two million newcomers suddenly set down in a strange country of only six million (70 per cent Uzbeks) were bound to tax everybody's endurance. The vast and complex undertaking could never have been accomplished successfully if the Soviets had not first won the loyalty of the native Uzbeks during the past twenty years.

Rodion M. Glukhov, the vice premier of Uzbekestan, is a tall, heavy-set, blue-eyed Russian who was the responsible government executive in charge of evacuation problems. In Uzbekestan the greatest shortage was not food, but housing. Civilian refugees began arriving in July, 1941. A complete census was immediately carried out which recorded every available square foot of space. Since this was not sufficient, the government embarked on a drive

for cheap, quick new housing made from available local materials. Glukhov said that every newcomer had a roof of some
kind over his head by the winter of 1941-1942.

Providing suitable and adequate space for evacuated industries
was not so easy. Glukhov was given about two weeks' notice in
October, 1941, to provide structures for a certain number of
plants which were heading his way on flatcars. The job was done
because it had to be done. "On an average transplanted factories
were able to start production within four weeks after their
arrival," Glukhov said, and gave us a few examples.

The Douglas aircraft plant evacuated from Moscow in November, 1941, produced its first DC-3 only thirty-five days after moving
into an old airdrome in Tashkent. In late April, 1942, a huge
munitions factory arrived from Rostov, complete with workers.
They had not been able to transport their foundry, which was
required before production could be resumed. A new one was
built in twenty-eight days. The old foundry had taken two years
to build. The Rostov arsenal is now producing 50 per cent more
in Tashkent than it ever did in the west.

Tashkent had a food supply shortage but it was not so critical
as that of Novosibirsk, since the southern area was a greater food
producer. The problem was tackled much the same way in both
cities. Each plant was given land to farm. The Uzbek government
helped out with horses, seeds and implements. A victory garden
campaign succeeded in increasing the amount of personal planting fifteen times in three years.

"The evacuated Russians and Ukrainians and Belorussians
and Jews were received by the Uzbeks as Soviet citizens and not
as strangers or foreigners," said Glukhov. "Uzbekestan has bene-
fited immeasurably in return. The country's industrialization has
been speeded up enormously. New plants required transforming
over ten thousand Uzbek peasants into industrial workers. It was
done. Now additional thousands are receiving such training."

One morning we went to visit the Old City of Tashkent. It was
a different world and a different age. The streets were labyrinths
of winding and narrow alleys. One automobile could not get
through them. Burros and camels, for which the passageways had
been built, still slowly clopped along as they had in the fifteenth
century. The houses of the Old City were thatch-roofed huts made
of adobe and mud, a sun-baked dun-colored brown. The Uzbek
men in their traditional long white kimono-like robes wore their

Tyubitekia ("skullcaps") woven with a traditional natural design. A few of the older women were veiled, but the younger ones had long since discarded their *paranjas.*

We wandered up one of these hot, dusty, ancient alleys and someone invited us to step beyond the adobe wall which faced on the walk. Inside was a delightful, cool oasis with green grass and sweet-smelling fruit trees. An ageless Uzbek, looking as old and lined as one of the high priests of Shangri-La, offered us tea and dried fruit. We started to take a few pictures. Presently the garden was filled with young Uzbek girls in eye-filling native costumes— rich multicolored silk brocade robes and turbans of picturesque design. They wanted to pose for us.

When we left to meet Johnston at the Douglas plant, the courtly Uzbek made a little speech. It was quite unrehearsed. No official had selected this street or this house. "I am an old man," said the Uzbek in a lilting singsong which is more Turkish than Chinese. "I remember well the days when the emirs ruled. In those days I was not a man. Now I am a man. I am treated like a man." He glanced at a familiar portrait hanging on the wall of his house. "For that I am a man I thank the Revolution and Stalin."

The part of the Douglas plant that we visited was housed in the hangar of a former airdrome. In this building the final plane assembly took place; parts were being made in four other buildings scattered over the city. Director Afanasy M. Yarunin, forty, had been chief of this plant since it first began turning out DC-3's in Moscow in 1939. When he evacuated in November, 1941, with most of his equipment, he also brought along seven thousand of his fourteen thousand workers. He now has twenty thousand workers in the plant, 60 per cent of whom are women.

The shift from Moscow to Tashkent marked some other changes in the Douglas operation. Metals, especially light steel and aluminum, were scarcer. Yarunin began using more wood in the construction; Siberian pine was employed as a metal substitute in the doors, the interior fittings, the partitions and walls.

The chief engineer of the plant, Boris P. Lisunov, had been to the Douglas plant in Santa Monica, California. He studied our methods there in 1936 and 1937 right after the Soviets had purchased the patent rights to the DC-3. But the ships that he and Yarunin are now turning out at the rate of six per day in Central Asia are not like the ones made in Southern California. The

Red Air Force had adapted the DC-3, originally intended only as a passenger plane, for service as a transport, for cargo, for parachutists, as a Red Cross flying hospital, and as a night bomber.

At this plant Johnston, very impressed by the general efficiency, pulled out his notebook and pencil and began figuring. He wrote down the number of workers and the number of planes produced at a huge new American plane plant built since 1940. He added and divided and multiplied for a few minutes and then came up with this observation: "This is the best plant I've seen in Russia and our ratio of efficiency is at least 2 to 1." This is the kind of "cold logic" which infuriates the Russians when they read it in American reports on the Soviet Union. It fails to take into account many factors which cannot be readily computed, i.e., that the workers in the Tashkent Douglas plant are not second or third generation Poles in Detroit who have developed their mechanical skills to a higher degree than either the Uzbek or the Russian peasant; that the plant in Tashkent was not built primarily for up-to-the-minute aircraft assembly-line production at a cost of millions of dollars and many months' time—but was, in fact, just a converted hangar; that the entire plant had been moved bodily from Moscow during the Nazi invasion to a point thousands of miles from many raw materials.

Johnston pleased the plant officials by offering this preamble to a toast at a banquet that afternoon, "I have seen what great things Communism and the Soviet system have done for Uzbekestan. I can see what this country was like thirty years ago, and the progress you've made is notable."

Everywhere we went in Tashkent we not only saw the obvious signs of the tremendous progress in the past few decades, but we heard how that progress had been utilized and accelerated during the war years. Since 1941 the republic's industrial output has been increased by 150 per cent, with almost half of it in heavy industry. Before the war only 14.3 per cent had been in heavy industry. Steel was being produced at the Begovat Metallurgical Combine, oil production had been raised to twice its peacetime level, coal mines were opened and being exploited.

While irrigation projects are the touchstone of Uzbekestan's agricultural advances, the development of hydroelectric power is frequently used by the Soviets as the mark of industrial progress. Four power plants with a total capacity of 72,000 kilowatts have been constructed since the war and nine new ones are being built.

"We need turbines from America," Vice Premier Glukhov kept reminding us. "I hope Mr. Johnston carries that message to your President."

Glukhov, as our official host, toured us through the great Stalin Textile Plant. This enterprise with its 250,000 spindles is housed in six huge, modern, well-ventilated brick buildings grouped around a lovely green park. The park contained benches, recreation equipment, an outdoor lunchroom and a dance pavilion for the workers. Of the plant's 14,000 workers, 80 per cent are women. Practically all the equipment in the plant, which was built in 1934, is Soviet-made.

As we walked through the various buildings the barefooted girls seemed incredibly busy overseeing as many as ninety of the automatic looms at once. They were dressed in pleasant-looking cotton dresses, obviously made from the plant's own produce. The average wage which runs well over 1,000 rubles is augmented by a monthly premium of 15 to 20 feet of cotton material. The factory is almost wholly devoted to making cloth for parachutes, tents, Red Army shirts and underwear, and only 10 per cent is produced for civilian goods.

I asked Nikita S. Ryzhov, the plant's manager, about patterns. They were able to use native dies but he said that "the demand for bizarre Uzbek patterns is decreasing. Even in the villages there are requests for more sober patterns. Perhaps it is the war."

Another afternoon we drove out to the Chirchik Electrical and Chemical Trust. Besides the usual feast we were given several pages of figures, but to one who doesn't understand the details of electric power and chemical processes they are not meaningful. But they did indicate to Johnston, who knows the field, the giant steps in local production since the war. And here again the growing dominance of women in all fields of Soviet war industry was emphasized: of 1,500 peacetime workers in the trust, only 10 per cent had been women. Today 90 per cent are women, most of them Russian, most of them under eighteen years of age.

Signs of agricultural progress were impressive, too. Directors of the Lenin Experimental Cotton Institute near Tashkent claimed that due to controlled irrigation they were getting a constant cotton yield which was two and a half times better than the average in the United States. But during 1944 Uzbekestan's cotton acreage had been curtailed for wartime conversion to sugar beet. The Ukraine formerly produced the bulk of Russia's sugar, and when that was lost Uzbekestan became the chief source. The republic has about 85,000 acres of sugar beets for industrial production in four great sugar refineries which were evacuated from the Ukraine. Another 37,500 acres of sugar beets have been planted for seed which will be transplanted in the Ukraine during 1945.

Uzbekestan, like Kazakhstan, has made progress with synthetic rubber production. The two chief types being grown are *Tau Sagiz*, meaning "mountain gum," and *Krim Sagiz*, "Crimean gum." The former is a bush plant which grows to three or four feet in height, takes two or three years to reach maturity and then dies after its fourth year. *Tau Sagiz* produces only one crop but it has a 30 per cent rubber content which is extremely high. This plant fares better in Kazakhstan, while the *Krim Sagiz* has proven a more economical crop in drier Uzbekestan. The latter is a grass of the dandelion family, which yields a crop every other year with a 5 per cent rubber content.

Between our tours of inspection we lived like grand dukes at the *dacha* of the Uzbekestan Council of People's Commissars. Between meals we were served a local *pivo* which, unlike most Soviet beer resembles Pabst, Ballantines, or any good U. S. brew; or, if we wanted it, we were given a sweet soft drink called "Krem-Soda" which tasted like cream soda.

At meals we were surrounded by pongee-clad Russian-born commissars, and the mayor of Tashkent who was a silent Uzbek. Glukhov was the reigning big shot (the Premier was in Moscow) and when he wasn't telling us about the evacuation or his great irrigation and hydroelectric projects, he was warning us, "I hope you will write this objectively and not give it to the press of Hearst." He looked meaningfully at Bill White of *Reader's Digest*.

Glukhov had been the "boss" of the fantastic Ferghana Canal which now irrigated 1,250,000 square acres of former wastelands north and west of Tashkent. The 80-mile-long canal was built in 45 days by the collective labor of 220,000 people. It is 60 feet wide and 40 feet deep. "We mobilized people from every section of the population to get the job done," Glukhov said. "We built a dam at the confluence of two rivers that form the Syr-Darya." The size of the undertaking can be gleaned from these figures: 18,000,000 cubic meters of soil were excavated; over 1,000 trucks, 17,000 horses, oxen and camels were used.

"We are now building a new canal, the Farkhad," Glukhov told

us, "which entails changing the entire course of the Syr-Darya.
It will irrigate amost a million and a half square acres of the
Starvation Steppes. The digging is already finished but we need
turbines. The Farkhad hydroelectric station will be one of the
largest in the Soviet Union and in the whole world." He sighed.
"I hope Mr. Johnston makes sure that we receive those three giant
turbines we requested from America."

"What else do you need from America?" we asked.

"Mainly structural steel—for the ammunition industry. Also
some excavators and other machinery for our very young coal
industry near Tashkent."

Tashkent's Uzbek mayor, Sadik Khusainov, was most anxious
that "you write about the friendship of our people for the Russians." The mayor was a slight, dark-skinned man—café au lait
color—with fine gold teeth and a shaved head. He couldn't tell
us much about industrial figures; that was outside his ken. But
one night at supper after a wonderful excursion to the local
opera and ballet, he told me about Tashkent's care for war children. "We are taking care of 25,000 children who are here with
their mothers—their homes have been destroyed. We have another 7,600 orphans, children without any known relatives. More
than 3,000 have been adopted. A Uzbek blacksmith named Shoma
Khmudov has taken twelve children—a Russian, a Jew, a Ukrainian, a Belorussian and so forth. He said he had no sons of his
own to offer the Red Army, so he can at least adopt some."

After a few days in Tashkent, Johnston and his party flew on to
Ashkhabad, Teheran and then back to the United States. Before
he left Eric had arranged with Glukhov that we be allowed to
remain behind and go by rail to Samarkand, the heart of ancient
Central Asia. No Moscow correspondents had been there in a
very long time, and the suspicion had grown up that "maybe the
Russians are hiding something." Johnston had been told that
he couldn't go there "because the airfield was too small for a
transport plane." This made us all the more anxious to see
Samarkand.

When Johnston left we had another day in Tashkent before
catching the train across the desert. We were alternately entertained and bored by a continuously convivial Tass correspondent
named Mike who regaled us with stories of his journalistic
triumphs.

"I was in Spain during the civil war," said Mike, a small, fat, red-faced man with thinning hair and blue eyes. He could have been any Third Avenue barroom Irishman with his flushed nose and bloodshot eyes except that he had a vodka and not a whisky breath.

"With the Loyalists, eh?"

Mike was hurt. "Certainly *not*. With Franco. I interviewed him."

"In what language?"

"Swedish. I was stationed in Stockholm for a long time. I used to play tennis with the King of Sweden."

"You did?"

"Certainly. Center court of the palace." Mike ordered more vodka for us, and then poured himself a glass. "Well, I walked in on Franco. I asked him right off, 'What language do you speak?' He said, 'Spanish.' I said, 'That's too bad. I speak Russian, German, Swedish, Estonian and a few others.'"

"How did the interview go?"

Mike drained his glass. "I had the same trouble with Chiang Kai-shek." He spoke very fast, garbling his words.

"You mean you interviewed him?"

Mike never smiled, always remained very serious. "I was in China. Shanghai, I think it was."

"What language did you speak?"

"Swedish. Through an interpreter. Chiang didn't speak any Swedish."

"How strange."

"I thought so," said Mike, "but I was stationed in Stockholm and knew the language well."

Conversations like this with Mike could be picked up or left off whenever he was awake. He spent a good deal of time sleeping off the vodka. He disappeared when Glukhov was around. But when we caught a midnight train for Samarkand, Mike was in our private car dressed in a straw hat, white linen jacket, silk shirt, and white sport shoes. Before he locked himself in his compartment with a bottle, he came down to see if we were all right.

"Have you been to Samarkand before?" we asked him.

"No." said Mike. "Funny thing. I always wanted to go there, do you know that? Been in Berlin, Lisbon, Madrid, Shanghai, Calcutta, but never in Samarkand. Probably because I come from Moscow, it's so far away." He was sweating profusely and began cooling himself by waving his hat.

"Where'd you pick up the hat, Mike?" I asked.

He stared at it blankly for a minute. "Sweden," he said. "Good night. Sleep well." He slid the door closed. While we were still laughing he opened it again and stuck his head back in. "Anyone got a deck of cards? I know some swell card tricks." We threw the Baedecker at him and he went to bed, mumbling.

8.

Samarkand is hotter than Tashkent. It lies two hundred and fifty miles west of the capital across the Starvation Steppes. Samarkand is without age. It is older than Communism or Christianity. It was a world capital centuries before Moscow or Rome. For centuries progress has by-passed Samarkand, leaving it to dry up and shrivel. Now progress is seeping back into its rich, ancient soil, bringing it new life, new vegetation, new techniques, new ideas.

Thus far the physical impact of modern times on Samarkand has been like a nick on a pyramid. The new Soviet-built stores and offices are blurred out in the maze of yellow-gold houses from which arise the silent turquoise cupolas of bygone ages. At last, I thought, we have come to a place where the war means nothing, where the temperature is 161° F., where a rocket bomb wouldn't want to reach—if it could. . . . The railroad that had brought us to Samarkand, the station where we got off, had no reality. It wouldn't have seemed like 1944 or the Soviet Union except for the inevitable tourist bus which met us.

We were also met by Mayor Askar A. Danierov and several of his assistants. The mayor was a very handsome young Uzbek. His aides were older Russians. They all wore neat silk pongee suits and silk shirts, open at the neck. We climbed aboard the rickety, light blue bus of Zis construction, and rode off toward an experimental farm. The country around us could not be compared to anything. Sometimes it looked like the Hopi Indian reservation in New Mexico, sometimes like the Egyptian desert, and sometimes like the front side of a Camel cigarette package—only the minarets were blue-green rather than golden. As we drove through the modern part of the city, I saw signboards advertising the showing of Lillian Hellman's Hollywood movie, "North Star." I thought, They shouldn't show that *here*—it's a war picture.

Along the bumpy road to the farm—we had to back up twice because the road wasn't wide enough for the bus—we saw some strange and wonderful sights. A few veiled women carrying water jugs on their heads. Corner open-air tea shops called *Chai-Khannas*. Old Uzbeks, solemn and bearded, wearing turbans, mounted on little donkeys. Most of the houses were well hidden behind walls of sun-dried bricks. There were no windows fronting on the cobbled streets. The roads we were riding over were the ancient camel routes of the East, and except for the main boulevards of the modern town, they had not changed much.

Suddenly I spied something which made me jump.

"Look at that!" I shouted.

"Where?"

"There."

"Good Lord!" said Magidoff, "it's a Red naval officer—in Samarkand!"

We put the question to the officials. But neither the Uzbek mayor nor his Russian assistants seemed to be able to explain what a Russian naval officer was doing walking down a dry road in Samarkand.

The experimental farm in Samarkand, which we finally reached, was remarkable for "the world's most complete catalogue of apricots"—three hundred different varieties. The most incredibly delicious fruit I have ever tasted is a unique Samarkand apricot called the Kursadik. This is an apricot which dries on the trees and can be picked dried. It has a 50 per cent sugar content when dry and tastes a little like a fig. Developed by five years' work in the process of selection, the Kursadik has simplified the harvesting problem as fewer laborers can work a larger number of trees. The fruit, when it does fall to the ground, will remain there a full month without spoiling.

The farm is also experimenting with American peaches and all available varieties of apples. The problem is to plant apples that will ripen in rotation throughout the summer so as to keep the pickers and canners busy all season. The Samarkand station has already discovered an apple that will ripen by mid-June and is now perfecting another hybrid which can be picked in early June or late May.

Full of a rich and assorted variety of fruits, both fresh and dried, we headed back toward the products of more ancient civilizations. Salisbury's 1914 Baedecker had forewarned us that there are twelve layers of civilization in Samarkand dating far back before the Christian Era. The city, when it was known as Maracandia, had been captured and destroyed by Alexander the Great in 329 B.C.

"Right over there," said the mayor, "is where Alexander stabbed his favorite general, Clitus, during a banquet. I think it was 328 B.C." Beyond the sand dunes were excavations.

After Alexander, the Arabs came as conquerors, and after them, Genghis Khan. He, too, built a great new city. After Genghis Khan came another famous monarch, Timur, called "Tamerlane" which means "crooked one." For generations he and his Mongol descendants ruled as emirs. "The Uzbeks didn't arrive on the scene until the fifteenth century, and the Russians as recently as 1869.

Only an archeologist could make much of the first ten layers of civilization. But Samarkand remains rich with relics of the fourteenth and fifteenth centuries. It is a museum of Islamic glories, of Mohammedan architecture, full of exquisite mosques with hand carved mosaics and towering turquoise minarets.

The Soviets are equally busy restoring the monuments of the old cultures and building a new civilization of their own. Reconstruction work under the direction of the Soviet Union's foremost authority on Uzbek culture, Boris Zasipkin, was proceeding despite the war. Zasipkin is a remarkable-looking old man with a perfectly round face, large brown eyes, and dark, almost unwrinkled, skin. He was dressed in traditional flowing Uzbek robes and a green skullcap. Also acting as a guide was a pretty blond Russian girl from Leningrad named Taisia Smirnova. Taisia said she was an architect writing a thesis on ancient architecture. She had come to Samarkand to study under Zasipkin. An Uzbek family had invited her to stay with them for a few days. "They are very hospitable," she said. "I have already been with them three weeks."

As we stood in the middle of the great market place, Registan, and gazed at the beautiful buildings around us covered with sparkling blue-green mosaics, Taisia asked me, "Do you know how the Uzbeks court?" I couldn't have been more surprised if she had asked me who won the National League pennant, the Dodgers or the Cards. She didn't notice my surprise, but went right ahead with her story. "The man sends a bowl of fruit, perhaps grapes, to his beloved. If she is interested, she sends something back in the same bowl. Usually it is something she has cooked herself, perhaps a mutton dish. Then he sends her something. The bowl must never be empty. If she once sends the bowl back to him without an offering, it means she doesn't love him."

"Do they still do that?" I asked.

It was her turn to look surprised. "The Uzbeks are a very formal people," she said. "They do not change their habits of courting so easily." Then she added, "And besides, why should they? There is nothing un-Marxian about it, is there?"

The bus next pulled up in front of the fourteenth century. We got out and began slowly climbing hundreds of stone steps.

"This is the Shakh-Zinda," said Taisia. When we finally reached the top there was a long stone corridor. On both sides were mausoleums. "This is the Street of Mausoleums and these are the graves of kings." We went into one tomb. It was much cooler. "This is the tomb of Mohammed's cousin. The legend says he was captured here and beheaded but he jumped down this well without his head and is still alive."

I leaned over the well, slightly giddy from the sun and yelled, "Hello, down there." The answer echoed back, "Hello, down there."

The tomb itself was in an inside room; it was a beautifully carved piece of marble about 6 feet wide, decorated with delicate blue stone flowers. From here we went next door to the tomb of one of Timur's sisters. Its walls were covered with terra-cotta flowered mosaics. "Look here, please," Taisia called. "See the flowers are missing. When a Uzbek had a toothache he used to cure it by chipping out a flower and putting it into his mouth. Then if that didn't stop the ache he would have his tooth pulled and place it in the cranny of the wall where the flower had been. That nearly always stopped the pain." She smiled and winked. It seemed very sacrilegious to wink in a fourteenth century mausoleum belonging to a princess named Dshushuk-Bika.

Walking back down the stairs Taisia told us, "Until the Soviets came to power it was the religious custom that no woman could walk up the holy stairs of the Shakh-Zinda. She had to crawl up on her knees."

The bus, which by this time had become an inferno under the midday sun, took us on a trip out to the astronomical observatory of Ulug-Bek, a very wise fifteenth century ruler and a grandson of Timur. He had been a pioneer astrologist. The ruins of his observatory had been discovered in 1908. Taisia said, "It was the largest observatory in the world in the fifteenth century." I was too groggy to care much except that its interior was cooler. You could see the marble rails for the giant 124-foot radius quadrant which Ulug-Bek had used to chart the heavens.

"How hot it is?" The Uzbeks consulted. By the time it was translated into Russian and centigrade and then into English and Fahrenheit it came out: 131° F. in the shade, 160° F. in the sun.

Next stop was the Gur-Emir, the massive mausoleum of Timur himself which is topped by a lovely melon-shaped blue dome. The building had been constructed for Timur and his two sons. There were nine tombstones on the main floor, eight of them surrounded by marble railings. Timur's tombstone, Taisia told us, was covered by the largest known piece of nephrite. The other stones were made of gray marble or alabaster. On Timur's gravestone his biography was hand carved in Arabic.

Timur's actual coffin was downstairs in a crypt. We took some kerosene lamps and descended into the cool depths. The place was thick with common ordinary house flies. "Flies are very intelligent," said Zasipkin. "This is the coolest spot in all of Samarkand. And the flies stay here."

Timur's coffin was wood, covered with gold and silver leaf. It had been opened on June 22, 1941—and someone who looks for religious omens might note that this was also the day the Germans invaded Russia. The investigators had discovered that Timur was called "Tamerlane" or "crooked" because his right arm was one solid bone and so was his right leg; he could bend neither of them.

A couple of ancient Uzbeks and the fourteen-year-old son of Zasipkin were busy cementing mosaics into the outside walls of the tomb. The state had appropriated three million rubles for the restoration, which is expected to be finished in the autumn of 1945.

The heat at this point was more than any of us could stand. We went off to take a shower at the mayor's house. After that we sat on a shaded terrace and fought a big Uzbek banquet with all the traditional native dishes. The handsome, twenty-nine-year-old mayor seemed to sympathize with our inability to eat this twelve-course meal in the 131° heat, but his Russian assistants were adamant.

Mayor Danierov had been a teacher of physics and mathematics before his election as a city official. He was a native of the city and had graduated from the Uzbek State University in Samarkand.

"We had 40,000 evacuees in Samarkand—from Kharkov, Kiev, Rostov and many Ukrainian villages. Most have gone back. Our prewar population was 140,000. It's slightly more now," Danierov reported. Then he told us about the increase of schools since the coming of the Soviets. From education he passed to religion. "We have three mosques open in Samarkand, one Russian Orthodox church, and two synagogues—one for Bukhara Jews and one for European Jews. The Bukhara Jews are a very special sect. They ordinarily speak Tadzhik but they pray in Hebrew."

Samarkand's population is 60 per cent Uzbek, 25 per cent Russian, and the rest are Jews, Tadzhiks, Tartars and Armenians. Like Omsk, Samarkand is becoming a center for retraining war invalids. It already has a large factory for the manufacture of artificial limbs, and two homes where patients receive individual fittings and job rehabilitation.

There are a great many Poles in the Samarkand area, too. They were brought there in "protective custody" after the Soviets went into the Lwow area in 1939. Now most of the men are said to be fighting with General Berling's Polish Army in conjunction with the Red Army. The women and children who remain behind work on farms and are cared for jointly by a special committee under the Commissariat of Education and a branch of the Union of Polish Patriots. German prisoners were also kept in this section after the Battle of Stalingrad, but now they have been shipped off to build roads in the Urals and Siberia.

"We in this province have sent over 100,000 men into the Red Army," said Danierov, "yet we have increased the amount of land we have sown by 425,000 acres since the start of the war." The Samarkand area is the biggest cattle-breeding region in the Uzbek Republic; it supplies one-third of the republic's bread; it is the biggest producer of dried fruits; silk is being made; neighboring Bukhara Province is the largest producer of black and gray karacul in the Soviet Union, and Samarkand is second.

"We export only about 100,000 skins a year," explained one of Danierov's Russian aides, "but they are finer in quality than Bukhara's."

"Do not lose sight of the fact that Samarkand is the Leningrad of Central Asia," said the other Russian assistant. "It is a seat of culture. We have medical, agricultural, economic planning, cinematic engineering, teachers, tropical diseases institutes."

He then went on to emphasize a point which the newspaper

editor had told me in Alma Ata. In schools of the fifteen non-Russian republics, it is compulsory for students to learn Russian. But Russians living in any one of these fifteen republics must study the language of the republic in which they live and work.

"Before the revolution literacy was only 7 to 8 per cent here," said Danierov. "Now it is 92 to 93 per cent. And we have special courses to liquidate that remaining illiteracy which is mostly among the older people. We have many classes for adults."

Samarkand produces three-quarters of all the Uzbek wines, sixty-two different varieties, and our hosts wanted us to sample them all. "Our wine would be world famous if we only had big beautiful bottles," mourned one of the officials. "Isn't it good?"

"But of all things," Danierov spoke up with much feeling, "the greatest Soviet contribution has been spurring our cultural growth. We were just a colony, a source of raw materials for absentee landlords. But now. . . ." He went into statistics on operas and theaters, on the new cotton-ginning plant, on the wolfram industry, on new coal-mining operations, on the great canals they were digging and the electric power they were developing. "We were counting on Leningrad to send us turbines," Danierov concluded. "But Leningrad has not made them. Now we ask you in America to send us turbines. It will mean a tremendous forward leap in our production."

At the station the pleasant young Uzbek mayor said, "Come back again. Bring your wife and children. We have everything very healthy here, especially fruit."

9.

Back in Tashkent to pick up our plane for the return trip to Moscow, Glukhov was anxious to learn our impressions of Samarkand. We gave him a confused picture of pilaff dishes, wines, dried fruit and heat.

"I cannot understand about that Red Navy officer," I told him.

"Oh," he said, "that's understandable. The Leningrad Naval Academy was evacuated to Samarkand."

I couldn't understand, then, why they hadn't told me.

Glukhov's large blue eyes twinkled. "A military secret," he joked.

We thanked Glukhov for his hospitality.

"I am glad you were able to see everything you wanted." Glukhov looked each of us straight in the eye. "I hope that many

more correspondents will be able to come to Uzbekestan and report what we have done." We toasted that hope. Glukhov went
on. "There are many things here that are not perfect. We have
not always done as well as we might have."

Several correspondents told him he was being too modest.
"No," said Glukhov, very seriously. "Just write objectively about
what you saw, that's all I ask."

10.

The development of Central Asia under the Soviets is obviously
impressive. At prewar levels Central Asia had an industrial output
far greater than the combined production of Iran, Afghanistan
and Turkey. Neighboring Iran, for example, has been open to
western European influences for generations. There are more consumer goods in Iranian shops, but there has been nothing like
the widespread advancement in public health, education, mechanized agriculture, industrialization and what the Russians call
"the raising of the cultural level"—meaning more theaters, operas,
ballets, movies and artistic expression for everyone.

The Uzbeks and the Kazakhs have already achieved a solid
economic base for their future which will certainly be great.
They are not only learning how to use the tools of the twentieth
century to their fullest, but they are slowly learning how to
govern themselves. Individual republics run their own commissariats of education, public health, justice and agriculture. Recently they have been given some rights in the fields of defense
and foreign affairs.

The natives of Central Asia were once just as ignorant, just as
superstitious and backward as the natives of neighboring countries. Scientific farming was made to work in Central Asia by a
system of centralized government. Intelligent, trained experts
studied the agricultural problems, decided what was economically
best for the area and then saw to it that the policy decided upon
was carried out.

No doubt the peoples of Central Asia gave up certain liberties
as a result of this centralized government. They gave up the right
to criticize some of its measures; they couldn't grow cotton when
they were told to plant sugar beet. "But," say the Russians, "they
also gave up their right to starvation, to disease, to ignorance."

The six thousand-mile journey through the Urals, western

Siberia and Central Asia left some conflicting impressions, the inevitable paradoxes of the Soviet Union. Why were plants dirty in Magnitogorsk and clean in Novosibirsk? But certain things were, for me, beyond controversy. First, the government had successfully carried out a fantastic evacuation of people and plants which no figures can mirror completely. Second, production in the east, while not up to American standards, is breath-taking, judged by Russia's own industrial background, tradition and experience. Third, the Soviet policy toward national minority groups within the Union has withstood the acid test; in time of crisis, former "colonial" peoples like the Uzbeks and Kazakhs voluntarily stood shoulder to shoulder with the Russians. The Soviet national policy has given them new dignity, new economic freedom, new hope.

We Americans like but still distrust, "facts and figures." They can be made to add up to anything. Yet it is difficult to cast any doubt on these facts: during 1941 and 1942 the Soviet Union lost two-thirds of its industrial capacity and one-third its population as a result of German conquest and destruction. By the end of 1944 the industrial capacity was practically back to its 1940 prewar level. This miracle depended very largely on the development of resources in the Urals, Siberia and Central Asia, on the success of the evacuation, on sound leadership, and on the complete co-operation of all the Soviet peoples. The continued speedy development of Russia's industrial capacity will also be due, more and more, to the people's untiring passion for reconstruction in the liberated areas.

Book 7

The End Is Only the Beginning

I. Reconstruction of the Cities

THE planning, initiative and spirit which characterized the building of the Urals, Siberia and Central Asia, carries over into the rebuilding of the west even during the war. The enormity of their reconstruction problems has given the Russians a longer term view of the war than the one we have. While United States automobile manufacturers have been competing on drawing boards to see whether it will take four or six months for Americans to get a new car after the war, Russians are wondering whether it will take four or six years before they have enough glass to repair thousands of millions of shattered windows.

On the train from Stalingrad to Moscow, a Russian professor of mathematics who was traveling in the same car, asked me how soon I thought the war would be over.

"I don't like to guess," I said, "but probably two more years. Unless, of course, there is an internal collapse in Germany."

"That long?" he said, surprised.

"After that," I reminded him, "we will still have the Japs to finish."

"True," he said, "but if all your fighting men and ships were concentrated against Japan, that would not take so long."

"Especially if you help."

He shrugged. "I do not like the Japanese. Russians have many old wounds to settle with them." He accepted one of my cigarettes. "Do you still have plenty of these, or are they strictly rationed as in Russia?" I assured him that we had plenty—that was in 1943.

He rolled the cigarette, loosening the tobacco. "That's the whole thing," he said.

"What?"

"Your economy is well preserved. Your homes, too. When the war is over for you, it's over. That is, when the fighting is over for you, the war is over. When the fighting is over for us? . . . Well, you saw Stalingrad just now. Even the earth must be restored—the bombings have made it sterile. For us the end is only the beginning. You can just go back to peacetime ways and peacetime production. We must rebuild. That will be a hard fight, too. And we are very tired."

The professor was a member of the generation which had worked to repair the damage wrought in Russia during World War I and the civil strife that followed. He remembered how difficult it had been to get started. Everything began at scratch. The blast furnaces were dead and the mines flooded. The railways were in a state of complete ruin. Agriculture had collapsed. The country was starving. Rehabilitation could be tackled only after the war was over because there was no economic base that would permit the country to fight and build simultaneously.

But during this war the economy of the Soviet Union has grown stronger. Plants which yesterday had to work exclusively for the armed forces today can already devote some of their production capacity to the output of equipment and materials for rehabilitation. Collective farms in the east have voluntarily sent part of their own farm machinery, livestock and seed supplies to the areas which suffered from German occupation. The whole country has pitched in to help, and state grants for rehabilitation have been swelled by contributions. Eastern regions and eastern plants have become "patrons" of similar regions and plants in the west. Plants in the Urals, for instance, have sent both equipment and skilled workers to the Donbas.

The result is that reconstruction in Russia is a process as amazing as Soviet prewar industrial expansion, as well organized as their evacuations, and full of the brilliance and initiative which characterized the Red Army's victories in the field.

One of the first foreign experts to study Russian reconstruction was Pierre Cot. The former French Minister of Aviation came to Moscow in the summer of 1944 to study Soviet methods for the De Gaulle government. He was given whatever figures were available and allowed to tour around the country to inspect various liberated areas. He has estimated the material destruction in the Soviet Union at 250 billion gold rubles which is twenty-five times greater than the destruction in France and Belgium during the last war. He told me that he had discovered the secret of Russia's incredible speed in rebuilding: "The willingness of workers to rebuild factories before their own homes and to let personal comfort wait until production for the front was resumed." Unfortunately, Cot said, he didn't think the individualistic French would be willing to do the same thing.

The Soviets, however, are paying attention to some aspects of individualism in their plans for reconstruction. At every exhibition of postwar architectural plans, the stress is on small, private homes. Large prizes are being offered for the best bungalow, the best two-family house, the best cottage for southern climates, the best log home for northern temperatures. In August the government announced that it had allotted 257,000,000 rubles for the construction of private homes and for repairing privately owned houses wrecked and damaged during the German occupation. Under this new appropriation, Soviet home builders can borrow as much as 10,000 rubles from a state bank and take seven years to repay it at low interest rates. Servicemen, their families, all war invalids will be supplied with building materials by the state without cost. Citizens of former occupied areas are exempted from taxation for the next four years.

The law has a few other interesting provisions. Building plots are to be assigned on the outskirts of towns. New homes must blend with the general architecture of the township. Building lots "are to be granted in areas providing water supply, electricity and transport facilities, and are to be large enough to accommodate the necessary outbuildings and garden plots."

According to Alexander Dubrovolsky, manager of the All-Union Bank for Municipal and Housing Construction, the trend toward privately built and owned homes was evident even before the war. Between January 1, 1938, and June 1, 1941, more than 400,000 persons moved into new houses which they had constructed under the state credit scheme with loans advanced by Dubrovolsky's bank.

The central government is also making both credits and live-stock available to farmers. The special reconstruction decrees of August, 1943 ordered that 600,000 head of cattle be immediately returned from the east to the liberated territory. The Commissariat of Agriculture had the tremendous problem of carrying out this transfer. Logistics for moving cattle can be just as exacting as logistics for moving men. Trains and trucks were crammed with essential war materials. The commissariat had to plan special overland routes and see to it that water, proper feed and care could be provided all along a trek which averaged between one thousand and two thousand miles.

Hundreds of scouts were dispatched on motorcycles, bicycles, horseback and on foot. They mapped twenty-three routes totaling a distance of 25,000 miles. Along these were set up 250 control and 540 veterinary stations where cattle experts were on duty day and night. The unique migration was so skillfully accomplished that reports claim the herds averaged heavier when they reached their destination in Western Ukraine and Belorussia than when they left Kazakhstan. Within ten days after the decree was promulgated the "roundup" got under way. In addition to the original 600,000, eastern state and collective farms sent along 40,000 head additional as a gift. Another million or more head were purchased by the commissariat on credit to help the quick revival of western agriculture. The timber commissariat arranged for the shipping of thousands of cords of wood so that farms could repair their homes, sheds and fences. By January, 1944, less than five months after the decree, farms in liberated areas had received 1,700,000 head of cattle.

The swiftness of Soviet reconstruction can be gathered from a few examples. The Red Army entered Kharkov before dawn on August 23, 1943. By nine that morning city officials arrived with a truck convoy carrying food. It was distributed all afternoon despite shell fire. The Germans had destroyed the city's communications. On August 24, transport planes landed with equipment to rehabilitate radio, telegraph and telephone systems. A day later the state opera company returned from evacuation in Irkutsk and gave a show. Four days after the Germans had gone, a daily newspaper appeared printed on presses flown into Kharkov, two movie houses were open for business, and a visiting Moscow theater group performed.

As soon as a town or city is liberated, civilians begin flocking back from the woods, from farms, from underground hideouts. Almost immediately representatives of the commissariats are sent in from Moscow to appraise the damage and to report on what essentials are required from outside. Since it takes some time for state projects to get going, local officials encourage a brief return engagement of the kind of free enterprise which existed under the German capitalists. Privately owned and operated restaurants, shoe repair shops, groceries, secondhand stores and dressmaking establishments are allowed to continue. If they don't already exist in sufficient numbers for the needs of the town, people are urged to open them. But as state-operated projects are set up, the privately owned businesses evaporate. I asked the mayor of Kharkov how this was done. He smiled and answered, "Competition. We can do it cheaper. Why would anyone continue eating at a private restaurant where a meal cost ten rubles when he can get the same thing, often better, at a co-operative dining room for half that price?"

Things do not always go so smoothly in liberated towns. When I was in Smolensk in January, 1944, I bought a copy of the local paper *Worker's Path* and read the report of the local party secretary on restoration. This was four months after the city had been retaken by the Soviets. After praising the workers of the "Stalin section" of Smolensk, the official began finding fault. The construction work had been badly organized. The building was not of a satisfactory quality. Not enough attention had been paid to the living quarters of the construction workers. The socialist competition (seeing who could build the most the quickest) had been "purely formal." But the worst thing, said the comrade, was that elementary household articles could not be bought in Smolensk for love or money. The city's leaders had failed to organize workshops (artels) for clay pottery, for making kitchenware, buckets and basins which Smolensk housewives must have. "There are plenty of raw materials around Smolensk," concluded the report. "They can be utilized. All that's lacking is the local desire to assume the responsibility for taking care of the people's urgent needs."

2.

Kalinin, Stalingrad and Leningrad are interesting examples of Russian reconstruction efforts. Kalinin is a small city which was liberated very early in the war after a brief, but highly destructive Nazi occupation. Stalingrad is a middle-sized city which was itself a battlefield and was as completely destroyed as any modern city can be. Leningrad is a very large city which suffered relatively slight damage and was never under German control.

In every case where the Red Army frees a town from the Germans, the first step is cleaning the area of mines and filth. In many instances the Germans systematically infected the places which they left. They dropped corpses in artesian wells, put cyanide in reservoirs, turned patients with contagious diseases out of hospitals, spread typhus even by inoculation. Red Army statistics show that 90 per cent of the people still living in occupied areas required some kind of medical treatment. This they receive immediately from the physicians and medical workers who travel with the Army. Their problem is not only to clean up the newly liberated sector but to establish rigid health control so that disease cannot spread behind the lines or into the Army itself.

The increase of venereal disease under the Germans is especially disheartening to the Russians. Before the war V-D had been almost completely stamped out in the Soviet Union. Now it is once again a major problem in special regions.

Kalinin, often called the "test-tube" city of Russian reconstruction, was held by the Germans for a period of less than two months in the summer of 1941. But for good parts of the two years following its liberation on September 16, 1941, the city was under attack by either German guns or bombers. Situated on the main rail line between Moscow and Leningrad, the city is about 100 miles northwest of the capital. Kalinin, formerly known as Tver, had a prewar population of 225,000. When I visited it in May, 1944, its population was about 170,000.

The city was famous as a textile center. It also had one of the largest car foundries in the Soviet Union. The textile industry turned out 900,000 yards of finished fabrics daily and the car foundry produced 40 flatcars per day in addition to 300 passenger cars per year.

Five days after the Red Army retook Kalinin, the Commissariat of Light Industry in Moscow sent in fifty-year-old Vassily Nazarov with instructions to investigate the condition of the textile industry in Kalinin and "get it going as fast as possible producing for the front." Nazarov's most immediate problem was finding workers. He went to the city soviet and told them what he would need. Finally by Christmas Day he had enough men to begin clearing the ruins of the Volodarsky Mill. A month later he was ready to operate his first small shop in the basement of one of the demolished buildings. On February 1, Nazarov sent the first shipment of garments to the near-by front.

Nazarov's problems during 1942 would make an ordinary executive quit. It was bitter cold in Kalinin, and Nazarov had to get his boilers repaired. Since there was no way to obtain new equipment or furnishings, he had to arrange for the millworkers to make their own. They set up a carpenter shop in the old firehouse and nailed together crude unpainted tables and chairs. The lathes were pieced together with bits and parts which the Nazis had considerately left behind. In fact Nazi efficiency contributed to easing the reconstruction problem. They had gathered light machines and household belongings (everything that was movable) into a central warehouse. The Red Army counteroffensive moved in so rapidly that the Nazis did not have time to destroy their loot.

The textile industry by May, 1944, was only back to 20 per cent of its peacetime level. The chairman of the Kalinin district soviet explained this figure by saying that it was still impossible to procure machines. Soviet machine plants were still not making spindles, and so Kalinin had to struggle along with what could be salvaged and repaired.

After two and a half years, the car foundry was operating at 50 per cent of its prewar peak production with 60 per cent of its former personnel. The plant had been burned, and it cost Kalinin over 16,000,000 rubles to restore it. The buildings were patched up with burned bricks and old boards and some new machinery had been shipped in.

While large-scale industry had not been able to achieve a full comeback in this city, small local businesses have doubled their output. Among the new enterprises begun in Kalinin since the Germans left were a match factory, a winery, brewery and a small candy factory all producing for local consumption.

Prewar Kalinin had 11,033 houses with 811,000 square meters of floor space. When the town was recaptured the habitable buildings numbered 1,630 containing 84,000 square meters of living area. Up to May, 1944, the people had restored 6,900 houses with 580,000 square meters of space. Wherever possible old foundations and walls were utilized. In many cases construction was simplified by the substitution of wood for metal. Local wood, stone and bricks were employed, together with as much salvaged material as possible. If the walls and foundations of a house were especially strong, additional stories would be added.

Kalinin's water system was repaired, its bathhouses and laundries were functioning and its still windowless trams running. The hospitals were open. There had been 72 schools with 40,000 students. Last May about half this number of schools were restored and 21,000 pupils enrolled. Of the city's 41 libraries, 9 had been completely destroyed and with them 564,000 books.

Only now is Kalinin able to think of more permanent town improvements. While the 1944-1945 housing budget of 25,000,000 rubles does not call for any new buildings, the city soviet expects to restore the regional theater which was seriously damaged in 1941. When reconstructed this 150-seat house will have room for 1,500 plus a concert hall for 500 additional.

3.

Stalingrad had a prewar population of over half a million. When the Red Army conducted a census on February 2, 1943, there were exactly 1,500 inhabitants left in the city. By the end of 1944 there were more than 250,000. Over 11,000 houses had been built or restored. The Red October and Red Barricade war plants had been restarted. They were making some tanks, but chiefly parts and munitions. Everything that was shipped from the city to the front was marked with this inscription: ANSWER FROM STALINGRAD. By the end of 1944 there were 187 shops, 20 hospitals, 125 communal dining rooms, over 40 schools, 50 kindergartens, 6 movie houses and 8 clubs functioning in Stalingrad. All of them reconstructed.

By November, 1944, just two years after the battle which practically leveled the city, Stalingrad had the same percentage of teachers and schools, of beds and hospitals, that it had before the war. By the end of 1944, Stalingrad had restored 45 per cent of its peacetime industrial capacity.

The rebirth of Stalingrad, inch by inch and step by step, has been carefully set down in the diaries of Alexander Chuyanov, secretary of the city's Communist party. Here are some extracts:

Jan. 21, 1943—Remnants of German army still holding out in parts of city. Party executive meets to prepare plans for rebuilding city.

Feb. 2, 1943—4 P.M. Last Germans wiped out in grounds of tractor plant. Military operations declared ended. Red Army takes census. Population, 1,500. In city's largest residential district only 33 people remained alive, 20 adults, 13 children.

Feb. 5—Work begins clearing rubble.* German corpses counted and cleared. Number: approximately 100,000.

Feb. 16—Big drive begins for complete removal of mines and unexploded shells. Total from all sappers' reports exceeds one million.

March 1—New census taken. Population up to 12,000. Housing shortage critical.

March 16—First turbine repaired. Power station functions slightly.

April 3—Engine driver Nikolai Lunin arrives in city from Novosibirsk bringing with him a trainload of coal which he bought with his savings. Coal presented by Lunin to President of City Soviet.

May 10—Special group of architects arrive by plane from Moscow to draw up plans for a new Stalingrad.

June 1—Population now 65,000. Housing situation bad but warmer weather eases immediate problem. Drive opens to prepare for winter months.

June 23—Kindergarten teachers organize spare-time brigades. Idea should be spread.

July 19—Siren at tractor plant sounds for first time.

Aug. 27—Report to party executive shows 6,618 houses have been restored and judged "livable."

Sept. 28—"Livable" houses up to 7,232.

Oct. 31—Party and City Soviet issue decrees that all those still living in tents and dugouts must move before winter.

Nov. 7—Revolution anniversary. Fifty thousand in city pay tribute at graves of Red Army dead.

Dec. 27—Trams are running! But thus far only 14 kilometers in operation compared to prewar trackage of 60 kilometers.

The major credit for organizing the rebuilding of Stalingrad has not gone to the party secretary, however. The new hero of the new Stalingrad is fittingly a woman. Her name is Alexandra Cherkassova. As the name of Alexei Stakhanov became inseparable from the movement to increase production, so the name of Alexandra Cherkassova is now identified with the determination to rebuild fallen cities.

Cherkassova is a schoolteacher. She has two children. Her husband died defending Stalingrad. "I remember our first Sundays given up to clearing the streets and factory grounds," she says.

---

* Although Soviet officials do not publicize the fact, much of this cleaning up and early reconstruction was carried out with the help of German prisoners of war.

"Everyone took part, both young and old. And then one Sunday I got an idea: could not we inhabitants think of something to rehabilitate our city quicker? What if we whipped together volunteer brigades of women and went out every day after work to rebuild and repair the houses? Surely somehow we could find three or four hours a day for the job. True, we were not bricklayers, nor plasterers nor carpenters—but these are made, not born. Our Russian woman isn't the kind to shrink at difficulties. We would try. . . ."

So Cherkassova got together eighteen women. Most of them were, like herself, working in kindergartens. She didn't make a long speech. She said, "For all of us Stalingrad is our life. We cannot look at its ruins without pain. Let's start building."

The others talked it over and agreed with her. But no one could agree where to start. Work was already going forward on the war production plants. An apartment? A bathhouse? A theater? Everyone had a suggestion. Finally someone said, "Pavlov's house!" and there was no more discussion. Pavlov's house was a building which was defended for two months by a handful of men of the 62nd Army. On the façade of the house they wrote: "Motherland! Here some of Rodimtsev's guardsmen stood until death. . . . This house was held and kept by the guardsman Sergeant Yakov Fedorovich Pavlov."

The kindergarten teachers and some of their friends called themselves the "Pavlov Brigade" and set about restoring the historic house. There was not a professional builder in the brigade. Everyone had a full-time job in addition to their work in the volunteer effort. "We did not think," Cherkassova admits, "that our initiative would start a whole movement, that it would stir the whole city. Now, of course, I realize that if we hadn't set the ball rolling somebody else would have done it because everyone had the same desire."

Cherkassova and her brigade wrote a letter to the local paper and asked for more volunteers. Five days later over five thousand Stalingrad citizens were out at the job of rebuilding their city. It was suddenly coming alive again. Some groups were restoring a drugstore, some a school, some filling in street craters. But it wasn't all fun. "It was somewhat tough at first," Cherkassova recalls, "there were moments when you just wanted to sit down and weep: five times you would build a Dutch oven and there'd be something wrong every time. Or you had to make a door and you couldn't think for the life of you how to fix the frame. . . ."

Several days later seven thousand turned out, and the number kept increasing until by the fall of 1943 over thirty-five thousand volunteers were giving two or three hours a day. By the winter of 1943-1944 the people of Stalingrad had some place to live, even if it wasn't perfect. There were warm schoolhouses for the kids and enough baths and laundries and dining rooms for all.

All during this period the volunteers had to watch out for hidden mines. A year and half after Stalingrad's liberation, over three hundred a month were still being discovered. They were hooked to water pails and desk blotters, to phonographs and coffee grinders, even to coat racks so the hanger would explode when used.

During the winter months the building stopped. But the volunteers still gave their two or three hours a day to the task of reconstruction. They spent the time learning carpentry, plastering and other trades. Cherkassova was invited to go to other liberated areas and tell how she had organized things. The central government in Moscow honored her with a decoration. And the volunteer rebuilders of the Soviet Union became "Cherkassovites."

The Soviets are fond of statistics. In an editorial praising Cherkassova one of the Moscow newspapers figured out that she and her brigades had voluntarily contributed 650,000 work days between July and December, 1943, to reconstructing Stalingrad.

The people of Stalingrad have never been alone. Everyone is pulling for them or with them. Nearly every week I read in the Soviet press that some factory or some group of workers had raised money to rebuild Stalingrad, had worked in excess of plan for Stalingrad, had sent furniture or clothing to Stalingrad. We cannot imagine what a terrific driving force this desire to rebuild, rebuild, rebuild can be. In April, 1943, I am told, five hundred members of the Moscow Komsomols volunteered to go to Stalingrad and work; that same month three hundred men and women volunteers reached the Volga city from the Tatar Republic and six hundred construction workers from Kirov also turned up to help Stalingrad arise from the ashes.

In Moscow last summer I saw some of the architect's plans for the new Stalingrad. From these and drawings for other Soviet cities, whose names are themselves monuments, it seems obvious that the Russians are going to have a huge number of colossal war memorials. In the central square of Stalingrad there will be

a 180-foot "victory" tower topped by a bronze statue of a Red
Army man. At noon, daily, hidden loud-speakers will send forth
the strains of the Red Army victory march. At night the tower will
be lit by floodlights as a beacon for the Volga boatmen. And on
the sides of the tower will be engraved the names of all the
divisions which defended Stalingrad.

4.

No city in the Soviet Union was better prepared for reconstruction than Leningrad. When I visited the city not long after the
siege was broken, work was already in full swing. Russians, as a
rule, do not like to talk about anything until it has been accomplished. Officials like to say, "We do not deal in prophecy." But
in Leningrad, at a time when we were still measuring our wall maps
to figure out how far away the nearest German and Finnish cannons could be, we found a highly intelligent, well-developed program for reconstruction. The man primarily responsible for the
city's reconstruction activities is Chief Architect Nikolai Baranov.
It was he who toured us around the city and its suburbs, reciting
the damage with intimate knowledge of every brick and tree.

Baranov is only thirty-five. He would be an excellent lecturer
on housing and town planning in one of our universities. I heard
him give his talk twice to different groups and found his ideas
fascinating both times. Baranov was in Leningrad throughout
the siege. He drew up all the plans for the city's defense works
and directed the camouflaging. He is highly educated and speaks
with vigor and clarity. First he stressed the fact that those who
rebuild Russian cities must make a positive factor of the destruction. In Leningrad, this is more difficult than elsewhere, because
they cannot always tear down damaged buildings and create
parks. Leningrad to a greater degree than any other city is a
museum of Russia's history and architecture. The war has intensified the sense of history which the Russian people have. To do
away with the palaces where Peter the First or Catherine the Great
lived, although they are badly damaged, would deprive the Russians of cherished landmarks.

In 1935 the Leningrad city soviet approved a project for the
replanning and rebuilding of Leningrad. Work had been begun.
Then it was interrupted—first by the Finnish war and then by
the German invasion. But in March, 1942, while the Germans

were still attacking, Leningrad's architects received orders to go ahead and concentrate on reconstruction. "Why did we start work with the front so close and no chance actually to build because of material shortages?" Baranov asked, using that peculiar Bolshevik monologue-in-dialogue form—asking and then answering his own question. "Because we Leningraders love our beautiful city—one of the most beautiful in the world, and so for us to do our own work proved to be the best medicine against privations. It took our minds off our stomachs."

In the much-bombed outskirts of the city Baranov and his associates now plan to undertake large-scale developments of small houses modeled on the American suburban community. Work started in the spring of 1945 on plans which were completed late in 1944. Some of the small homes, bungalows actually, will be built of gypsum, some with prefabricated parts. In Moscow, before I left, I saw a partly prefabricated house constructed with a new type of building block made of pressed wood. Moscow architects hope this new wood block can be mass-produced to partially solve future housing needs.

Baranov does not feel that this kind of informal bungalow would "suit the mood" of Leningrad. But he is willing to try it in the outskirts. He has very definite ideas about the style and design of Leningrad's architecture. "Nothing must violate Leningrad's personality," he said. For that reason Baranov is not planning on any more temporary housing than is absolutely necessary to meet the immediate requirements of returning evacuees. "It would spoil our city's looks," he explained. He feels strongly, too, about skyscrapers, and his reasons are aesthetic. Most of Leningrad's buildings are fairly uniform in height, not more than six stories except for a few of the newer apartment houses which rise as high as eight or ten. The dominating building in Leningrad is, has been, and will be the Admiralty. Its thin, graceful spire is only slightly more than two hundred feet high. Yet it can be seen along prospects and boulevards for two or three miles. "Any tall building would spoil this effect," Baranov said. "We have plenty of room to expand sideways, so why go up?"

The direction of Leningrad's growth will be southward, away from the swamp area around the Gulf of Finland. This section will be converted into a large six hundred-acre park with a fine motor parkway like Chicago's Lake Shore Drive. Baranov insisted that Leningrad's reconstruction will not be "mechanical." Except for historical monuments, ruined buildings will not be rebuilt if it is more economical and sensible to tear them down. Buildings which stand inside city blocks will be dismantled to give more inner air space. In the central area where a solid mass of buildings were pretty well destroyed, another park is being created. Work had already begun in February, 1944, on my first Leningrad trip, and it was fairly far advanced when I returned in June.

Baranov said that Leningrad will be doubled in size without a proportionate increase in population. That is to be stabilized at 3,500,000 people. The city has no special slum area like London, but housing conditions have always been crowded, especially in the "downtown district." Baranov blamed the density of population in this central section on prerevolutionary private ownership of real estate. In the future, density will be limited to two hundred persons per acre, which compares favorably with newer, better planned cities.

The present trend toward greater privacy and away from collectivized living will be reflected in Leningrad's center, too. When large new apartment houses are built they will contain small, family suites of two, three and four rooms. Old buildings, where four and five families once crowded into a single ten-room apartment are being cut up into much smaller, single-family apartments, usually with private baths and kitchens.

Baranov believes that Russian style and design must be in the spirit of Russia's heroic tradition—reflecting not only the glory of the tsars but the triumphs of the present war. He realizes that what will be acceptable in Leningrad will not be acceptable elsewhere. "Architecture must be functional," he repeated. "It must be in keeping with national and local characteristics, with climates, with the customs and the lives of the people." He deplores some of the "modern" architecture which sprang up throughout Russia in the thirties. He scoffed at the Bauhaus school, calling their designs "depressing." After visiting Magnitogorsk, which is largely Bauhaus-influenced, I would not argue the point.

The Central Architectural Committee in Moscow has raised no objections to Baranov's thesis that Leningrad must be a city apart. The chairman of that body told me in Moscow that no city would be regimented. "Our goal is clear," he said, "we must have more air, light and privacy for our people. More comforts. We encourage different cities to build in different styles. Wouldn't it be silly as well as uninteresting, if Asiatic Alma Ata looked exactly like European Minsk?"

II. Rehabilitation of the People

The problem of reconstruction in the Soviet Union is not limited to restoration of farms, factories, oil fields, buildings, railroads, power stations, cities and homes. In the huge area which was under Nazi occupation for more than two years the problem extends into the realm of family relations, education, and ideology. The human wounds—physical, mental and spiritual—will take more time to mend than the cities.

The population itself must be reborn. Since that is impossible except in a figurative sense, the rate of birth must be stimulated. The Russians have lost between fifteen and twenty million dead, soldiers and civilians, in this war. Millions more were deported by the Germans as slaves. The usually high Russian birth rate has fallen. This is due not only to the loss of men. Families have been separated by evacuation. Millions of women have joined the Army and millions more have entered war industries. For example, over one million women have become railroad workers in the Soviet Union since the war's start.

On July 8, 1944, the government in Moscow took measures to increase the birth rate, make marriage more secure and divorce less desirable. Under this decree maternity leaves for expectant mothers were extended and their food rations were doubled.

Divorces are now as difficult to obtain in Russia as in most parts of the United States. And so are abortions which have been illegal, except in special cases, since 1936. Incidentally, the lurid picture of free love in the Soviet Union which lingers in the American imagination has not actually existed for almost a decade.

The publicity given the new decrees has done much to correct American concepts of Soviet morality. Monseigneur Fulton Sheen, prominent U. S. Catholic spokesman, remarked in a speech last November that "the family is higher in Russia than in the United States, and God, looking down from heaven, may be more pleased with Russia than with us." Soviet editorial writers, while not making any predictions about God, have referred to the Russian family in equally lofty tones. One commented, "First and foremost it is a new assertion of the inviolability of the family, of the sanctity of family ties as some of the fundamental bonds which knit civilized society into one indivisible whole." Another added, "Sound society is unthinkable without a sound, economically secure family."

Few subjects caused so much comment and discussion among the people in Moscow during my stay there. I walked out to the Hermitage Park one night shortly after the decree was printed. The park, as usual, was crowded with young soldiers and their girls walking up and down and chattering. I sat down on several park benches just long enough to hear snatches of conversations and to ask a few questions. The girls were not too happy about the decree. One said, "Well, comrades, the new slogan will be—for women—'Children and not careers.'" The Red Army men thought the whole idea was good. It made for stability, they said. Sons were needed, and daughters, too, if they happened to be born. But mostly Russia needed sons.

There was considerable fun about some aspects of the law, especially those provisions which stipulated that heavy premiums would be paid to mothers for each child beyond the third. And as in every other line of Soviet competition, medals and titles were to be awarded to those who excelled in production. The title "Mother Heroine" is conferred upon mothers who have borne and brought up ten or more children. The Order of "Glory of Motherhood" is awarded to mothers who have borne and brought up seven, eight or nine children. For seven children the order is only third class, for eight it is second class, and for nine it is first class. The Red Army men jokingly demanded that there be a "Father Heroine" title, too.

Subsidized procreation will undoubtedly increase the birth rate, especially as it is already being backed up with the full weight of the government and party press and other arms of their propaganda and educational machine. Unfortunately it is easier to increase the birth rate than to solve the enormous problem of those homeless children born amid the horror of war and invasion. A million are reportedly suffering from severe cases of rickets and other nutritional diseases in the former occupied area of the Soviet Union alone. I tried for weeks to obtain a figure on the number of children who were made homeless or parentless by the war.

But even the Council of People's Commissars (of which Stalin is chairman) admitted that such figures could be approximated only roughly. "It is better to say 'countless millions,'" I was advised.

No Russian has ever forgotten the years after the first World War when millions of orphans roamed the country in wolf packs. They were cold, hungry, ragged, amoral. Everywhere they went they begged, stole, died. The story of their round-up and eventual reformation was the theme of a Soviet movie which Americans knew as "The Road to Life."

So that there will be fewer "wild boys of the road" after this war, the Soviets have expended great care and effort, infinite patience and foresight, and millions of rubles. They have established a network of homes and special schools where orphans and children of men at the front are looked after. These are in addition to the unusually large number of nurseries and child care centers which have existed since the early days of the Soviet regime. In 1913 there were 550 nurseries. In 1941 there were 854,000.

In spite of the war, the number of Soviet kindergartens, for example, has doubled since 1941, and the number of children enrolled in them has tripled. These figures are all the more amazing because of the Nazis' systematic destruction of the Soviet educational system. While no statistics have been available for Belorussia or the Ukraine, large Soviet republics which were completely dominated by the Germans, they do exist for the Russian Republic. This republic was only partially under German occupation and not for as long periods as those farther west. In the Russian Republic the Nazis destroyed thirty-five thousand schools which before the war had been attended by five million children. At the end of 1944 the Russian Commissariat of Education announced that thirty-three thousand of the schools in liberated Russian territory had been restored and reopened, and that four million children were now back attending them. Another two million youths are in apprentice schools, and many more have not yet returned from evacuation points in the east.

Soviet postwar plans call for an educational system so extensive that it will reach literally from the cradle to the grave. Every mother who wants to work will be able to find a nursery for her child or children. This plan was so well developed that by 1941 nearly half of all the children in the Soviet Union were receiving nursery care. Since the war the nursery system has been further expanded to include evening care for the children of parents working on the night shift; and many more quarantine stations have been established so that children with communicable diseases can be left at these centers for expert treatment.

2.

The Russian Republic has made the greatest advances in child care of any of the Soviet states. It has 17,000 special homes which accommodate 1,200,000 children, most of them orphaned by the war. The state spent 1,700,000 rubles during 1944 on the maintenance of these homes. In addition, it appropriated a vast sum so that 2,000,000 children could enjoy summer vacations in state-controlled camps.

One of the Russian Republic's 17,000 children's homes is located at Babushkino, a suburb about ten miles north of Moscow. Children from three to seven, whose parents are dead or at the front live in a rambling two-story green frame cottage surrounded by an acre of trees and gardens. Slightly more than one hundred of them are cared for by eleven women teachers, fifteen servants, a doctor and a nurse. Before the war the cottage was a small day nursery for the children of working mothers. In 1941 these children were evacuated, and for over a year a military unit was quartered on the premises. Then the unit moved up to the fighting lines. When the front receded from Moscow the Commissariat of Education took over the building for child war refugees.

The first refugees arrived in July, 1942. Many of them had just been evacuated over Lake Ladoga from Leningrad after managing to survive the terrible winter. They were children in age only. They did not play. They did not smile. "Little old men, little old women," was the way the director, Faina Yefimova Rutkovskaya described them when they arrived. They cried. They hid under their cots at night for fear of air raids. They jumped at sudden noises and burst into tears. They did not talk but hung their heads in silence.

One of the first Leningrad arrivals was five-year-old Genya Terentyev. His mother had been killed by a Nazi bomb, his father was at the front. His body was covered with hunger sores —he suffered from dystrophy, a disease of malnutrition. He was near collapse from exhaustion. He could neither move nor make a sound. For two weeks he lay in a Moscow children's hospital, close to death. At the end of the second week he feebly uttered his first word—"give." Soon he was saying "eat," "want," "give." The nurses resorted to every possible trick to encourage speech and movement in the thin, listless boy: games, stories, dances, songs, anything to stimulate his interest in living. The battle for Genya was finally won, but it took long months before Rutkov-skaya saw the first sign of victory: Genya smiled.

Genya was one of the most difficult cases. But on an average it takes at least two months before the evacuees are anything like normal, gay children. They have few comforts, although the whole country is trying to make their lives progressively easier. Help comes from America, too. In fact most of the clothing worn by the children at Babushkino and a part of their food is supplied by Russian War Relief, Inc. Even the crates and boxes from the American food and clothing are utilized at the Babushkino home. From them the children make many of their own toys. Their "ships," "trains," "tanks" and "guns" might not be easily identified by adult eyes, but children have enough imagination so that three Kraft cheese boxes tied together with string can be a "truck convoy."

The children all know about the generous gifts from Russian War Relief and are very grateful. Incidentally, in the Soviet Union this organization is referred to as *Amerikansky komitet pomoshchi* ("American Aid Committee"). The reason for this change is that "Russian" signifies only one of the sixteen republics, that "war" when translated infers only military aid, and the Russian word for "relief" is "aid." Last spring when Leo Gruliow, Russian War Relief's American representative in Moscow, visited Babushkino he was plied with questions about where the new shoes, sweaters and coats came from. The children gathered around him while he traced the long route over which the clothing had traveled.

Currently the Soviets are conducting a campaign urging families to adopt these waifs who have lost both their parents. The Moscow press carries frequent stories about patriots who have taken one or more orphans into their homes. They have made a sort of slogan out of the simple words of Ovchinnovka, a woman worker at the Krasny Bogatyr plant, who said, "There are no unwanted children in our country. They are all wanted." In the latest compilation released, 239,000 war orphans have found foster parents in the U.S.S.R. since the war.

3.

Babushkino is typical of thousands of preschool homes. They are open to all children, regardless of aptitude. But as a result of the war a new type of institution has been started in the Soviet Union. In the fall of 1943 the Suvorov Military Schools were established by decree of the party and government. The purpose was not only to create a reservoir of trained personnel for the Red Army of the future, but to help solve the problem of talented war orphans. At the time the schools were established foreign observers viewed them as a resurrection of the old tsarist Cadet Corps, which were socially correct military academies for the sons of the nobility and the elite of the Russian Army.

But the children who applied for the new Suvorov schools came from a different class background, with a different preschool kind of environment and experience. They were the children of Red Army generals and officers, of Heroes of the Soviet Union, of partisans and prominent party people, or just stray waifs who had also lost one or both parents in the war. The schools, which were first opened in December, 1943, were under the supervision of the Commissariat of Defense, and received the special attention of Stalin's aide, General Golikov. They were set up in Kalinin, Chuguliev (near Kharkov), Stavropol, Novocherkass, Voronezh, Orel, Maikop, Stalingrad and Kursk, with new ones planned for Leningrad, Moscow and Kiev. Similar naval training schools named after tsarist Admiral Nakhimov, were also founded during 1943-1944. Students at all these schools receive room, board, tuition, clothing and incidental expense money from the government which considers them wards of the state.

About five hundred children were chosen for the Suvorov school at Kalinin out of fourteen thousand applicants. They came from all over the Soviet Union, from Karelia to Vladivostok. They represented twelve different nationalities. Their ages varied, but they were all old with the special kind of aging everyone experiences who lives with the rat-tat-tat of machine guns and the howl of mortars. More than 75 per cent of them were war orphans. "I know what war is," said Nikolai Mishchenko when he arrived in Kalinin. "For two years I have learned to fight and be afraid of nothing." Nikolai was thirteen and an orphan.

Last May I went to Kalinin to visit this school. It was housed in a rambling wood-frame building which had been the Kalinin

Theological Seminary before the Revolution. There were several other newer buildings and a campus or drill ground, and the entire place was surrounded by a combination stone and iron fence. The school is presided over by a headmaster, Major General Viktor Vizzhilin. He is a forty-five-year-old former factory worker from Saratov who joined the Red Army during the civil war. After that he was trained as an infantry officer in the Frunze Academy. In 1939 he participated in the Bessarabian campaign where he twice suffered from shell shock. In the fall of 1943 Vizzhilin was appointed to the school at Kalinin. He was given less than three months to gather a staff and get the school into serviceable condition. The main building had been used as a base hospital by the Germans during the occupation of Kalinin and had not been severely damaged. It did require considerable redecoration and refitting.

With the help of wounded army officers and a staff of seventeen women teachers, Vizzhilin managed to have things in readiness for the first day of classes on December 1. The 510 children, ranging from eight to fourteen in age, were roughly divided into four classes. Each class was then subdivided into five sections. Over each section there was a former Red Army officer who acted as a "housefather."

Other Allied correspondents and myself interviewed the members of the staff, inspected the dormitories, the military exhibits, the natural science museum, the bathhouse, the infirmary, and the mess halls. We sat in on various classes, were entertained at a concert given by the students, and talked to a hand-picked group of the boys.

The dormitories looked neat but austere. Each student has a bare iron cot and next to it a night table. On the top of every table was a military hat. The walls were whitewashed and bare—not even any slogans. Attached to each cot was a little sign with the cadet's name and year of birth. The rooms were heated by old-fashioned Dutch ovens. In the student's mess the food was not fancy, but it was certainly more plentiful and better balanced than the fare the same children would eat in an average Russian home. Their diet averages 3,600 calories daily. For "first" breakfast at 7 A.M., a half hour after reveille, there was tea and black bread. "Second" breakfast at 11:30 A.M. consisted of eggs (or hot grain cereal), sometimes potatoes, more bread and tea, and frequently fresh fruit. The main meal or dinner was served at 3 P.M. and included a thick, rich soup, meat, potatoes, vegetables, stewed fruit or a sweet, and milk. Supper at 9 P.M. was light—bread, a little fish, cereal and milk or tea. Students ate their meals in solemn silence, although whispering was permitted. Napkins were tucked in under the chin, but I don't think any of them ever spilled a spoonful of food. They ate with studied preoccupation—the kind of expression people have when learning to drive a car.

The schools were using the same textbooks as the regular public institutions for the same age level. But we were told that special books would be published based on the first year's experience. For the Suvorov curriculum is meant to be broader in its scope than the ordinary Soviet ten-year school, and the standards of scholarship are definitely higher. Each class lasts fifty minutes. The younger boys, eight and nine years old, have four hours of classroom work per day, while the older ones have six hours. On an average there is an additional two hours daily of homework. Backward students are given special tutoring so that the general class program does not lag behind schedule. According to General Vizzhilin the results of the first semester were extremely satisfactory: only twenty boys failed to receive marks of "good" or "excellent" in all subjects.

The actual instruction in the classes which I visited seemed to be handled with intelligence. The atmosphere, however, was stern and almost forbidding. The serious, white-faced youngsters with shaved heads marched to their classrooms in uniform, snapped to attention when confronting an officer or civilian teacher. They were not permitted to speak unless they were first questioned. Everything was very formal—even dancing class. I heard no sounds of laughter, not even in the play yard.

When the teacher entered the classroom the cadets rose. The teacher said, "Good morning, comrade pupils." In unison the boys replied, "Good morning, comrade instructor." The cadets then sat at their wooden desks with their hands folded in front of them. When called upon to recite a student jumped up, stood rigidly and began his answer by announcing his name. Notes were taken with pen and ink. The women teachers wore black dresses with gold buttons down the front and high white, formal collars. The boys themselves must be in uniform—except when they sleep. Cadets have five separate and complete outfits including two parade uniforms. The everyday uniform is black with brass buttons and red epaulets. A red stripe runs down the side of the long trousers. There is a wide leather belt around the waist of the tunic with a bright brass buckle on which the Soviet star gleams.

The children did not object to the military discipline. The

teachers believed it advisable because the boys had been on their own for so long and unaccustomed to social behavior. General Vizzhilin reported that there had been very few infractions of the rules. He said he had employed "prophylactic methods" of reprimand. The mildest was depriving the offender of his dessert at dinner, the severest, stripping off epaulets and ordering the culprit to stand two paces out of line during parade drill for from five to ten days. The tenets of the school system permit solitary confinement up to three days, but this form of punishment has never been utilized at Kalinin. In only one instance had severe discipline been required. A wild boy named Arkady Kisilov indulged in coarse language, smoked and was guilty of several thefts. Since he did not prove responsive to any kind of correctives he was expelled. Looking through a copy of the school's paste-up magazine, I came across a letter from Arkady to his former mates. He had been sent to a children's home in Kalinin. He wrote: "How happy I should be to come back to the school. I am being badly fed, not the way you are being fed at school where you have everything and are being taken care of. Do your work properly and do not follow my example. I wish you all success."

While the discipline is strict, or seemed so to me, the academic emphasis in the Kalinin school was not on military subjects. Vizzhilin noted this immediately when he pointed out that the program was much broader than that of the old Cadet Corps. Stress is on a well-rounded education, plus the development of extracurricular activities such as dancing, singing, painting, music, writing, riding and outdoor sports. At first students are given a choice of studying either English or German, but before they can graduate they must be able to read, write and converse in two foreign languages. When they pass their final tests they have a rank tantamount to that of a junior sergeant. They may enter any advanced military school without further examination. After three more years of study they become officers. If specially recommended by the headmaster they may even be admitted directly to the Frunze Academy from a Suvorov school.

But a military career is not at all obligatory. Suvorov graduates can qualify for advanced studies at institutes for medicine, chemistry, engineering, music, railroading or anything else. Most of the Suvorov cadets that I had a chance to question were uncertain about their future careers. In the older age group out of fifteen boys, three said they wanted to become officers, two wanted to be painters, one a composer, another a construction engineer. Dmitri Vassiliev said, "I am thirteen years old. My parents are dead. When the Germans took the town of Kalinin where I lived, I evacuated with my family to Nezdillo. One of our divisions was stationed there. I asked to be taken into the Red Army and I was accepted. I was in the army for six months. During this period I was a scout. Now I am in Suvorov school. I came here to become an officer. My dream is that I want my life to resemble Suvorov."

They all sounded so composed, so old. Even when they hadn't thought things out, they said things like: "My fate hasn't been settled," or "I have not fully pondered the matter."

During the concert which the cadets staged for us I asked some of the younger boys sitting near me what they wanted to be. Only three would say that they definitely wished to follow a military life. One large-eyed, chubby little boy bounded out of his seat, saluted me and replied: "Gentleman officer, I wish only to become a cultured and intelligent gentleman."

Many of the students are sons of men who are well known in the Soviet Union. There are two grandsons of a former commissar, Ordzhonikidze, and two grandchildren of the great civil war guerrilla, Chapayev. One of them, Valya Chapayev, said: "I want to be an artillery officer. My father is an artillerist. He strongly beat the Germans with his guns. I will be such a fighting officer as my father. I must graduate from school as a disciplined and educated warrior. This is my dream of my future."

One of his classmates is the son of Captain Viktor Gastello, a Hero of the Soviet Union. In the early months of the war Gastello, a brilliant fighter pilot, ran out of bullets during a dogfight with a Messerschmitt. Rather than let the Nazi escape, he rammed his plane into the German's. We talked to young Viktor who is twelve. He is a dark, handsome boy with almond-shaped eyes and firm, thin lips. He, too, would be a great pilot. His favorite subjects now were Russian grammar and history. Later in the day we heard him recite in his German class and he seemed to be having difficulties with that language. "I prefer chess or skiing," he admitted. He never smiled, not even when we tried to joke about the universal difficulty with German and the Germans. We asked him why he wanted to become an officer. He thought for a moment before answering, "To defend my country."

The most interesting cadets were those who had won decorations for their own valor before coming to the school. Lazar Burstein, thirteen, wore on his black tunic the Medal for Bravery. He told his own story with amazing poise. He said, "I am a Jew. I come from a village near Orel. In July, 1941, the Germans entered our village. They started to shoot the population. They shot over half of them including my father and mother. When my parents died I went away. I didn't know where I was going. I just wandered. After two days I was picked up by some partisans. The commander said, 'Stay with us.'

"We fought. We ambushed the Germans, we attacked them on the roads, we derailed their troop trains, we prevented their machines from reaching the front, we blew up munitions dumps. One time I was a scout, one of nine. We met some Germans. I had to use a gun. A German revolver. I killed some Germans. I do not know exactly how many."

He paused. Someone asked him about his background. "My father worked in a factory," he said. "He had one brother. I do not know where he is. When I left home I spent the first night with neighbors in another village, the second at an outpost."

"How did you get the medal?"

"The Germans were coming through with reserve troops and ammunition. I was sent to find out the type of troops and vehicles and munitions and how many. In the evening I left the woods where my partisans were. I walked to the village where the Germans were. I arrived at ten in the morning. I knew everybody in the village. They hid me for an hour and a half. Then the Germans started moving through the local station. I counted. Fifteen trucks. Three hundred motorcycles. The village had been burned by the Germans. I was in a new hut. It was made of birch twigs. I kept count, peering through the twigs. I counted a great many of cavalry. Then I made my way back to headquarters and reported everything I saw. But first I was held up by the German sentries. I had no weapons. I wore a simple peasant shirt. I had a sack on my back containing new straw shoes. The sentries spoke bad Russian. I said 'I have been to see my aunt. I am on my way to trade shoes for bread. There is no bread in our house.' The Germans looked into my sack. They saw the shoes. So they let me go."

As the result of Burstein's information the partisans surrounded and wiped out the German detachment. The boy was recommended for a decoration, and "officially entitled to have a rest." He was picked up by a plane and carried to Soviet-held territory where he entered a children's home like the one at Babushkino. When he read in the *Pioneerskaya Pravda* about the formation of the Suvorov schools, he applied. "And now I am here. When I grow up I want to be a mining engineer."

"Are you sure you won't be an officer?"

Burstein almost allowed himself to smile. Not quite. He replied, "Well, we'll see."

But his new friend Nikolai Mishchenko definitely wanted to be an officer. He was Belorussian, born near Vitebsk. "I was two years in the active Army," he reported to us, standing at attention, his large brown eyes focused straight ahead. "Two years from the age of eleven. The Germans came in July, 1941, but my parents had taken me away. We lived in a village. My father, a doctor, had been shell-shocked at the Finnish front so he could not join the partisans. But he secretly helped them with medicines, with treatments. The Germans shot him when they discovered this. Three days later they came to the house and shot my mother. Soon after this the Red Army returned. My brother and sister and grandmother were sent to the rear. I remained. I wanted to join the Army. One officer sort of adopted me." We later found out that the officer was Lieutenant General Mishchenko, and that the boy had assumed his name. Nikolai was decorated with the Medal for Military Service. "I went many times to the German rear, behind their lines. I was with a reconnaissance unit. Once I led our scouts over a forest path at night. I knew this path as a child. We had to capture some German prisoners. We needed certain information. It was successful. Shortly after this I received my medal."

Nikolai was permitted to sit down. We turned to a tall very serious-looking boy with big ears and bright intelligent eyes. His name was Leonid Kaplun. He was thirteen and a half and he came from Moscow where his mother was still alive. Kaplun was at the top of his class in his studies. He talked on almost every subject with quiet confidence but without cockiness. He held a press conference as if he were used to doing it every day. He thought the war would be over soon. After the war he would like to go abroad, to the United States, to England, to Germany.

"What would you especially like to see in these places?"

Kaplun answered: "The army officers and their life, the techniques in the factories."

"What do you know about the Allied war effort?"

"England and America help Russia very much in the war against

Germany, they fought in North Africa and they are also fighting Japan."

"What do you think about Japan?"

Without hesitation, Kaplun said: "Japan is an ally of Germany which is an aggressor country." In response to other questions he said he wished to devote his life "to the military arts." Why? In order to become a polished officer and to defend his country.

"Against whom do you think you will have to defend your country?" a reporter asked. This was a tough question. I expected a possible reference to world capitalism. But Kaplun had more tact and diplomacy than one could rightly credit to a boy under fourteen. "Against any enemies who attack it," Kaplun said after a pause.

One of the British correspondents had been trying to discover what the boys were being taught about the British Empire. He asked Kaplun if he could define the difference between a "dominion" and a "colony." Kaplun did it in economic and political terms and then added, "A dominion is only a semistate and not able to defend itself. A colony—well, if it could defend itself, it wouldn't be a colony." When I tried to report this answer from Moscow it was censored. The reason for the censorship was that the remark was not flattering to the British Empire and might be picked up and used by the Berlin radio.

After we had talked to the boys, about fifteen of them, for several hours, I asked if they would like to question us. They did not mention the "second front." Instead their interest seemed to be in education. Were there similar schools in England and America? Who were taken into such schools? What was the curriculum in the British naval training school?

During supper I talked to one of the young Red Army instructors who sat at my table. He wore the uniform of a cavalry captain. He was only about twenty-five, but a bullet had pierced one of his lungs during the fighting for Kharkov, and he was now on detached duty. The captain told me that "a hundred and sixty students are taking English. Four hours a week," he said. "Everyone must have singing and riding. Two hours a week. And two hours a week for individual music lessons."

"I saw them dancing," I said. "Doing the polka. Maybe they will all be diplomats or military attachés in foreign countries some day."

"Yes," mused the captain. "they have many advantages here.

Showers once a week and a haircut and clean underwear at the same time."

I inquired about vacations. When the year is finished in July, the cadets go off to an outdoor camp. They will have a little military training, but most of it will be recreation: games, nature study, dramatics. Those boys who have relatives are allowed from fifteen to thirty days at home.

During the midyear holidays many of the boys were taken on a junket to Moscow. "You know what they enjoyed most?" asked the captain. "I'll tell you. It was your movie 'The Thief of Bagdad.' I liked it very much, too."

"Do the boys enjoy the drill?"

"Oh, yes. One boy, he is nine, named Vanya Kolpakov wrote to his grandmother. He said, 'I am a military man now. We have the military uniform, discipline and order and I liked them. Only now I see how much disorder we had at home with you. As soon as I will come home for my vacation we will establish discipline.'"

"Are there any student organizations in the school?"

"Only the Komsomols."

"Why only that one?"

The captain shrugged. "Perhaps because that is the best," he said.

I went back to the subject of the discipline. I know nothing about military schools in the United States, where perhaps things are just as strict. Did the captain think the Suvorov routine would be less severe in peacetime?

He thought for a few minutes, gulped his vodka, and then said, "There is a famous saying of Suvorov. 'A hard drill makes an easy battle.' Perhaps the same is true of the battle of life, in war or peace. Anyhow you must remember that there will be no easy road for these boys even after the Germans are crushed. Our Russian life is hard. There is so much to do."

Walking down the hall after we had finished the usual toasts, the captain asked me if I was a Republican. "No," I said, "why do you ask?" Then he wanted to know if any of the other American correspondents were Republicans. I didn't know but didn't think so.

He shook his close-cropped blond head sadly. "I feel in a mood for argument," he sighed. "I have been reading a life of Abraham Lincoln who was a Republican, you know, and I have studied his theories. The Republicans must not be a very firm party because

they do not seem to follow the Lincoln theories. Is that correct?"
I nodded.

"You are not a Republican so perhaps you do not know about
Lincoln's theories?" he asked. I thought I detected a note of hope
in his tone.

"All Americans of every American political party know about
Lincoln and what he said and wrote," I explained.

When the captain recovered from his surprise he mumbled,
"Here it is Lenin, the same way."

4.

For boys and girls in the next age group—fourteen to seventeen
—the governments of the liberated areas are rapidly opening
trade schools. By the end of 1944 an estimated 140,000 were
receiving technical training in the liberated Ukraine. These
students have been rendering service in the restoration of industrial enterprises while at school. Every few weeks specially picked
crews are sent to some town where help is badly needed in rebuilding. Such crews have been especially successful in reopening power
plants, telephone and telegraph stations.

The Ukraine has also established nineteen vocational schools
for war orphans in eight different cities and towns. Without cost,
the orphans will receive the equivalent of a seven years' academic
course compressed into four. And in addition each student will be
given a thorough grounding in a mechanical trade so that he will
be able to make an immediate contribution to reconstruction upon
graduation. The outstanding pupils will be given an option of
continuing their work at technicums in Kharkov, Kiev and
Stalino which will turn out highly skilled specialists.

Teachers for these schools have come from the Urals, from
Siberia and Central Asia. Many of them are former instructors
who were evacuated, but thousands more have been preparing for
pedagogical duties during the war.

In reconstituting their educational system, Soviet authorities
discovered that practically every age group will need some special
training. Millions of adult Soviet citizens who lived under Nazi
rule in occupied regions now required reorientation. The Germans
not only destroyed schools, burned books and educational equipment but they also came completely prepared to demolish Soviet
ideology and to substitute the ideas of Hitler's New Order.

Special instructors trained for years in Berlin taught the virtues of state-controlled capitalism. They also introduced their racial and political theories. During the occupation, many boys and girls brought up under the Soviets heard about anti-Semitism for the first time. The Germans used this weapon with some effect in the Ukraine. The local Soviet governments, when war was declared, realized that the Jewish population would be subject to very special persecution by the oncoming Wehrmacht. Therefore Jews were among the first to be evacuated to the east. When the Germans arrived they killed or deported nearly all the remaining Jews and then told the Ukrainians, "You have to stay here under hard war conditions while your Jewish 'friends' are all making thousands of rubles in soft jobs in Tashkent." Some of this poison seeped in.

Last December the Central Committee of the party in Moscow recognized the danger of permitting this propaganda to pass unchallenged and took measures to counteract it. Biological documentary films were prepared in Moscow to disprove Nazi racial doctrines. Other documentaries were filmed to show the special contributions and the growing unity of all the peoples of the Soviet Union. The educational campaign undertaken for the liberated areas also stresses this: that the principal factor in Russia's victory over Germany was the *Soviet socialist* structure of the U.S.S.R.

5.

Russians are hoping that their friends in England and especially America will help them in the great task of physical reconstruction. Many of them count on it. If for any reason we don't aid them, they will do the job alone anyhow. It will take them a little longer, every one of them will have to sacrifice a little more, but they will do it.

They will do a better job in the next twenty years than they have in the past twenty years. It's the old story of the fighter never realizing how good or how strong he is until someone really hits him hard and hurts him. The war has made the Soviet people understand their own terrific potential as only Stalin and maybe a few hundred other leaders realized it before.

Self-confidence helps. Unity helps. The future now glitters in the mind's eye of every Russian. So much was done in war, so much more can be done in peace. I recall what the late Alexei Tolstoy said on this subject: "After the war, when we will have healed our wounds, our entire native land will flourish as never before," he predicted. "After the war each fighting man of the Red Army will make a 'stand for life' as he stood to the death, and he will turn all the initiative, wisdom, courage and skill he has gained toward peaceful victories, toward building up the country."

But Tolstoy also stressed that no glitter of peace will ever make the Russians forget what Germany has done. And he believed it is his task, and that of every writer, to record the crimes of Fascism as a warning to posterity.

Book 8

Red Blood Is Russian Blood

1.

THE Soviet Union is emerging from this war changed in many ways. The stresses and strains of the war, the almost mortal blows of the Wehrmacht have had a dialectically hardening and softening effect on different aspects of the Soviet system. How many of these changes will continue to develop and be permanent no foreign observer can rightfully say. Many well-informed Russians do not know themselves.

Most of the changes made during the war had their start in pre-war years. But the conflict has accelerated them: restrictions on divorce and birth control; new stress on the family as a nucleus of Soviet life; the shift from coeducation to separate education for boys and girls; the trend toward individual home ownership and the building of smaller dwelling units; fostering of Russian nationalism—as well as the indigent nationalism of the other republics within the Soviet Union; the rekindling of pan-Slavism as a bulwark against future German aggression; the strengthening of the position and function of the Orthodox Church; and the increase both in the membership and the prestige of the Communist party.

There will be other changes in the Soviet Union. But one thing has not and is not to change: the basis of the Soviet economic system is still the teachings of Marx and Lenin; and Russians, especially the Communists, still believe this system is better than any other.

Foreign observers, writing from the United States, have from time to time discovered a "new capitalism" in the U.S.S.R. The most recent claim of this kind is based on one particular article in a Soviet economic journal and on the tendency of the Russian press to say nice things about capitalism as it exists in England and America.

The economic article which was cited in America was quoted out of context. On the whole it stressed the reaffirmation of Marxist-Leninist-Stalinist practices, claiming "socialism is the highest stage of development of society compared to all preceding systems of production" and "the Soviet structure has saved our fatherland."

Soviet leaders are quick to acknowledge the help of capitalist Allies in aiding Russia. They find no contradiction between praising Allied aid and Allied production and stating that "the Soviet structure" saved Russia. They have even been careful to differentiate between capitalism as it exists in England and America and as it exists in Nazi Germany. Stalin made this point clear early in the war when he said:

> In an attempt to camouflage their reactionary blackguardism, the Hitlerites denounce the domestic Anglo-American regimes as plutocratic. But in England and in the United States there are elementary democratic freedoms and there exist professional labor and employees' unions, labor parties and Parliaments, while in Germany under Hitlerism even these institutions have been suppressed. It suffices to juxtapose these two sets of facts in order to grasp the reactionary essence of the Hitlerite regime and the hypocrisy of the fascist babble about the plutocratic character of the Anglo-American regimes.

Despite this defense of England and America, and despite the fact that the Soviet press has restrained itself from attacking the capitalist "system" as such, there has been no fundamental shift in Russian economic thinking. During the war period they have frankly used every type of production incentive imaginable with one exception: they have not allowed some people to make a profit from the labor of other people.

Although it has been stated and printed often, Americans are still surprised to discover that Russians can own their own homes and everything in them. They can own their own cars, cows, pigs, chickens and gardens. Furthermore they can sell such belongings or will them to relatives when they die.

Strictly private businesses are permitted, too, if an individual handles the entire operation himself. For example, many people make and sell pottery, hats, shoes, jewelry and handicrafts. But no matter how successful, a private business cannot be "expanded" so that an individual makes a profit on someone else's labor. The individual proprietor might convince the state to finance a larger enterprise, and in such cases the originator usually remains as director or manager.

2.

There is a growing feeling in Moscow that the value of the socialist system as such in winning Russia's war against Germany must be emphasized. Admittedly, the exigencies of the invasion and the all-out effort to beat the Nazis resulted in a slackening of Marxist study and concomitantly in Marxist internal propaganda. More important things had to be learned—how to survive, how to kill, how to make a hand grenade.

Soviet authorities are perfectly aware of this slackness. The party press has recently been nagging about it. Responsible party functionaries have been reminded that political debates and the self-study of Marxism must be promoted among the workers. One editorial categorically stated that the successful outcome of the war as well as the solution of peacetime problems depended upon the thorough Marxist education of party members and the entire Soviet intelligentsia.

Several times last year Andrei Vishinsky, First Vice-Commissar of Foreign Affairs, and a member of the Academy of Sciences by virtue of his pre-eminence as a jurist, lectured in Moscow on the "Soviet State in the Great Patriotic War." Excerpts from this long three-hour analysis appeared in the newspapers and it was later published in booklet form. The central theme was that Soviet successes in the war are traceable directly to the historical correctness of Marx, Engels, Lenin and, of course, Stalin. In fact the first part of the speech makes special references to Stalin's contributions to Soviet thought.

On the basis of theoretical prerequisites and practical experience [Vishinsky said], Comrade Stalin built up laws of socialist construction, struggle and labor. As an instance I will mention "The Law of an Offensive," formulated by Comrade Stalin in 1930 in his reply to "Comrade Collective Farmers" which reads: "An offensive without consolidation of captured positions is doomed to failure. An offensive can only be successful in case people are not only advancing but at the same time fortifying themselves in captured positions, regrouping their forces in relation to conditions prevailing at the moment, and bringing in reserves and rear units. This is necessary in order to be protected against surprises, and to close up breaches in the line which may be caused in every offensive, and thus prepare for a complete rout of the enemy."

The reader will note that although this statement of Stalin's was written in 1930, it is couched completely in military terminology. It is a sharp reminder that the Soviets, since their coming to power, have felt themselves to be constantly waging war in a political and economic sense.

Vishinsky made other interesting points. He claimed that in the Soviet state there are no contradictions between public and private life, between public interests and private interests. "The basis of the Lenin-Stalin theory about government lies in the welding of persuasion and coercion," he said. I saw how clearly this applied in Central Asia, where the Bolsheviks had successfully introduced scientific agriculture and industrialization by methods which were a combination of "persuasion and coercion."

Reasons for the Soviet victory over the Germans, according to Vishinsky, were the strength of the Soviet state, the creative energy of the Soviet people; their high moral and political qualities, their devotion and love for their socialist fatherland; public socialist ownership; friendship of the nations (in the U.S.S.R.) and the invincible unity of the workers and peasants; the determining role of the Communist party as the leading force in the dictatorship of the proletariat.

Being Americans, we are overprone to look for developments in Russia which indicate that the Soviet Union is becoming more like ourselves. And often the Soviets do nothing to discourage our vanity. Objectively, however, I believe the most significant development in the Soviet Union during the war has been the growth and the strengthening of the Communist party.

One of the questions for which I wanted to find an answer in the Soviet Union was: did Russia win *in spite* of the Communist party or *because* of it? It is impossible for anyone but a sentimental romanticist to reach any conclusion but the latter.

The Communist party of the Soviet Union is a well organized, well integrated, highly centralized party. When Hitler struck, it was the cement which held together all the bricks in Stalin's fortress. A message tapped at the top of the building was felt in every nook and corner and conversely a frantic plea in the cellar echoed almost immediately to the top. The party was everywhere, reaching into the depths of the Belorussian forests to organized guerrillas, into Siberian factories to step up the production, onto the collective farms, into the press, the theater, the radio, the Army. What was true to a lesser extent in the smaller countries outside of the Soviet Union was true inside of it: the Communists had the leadership, the program and above all, the means. When slogans were needed, they had them by the pamphletful. When a song was needed to improve morale, they had the songs—and stirring ones, too. When a plant urgently required a high-priority building material, the party channel was the quickest way around wartime red tape. The party recruited, trained, propagandized. Every day it spoke to millions in *Pravda*; it spoke through the political advisers in the Army and Navy; it spoke through the underground, through trained members who remained behind when the Germans moved in; it cemented the fortress.

The Communist party during the war years has found and developed new, young leadership. Where the new leaders did not come directly from party ranks, they were invited to join. The generals of the Red Army are almost 100 per cent party members. In fact, no one is promoted to this rank unless his "political level" is passed upon by Alexander Shcherbakov, chief of the Red Army's political department.

Through the huge Army the party, which was always stronger in urban areas, has recruited millions of peasant youths. Millions more have become Komsomols. Once a party candidate required three witnesses who had been members for eleven years; now one sponsor, who has been a member only one year, can vouch for a recruit. Prewar party membership was 3,400,000, Komsomol membership, about 7,000,000. A responsible government official told me that "party membership may be considered to have almost doubled, Komsomol membership to have more than doubled since the war."

In connection with the current campaign to identify the country's military and production successes with the Soviet form of government and the Communist party, it should be noted that many of the old Bolsheviks have been awarded high military ranks. Commissars have an honorary rank equivalent to that of a marshal, and many of them wear impressive uniforms. Nearly all have been awarded war medals and orders.

The new Communists know about flying Airacobras or welding tanks, about farm prices and fertilizer, about writing symphonies and inspirational editorials, about planning reconstruction and running hospital clinics. Their present training contains no more orientation toward world revolution than an American G.I. receives in officers' candidate school.

Of course they do learn to respect the old Bolsheviks and they read their old revolutionary pledges and their old speeches. But the basis of their respect for the old Bolsheviks can best be expressed in the words of Foreign Trade Commissar Mikoyan, who is one himself: "One respects the old Bolsheviks not because they are old but because they never grow any older."

In Soviet schools there have been revisions of some Marxist tenets. But the revisions are in the letter of the word and not in the word. The trend is to regard Marxism not as a fixed and closed body of dogma, but as a dynamic system capable of development and expansion. The rigid, pedantic attitude of the convert to a "faith" is gone in Russian economic theory. "The science of Marx and Lenin does not and cannot stand still. It grows on the foundations of general historical experience. Its various theses and statements change, conforming to new historical situations and conditions," stated the authoritative Soviet magazine *Bolshevik* in a recent issue.

All this does not mean that the Communist party no longer considers itself a revolutionary force. "We are no longer the revolutionary center of a world revolution," a new party member explained to me. "But we are making revolution by example and we will continue to do so." He gives as an illustration of how this operates the "movement" in Yugoslavia where Tito's followers were inspired by the example of the Red Army and not by the doctrines of Marx or Engels.

Through the efforts of the party Russia has achieved a remarkable degree of social and racial equality and hopes to attain much in economic democracy. Whether or not the party has become sufficiently strong so that it is willing to foster political self-expression I do not know. But with such widely divergent groups entering the ranks during the war one of the results may be a slow liberalizing of inner party debate and discussion.

Anyone who has seen the party functioning in wartime Russia cannot hold with the sentimental notion that this is a triumph of "Russia"—vast, rich, overflowing with masses of people—and not per se a triumph of the Soviet Union, i.e., the Soviet system. Without its dictatorship, without the Communists (or their counterpart) in the leading role, without singleness of thought and purpose, Russia could never have achieved the truly amazing industrial progress of the two decades between wars.

In the peace that follows there will be no "withering away" of the state. There will be work to do for the dictatorship. Party leaders view the coming decade with its giant task of rehabilitation as a period of crisis as vital to Russia's security and Russia's future as the two Five-Year Plans. There will be no freedom of speech for those who advocate any change of basic concepts. And there will be no freedom of religion for those who use the church as a weapon against the state or party.

3.

For the past four or five years the Soviet government has been extremely concerned about the question of religion, not only as it affected the state and its citizens internally but also as it reacted on the Soviet Union's relations abroad. Over the years there had been a gradual *rapprochement* between the government and the Russian Orthodox Church. The government began to realize that the church was no longer a menace; it had no property; it had no foreign commitments; it had not only ceased inveighing against socialism, it had, in fact, preached against wealth and exploitation and attacked Fascism. Party oracles were ceasing to stress Marx's "religion is the opium of the people" and were placing fresh emphasis on the same man's, "It is not religion that creates man but man who creates religion." In Metropolitan Sergei of Moscow, the head of all the Orthodox believers, the state quite literally saw a man who had "created" a religion which potentially could help the state. When he was made acting Patriarch in 1925 he had proclaimed that the main function of the church is the salvation of souls and not politics.

The 1936 Constitution guaranteed "freedom of religious worship and freedom of anti-religious propaganda," and United States Ambassador Joseph Davies was moved to write, "Christianity could be superimposed on Communism without doing violence to either." In a census soon after (1937) it was discovered that two-thirds of Russia's peasants and one-third of the city population still held frank religious beliefs. As the Soviet Union prepared for possible war, Soviet leaders realized that Hitler intended to pose as a "defender of Christianity" against Bolshevism. At government expense he had restored the Orthodox Church in Berlin and in nineteen other German cities. Dissident Ukrainian and White Russian émigré priests were highly paid to establish training centers for new clergymen who would go into the Ukraine hand and hand with the Wehrmacht and bring the word of Hitler and the word of God in that (new) order.

When Russia was attacked, the Orthodox Church and its hierarchy fervently supported Stalin, the Soviet state, and the Red Army. Sergei sent a holy call ringing throughout the land: "Our country is in peril and calls to us: All into the ranks! All rise in defense of our native land, of her historic sanctuaries, of her independence and freedom from the alien yoke! Shame on all those, whoever they may be, who remain indifferent to this call!"

The state responded by closing antireligious museums and halting antireligious propaganda (although anyone was theoretically free to indulge in it); the journals *Bezbozhnik* ("Atheist") and *Antireligioznik* ("Antireligious") were suspended due to the paper shortage; the Society of the Militant Godless, which once claimed 5,500,000 members, was disbanded. Incidentally, in 1941 the Soviet calendar with its five-day week was dropped, and the standard seven-day week resumed—with Sunday the universal "free day." This pleased the church, and increased attendance.

On November 7, 1942, *Pravda* published this telegram from Sergei to Stalin: ON THE DAY OF THE 25TH ANNIVERSARY OF THE SOVIET REPUBLIC, IN THE NAME OF THE CLERGY AND BELIEVERS OF THE RUSSIAN ORTHODOX CHURCH, FAITHFUL SONS OF OUR COUNTRY, I HEARTILY AND WITH PRAYER GREET YOU PERSONALLY AS THE LEADER APPOINTED BY GOD OF OUR MILITARY AND CULTURAL FORCES. . . . LET GOD BLESS WITH SUCCESS, AND WITH GLORY YOUR GREAT DEEDS FOR THE SAKE OF OUR COUNTRY.

The church collected millions of rubles for the Red Army, excommunicated clergy who collaborated with the German invaders, and asked true believers in the Rumanian Army not to fight against their Russian "brothers in religion."

On September 4, 1943, a few days after Sergei returned from Ulyanovsk where he had been evacuated, he went to the Kremlin for his first audience with Stalin. Accompanied by Metropolitan Alexei of Leningrad and Metropolitan Nikolai of Kiev, Sergei talked with the Marshal and Molotov for two hours. Sergei informed Stalin "that in the leading circles of the Russian Orthodox Church there is a wish to call in the near future a *sobor* of bishops for the electing of a Patriarch of Moscow and All Russia and the formation by the Patriarchhood of a Holy Synod." Stalin's attitude was sympathetic and he declared there would be "no objection on the part of the government."

The bishops met and elected Sergei as Patriarch. This seventy-seven-year-old scholar died in May, 1944, but in his brief months as recognized ruler of the church much was done to solidify its position. The Patriarchate had moved into the former German Embassy on Chisty Street in time for the Moscow visit of the Archbishop of York; the latter was greatly impressed by the church's emergence and last spring publicly declared that the Russian church today enjoys a freedom it has not had for centuries. The Patriarchate began printing a monthly magazine, a holy candle factory was started, a religious seminary was opened for the training of clergy, Soviet President Kalinin urged that nobody make fun of Red Army men who wore religious medals, and Metropolitan Nikolai was appointed a member of the State Atrocities Commission, the first clergyman to receive a government post under the Soviets.

To deal with the newly created church-state relationship, the Soviet government appointed a Council for the Affairs of the Russian Orthodox Church headed by Georgi Karpov. Several months later another council, one for the affairs of religious creeds, was appointed to function as a liaison between the government and the Roman Catholic, Greek Catholic, Mohammedan, Jewish, Evangelical and other non-Orthodox religious groups.

4.

Before Christmas, 1944 (the Orthodox Church uses the old Gregorian calendar which is thirteen days later than ours) I was cordially received at the Patriarchate. It was evident that Sergei and Alexei and Nikolai, his intimate aides, were very pleased with developments; they believed that the new government attitude toward religion was permanent and not a wartime measure, and that religion would have a rebirth in the Soviet Union. In 1941, they estimated, the Orthodoxy had slightly more than four thousand churches open. Counting those reopened in the liberated areas, the total number in operation was over five thousand by 1944, despite the war. They told me that attendance had increased and contributions—always an index of a cause's popularity—had increased many times.

The old Patriarch was very obliging. I had an assignment to do a story about him for *Time*. I was expected to describe the ritual enacted when Sergei officiated at a Christmas mass, but I discovered that he was not expecting to serve before my deadline. I telephoned his office and explained my predicament to Father Kolchitsky, one of his assistants.

"When must you attend this mass?" asked the Father.

"This coming Sunday."

"I cannot say. The Patriarch is not very well. Call back in two hours, please."

Two hours later it was arranged that the Patriarch would take part in a special high mass the following Sunday. For almost three hours I stood and shivered through an elaborate service—so close to the Patriarch that when I left, my army trenchcoat smelled of holy incense. The Bogoslovensky Cathedral was packed, much to my surprise. There were whole families in the congregation, including many well-dressed men and several Red Army soldiers. There were the very young as well as the very old.

The tolerance being shown the church is one example of the "loosening up" process which I believe will take place in the Soviet Union once they have a feeling of security. They feel secure about the Orthodox Church; they feel sure it can never be used again as an instrument of tyranny and oppression.

Cathedrals are being repaired, Bibles are being printed, and most extraordinary of all, Georgi Karpov went on record that there could be religious instruction for the young—a practice hitherto completely foreign to the Soviet system. Karpov said that "parents may educate children themselves in the privacy of their homes or may send their children to the homes of priests for such education." The question of Sunday schools does not arise since there was no such practice at any time in the Orthodox Church.

When I repeated Karpov's remarks to Natasha Denisov, who is an atheist but not a party member, she moaned, "When we do things here we certainly do them. Do you suppose in five years from now my son Petya will *have to 'go* to church?" She didn't really mean it, but the point she made was worth making.

One day last August I walked out to Ostrovsky Street to call on Ivan Vasilevich Poliansky, chairman of the council on non-Orthodox creeds. He and Karpov are now installed in a fashionable beige-colored stone building next to the Foreign Office guesthouse; it is the former home of the dancer, Isadora Duncan. Poliansky is forty-seven and a native of Moscow. Under the Tsar he attended church and "was sometimes interested in religion." His career has been in the field of adult education.

Poliansky outlined the duties of his council: to postulate all future laws and decrees connected with the non-Orthodox churches; to see that existing laws and decrees are carried out and when necessary to take measures guaranteeing the interests of the government or the believers as the case may be—i.e., the council might intervene to correct abuses if a church claimed it was over-taxed; to make recommendations to the Council of Peoples' Commissars on any requests from leaders of the faiths; i.e., obtaining building materials for churches, textbooks, or permission to open new churches or theological schools.

I told Mr. Poliansky that from my observations the Orthodox Church seemed to be in a favored position under the new setup. Would the Orthodox Church continue to benefit by favoritism? He replied, "In the Soviet Union all religions are equal. There is no single superior religion. The government's position in respect to them all is the same." He emphasized that the decree of July 1, 1944, establishing the councils in no way abrogated the fundamental law of January 23, 1918, providing for the separation of church from state.

Poliansky said that any group of twenty people could apply to have a church opened for them. He also cited the fact that the Gregorian Armenians had been granted permission to open theological schools, and the Mussulmans (Mohammedans) wished to start madrasahs in Uzbekestan for training mullahs. He thought this would be approved.

At this point I asked him whether all creeds, specifically the Roman Catholics and the Jews, could open theological schools in

Russia He answered quickly, "If any of them want to have schools there will be no barriers for them."

To date there are many preliminary barriers to be hurdled before the Soviets and the Roman Catholics can even get around to discussing the subject of schools. Relatively, there are not many Catholics in the Soviet Union. Father Leopold Braun, resident priest in Moscow—and the only one for over a decade—estimates a possible ten million Soviet Catholics, while a Russian source says about seven million. Shortly after I interviewed Poliansky he refused to discuss church matters with Father Braun, stating that his government did not recognize Braun as the Vatican's Apostolic Delegate but only as pastor of the Church of St. Louis in Moscow.

The chief cause of the friction between the Soviets and the Roman Catholic church has little to do with particular Communist animosity toward that faith as a religious belief. The trouble is political. The Vatican has been anathema to the Communists for twenty-five years (and vice versa). Stalin knows from his own embassies' reports and from conversations with foreign diplomats, that a large body of Catholic opinion in western Europe, the United States and especially South America has been anti-Soviet partly because of the Vatican's stand. Stalin, who realizes "that facts are hard things," understands that there must eventually be an agreement or at least a truce between the Soviets and the Vatican before there can be peace and security in the world.

Father Stanislaus Orlemanski, the Polish-American priest from Springfield, Massachusetts, flew to Moscow "as a private citizen" to visit Polish troops in Russia last spring. Once there he was surprised to receive an invitation to talk to Stalin. They discussed many questions, including religion, and the priest found Stalin making some very reassuring statements about Catholicism and the Vatican. He subsequently mentioned this to some American correspondents in Moscow, who told him he had better get it on paper. So Orlemanski, the second time he saw Stalin, remarked, "All that you said is marvelous. But there is one trouble. Some people in my country, if I dare say so, sometimes do not believe you. So what shall I do?"

Orlemanski appeared so genuinely distressed that Stalin could not become angry. He asked the priest, "Why are there some people in your country who do not believe me? Have I ever broken my word? If so, I shall not mind if you give me but one instance."

The priest protested that he couldn't think of a single such example. "But that's the way some people think, anyhow. . . ."

The upshot was that Stalin agreed to put on paper the answers to any questions which Orlemanski wished to have on the record. The priest dug out two strong ones which the correspondents had helped him to concoct.

The first: "Do you think it admissible for the Soviet government to pursue a policy of persecution and coercion with regard to the Catholic church?"

Stalin wrote: "As an advocate of the freedom of conscience and that of worship I consider such a policy to be inadmissible and precluded."

The second: "Do you think that co-operation with the Holy Father, Pope Pius, in the matter of struggle against the coercion and persecution of the Catholic church is possible?"

Stalin wrote: "I think it is possible."

Soon afterward, as concrete evidence that Stalin meant business, Polish children in Russia were permitted to have Roman Catholic education from their own priests (formerly in detention camps). Bibles and prayer books were printed at state expense, and Catholic chaplains were attached to General Berling's Polish Army Corps.

In a clumsy way, the Kremlin believed this was an overture to the Vatican to explore further possibilities of peace between them. Evidently the overture was coldly received. Since then the Soviet press has been sharpening the pitch of its screams against the Vatican—as a proponent of a soft peace for the Germans, as a stanch supporter of Fascist Franco "not to strengthen its internal position in Spain, but for the purpose of foreign policy."

It is, therefore, in the realm of foreign policy where Moscow and Rome have their chief conflict. The Soviets believe that these matters must be settled before the Roman Catholic church can get back on an equal footing with other creeds in Russia. They believe, rightly or wrongly, that the Vatican is a threat to future Russian security. And security is the measuring rod for judging friends and enemies even in the realm of religion.

In the realm of foreign policy the Soviets are finding it much easier to work with the Russian church. Church propaganda helped win support for the Red Army in Rumania. Invitations were sent to patriarchs, metropolitans, bishops in the Balkans, the Near and Middle East to attend the Orthodox congress held in Moscow early in 1945 to name Metropolitan Alexei as successor to Sergei. The warmest and most cordial kind of relationship is being fostered between the Holy Synod in Moscow and "brothers in religion" in Constantinople, Jerusalem, Antioch, Egypt and elsewhere.

The government's new orientation toward the Moslems is also gaining friends for the Soviet Union, especially in the Middle East. The mufti, Abdul Rahman Ibn Sheikh Zinulla Rassuli, spiritual head of Soviet Moslems, has been active in his support of the war against Hitler. His religion still has roots in parts of Central Asia and the Caucasus. The Soviets are now allowing more mosques to be reopened in these areas, and the state has even appropriated funds to restore historic mosques in Samarkand and Bukhara. Another indication of the new attitude is that this year for the first time since the Bolsheviks took power, Soviet Moslems not only have been granted exit visas but also aided with transport so they could make the pilgrimage to Mecca.

Paradoxically, some of the factors which increased the internal security of the Soviet state and led to more religious tolerance may also militate against a really widespread revival of religion in Russia. By this I do not suggest that the government has any notion of restricting freedom of religion in the future. But the upheaval caused by the war, the rebirth of nationalism, the growth of the armed forces and the party, have given more Russian citizens new faiths. Russian Communists argue that the rich ritual of the church is compensated for by more movies, theaters, ballets. They claim that instead of the inspiration of Orthodox chants, there are patriotic songs. Instead of the fatherly guidance of prelates, there are Red Army political advisers, schoolteachers, party functionaries. Incidentally, a U.S. Army officer stationed at our air base in the Ukraine told me the Russians were amazed that our chaplain was a good guy who liked to play baseball and arrange entertainment and was not always spouting religion. Similarly, the Americans discovered the Red Army "political advisers" performing about the same kind of work as our chaplains—without the spiritual undertone, and with educational overtones. The spread of science, of education, has removed much of the mystical lure of the church. Instead of God at the front, as the Red Army doctor said to me on the steamer coming across the Caspian, "there is Stalin and science." Certainly the opinions expressed on that ship would not indicate a wide desire for religious expression.

For those who feel the need of spiritual communion there will be a place for religion in the Russia which emerges from the war. In fact, there already is a boom in church weddings as a result of the new decrees on the family, marriage and divorce published last summer. Marriage in Russia is no longer a private affair; the state is very much concerned with making nuptials solemn and binding, and one way of doing that is to take the ceremony out of the "get-your-driver's-license-here" routine and exalting it to the status of a ritual.

5.

At first glance, those who look to Moscow for the last word in "progressivism" may be disturbed by developments in Soviet education. Progressive pedagogues in most countries have been agreed for many years that coeducation is a superior system to separate education. On July 16, 1943, the Soviet government dropped coeducation in the schools of large cities and industrial centers. Russian educators explain the move this way:

In tsarist Russia women did not enjoy equal rights with men; usually they tended home and family. Working-class women could have "careers" in factories, as domestics, or as hired hands on large estates. Relatively few had an opportunity to learn reading and writing; even those well off by birth or financial position found it difficult to enter universities. For the average Russian woman in those days the acme of educational opportunity was the local parish school or a seminary, and their standards were not strict enough to qualify graduates for advance studies. For non-Russian subjects, for the Uzbeks, Tadzhiks and others, illiteracy was the general rule.

Before the Revolution those who championed equal political and economic rights for women also advocated a coeducational system; those who fought equal rights for women opposed coeducation. By the decree of May 1918 the Soviets established the principle of educational equality enabling girls to enter every elementary and high school in the country. The principle was subsequently backed up by a law requiring universal education and by the continuous construction of new schools and the training of new teachers. In the decades of Soviet power women have been encouraged to utilize their equal opportunity. They have flocked to the technical schools and universities, they have become skilled workers, doctors, lawyers, engineers, teachers, scientists. By 1926 women comprised 13 per cent of the Communist party's membership, and by 1941 over 30 per cent. In the last prewar elections to the Supreme Soviet, almost 17 per cent of the delegates chosen were feminine—a proportion far greater than that of any similar national congress.

Discussing the educational changes, a member of the Russian Board of Education employed these statistics to prove that the idea of sex equality is accepted in the U.S.S.R. "Thus," she concluded, "the main problem which the introduction of a coeducational system was intended to solve—realization of the equality of sexes—has been solved. But the question of the value of that system is far from being settled."

Soviet educators claim that boys and girls have different rates of intellectual and physical development at different ages. Girls develop more rapidly in the eleven to thirteen period and boys in the fourteen- to seventeen-year-old stage. After a year of the experiment, experts reported "a higher level of military and physical training, a better order of school life and better discipline" as well as better classroom work. There is no doubt that the immediate reason for the switch to separate education grew out of wartime practices. While upper-class boys were receiving three and four hours of military training per week, girls were taught rudiments of civilian defense and then trained for emergency work in the fields of sanitation, nursing and communications.

In one Moscow girls' school which I investigated, the regular curriculum had not been curtailed. But the girls had been given additional courses in housekeeping, pedagogics, and psychology. An hour each week was set aside for lectures on discipline, morals and politeness. The girls were encouraged to form after-school sewing circles and to make their classrooms more beautiful and "dainty." In a corresponding school for boys, new courses had been added in carpentry, metal work and electricity so that on graduation the students could more quickly fill technical jobs if they showed an aptitude.

The Russians, while they scoff slightly at the new marriage and divorce laws, are not objecting to the separation of sexes in schools. Boys and girls still mix freely at social gatherings. Most clubs and the omnipresent political discussion groups (including the Komsomols) are coeducational. Sex relations between young people in the Soviet Union are still healthy and natural; even the tensions of war have not seduced Russian youths to the level of "pin-ups."

But it cannot be denied that the changes in education dovetail neatly with the new Soviet stress on the sanctity of home and family. *Izvestia* in a front-page editorial advised:

Girls' schools must bring into being girls who are equipped for useful work and useful social activity and who have access to any profession. But at the same time the schools must make these girls good members of the family, loving and capable mothers and rearers of children. While girls' schools must give the same profound and many-sided scientific training as the boys' schools, they must also develop in the girls femininity, modesty and the feeling of the great worthiness and honor of women. They must teach girls how to think and how to work with books; and at the same time they must give them a whole set of practical habits which are necessary in life and in the family.

When the Soviets adopt something new they really go at it with overweening zeal. In time perhaps they will drop the frills. But, for example, they are now officially recommending that pupils in girls' schools must be tidy and "comb their hair straight and smooth and wear braids in the back." Girls with torn dresses will not be admitted to class until they have repaired the damage.

Last summer at a conference of high school principals in Moscow, Russian Commissar of Education Potemkin delivered the final report. In it he summed up the results of the first year of separate schools. He found them excellent for the most part. "But," he warned, with a smile, "we have on occasion gone too far, comrades. I find in some districts that when Tolstoy's *War and Peace* was studied, teachers read the parts about war only to the boys and the parts about peace only to the girls."

I did meet some Russian girls who felt that the "developments" (Russians dislike to use the word "changes" in reference to new laws or decrees) of the past years indicated a restricted future for them. They pointed out that the party, which is the barometer of Soviet life, had not promoted many women to prominent positions. They feared that their government was being influenced by England and America. "Once we all thought we could become foreign representatives or ambassadors like Madame Kollantai. But now they are sending out only men—and some of them not as talented as women," girl students of international affairs at Moscow University told me.

They hope that after the war it will "develop" differently, but they are not too certain. One thing is certain. Soviet women will never become mere household drudges. "A woman who confines herself purely to domestic life deteriorates mentally as well as in other ways," said Olga Mishakova. Mishakova is the responsible secretary of the Komsomols—an attractive, intelligent, smartly dressed woman in her thirties. Her career is one answer to fears that Russian women are being forced into a permanent back seat. Continuing on the subject of the household drudge. Mishakova said, "She is in danger of becoming an idler and a gossip and of frittering away her time and energies on dull hobbies and useless practices. A woman must combine socially creative work with family life and she must be well prepared for both. We will do all that we can to lift the burden of domestic duties from women's shoulders. We may find it necessary to reduce her hours of outside work to six or even four hours a day. But not for one moment do we intend to draw her away from a career."

6.

If one wants to find revolution in Russia today the best place to look for it is in the hospitals, clinics, experimental laboratories, and field stations where Soviet scientists are smashing atoms, breaking traditions and turning accepted formulas upside down.

I had a discussion on the subject of the great flowering of Soviet science* one afternoon last summer at a reception for the noted physicist, Peter Kapitza. He had been awarded the Franklin Institute Medal for his most recent discoveries. Kapitza has produced the world's strongest magnetic field and lowest temperatures in his studies of the electrical properties of matter. The party was attended by leading scientists many of whom spoke English. After the food and a few rounds of the usual drinks they were not unwilling to talk. Kapitza, who is about fifty, has soft smooth-shaven skin and eyes like very blue marbles. He had a yen to see some American movies, and almost immediately after the presentation he disappeared while they showed him the latest Deanna Durbin songfest in the adjacent auditorium.

There was one sixty-year-old chemistry professor with a chest-length gray beard, who undertook to deliver me a lecture on why Soviet science was making such strides even during wartime. "Do you know that in 1944 my government is spending thirteen billion rubles (about $2,600,000,000) on scientific research institutes and an additional forty-four billion ($8,800,000,000) on the training of scientific specialists at universities and technical schools?"

I didn't know that (I later checked the figures and found them

* Even before the 1917 Revolution, Russia had a distinguished tradition of individual scientific achievement.

correct) and I couldn't give him any idea how much was spent in the U.S.A. I said that science was not primarily a government problem.

"Our Soviet state can afford to pay for abundance in science. In your system, if you will forgive me, private industry will often pay more to restrict a scientific advance, even to hold it back. You need not bother to deny this for I have been abroad. Also I was a chemist in Russia before 1917. Today in Soviet Russia a wonderful new invention or an amazing technological improvement— they cannot upset a capitalist's investments. We welcome them with banners, with hallelujahs. The Soviet state invests only for its people. If something new and incredible is found that makes work easier, that improves a product? . . . We welcome it." He smiled and stroked his beard thoughtfully. "Perhaps I would be dogmatic to say that in my country science is the servant of the people. And in your country? You have done outstanding things, technically. But I cannot say that there science is always the servant of the people. Is it possible for you to say so?"

We argued. But the professor didn't give an inch of ground. "I should warn you, my friend, that I have been preparing a paper on the superiority of Soviet science. Therefore, I am perhaps better prepared in advance for this discussion than you."

In the next hour or so I probably heard most of that paper translated into highly stylized English. When Kapitza had seen Deanna Durbin he wanted something else, and they dug up another American movie. The chemistry professor lectured on. There is in the U.S.S.R., he said, a constant interchange of information between all research laboratories, universities and experimental field stations. Nothing was withheld. He claimed that science in America was so highly competitive that a chemist in New York could not share the latest findings of a California chemist who was working in the same field.

Somehow I managed to get in, "That certainly isn't true in wartime. Every chemist worth his salt is helping."

He just said, "And after the war?" Again he emphasized what a "satisfying of the soul" it was for a man to have his research immediately utilized. He did not feel that such was the case in other countries.

In peacetime the Soviets were almost as worked up about science and scientists as they have been in recent years about the war and the Red Army men. Science is still something glamorous and exciting and profitable. It is still one of the nation's major goals;

girls and boys yearn for careers as chemists or botanists or geologists. From the earliest grades school children are taught the value and importance of science. Popular science magazines for all ages are more eagerly devoured in Russia than comic books or movie fan magazines are in the United States.

Even in wartime, new achievements in any scientific field (and Russians use the word "scientific" more widely than we do) receive wide publicity. In keeping with the constant effort to identify present-day Russia with the old Russia (in its better aspects), the rich tradition of the nation's inventiveness is frequently recalled in the press. I have read about a Russian who perfected the radio before Marconi and another who perfected the airplane before the Wright brothers. A Russian named Zelinsky invented the first gas mask, and one named Lebedev found out how to make the first synthetic rubber. Russians pioneered in the preparation and use of helium, of blood plasma, of winter lubricants for planes and tanks. These are not fictions of Russian boastfulness. In military science, the Soviets were the first nation to develop and use parachute troops and rocket projectiles. They also claim to have been the initiators of jet-propulsion.

All the stories which appeared in the Moscow press about new findings would fill several volumes. Here are a few samples: Georgi Babat invented an automobile which can receive power from a wire that runs below city streets. The machine itself has no actual contact with this underground wire. The automobile has been tried out on a small scale in Soviet factories and found practicable. It may revolutionize surface conveyances on city streets, eliminating the need for overhead wires or contact conductors.

Dr. Vladimir Begovsky, specialist in pathological physiology, and one of his students, succeeded in restoring life to battlefield casualties who were in a "state of clinical death." Begovsky's system is based on injections near the heart of blood enriched with adrenalin and permeated with oxygen. When the heart begins to respond by beating, more blood is injected and artificial respiration is applied. This is done with a bellows and hose attachment which is introduced into the windpipe of the subject through the mouth.

According to Begovsky, fifty cases of men in a state of clinical death, of death agony, of third-degree shock and asphyxia were treated. Of this number, twelve have completely recovered; three were brought back to life but later died from pneumonia and gas gangrene: twenty-one were restored to life and lived as long as three days, some regaining consciousness; another twelve were partially revived. Only two cases failed to respond at all to the treatment.

The Russians are careful to point out that these cases are far from conclusive.

This front-line attempt at raising the human dead stemmed from experiments which have been carried out for a number of years at the Moscow Institute of Experimental Physiology and Therapy. While in Moscow I saw a movie based on preliminary stages of this work. Blood was drained from a dog. Fifteen minutes after its heart had ceased to beat, blood was pumped back into the lifeless body with a machine called an autojector which served as artificial heart and lungs. Soon the "dead" dog stirred, began to breathe and its heart began to beat. Twelve hours later the same dog was on its feet, fully recovered, barking and wagging its tail.

The autojector, operating on the "bellows" principle, has a "lung" in which blood is supplied with oxygen, a pump that circulates the oxygenated blood through the arteries, another pump that takes the blood back from the veins to the "lung" for more oxygen. The experiment was first performed in 1939, and two of the canine subjects used at that time are still alive and healthy.

The list of fresh Soviet discoveries seemingly never ends: a honey which is impregnated with quinines, sulfonamides and vitamins; a portable movie projector which can be used anywhere and requires no electric outlet since the electrical energy is generated manually; a radical and effective new technique for feeding patients with abdominal wounds; a cotton which can be grown in colors—red, green or black; a hybrid mountain sheep that bears fine fleece wool, and a new formula for steel which may make it *transparent* but just as strong.

They are also in the process of checking startling new findings which may give the world effective weapons against cancer, tuberculosis, encephalitis and the common enemy, grippe. At the moment all the scientists are closely integrating their work with the war and with rehabilitation. Such an abstract physicist as Peter Kapitza won a Stalin prize in 1942 for his practical analysis "On Developing the Economy of the Urals in Wartime."

I have met and talked with three very great Soviet scientists who are working toward these goals: to abolish famine, to increase the span of life, to alleviate one of the greatest horrors of war. I refer to Nikolai Tsitsin, Alexander Bogomolets and Anatole Frumkin.

Nikolai Tsitsin looks more like one's conception of a revolutionist than a scientist. He is a small, dark man with a mop of unruly black hair, a black mustache and glittering black eyes which spark when he talks about his experiments. Only forty-seven, he is one of the youngest members of the Academy of Science.

Tsitsin has his own institute at a village called Nemchinovka, which is about a forty-minute ride from Moscow on the suburban train. His "Institute of Grain Economics for Non-Fertile Soil" turned out to be the general heading for a collective which included special farmland, hothouses, laboratories, offices and some students. The government thinks so highly of Tsitsin and his institute that they give him a yearly appropriation of fifteen million dollars for research.

Last summer Tsitsin was about ready to exhibit a bumper crop of agricultural miracles. He had produced a new annual wheat crop of 144 bushels per acre which quadrupled the best previous yield for the Moscow latitude. He was growing fruit on vegetable vines and vegetables on trees. (I saw some large lush tomatoes grafted on a South American fruit tree called "tsfamalda.") He had just gotten the first live seeds from many attempts to cross wheat and rye with a wild desert plant (elymus giganteus) which might make it possible to raise these grains on almost any kind of soil. This, Tsitsin computed, would open to cultivation 150,000,000 acres of hitherto untillable Soviet land.

The greatest miracle had been occupying his attention for fifteen years, and last summer Tsitsin was finally close to pronouncing it performed. For fifteen years he has worked toward a perfect wheat: one which would come up year after year without reseeding, resist drought and disease, survive freezing winters, wind and rain, and when ripe not shell except in a threshing machine—and yield at least twenty-five bushels per acre per crop.

The magic number at Nemchinovka is 34,085. That is the number of the perennial which meets most of the specifications. This strain, a cross between wheat and couch grass, grows summer or winter, is drought- and disease-resistant, pollenizes itself (bisexual), thrives even in salty soil (producing salty wheat) and has a gluten content of sixty per cent, which is equal to that of the best U. S. or Soviet annual wheats. Experimental plantings have thus far yielded two crops per year, totaling about sixty-eight bushels an acre.

Tsitsin is not satisfied with 34,085. It has some serious flaws: the grain it bears is wrinkled and hard to mill, and the strain is not as frost-resistant as Tsitsin would like it to be for the vast barren stretches of Siberia which require cultivation.

It may be many years before the perfect perennial wheat is ready for large-scale commercial purposes, but when it is fully developed it will have revolutionary effects on agriculture throughout the world. Not only will it make tremendous land areas both habitable and profitable—thereby "abolishing famine," but it will also cut down the labor force needed in wheat fields by at least 50 per cent.

For the immediate present, Tsitsin is concentrating on the possibility of crossing wheat or some other glutenous grain with rye, thus producing a super-grain which would revolutionize the world's bread and cereal economy. Rye is cheaper and easier to raise than wheat; it can get by on inferior soil and with poorer fertilizer and can be grown further north even in the sourest of soils. Prewar U.S.S.R. produced about 60 per cent of the world's rye, which may explain Tsitsin's concentration on raising that grain's glutenous content. If he achieves the goal rye could easily crowd wheat from the bread market and become the No. 1 cereal.

"The battle between wheat and rye in my laboratory is one of the most momentous in the world," Tsitsin told me.

I asked him what the prospects were for this super-grain, and how far along he was on the fruit-vegetable grafts. He then invited me to inspect the samples for myself and said, "In science nothing is more futile than prophecy. Science means work and work which is often without the least results."

7.

Alexander Bogomolets, President of the Ukrainian Academy of Sciences, member of the Supreme Soviet, is more than six feet tall, thin and supple like a birch tree, with close-cropped, bristly silver-white hair. Last year he was awarded the rank of Hero of Socialist Labor (home-front equivalent of Hero of the Soviet Union title for military men) and the Order of Lenin "for outstanding accomplishments in the field of science, for creation of the most valuable prescription for healing wounds and fractured bones."

Bogomolets has had a remarkable life. He was born on May 12, 1881, while his mother was in a solitary confinement cell of the

Lukanovskaya Prison in Kiev. She was then awaiting the death penalty for revolutionary activities. Shortly after her child was born the mother's sentence was commuted to life in a Siberian prison. Alexander's father, a liberal doctor who was prominent in the South Russia Workers Union, had been exiled for ten years. Bogomolets was raised by his grandfather in Kiev. When he was almost ten, his father returned and took him to Siberia so they could be near his mother. Young Alexander saw great suffering on this trip and in Siberia; he determined to dedicate his life to a fight against violence, brutality and ignorance.

When he came back from Siberia he entered school in Kiev. He was far ahead of his classes in every subject. He graduated with the gold medal, attended Odessa University and then took his medical degree at Novorossisk University in 1906. He was sent to the Sorbonne in Paris to prepare for a professorship in biochemistry. Both before and after the Revolution Bogomolets held important posts at various Russian Universities. In February, 1925, he became a professor at the Second Moscow State University. Later he returned to Kiev and became active in the Ukrainian government.

For nineteen years Bogomolets has been working on what he calls "anti-reticular-cytotoxic serum" (U.S. doctors abbreviated it to ACS) which hastens wound healing, mends broken bones speedily, increases the body's defenses against infection and cancer, and may ultimately hold the key to longevity. "Although," Bogomolets says in his careful, slow speech, "the age of a hundred and fifty is probably the limit at the present stage of the evolution of the human organism." His book on that subject called *The Prolongation of Life* was printed in millions of copies before the war, and he still hopes that it will be translated and printed in America.

The ACS serum is not new in Russia. Professor Elie Mechnikov was experimenting on a similar preparation back in 1900. ACS is made by injecting horses with cells from the spleen and bone marrow of human corpses, usually healthy young people who died by accident. The serum is then derived from the horses' blood.

In treating patients, Bogomolets uses a tiny dose ("measured by the hundredth part of a cubic centimeter") injected into the patient's vein or under the skin. Three such doses every three days until twelve are given comprise a full "course." The course may be given again without harm; one of the professor's cancer patients gets three courses a year.

Controlled experiments on a large scale in Soviet military hospitals show that with ACS treatment a wound which ordinarily takes six months to heal takes only one month. This is not an infallible ratio as it depends to a large degree upon individual constitutions.

There have also been checkable experiments in the application of the serum as a scarlet fever cure for children; it has proven amazingly effective if introduced not later than the third day after the patient has fallen ill.

Bogomolets and his active associates, including his son, Oleg, believe that ACS can also reduce the severity of typhus, prevent the recurrence of cancer after operation, help correct schizophrenia and other insanities by improving the health of nerve fibers, speed recovery from second and third degree burns, frostbite, ulcers, and rheumatism. Bogomolets told me, "Against acute arthritis the serum is a quick and certain cure but only in cases where there is no endocarditis (heart disease) in which instance the application of the serum produces a bad effect."

When the war came ACS, still in the experimental stage, was immediately put to use. Now it is used in most Russian hospitals. *Red Star* has published stories about the men now at the front who would have been legless or armless but for ACS. At a Moscow hospital I talked with wounded men who expect to be fighting again in several weeks, and their doctors told me that such cases would have required several months to heal without ACS.

In 1943 over 3,000,000 doses were used, and last year this was increased many times. The serum does not cost much—less than ten cents a dose—and is now being mass-produced. Bogomolets, who has now returned to his own laboratories in his native Kiev, said, "Our future plans are very extensive. I regard it as our task to use this serum as widely as possible. I personally attach very great significance to it in the fight against the aging of the organism." The professor summed up the action of his serum this way—("for the nonscientist," he said with a smile): It stimulates the connective tissue, speeds up the process of regeneration of the bony tissue and of bone corn.

American and British doctors are interested but still skeptical about the properties of ACS. Meanwhile a very high percentage of Red Army wounded are returning to the front to fight again, and the death rate among wounded in Russian hospitals is only 1.1 per cent.

8.

In Moscow's Botkin Hospital works an animated, sensitive red-headed doctor named Anatole Pavlovich Frumkin. He is forty-eight years old and, as chief urologist of the Red Army, he holds the rank of colonel. Frumkin has big ears, a long nose, bushy red eyebrows and a lot of freckles on his very white skin. He is a pioneer, a revolutionary in an exciting, vital field of medicine.

Almost every foreign correspondent who reaches Moscow visits Botkin Hospital. It is one of the finest in Russia. The rooms are not always well furnished or bright, the enamel of the bedpans is sometimes chipped, and wards are often too crowded. But I doubt if there are many hospitals in the world which can excel it in the fundamental function of all hospitals, new or old—restoring unhealthy human beings to health.

Dr. Frumkin likes American visitors. He has an enormous and deserved pride in his unique work. He likes to explain every detail of every step, and when he feels a translator is not doing him justice, he helps out with a useful smattering of Latin, French, German and even English.

The urologist in this war, Dr. Frumkin explains, has had more to do than ever before. Every step of every battle may be paved with small anti-personnel mines. When they explode at the touch of a soldier's foot, death does not always result. The heart may still beat. But in a great many cases the mine severely injures or destroys a man's reproductive organs.

"I have seen men at the front, carried off the battlefield. They plead for death. They do not want to live. And so," Frumkin said, "my first job is always to convince the wounded that there is hope. Two years ago, three years ago—I had little faith myself. Now I can speak concretely of results. I can show them pictures. I can even let them speak to men who have been restored fully—both mentally and physically."

Frumkin is not the first doctor to graft new male sex organs, but he is the first to apply it widely and he has been more successful than anyone else. His office is covered with plaster models showing the various stages of the graft. When a new patient arrives he is wheeled into this office and Frumkin explains the entire process. He brings in other patients who have recovered or who are recovering. Then he allows the wounded man to select the "model" that pleases him from Frumkin's catalogue of sizes and shapes.

Described in oversimplified terms,* Frumkin makes a new genital organ from the cartilaginous portions of the eighth and ninth ribs. This remains attached to its original location while a tube is formed inside the flap of skin. "It looks like the handle of a suitcase," Frumkin said, indicating one of his patients who was in this first stage of the process. After three or four weeks, the top of the future organ is severed from its original position and transferred to the abdomen.

The entire process takes from six to nine months.. Frumkin showed me patients who were in all the various stages of recovery. It was a wonderful experience to talk to them—men who had been without hope suddenly handed a reprieve.

Alexander Karachevits was typical of the one hundred or more men under Frumkin's care. He was nineteen, a dark-eyed Georgian from Tiflis. He told his story: "I was injured by a mine. We were on the central front. I cannot tell you more. But I lay for six or seven days on the battlefield, wanting to die. I knew at once what had happened. I wanted to kill myself, but my gun was missing. Then they brought me back to the field hospital. I lost consciousness. When I came to—they quickly told me about Colonel Frumkin."

"Did you believe it?"

"Not entirely. Not until they brought me here and I saw the pictures and some of the men. Now I am staying to tell others. Soon I will go to the front to lecture about it to the men. Then I would like to fight."

"Are you married?"

"No. Time for that after the war. But I shall be married and I shall have children. The doctor says so, and he has not been wrong until now." He grinned at Frumkin who slapped him on the back, told him to dress and go back to writing letters.

"He is a bit of a skeptic," Frumkin said. "He refused to write to his mother and father in Tiflis until he was *absolutely* certain that he had all his functions restored. He would rather have

---

* Readers interested in a full, technical explanation are referred to Dr. Frumkin's illustrated article called "Reconstruction of the Male Genitalia" in *The American Review of Soviet Medicine* for October, 1944.

had them think that he was dead if he were not a whole man. Well, now he is convinced. Maybe he was a bit premature, a trifle overanxious. . . ." Frumkin winked. He had an uninhibited, scatological sense of humor.

Frumkin, personally, has had 180 successful cases in which urethras that had been shot away were restored. In 70 cases he has grafted new genitals, all successful. "My patients have been happily married, they have produced normal offspring," Frumkin boasted. "Quentin Reynolds said there would be a lot of postwar babies named Frumkin. I hope he meant named in honor of Frumkin and not that I was their father. Be sure not to confuse your readers."

When I first visited Frumkin early in 1944 he was quite satisfied with this genital graft and was busily training other doctors as missionaries. "After the war," he said, "I could open the damnedest mail order business in the world, right?" He said he had received letters from America as a result of a Quentin Reynolds article. "One woman wanted to know if I could graft new breasts." He laughed.

Frumkin told me that he was working on the incalculably more difficult problem of grafting testicles, but he had nothing concrete to report. I checked with him again last August and he was in a state of great excitement. He believed that the testicle graft was also feasible.

During the spring a Red Army colonel was sent to Botkin Hospital. He had been wounded by a mine explosion. His penis and a portion of his scrotum were left, but his testicles had been blown off. For weeks Frumkin nursed the colonel, wondering whether or not to try the new graft. The colonel began to develop some of the outward signs of a eunuch; his hair stopped growing, his body fattened abnormally, his voice grew shrill. Finally Frumkin put the decision up to the patient himself. The patient was willing.

Moscow hospitals were alerted. When a young man in the same blood group as the wounded colonel was mortally injured in a streetcar accident, he was rushed to Botkin. As soon as he died, Frumkin operated. He removed the right testicle along with the vessel's pedicle. This he immediately placed under the skin of the colonel's right thigh about eight inches below the pelvis. He then sewed the arteria to the *arteria femoralis* and the vein to the vein *femoralis*.

Four months later when I talked with Frumkin again, he termed the operation at least a partial success. The testicle seemed normal. It was drawing a blood supply; Frumkin supposed that it had acclimatized. The patient's hair had resumed growing, he had lost his surplus fat, his high, piping voice had deepened. "The testicle is working," Frumkin pronounced, "you should hear that colonel talk about women!"

After several more months Frumkin planned to operate again, removing the testicle together with a portion of the thigh's skin into the scrotum. "This portion of the operation will be less difficult than what has already been accomplished," Frumkin claimed.

When the graft is completed Frumkin thinks that the patient will be able to function more or less normally as a husband, although not as a father. "At this stage of my experiment—and mind you, it is premature to call this anything but the purest kind of experiment—I have not gone so far as to consider making a connection with the spermatic cord."

Frumkin did not want any publicity on the testicle graft because it was still unchecked.* I cite it here only as an illustration of the prevailing Soviet attitude toward science and medicine: everything is possible no matter what the standard rule books claim.

* *Time* reported on April 2, 1945: "The colonel now feels fine, commands his regiment, enjoys a normal sex life. (*He is sterile; Dr. Frumkin will not try to connect the delicate sperm-carrying tubules.*)"

BOOK 9

Justice But Not Revenge

E VEN before October 14, 1942, the Soviet Union had made it
quite clear what its policy would be toward war criminals.
In a statement issued on that date Molotov reiterated that "the
Soviet government hereby once more declares for the whole world
to hear and with utter determination and firmness that the criminal Hitlerite government and all its accomplices must and shall
pay the severe penalty for the crimes committed by them." By "all
its accomplices," the statement referred to all those guilty "of the
organization, encouragement or preparation of crimes on occupied
territory."

There are factions who have attempted to use the Russian
position on war crimes as a political weapon against the U.S.S.R.
They have hinted, or even stated in so many words, that the
Russians were going to destroy as many Germans as possible in
order to bring their own people (i.e., Communists) into power.
Some said the Russians would "wipe out" Germany. Stalin, in
his speech on November 6, 1942, denied this: "We do not pursue
the aim of destroying Germany, for it is impossible to destroy
Germany, just as it is impossible to destroy Russia. We can and
must destroy the Hitler State. Our first task is to destroy the Hitler
State and its inspirers."

It is extremely difficult for us to feel as strongly as the Russians
do about the Germans. Our country has not been ravaged. We
have been taught to be skeptical, even cynical, about atrocities.
We remember the debunking of such stories which followed the
last war. Some of us suspect that these current atrocities are exaggerated or even made up to play on our sympathies. Nothing
could be further from the truth.

I belong to the postwar generation, a very cynical generation. I
also belong to a cynical profession. Almost every day that I spent

in the Soviet Union there were fresh atrocity stories in the newspapers. We rarely ever went on a trip toward the front that we
didn't hear about Nazi barbarities or see the results of German
viciousness. After awhile, like other correspondents, I became
calloused to such things. We even had the feeling that no matter
how many people were massacred the story was "old," or not
"news." In the end the death factory at Lublin shook me up enough
so that I can never again be "sophisticated" about Nazi atrocities.

After the Kharkov trials, after Katyn Forest, after Maidanek
(Lublin) I began to understand the Russian attitude toward the
Germans, and toward the Finns and Hungarians and Rumanians
and Spaniards, too.

2.

The night before we left for the Kharkov trials we attended a
special Red Army concert staged in honor of President Eduard
Beneš of Czechoslovakia, who was in Moscow to sign a new treaty
with the Soviet Union. It was a wonderful concert full of rich,
traditional choral singing and wild Cossack dancing. The Red
Army boys sang a few humorous songs, too, and Molotov and
Beneš who were sitting in the very first row seemed to enjoy these
the most. Once during the concert a Narkomindel aide came
down the aisle and whispered something to another aide who got
up and whispered something to another aide who leaned forward
and whispered something to Molotov. Molotov excused himself
and walked out of the auditorium. As he did so a dozen or more
men wearing shiny blue serge suits also rose and left. They were
scattered in seats all over the theater. When Molotov returned
ten minutes later, the "angels" obtrusively went back to their
posts.

Between the acts Mr. Molotov gave a reception for Mr. Beneš
in one of the elegant buffets. The usual lavish table had been set,
and the room was jammed with milling dignitaries. I hadn't had
a chance to see Mr. Beneš since his arrival. He was talking to
Litvinoff. When Litvinoff caught sight of Bill Lawrence and myself
waiting around on tiptoes like anxious substitutes ready to make
their "Y" in life, he beckoned us to come over. Beneš was extremely cordial and promised to hold a "frank" press conference
before he left Moscow.

We let some of the other correspondents get to Beneš and
turned to the host. Molotov was in an unusually friendly mood.

He chatted with correspondents as if they were old friends. I joined the group around him. He was speaking in Russian, and little blond Pavlov, who did the honors for Stalin at Teheran, was translating.

"So you are going to the Kharkov trials tomorrow?" Molotov beamed.

Someone shot right back with "Yeah, but we should have been there all along." Molotov did not lose his good humor. "You should have asked," he said, "it would have been arranged."

Harold King, of Reuter's, an excitable type, blew up. He has a habit of talking fast and furiously when he gets mad, which happens often. Pavlov looked completely bewildered, and Ed Stevens took up the translating. What King said, in brief, was that he and several others had demanded to go to Kharkov as soon as they had heard about the trials. Molotov made some noncommittal reply, and we threw in a few more digs about the inefficiency of the press department. Molotov, not minding, complimented Stevens on the excellence of his Russian.

I said to Pavlov, "If you are not careful, you'll be out of a job." Pavlov didn't think I was funny, but the others had had enough schnapps to laugh. Molotov wanted to know what the laughter was about. Pavlov kept giving him "*Neechevo*" and "Not important," but Motolov persisted. I began to tell Molotov in my reluctant Russian. At this point Pavlov quickly explained. Molotov said he liked the idea. "Pavlov has not been working twenty hours a day since the Moscow Conference," he said. "He's sick. He needs a rest. Mr. Stevens would be very good. That's a fine idea."

One of the Narkomindel boys appeared and signaled to Mr. Molotov that the forty-five-minute intermission was over, and they were ready to resume the concert. Molotov was enjoying himself, and ordered the second act held up for another fifteen minutes or more.

He asked me how I liked Moscow, and I was on safe ground with my vocabulary. I had gone through the speech so often that I sounded almost fluent to myself, if not to a Russian. I said that I had been in Moscow before the war, and that I was amazed by the great determination and the great energy of the people. This little speech seemed to please Molotov, probably not because the sentiments were new but because most Russians felt flattered when someone was making an attempt to talk to them in Russian— no matter how badly.

Before we returned to the concert, Molotov said he was very glad that we were going to Kharkov, that it was very important that the foreign press hear and see things with their own ears and eyes. I don't think he ever got a faster, more affirmative, more heartfelt, or more collectivized *"Da, Da!"* For the first time he looked a trifle nonplused.

3.

The next morning we flew down to Kharkov. It was a gray day with a low ceiling and the plane only went above church steeple level to avoid church steeples. When we arrived it was still only midmorning. We went straight from the airport to the Ukrainian Musical Comedy Theatre on Rymarskaya Street where the trial was being held. The theater was old and smelly. The central auditorium was packed with a thousand spectators, many of them standing. Tickets to the proceedings went to wounded Red Army men, front-line heroes on leave, outstanding production workers, and families of Kharkov citizens who had been slaughtered by the Germans during the occupation. The design of the theater was baroque, and white-sculptured nymphs arched against the upper boxes like so many little daughters of Atlas supporting the world. Despite the seriousness of the occasion, the setting seemed like a Hollywood première—klieg lights, microphones, cameras, celebrities and photographers. Perhaps the courtroom of the Lindbergh (Hauptmann) trial in Flemington, New Jersey, would be a more accurate comparison.

We were ushered into a box at the left, just opposite the prisoners' box. Prominent Soviet writers had boxes behind ours. On one door was a printed sign which read simply, TOLSTOY. That rotund writer appeared presently. When a photographer shot off a flash bulb in his face he cursed him out just as the Grand Duke So-and-So might have done thirty years before. Only the photographer talked right back—a big difference.

Death in battle is too easy a death for their crimes [Tolstoy wrote in *Pravda* when the trial of the Nazis and one traitor opened]. Hitler freed the Germans from moral feelings of pity, nobleness, honor and respect for man, but we haven't freed the Germans from their obligation to be men. When the Soviet Government said that the Fascists would be judged strictly, Hitler didn't throw the words into the wind. Today Kharkov began the first trial which opens a whole epoch of great and dreadful judgment for the Germans who have overstepped the laws of humanity. Today three Germans are being tried among the ruins of the town, surrounded by the tombs of their victims. They have behaved not like soldiers, but like bandits, torturers, licentious half-men. . . .

The "licentious half-men" took their seats in their box. The trial was resuming. There were sneezes in the audience. Girls focused opera glasses and others craned their necks to see the accused. The Germans were all in uniform. Captain Wilhelm Langheld, fifty-two, a Nazi counterespionage officer, sat straight and correct. He was clean-shaven with a long, puffy pink face, thin lips and slick red hair. Rheinhard Retslau, a member of the German secret police, had a bored expression, a chinless face, and spectacles. He sat very calmly and seemed to be listening to the testimony in Russian as well as the translation into German. He was thirty-six years old and wore a medal which Hitler had given him two years before. Lieutenant Hans Ritz, twenty-four, had a gnome-like head with a large skull, a sharp German nose, a caved-in chest and a silly mustache. He was an assistant commander of an SS company. He beat people with canes and rubber hoses, and in June, 1943, he took part in a mass shooting of Soviet civilians near Kharkov.

Mikhail Bulanov, called by one of the Russian writers "the black lining of the blue German uniform," was a Russian traitor. His black eyebrows had grown together over his closely set black eyes. He looked like a jackal.

The trials were being run by the military tribunal of the Fourth Ukrainian Front. The chief judge was Major General Miasnikov. The defense counsel, appointed by the judge, was N. V. Kommodov, who is the Soviet Union's Samuel Liebowitz with a bit of Clarence Darrow thrown in. He had two assistants, S. K. Kaznacheyev and N. P. Belov. Both lawyers were well known. The prosecutor was N. K. Dunaev, a young Red Army colonel. The accused made no objections to the judges or the defense lawyers.

The testimony thus far has been incredible. The Germans, pretty sure that they were going to die, took the long chance that they might get life imprisonment if they made a clean breast of things. They knew, too, that there was not much point in hiding facts. The Soviets had volumes of proof, cemeteries full of evidence. The accused had only to look into the eyes of the crowd at the trial to realize the hopelessness of claiming innocence. Langheld, a veteran of World War I, had related in his cold, expressionless voice how he beat women and starved prisoners without thinking of good or bad. He was almost the dramatic monologist or raconteur telling how he flogged an innocent young Soviet woman while her small son cringed in a corner watching his mother being tortured. Langheld said he beat the woman until she was covered with blood. She fainted. Next day she died. And what happened to the child? Oh, Langheld forgot that part momentarily. The child refused to be torn away from the dead body of the mother. That's why they shot him.

The audience listened in quiet horror. It was like a page from Wanda Wasilewska's *Rainbow*. Langheld was businesslike, accurate, choosing his words as if he were talking about a grocery store where certain foods had spoiled. They asked him, "How many innocent people have you personally killed or tortured?" He lifted his piggish little eyes to the ceiling, mentally counting. Then he replied like a bank clerk. To his regret he could not say definitely at the moment, but approximately he had shot, tortured or otherwise destroyed, say, a hundred people.

The Soviet writers hated Langheld more than they did the others. They couldn't forget that he had been a British prisoner of war in 1917 and had been allowed to return home to resume his militaristic Prussian career all over again. The sharp-tongued David Zaslavsky wrote about him:

In his person is seen the limit of savagery which Hitler's Germany attained when nothing is left that is human except the outward appearance. Langheld is Hitler reduced to the scale of one torture chamber. If, on the accused bench Hitler sat, he would say nothing different. Langheld, if he were an officer of the German High Command, would repeat that Germans are a super-race and that they can and must destroy others. Langheld speaks in German. He is translated into Russian. Words can be translated but it is impossible to translate in human language the feelings of Langheld. Of course, Hitler Germans are not a special race but a special breed of two-legged animals trained under unique conditions for artificially becoming savage. This is a dangerous breed. It must be wiped out and rendered harmless in the interests of mankind and humanity.

The prosecutor was making his long summation. The newsreel men took their pictures. Retslau kept staring at the speaker. Bulanov, in his black turtle-neck sweater, looked terribly uneasy.

Ritz had the manner of an Austrian provincial dandy. But he shivered occasionally as he felt the vindictiveness in the prosecutor's voice. Langheld seemed completely unmoved as if he were at a lecture on the weaving methods of the Navajo Indians and not at a trial where his life was in the balance. Often he closed his eyes or stifled a yawn.

The prosecutor paused to drink some hot tea. Then he continued, "The men who are in the dock are not responsible, we know who they are and they will have to answer. We try these three for their personal crimes, for what they have done with their own hands. . . ." He began to picture their crimes. He recreated scenes in which little children, thinking they were going for a joy ride, hopped into German vans. They turned out to be the notorious gas-wagons or *doushagoopkas*. In them the children, with or without their parents, were asphyxiated by carbon monoxide while the van was already on its way toward some dumping ground. There was quiet weeping among the spectators. Handkerchiefs appeared. Even the tough Red Army men had to keep clearing lumps from their throats. "Retslau," charged the prosecutor, "is a professional killer. The Red Army stopped his career. You judges must decide his future. . . ."

Next he delved into the triumphs of Ritz. "He wanted to get into the Gestapo because it was nice and comfortable and the first outfit to run away when there's danger." Ritz was the type who liked to have his picture taken hanging innocent women and children, and then sent it back to his mother and sweetheart.

For Bulanov, the prosecutor reserved his special scorn. He was a deserter from the Red Army. He helped repair *doushagoopkas*. He even drove them.

Near the end of the summation, the prosecutor struck a Tom Dewey pose. "The crimes are proved not only of those sitting in the dock but all those who will be!" he shouted. "For our mothers, wives, daughters, sisters—in their names, the state demands that you send these men to their death. . . ." There was a storm of applause.

We had lunch with Tolstoy, Konstantin Simonov, Ehrenburg, and Dmitri Kudriavtsev, secretary of the Soviet Union's Atrocities Commission. When it was over we returned to hear Defense Attorney Kommodov make his final plea. He was the man who defended the Trotskyist bloc in the 1936-1937 treason trials. He began talking slowly, analyzing the specific structure of Fascism. He showed how its very nature bred war and brutality. In all epochs there are atrocities, he pointed out, but none could compare with this planned, regular annihilation of a peaceful people. "I shall not recount all the terrors committed by the Germans, having respect for your nerves." He spoke without notes, a glass of tea held in his left hand. Once, when he read a quotation from Stalin, he put on his glasses. The burden of his plea was the same as the one the defense lawyer made in Richard Wright's *Native Son*. The crimes were committed because of the society in which the defendants lived. Only Kommodov was talking about German Fascism, not about the Negro problem in the United States. When he finished, a translator began reading the speech in German; Ritz sobbed as he listened to it. The others seemed unmoved.

Then, one by one, the accused made their last pleas. They sang echoes of Kommodov's tune, but with less effect. Retslau said it was useless to hide his crimes. He blamed German propaganda which said the Russians were torturing German prisoners, cutting off their hands. "I can say the opposite is true. We were well treated in prison." He asked the judges to consider his background and training under the Nazi system. Langheld dozed as Retslau asked to be spared. He wanted to return to Germany and prove himself by his deeds.

Shortly after six all the Red Army guards were changed, and the court announced that the curfew was being suspended for the evening so the crowd could stay. The next to speak was the hopeless Bulanov. When the Germans took him prisoner he had the choice of death or transgression. Of course, he said, most of the brave Soviet people preferred heroic death. But he, Bulanov, had no such high moral character. He asked the judges to imagine his feelings among the "German cannibals." He got only ninety occupation marks per month for his work. He said his guilt was tremendous, but he certainly hoped he could be used by the Soviets in some way; he would prove himself by hard work and good intentions.

When Langheld stood in front of the microphone the crowd stirred noisily and the judge rapped for order. The Prussian kept his hands behind his back. The klieg lights were switched on. Langheld blinked, faltered as he tried to speak. "I have nothing to add to the formal accusation," he said. "I beat prisoners, they were beaten under my orders, they were shot by my orders. I ask only one consideration. I am not alone. The entire German Army is like that, too. I do not mean to cover up my own guilt. The reasons for my guilt lie in the German government. The Hitler regime managed to suppress the generous feelings of the German people. And to bring out the beastly instincts. This is especially true in the Wehrmacht. This evil has shown itself particularly during this war. To contradict or not to fulfill the orders we were given meant to sentence yourself to death. And I was a victim of these orders. I ask consideration for my old age, and because I told the truth in the preliminary hearings."

I looked at the audience. There was no sympathy, only hatred. Ritz swayed as he stood up. He sounded like a whining boy. "I don't want to implore you, I don't want to blot out my crimes," he said. "It's unworthy of me as a man and a soldier. I wish to speak with frankness. . . . I want you to know that I did not relish killings. If so, I would have taken part in many more crimes as I had plenty of chances. I acted on orders. The system of our army forced me to do it. You do take into consideration the old Roman law. I was under orders when I committed crimes, under the sentence of death myself if I did not carry out these orders." He sighed. Then he began again. "The Hitler system is directed not only against other nations but against German people who do not obey him. Consider my life. I was a child of thirteen when the Hitler regime came to power. Since then I have been systematically educated." Ritz was something of an orator, and used his hands for gestures. I could not get all his testimony, but I checked it with one of the stenographers, and it is approximately correct: "I am young and I have my life before me. I want to live so I can testify against the other SS men who ordered these atrocities. . . ."

The court recessed at 9:15 P.M. We drove back to the hotel and had supper. About 11:30 a telephone call came that the judges were ready to announce their decision. We entered the packed hall. The prisoners were led in, under guard. The judges walked in from the wings. As they appeared on the stage everyone stood up, the Red Army men rigidly at attention. For the first time I noticed the light blue velvet curtain behind the judges, and the pretty Red Army girl court clerks.

At exactly 11:55 General Miasnikov read the findings of the court and the verdict: "Death by hanging." The audience applauded. Bulanov ducked his head down. Then a Red Army lieutenant stood up and read the same thing in German. Ritz looked incredulous. Retslau tapped his thick fingers against the frames of his horn-rimmed glasses. Langheld betrayed nothing. The guards led them out.

I asked Ehrenburg when they would be hanged.

"Sunday morning," he snapped back. "What better time? To-morrow."

On the way out of the theater I stopped to read a big billboard. It said, literally: NEXT WEEK—ROSE-MARIE.

4.

Sunday morning was overcast but not too cold. Naturally one of the Americans taking a deep breath of air, said, "A good day for a hanging." Nobody laughed. We piled into cars and went to see the end.

If the scene had been in a movie it would have jarred me by its savagery and unreality. Fitted into the context of time and place it had a stark but entirely believable reality. Around us Kharkov kids were scampering high on the snowy rooftops of shattered windowless buildings. Near by the great Kharkov Cathedral, damaged by Nazi bombs, was empty. Its proud spires were silent this Sunday morning, their tongues wrenched out and shipped to Germany where they were melted into shell casings.

About fifty thousand people dressed in their shabby Sunday best shoved into the enormous open market square. They were held in check by Red Army guards with fixed bayonets and low-slung tommy guns. Into the dismal gray light of that chilly December morning loomed four gaunt fifteen-foot gallows—stout wooden beams with strong thin nooses drooping from crossbars. Beneath the stiff nooses four open Chevrolet trucks were backed up. On each truck were three flimsy unpainted wooden tables.

Overhead two trim Lend-Lease Airacobras and a pair of ugly Russian U-2s hovered like vultures. Behind us a half-demolished office building still bore a German signpost on its crumbling façade. Its uncertain rafters were black with spectators. Photographers fought for vantage points. One newsreel crew was located on a platform twenty feet high opposite the gallows.

At 11:15 A.M. two cars plowed through the dense crowd. The first contained military and judicial officials. The second was a closed gray-green truck with guards and the condemned. The door was opened. The crowd stirred impatiently. With their hands tied behind them the Germans, Hans Ritz, Wilhelm Langheld and Rheinhard Retslau were led out, followed by the Russian traitor, Mikhail Bulanov. The crowd surged forward, straining against the cordon of guards. Despite their efforts the circle around the gallows tightened.

Red Army men helped each of the condemned onto a truck beneath the coiled rope. Then they assisted their reluctant feet onto the center table while two guards flanked them on the side tables. The necks of the condemned reached the empty nooses. Langheld's pink Adam's apple bobbed up and down. Cocksure young Ritz kept up his silly posturing. Retslau seemed as ruthless under his own death gallows as he had been when preparing to kill dozens of innocent civilians. Bulanov's knees kept collapsing and once the shaky table toppled over under him.

The Germans were in full uniform with epaulets and ribbons. They wore forage caps. Langheld had on a good pair of boots, high boots. As the moment approached, Bulanov's color became chalky. Ritz went pale and sickly like the sky. Langheld's pig-pink complexion reddened, Retslau's yellowed.

Suddenly the motors of the four one-ton trucks coughed, then roared. Major General Miasnikov, chairman of the military tribunal, mounted the rostrum improvised from packing cases. His voice over the loudspeaker system seemed to come from far off as he repeated the court's sentence. Then the general paused dramatically before he barked out the order:

"Lieutenant Colonel, fulfill the verdict."

The trucks lurched forward several yards. Retslau, the expressionless child-murderer, felt the full jerk of the cord first. Then the pathetic Bulanov and the dapper Ritz. And finally the correct Prussian, Langheld.

The gathering let out an involuntary screech like the escape valve of an oveheated boiler. Momentarily they broke forward. Four bodies, three in the dirty gray-green Nazi field uniform, swayed slightly. Death was surprisingly quick and simple. Ritz jerked and twitched, but not for very long. Soon the guards untied the cord from their lifeless hands. The populace stared. Some tried to squeeze closer for a better look at Langheld's pink face with its thin bloodless lips hanging crookedly open in death.

As I threaded through the throng I could see no expressions of horror, no remorse on their faces. After witnessing the courtroom trial and watching the spectators, I had not really expected to find horror and remorse. The people of Kharkov had lived with

terror and tragedy for so long under the Germans that the sight of
three Nazi barbarians and one traitor hanging cold and dead on
a Sunday morning in their snow-covered, cobblestoned public
square carried no modicum of shock. For the people of Kharkov it
was only the prologue of a new drama, not the climactic scene of
an old one. This was one of the small moments of justice, their first
satisfaction under law for months of unlawful brutality.

I asked a Red Army lieutenant how long the bodies would
hang.

"Three days and three nights," he said. "Let Hitler shake and
tremble in his bomb shelter."

Examining the strong-lined faces of these Ukrainians, you felt
instinctively that they would never put down their arms until
total victory was won. They will never and can never forget the
100,000 Kharkov citizens who starved to death under the Nazis.
Talking with them about "what it was like" I realized that in
every head there is a kind of projector constantly throwing slides
on memory's screen: scenes of thousands of women and children
being tortured, their lives snuffed out in the gas-wagons . . . of
rubber hosing and machine guns cutting down defiant old men
like a scythe cutting through a wheat field . . . of digging graves
and being shoved in, sometimes alive . . . of the mass slaughter
of the Jews . . . of barbed wire and bayonets ripping a tattoo on
honest flesh.

And if these scenes ever faded, the people only had to gaze
about them. There was always their beloved Kharkov, a living
tableau of Nazi artistic achievement . . . the once handsome, thriving Kharkov which they had built with their own labor, now
broken, twisted, wrecked.

The Red Army lieutenant followed me back to the car. The
crowd was scattering, slowly. The officer said to me, echoing the
prosecutor at the trial: "Their names are Langheld, Ritz and
Retslau. But in our hearts it is Hitler, Himmler and Göring who
are hanging there today."

Before I could find suitable words for a reply, a red-faced old
babushka who had overheard the lieutenant's declaration, said,
"*Skoro budyet.*" ("Soon it will be.")

5.

After we had written our stories at the hotel, several of us
walked around the town. Eventually we went back to the market

square, where little booths and stalls were open and doing a flourishing trade. I stopped and bought a secondhand *chainik* ("teapot") for forty rubles. It wasn't worth more than twenty cents at Woolworth's, but there are no Woolworths in Kharkov or anywhere else in Russia. And it was the first teapot I'd seen for sale anywhere at any price in the Soviet Union. Five minutes after I had bought it another correspondent came along looking for one. There weren't any more. He offered me sixty rubles for mine. Despite my capitalist instincts I resisted the profit.

The four bodies were still hanging in the center of the square. Only a few late-comers were looking at the bluish corpses. The three Germans had lost their forage caps. And Langheld was already minus his fine high boots. In Russia boots are boots whether they belong to dead Germans or anyone else. You take them where you find them and consider yourself lucky. I was to remember this fact later at Katyn Forest.

A kid with a macabre sense of humor was trying to stick a lighted cigarette into Bulanov's mouth. When a Red Army man shouted something at him he sprinted away.

We continued walking around the market. Somebody bought an old map in German. There were also German oil paints for sale, and German textbooks, and a sorry collection of Christmas tree ornaments including some frayed silver tinsel and a few large red balls. An old woman at another stall was selling empty German bottles with strange and wonderful labels—champagne from France, port from Spain, cognac from Poland.

About fifteen minutes later we left the market place. It was still crowded with Sunday strollers and shoppers and buyers. But nobody was paying any attention to the four bodies. A Russian photographer for *Pravda* who was with our sightseeing group said: "This must be very hard for you to understand." Then he went on quickly, "It's not that people have no feelings, it's because they have feelings. The business of death is everyday. The business of trade, the chance to buy things—can you imagine what that means to them? When the Germans were here they didn't dare to sell anything for fear the Germans would grab it. Of course, there isn't much here but it seems like much to them. Do you think this is bad? What is your opinion?"

I said I understood. "I have bought a *chainik*," I said, tapping the bulge in my coat pocket.

The cameraman sighed. "It cannot be a very good *chainik*. The Germans would not have left it behind."

As we neared the hotel he asked again, "Are you sure you understand how the people feel?"

"Yes." Then I said, "This is a nice hotel."

"Not very," he said. "You should have been here before the war."

"I was. I was here in 1935."

He brightened considerably. "Then you *do* understand," he said heartily. "You do understand." But as we went up the stairs toward our rooms he had another thought and he said to me, "But your home is in America. It is safe. Have you perhaps lost someone in the war?"

I said no.

"Then you only understand a little, just a drop." Then he seemed to be afraid that he had hurt my feelings and he squeezed my arm. "You will forgive me. Even if you are very sensitive . . . just a drop."

I thought he was wrong then. It wasn't until months later at the "murder camp" in Poland that I thought of him again and realized that he was quite right. People like me could only understand "just a drop."

6.

The hangings in Kharkov did a great deal for the morale of the Russians, but the repercussions elsewhere were not good. The Germans threatened reprisals against Allied fliers shot down over the Reich. Editorial writers in England and America decried the Kharkov trials, demanding that further judgments be postponed until the end of military operations. *War and the Working Class* cracked back at some of the critics. "It's easy to understand that Yorkshire (Mrs. Anthony Eden's Yorkshire *Post*) journalists can wait more patiently for the trial of the Hitlerite criminals than the people of Kiev and Kharkov who lived through the horrors of the Hitlerite occupation." The same article resented an assertion by the Manchester *Guardian* that the Soviets were solving the problem of war prisoner trials "in its own way." *War and the Working Class* claimed that the general declaration of the Allies had not been exceeded by the Soviet policy. It concluded that "Soviet justice goes 'its own way' in as great a measure as the valiant Red Army goes its own way, but in full unity with the Allies. . . ."

But there were no more public trials or hangings. In January the news broke that the Soviet government was undertaking its own investigation of the Katyn Forest atrocities near Smolensk. The roots of this controversial affair go back as far as 1939. In that year as the result of the Soviet invasion of Poland, the Red Army brought ten thousand Polish officers and men, all prisoners of war, to the western part of Smolensk Province. The prisoners were employed on road construction, under guard. When the Germans attacked Russia in June, 1941, the Poles remained around Smolensk and continued work. In mid-July the Germans effected a sudden and decisive breakthrough in this area with a tank column, and Smolensk was menaced. According to official Soviet sources, an attempt was made to evacuate Smolensk civilians as well as the Polish prisoners. But rail lines eastward were already under artillery fire, and the Russian authorities had to be reconciled to the fact that the bulk of civilians and prisoners would have to remain. The Germans took Smolensk on the night of July 15, 1941.

Suddenly in March, 1943, the Goebbels propaganda machine launched charges that the Germans had discovered dead bodies of some ten thousand Poles near Smolensk, and that they had all been massacred by the Russians in March, 1940. The Polish Government in Exile, which had been trying unsuccessfully to obtain information about missing Polish war prisoners from the Soviets, appealed to the International Red Cross to investigate the Nazi claims. The Russians were furious that one of their Allies would support any kind of Nazi charges to this extent. On April 25, as the result of this incident and other "provocations," the Soviet Foreign Office announced a suspension of relations with the Poles in London because the Poles had allegedly conspired with Germany by appealing to the Red Cross. The Soviet note stated that "the Polish Government, to please Hitler's tyranny, deals a treacherous blow to the Soviet Union. The Soviet Government is aware that this hostile campaign against the Soviet Union was undertaken by the Polish Government in order to exert pressure upon the Soviet Government by making use of the Hitlerite fake for the purpose of wresting from it territorial concessions. . . ."

The Red Army retook Smolensk on September 25, 1943. Almost immediately Soviet officials began digging into the Katyn affair.

On January 21, 1944, we set off for Smolensk to see for ourselves. Before I ever left Moscow my inclination was to believe that the Germans were probably guilty. But I had no conclusive proofs which would help me to convince anyone who believed otherwise. It did not seem plausible to me that a mass murder could go undiscovered for almost two years—the period of German occupation in Smolensk before they announced the "discovery." The killing and burying of ten thousand people cannot be kept a secret, not even in wartime. Besides, I had learned much about the Nazi taste for mass murder. And unlike some Poles in London, I had no reason to place any faith in Herr Reichsminister Goebbels' word.

It started out like a lark—just a bunch of amicable correspondents off on a skiing week end or house party. A special four-car train left Moscow's Belorussian station at four o'clock one afternoon and arrived at Smolensk, 230 miles southwest, at ten the next morning. Original plans had called for a rough trip by automobile with each correspondent bringing his own food and drink for three days. At the last minute the Soviet authorities decided to make available the Narkomindel's deluxe train—with well-heated, well-lighted, plush-carpeted *wagons-lits* and a cheerful dining car curtained in a pastel green. The reason for this pomp and circumstance was the unexpected presence of twenty-five-year-old Kathleen Harriman, the Ambassador's daughter.

War was remote from the conversation on the eighteen-hour train ride. The correspondents played bridge and gin rummy, sang songs. A slightly serious note was interjected when someone asked Ed Stevens of the *Christian Science Monitor* how he was going to write about so many dead people. Stevens, accustomed to such ribbing, lazily suggested that maybe they wouldn't be "dead" but just "passed on." Another reporter asked Stevens if the *Monitor* had such a thing as a "deadline."

In Smolensk the atmosphere changed. In this once great industrial city of 180,000 only 30,000 inhabitants remained. Once there had been over 7,900 buildings and now only 300 were left standing—of these only 64 were stone buildings. Bundled into cars we drove over slithery streets to the wall of the Smolensk Kremlin where we gazed at the graves of Red Army heroes recently buried. The graves were decorated with artificial flowers and pictures of the fallen heroes were tacked over the mound on a raised stick, not a cross. Above these new graves on the wall of the Kremlin were green plaques dedicated to heroes of the War of 1812. Near by was a great marble base for the statue of Kutuzov who halted Napoleon at Smolensk in 1812. The top of the statue had been stolen by the Germans and sent back to Berlin.

On the streets we stopped a peasant woman and asked where Hitler's Smolensk headquarters had been. She replied she didn't know just where but he had been there several times after the Germans entered Smolensk the night of July 15, 1941. When asked where she lived, the woman said that her house had been burned on Septmber 25, 1943, and now she lived in a boarded-up cellar.

Many important buildings of Smolensk were destroyed at that time, including the lending library's three-story brick building, the modern gray Agricultural Institute and the five-storied apartment houses along the Bolshaya Sovietskaya Street which the Germans unimaginatively renamed Hauptstrasse.

We drove west ten miles to Katyn Forest. The portion of the forest where the Poles were being exhumed was called Goat Hill, a high slope overlooking the banks of the Dnieper. This peaceful woodland scene had a lovely Breughel-like setting as a light snow fell, covering the slender birches, the leafless oaks, the tall firs and evergreens. Here the citizens of Smolensk came for berrying parties and picnics in the summer, here children came for sledding and snowball fights in the winter. Now from the bowels of the earth emerged a horrible stench as, one by one, stiff, mildewed Poles in faded gray-blue field uniforms were lifted out. Newsreel cameras ground and candid shots were made as we slogged over piles of wet, sandy loam to peer at the open graves.

We were shown around by Dr. Victor Prozorovsky, the director of the Moscow Institute of Criminal Medical Research, who wore a white smock and a white chef's cap, an orange rubber apron and gloves. In one great trench where Red Army men were digging, the Poles were neatly arranged like slices-of-seven layer cake, row on row. They all displayed decent-looking black boots sticking through the dirt at one end and their bare skulls with a fringe of snow at the other end. In other pits Poles were scattered loosely—as coal funneled down a chute into a cellar. Red Army men with shovels loosened the dirt around the bodies and other Red Army privates wearing rubber gloves carefully picked up the bodies and placed them on wooden stretchers. As the stretchers brushed past us, we could distinguish the Polish eagles on the tarnished brass buttons of the dead men's uniforms. Some Poles still had their hands tied behind their backs; the cord that bound their wrists had not yet rotted.

From the graves we walked to one of the large gray-green tents where Soviet doctors were making autopsies. It was warmer in the tent where a stove was burning wood. But the smell was stronger, sweeter. Dr. Prozorovsky ripped open Polish corpse No. 8. He explained that the condition of the bodies proved scientifically that the Poles had been buried only about two years. Since the Germans claimed the Reds shot and buried the Poles in March and April, 1940, this medical evidence would seem to invalidate completely the Nazi story. The doctor calmly carved off chunks of brain gray matter as if he were slicing Spam, then slit open the uniform, knifed through the chest, and, reaching in a red-rubber-gloved hand, yanked out the wizened organs. He said, "Heart." In his palm was a miserable object which looked like a large ladies' powder puff which had been first soaked, then squeezed dry and then frozen.

All the skulls in the autopsy tents and those lying out on the snowy field indicated that the Poles were killed by a revolver shot passing from the base of the skull at the neck through the forehead. The bullets were mostly 7.65 millimeters. At another table Dr. Prozorovsky ripped open a corpse's leg muscle to show us the relative freshness. "Look how well-preserved the meat is," he said.

We were told that eleven doctors with their assistants worked from nine to five daily examining corpses. About 1,600 were exhumed daily. Records were kept on each corpse. Here is the record for No. 808: "Body of male, middle height and build, good physical condition, no defects in physique, wearing Polish uniform, fully dressed without rank tabs on coat. Right foot fallen off. Half centimeter below base of skull is large bullet hole nine millimeters in diameter. No exit hole discovered. Epidermis dirty yellow color and partly mummified. Internal organs flattened out and partially mummified. No documents found in pockets which had been slit open."

The Russians found evidences that the graves had been disturbed and that at the time the anti-Soviet charges were made the Nazis had looted the pockets and put number tags on many corpses. After inspecting some trial soundings and some fresh excavations where they hoped to find the rest of the Poles, we walked about a half mile to look at the former rest house or *dacha* which had been used by the 537th German Construction Battalion said to be responsible for the murders.

During the afternoon and evening we heard testimony from members of the special committee "to investigate the shooting by the Germans of Polish war prisoners in Katyn Forest." On this panel were Lieutenant General Burdenko, Colonel General Y. E. Smirnov, director of the Red Army Medical Services, Metropolitan Nikolai of Kiev and Galicia, Lieutenant General Gundorov, chairman of the All-Slav Committee, Alexei Tolstoy, Sergei Kalashnikov, president of the Soviet Red Cross, and R. Y. Melnikov, chairman of the Smolensk Province Executive Committee. Dmitri Kudriavtsev, secretary of the permanent commission was present, too. He turned up with each new atrocity. This august body met on the second floor of the Smolensk Soviet, or city hall, in an oblong room with a sketch of Stalin on the wall and no other decoration. The tables for the committee and press were covered with a bright red flannel cloth.

In the afternoon a summary of the findings of the committee since they began work was delivered by Vladimir Potëmkin, now Commissar of Education for the RSFSR. The former Soviet Ambassador to Rome and Paris and onetime Assistant Commissar of Foreign Affairs was a smallish man in a plain business suit with pince-nez glasses, thin white hair and pinkish complexion. He concluded: 1) The Germans had killed the Poles during August and September, 1941; 2) Fearing their position was unstable and knowing they would have to leave, the Germans hastened to cover up evidences of their crimes, and thus opened graves, sought witnesses, transferred bodies and tried to create this provocation.

Between the afternoon and evening sessions Professor Peter Semenovsky of the Moscow Institute of Criminal Medical Research showed us documents and miscellaneous items found on 148 of the 700 bodies already exhumed. These included Polish gold coins, a United States $50 bill, crosses, pipes, prayer books, receipts dated as late as May 18, 1940, newspaper clippings (mostly 1940) and a postcard in ink from Stanislas to Irina Kuchinska of 15 Bagetella Street, Warsaw. The card was written from Starobelsky prison camp near Smolensk on June 20, 1940, two days before the German invasion of the Soviet Union. But it was never mailed.

"My little sunshine,

Thanks for what you sent me. Don't forget me. Don't forget you are the only thing I possess and please sell all my things and eat well. My dear girl I think only of you and every day I remember you. Please write to me often without waiting for letters from me. Keep a diary and send it to me in bits—it will fill up my time. I send you kisses. I love you very much. I miss you very much.

Stas

At the evening session the committee convened under the glare of klieg lights. A battery of cameramen photographed the press and especially the Ambassador's daughter from every angle. The opening remarks were by the chief surgeon of the Red Army, stocky, Lieutenant General Nikolai Burdenko. This famous old physician, a Ukrainian, has chalky blue eyes, a clipped mustache, thin goatee, high forehead, sparse white hair, and a wrinkled, lined face. He wore black-rimmed spectacles which he shoved up onto his forehead while listening to the testimony. He also cupped his hand over his ear as he is quite deaf. He talked too loudly in a deep, raspy voice.

Testimony was given for several hours. A seventy-year-old farmer, Parfon Kiselev, admitted he had falsely backed the German story about the killing of the Poles when they flogged him and threatened to pull his veins out. Mathew Zakharev, fifty, mayor of the village of Novoye Batekhi under the German occupation, said he had been rubber-hosed on a bench and threatened with a revolver until he signed a statement in German which he didn't understand; the document said the Russians shot the Poles in 1940. Twenty-eight-year-old Anna Alexeyeva, tall, blue-eyed, blond with a boyish bob, dirty hands, thick full lips, white skin, worked at the *dacha* near Katyn where the Germans lived. She said she had heard trucks turn past the house during August and September, 1941, with the Polish prisoners inside. After the trucks were in the forests there was a regular series of shots as if "someone was pounding with a hammer"—at this point she rapped several times on the table for emphasis. The returning German soldiers had fresh blood on their tunics and on such occasions received double ration of liquor plus good food. Boris Basilevsky, fifty-eight, a former professor of astronomy, testified that he was forced to become assistant burgomaster during the Smolensk occupation. He was thin-faced, with a long hook nose, iron-gray hair, black caterpillar eyebrows, and a scraggly chicken's neck—so that his Adam's apple bobbed as he talked. He quoted the Gestapo zone commander, Hirschfeld, as saying, "The Poles were good for fertilization of the land" and that they would be exterminated because they were an inferior people whose death would create more *Lebensraum* for the Germans.

Dr. Zubkov, an anatomist who had stayed in Smolensk during the occupation, had a high pompadour with a widow's peak. He spoke slowly, saying that he had visited the graves late in April or early in May, 1943, on one of the compulsory "excursions" which the Germans were running for the people of Smolensk. As much as he could see the state of decay of the flesh did not correlate with the amount of time the Germans said the bodies were in the graves. He saw no autopsies being performed but the Germans were "busily ripping pockets."

The last witness, Sergei Ivanov, thin and wan, dressed in a dark blue uniform of a railroad worker, was stationmaster in a near-by town. He said he had received orders from the Soviets to have a forty-car train ready to evacuate the Polish prisoners before the Germans took Smolensk. But as the railroad line was cut he couldn't do it. When he was asked to make false testimony by the Gestapo to prove that the Russians shot the Poles, he had pleaded, "I am sixty and I don't want to take this sin upon my soul." They finally forced him to sign a statement.

At the conclusion of the session the correspondents asked questions. I asked why some Poles were warmly dressed (in fur coats) if they were buried by the Germans in August and September. The answer was that the nights were cold and they probably had no other outer garments.

The special train left Smolensk at 1 A.M. Most of us stayed up for hours drowning memories, singing Soviet and American songs. In the morning we were still puzzling over some aspects of the Katyn Forest mystery. Like the other correspondents, I was sure the Germans had murdered the Poles and then had very cleverly "discovered" the graves for propaganda purposes. One of the strongest reasons was the advice given by medical experts that the corpses could not have been in the ground for more than two years because they were not far enough decayed. I lacked sufficient medical knowledge to puncture this diagnosis. The corpses we saw had skin and hair remaining, the flesh and muscles seemed well preserved.

Then there was a letter and several receipts dated in 1941. This would disprove the German claim that the Russians committed the crime in 1940. On the other hand there were many newspapers and documents dated February and March of 1940. I could not figure out why they would still be carried by the Poles if they had not been shot until August or September, 1941. Perhaps the Germans had planted the evidence when they exhumed the bodies in the spring of 1943.

In the peculiar technique for the actual killing, a case could be made for or against. In Kiev, Kharkov and elsewhere, the Germans had mowed down the victims with machine guns. But at Orel and Voronezh they had the pleasure of putting a bullet through each skull with a revolver.

When it came to writing my story back in Moscow, I found that the strongest bits of evidence were the boots. Even in 1940 boots were scarce in Russia. On a battlefield an American might first rush for a Nazi medal or a Luger, but a Russian would always look first for shoes. And all the corpses which I had seen were still shod with fine black leather military boots.

But the Narkomindel censors refused to pass this point in my story. They refused any explanation, but obviously they felt it did not show Russian character in its purest light. They were obviously worried about the whole story, as we had told them on the train coming back to Moscow that the evidence had not been prepared or presented in a manner which would convince a British or an American jury. The cables were held up for several days and when they were finally released they wouldn't let me say anything about the finery of the special train, or that the Poles had on fur coats.

At the time they happen, censorship stupidities like these seem quite important, and they tend to muddy a reporter's opinion of what occurred. It's the old story of not seeing the woods for the trees. Fortunately there was no "controversy" over any of the other atrocities. Sometimes there was a question of how many people had actually been killed, but nobody ever doubted that the Germans had done it.

7.

Because of our American sympathy for Finland and because correspondents never were allowed near the Finnish front, very little has been written concerning Finland's part in the war against Russia. When I visited Leningrad in February and again in June, I was surprised to find that the feeling against Finland in this area was almost as strong as the hatred for Germans. The chief reasons were, of course, the long-standing enmity between giant Russia and little Finland, and the role the Finns played in closing the Leningrad blockade. But among the Red Army men no difference was made between the terroristic methods of the Finns and the Nazis. An English-speaking major in Leningrad attached to the General Staff talked to me about Finnish atrocities for three hours. Later the Moscow papers printed many of these same stories, and in August the Extraordinary State Committee issued a statement as the result of its investigation of Finnish crimes.

Briefly, these are some of the things the major told me which were later backed up by the State Committee. I did not see them.

In areas occupied by the Finns, crops for the past three years had been shipped back to Finland. The Finns constantly searched the homes and barns of the Soviet people, seeking hidden foods and supplies. In Petrozavodsk, capital of the Soviet Karelo-Finnish Republic, and other towns and villages, civilians were not permitted to live in central districts, were not allowed to appear on the streets without red arm bands. The Karelian Red Army paper reported that the Finns organized a chain of concentration camps for civilians, each with 3,000 to 5,000 prisoners. Behind barbed wire "Finnish Hitlerities" beat, tortured and starved Soviet citizens, feeding them dead cats and dogs. They worked fourteen to sixteen hours daily at impossibly hard tasks. A prisoner who escaped from the Koochkovka camp claimed that 40 per cent died from beatings and starvation.

The major said that he had talked to Finnish prisoners. Toivo Pasonen, commandant of the village of Panila, rubber-hosed a sick and blind woman, Maria Petrova, who didn't want to dig Finn trenches. A prisoner had written: "We drank a lot and then dragged three girls with us . . . left them in their birthday clothes"; Moilanen Arne Ensida, soldier in the 101st Finn Division wrote: "In the village of Koikari we violated women, then shot them. Nobody was left." Will Soutari, of the Fifth Finn Chausseurs, confessed he had ordered two sixty-year-old men to dig graves and then shot them. Another Finn prisoner quoted Lieutenant Hapoia, Twelfth Regiment, Sixth Finn Division, who had received

special political training, that after the war "Russia will be
divided between Germany and her allies. Karelia, Leningrad and
other territories will go to Finland." An escaped Soviet soldier
reported that in a Finnish war prison camp called "Camp of
Death," Finns let individual prisoners loose and then allowed
hungry dogs to chase them. Also that an officer shot two prisoners
for picking up garbage from a dump, killed another who was too
weak to cut wood.

An orderly in the 30th Finn Infantry Division testified at a
hearing which the major attended that he was ordered to chop off
a Red Army man's head with an ax, which he did. The next day
Lieutenant Roosanen-Seppo ordered him to boil the head in a
kettle. The remaining skull was turned over to Roosanen who
took it home when on leave as an "original" gift. This was
evidently a common practice as a Red Army paper published a
picture of another lieutenant posing with a skull under which
was the inscription in Finnish: "Lieutenant Olkinoora admiring
the skull of Ivan" (Finns called all Russian soldiers "Ivan").

When I asked the major if such stories would make Red Army
soldiers savage, he replied: "If you mean will they chop off heads,
the answer is No. If you mean will they fight until they die, the
answer is Yes." Then he showed me this quotation from an editorial in a Red Army Karelian newspaper called "To Battle for
the Country." The major read it: "Warriors of the Karelian
Front: Do not rest day or night while hated Mannerheim robbers
prowl on your native land. It's not enough to find and destroy
Olkinoora and Roosanen-Seppo. Our holy duty to our country is
to put an end to corrupt White Finnish militarism so that these
gangs of beastly savages will never again attack Soviet villages and
towns and commit such atrocities."

The question of how these atrocities would affect the Russians,
especially the Red Army when it went into foreign countries,
bothered many of us. We soon had an answer. American and
British correspondents were taken to Rumania early in July. Reporters agreed that not only had the Soviets lived up to Molotov's
pledge ("The Soviet Government declares that it does not pursue
the aim of acquiring Rumanian territory or of altering the existing
social structure of Rumania"), but that the Red Army's conduct
appeared to be beyond criticism.

A few weeks later we had a chance to observe the behavior
of Russian civilians under rather unique circumstances. On July

18 a little notice was printed in *Pravda* stating that German prisoners would pass through Moscow at eleven that morning, and the commandant of the Moscow garrison requested that there be no vocal demonstration. The route of the procession was given.

I stood upon an iron railing outside of a bread store near Mayakovsky Square. It seemed as if every man, woman and child in Moscow had crammed the sidewalks along Gorky Street. Despite the instructions in *Pravda*, you expected some kind of outbreak, some kind of riot. It was impossible to imagine the same thing happening along the Grand Concourse in the Bronx or along Pennsylvania Avenue in Washington without an eruption.

By eleven all traffic in the area where the prisoners were due to pass had been stopped. Subway exits were closed. Busses were unable to move through the mobs. Spectators took them by storm and climbed onto the bus tops despite efforts of the drivers, all women, to chase them away.

Shortly after eleven the "parade" started. There were no bands. No cheering. No flags waved as the 57,600 prisoners captured during the great Belorussian campaign moved up Gorky Street. First came proud, immaculately tailored Red Army officers, mounted on perfectly groomed horses. Next came the Nazi generals. There was no rhythm in their ambling. They wore their medals, but without defiance. They needed shaves. Their boots were gray with the dust of Minsk. Company after company followed along. Tankists, parachutists, infantry, engineers. Once in awhile a group would attempt to keep in step just to maintain morale. But only the first two or three lines managed it. The others didn't care.

Russian newsreel and still photographers rode by on trucks. Every office and apartment window had a full quota of craning citizens. Young mothers brought infants and held them high over their heads. Schoolteachers brought their classes of youngsters. Everyone wanted to see the hated "supermen." Everyone wanted a taste of victory.

For more than two hours the Germans shuffled past. They didn't look good. A few were defiant-eyed. Mostly they blinked, incredulous in the sunlight. At last they were seeing Moscow. But not quite as Hitler had promised. They were two and a half years behind the Führer's blitzkrieg schedule and they were on the wrong end of the rope.

The discipline of Moscow's people was amazing. There was a holiday atmosphere, but that was understandable. For months the Sovinformbureau had been announcing enormous figures on the German prisoners. While the Russian reader believes these statistics, reading is not the same as seeing.

There were a few comments. A little quiet fist-clenching. A little quiet whispering. Many people said, "But they are dark, and small. They do not look like supermen. They do not even look like Aryans." Others said, "I hope they make them work, and hard."

I suppose they thought stronger things. Each spectator had lost someone. Each spectator had been affected by the Nazi atrocities. I asked a Russian friend how she felt. She said, "Each of us felt that he or she had to be dignified, that it was the duty of a Soviet citizen." I don't think anything ever made me feel the strength of these people quite as much as their staunch silence that July morning.

As I walked back to the hotel I was followed by a tough-looking eleven-year-old who had been attracted by my camera. "What did you think of the Germans?" I asked him. He spat before answering and ground out his cigarette butt on the pavement. "I saw them come in at the station," he said. "I saw them being inspected. They are all lousy, every one of them. I had to run away, the lice were hopping off so fast."

8.

In August, we went to Poland, to Lublin. There was a funny incident at the airport as we left. We had started out of the terminal toward our plane, when we were called back. "You are going to a foreign country," said the little man from the Narkomindel, "you must have baggage inspection." A frightened little girl began looking through our bags, aimlessly. Alex Werth told her, in Russian, that we could all save time if she would just tell us what she was looking for. Startled, the little girl stopped her inspecting and said, "I'm not looking for anything in particular, I'm just looking."

In Lublin we had further evidence of the Red Army's good conduct. I talked to some wealthy Poles who had no reason to like the Soviets or the Polish Committee of National Liberation (now the Provisional Government). But they admitted quite frankly that they were amazed by the Red Army. "They have kept to themselves, they have been extremely polite, they have not taken anything—it's so surprising after what we expected. They leave the police work to Polish troops. And they do not even fraternize with them." Everything I could see at Lublin substantiated this statement.

We arrived in Lublin on a Saturday. We had come to see, among other things, the death camp at Maidanek. We had read reports in the Soviet press by Soviet writers. The stories had sounded so horrible that our natural impulse was to believe them overwritten. I decided to go to Maidanek as a skeptic, and to keep careful notes on my personal reactions as well as my objective observations.

The sun was hot on Sunday morning and the Polish girls wore their best hand-embroidered dresses to mass and the men of Lublin chatted on street corners without a furtive over-the-shoulder look. We drove along the Chelm road about a mile from Lublin. Dmitri Kudriavtsev said: "They called this 'the road to death.'" Kudriavtsev always surprised me whenever I met him at each new atrocity. He is a short man, with curly hair and a nice face. He has such an even, soft way of talking. You could not guess that he has pored over more horrors in the past three years than any other living man.

Our car halted before a well-guarded gate. "This is Maidanek," Kudriavtsev said. I saw a huge, not unattractive temporary city. There were about two hundred trim, gray-green barracks, systematically spaced for maximum light, air and sunshine. There were winding roads and patches of vegetables and flowers. The grass inside was as green as the grass outside. As our car splashed through the dust I had to blink twice in the warm, strong sunlight to take in the jarring realities: the 14 machine-gun turrets jutting into the so-blue sky; the 12-ft.-high double rows of electrically charged barbed wire; the gaunt kennels which once housed hundreds of man-eating dogs.

We got out to inspect the bathhouses, which still had German signs: *Bad und Desinfektion*. Kudriavtsev said without emotion: "They came here for a shower. Their clothes are in the other room. The Germans said, 'Now you have had your wash, go in there.'" He led us into one of four gas chambers. It was solid gray concrete—walls, ceiling, floor, a room about 20 feet square and about 7 feet high. A single large steel door hermetically sealed the entrance. Everything was bare. There was a light switch, three apertures, nothing more. There were two openings for the pipes which brought in the gas from outside, one a thick glass peephole, protected by steel netting. The Germans watched through the glass after switching on the light. It took about seven minutes for this "cyclone" gas to kill the occupants, as many as 250 at once. Kudriavtsev was explaining: "The gas affects all parts of the organism. It is quicker when the body is warm, washed and wet."

I took notes calmly, feeling little emotion. It was all so cold and bare. It was like being shown through a scientific laboratory and everybody was talking in chemical formulae and equations beyond my comprehension. I wrote: "There are four chambers fed by cyclone gas—innocent, small, pale blue crystals which give off poison containing cyanide when exposed to air—two chambers for plain carbon monoxide. Maximum turnover simultaneously —2,000."

"On one day," Kudriavtsev said, "November 3, 1943, they annihilated 18,000 people, Poles and Jews, political prisoners and war prisoners."

We walked back into the sun. There was no horror left in Maidanek. It had evaporated with the Germans. We got in cars and rode a little distance to some cabbage patches. The big, leafy cabbages were covered with a sooty, gray dust, and next to them were heavy, high mounds of gray-brown stuff. "This," said Kudriavtsev, "is fertilizer. A layer of human bones, a layer of ashes—human ashes, a layer of manure. This is German food production. Kill people. Fertilize cabbage." We asked who ate the cabbages. He said the Nazis. He said most of the fertilizer was used on the big *SS* estates.

It wasn't very far to the crematorium. It might have been a big bakeshop or a very small blast furnace with its Dinas brick ovens and its tall, Dinas brick chimney. Here the Nazis carted the bodies, straight from the gas chambers. They cut them up to fit. They put them on iron stretchers which slid on rollers into the five greedy mouths, the five ovens which, heated by coke, reached a heat pitch of 1,700° Centigrade. "There was great economy," said Kudriavtsev, "these furnaces also heated the water for the camp." Like a blast furnace, the crematorium never was allowed to go out.

I kept jotting down phrases like "murder elevated to a branch of industry"—"the mass production of death"—"here's the peak in Nazi secret weapons—blitz burning."

But still the sun was hot and I was sweating, but it was the heat and not emotion. I tramped over some bones sauntering around the bakeshop. We heard about a young Polish girl who had refused to undress for a shower. The degenerate, sadistic Mussfeld who ran the crematorium ordered her shoved into the furnace alive. Her hair burned quick and bright and then she crisped up like bacon on an overhot skillet. A German witness confirmed this story later. By scientific chopping the Germans stuffed four to seven corpses into each oven. It took just fifteen minutes to charge the stoves and burn the bodies. They could disintegrate 1,900 people per day into ashes.

"On big days," said Kudriavtsev, "they had bonfires. There were too many victims. They reverted to more primitive methods. They shot them, poured benzine on them, and burned them."

A young Pole with us who had lived in Lublin during the occupation, pointed out a stack of urns. "They called on people in Lublin, and they wrote to families. They said, 'Your son has been killed. Would you like to buy his ashes, delivered in a special urn?' They charged as much as they thought they could get— from 500 to 10,000 zlotys. Of course they were not his ashes."

Near the ovens was the remains of a room with a big stone table. Here gold fillings were extracted from the teeth. When the trusties suspected that victims had swallowed rings or other valuables they dissected the bodies on the table. No corpse or piece thereof could be burned without a stamp on the chest: "Inspected for gold fillings."

Kudriavtsev led us to some large, open graves. Here were buried the bodies of the camp's personnel who had been hastily shot and buried on July 21 in the last hectic days when the Red Army was closing in fast. So fast, that the Germans had not the time to completely burn and destroy Maidanek and its witnesses, both living and dead. The pits smelled in the warm sun. I carefully walked around to the windward side. I remembered the cold and the snow and the smell of Polish bodies at Katyn Forest. These corpses were fresher. Around the pits, in the grass, poppies were growing. Orange-red poppies. Big ones. I kept my eyes away from the graves, not concentrating while Kudriavtsev talked on. I kept thinking, Nature doesn't much care. Here are dandelions and cornflowers, and very big poppies, and the sun is shining.

We filed quickly away from the stench. Crouching low we followed Kudriavtsev through an opening in the barbed-wire fence to a bordering barley field. More mass graves. A few yards away Jersey cows were peacefully grazing. I heard Kudriavtsev say: "The local people told us . . . we just began to dig . . . three layers of cut bodies." I looked closely and there were skulls and a piece of a Red Army service hat and a buzzing mass of large flies in the August sunlight.

We went back into the camp's grounds. It was a big camp—670 acres, with a fine view of Lublin. There were beds for the 40,000 who still lived and worked to build a bigger, better and more efficient death camp, and then died to make room for 40,000 fresh recruits. Once this had been the Lublin airport. The *SS* came in 1940 and began building. First they called it Dachau No. 2. But later it was renamed Maidanek after the district. While I made these notes, we came to a large, unpainted warehouse. Not suspecting, I stepped up and up and went inside. It was full of shoes. A sea of shoes. I walked across them unsteadily. They were piled, like pieces of coal in a bin, halfway up the walls. Not only shoes. Boots. Rubbers. Slippers. Children's shoes, soldiers' shoes, ersatz *valinki*, leggings, old shoes, new shoes. They were red and gray and black, some once white, high heels, low heels, evening slippers, beach sandals, suède shoes, and even wooden Dutch shoes. In one corner there was a stack of artificial limbs. There were shoes with open toes, pumps, oxfords, high laced old ladies' shoes, sneakers, galoshes. I kicked over a pair of tiny white shoes which might have been my youngest daughter's. The sea of shoes was engulfing, maddening. They overflowed through the high windows and through the doors. In one place the sheer weight of them had broken the wall and part of the wall had fallen out, and with it a mountain of shoes. It was like an overstocked corncrib in Nebraska.

Standing on the sea of shoes, all of Maidanek suddenly became grimly real and terribly horrible. It was no longer a half-remembered sequence from an old movie or a clipping from *Pravda* or chapters from a book by a German refugee living in Mexico City. The barbed wire had barbs which ripped flesh. The ashes on the big cabbage leaves were the ashes of the brothers of the worn, but pretty, peasant women who had spoken to us that morning at mass. The jutting leg bone in the pit, the piece of Red Army cap belonged to one jolly Ukrainian officer I had met at the front in the Crimea.

I had had enough of Maidanek. But there was more. Irrefutable evidence, as if bones and ashes and shoes are not evidence enough. A room full of passports and documents. Papers of Frenchmen, Russians, Greeks, Czechs, Jews, Italians, Belorussians, Serbs, Poles. Records left behind by some of the one million and a half who were brought to Maidanek. A million and a half of twenty-two different nationalities, including Chinese. People who were swept up from all over Europe. Little people who stood in Hitler's way because they were Jews or Slavs or because they liked to eat or talk or think. I picked up a card marked *La République Française*. Here was the Gallic face of Eugène Durane, metal worker, born in Le Havre on September 22, 1888. In less than a month he would have been fifty-six. He never knew that Paris was free. . . .

As we drove away from Maidanek I asked how many pairs of shoes there were in the warehouse. "Eight hundred and twenty thousand pairs," said Kudriavtsev, "and eighteen carloads of the best ones were shipped to Germany. You will see the receipts at the Gestapo warehouse." The Gestapo warehouse, a large, four-story building, was attached to a theater which had been built, but not finished, for the Polish Catholic Action Youth before the war. Here the Gestapo methodically fumigated and stored everything which the future victims of Maidanek hopefully lugged with them to Lublin. They had been told they were going to a "new settlement." "Bring or ship everything you can," the Nazis ordered. Everything, from their hats and suitcases to their underwear.

In the backyard were huge bins of locks ripped from suitcases. Inside, on the first floor, were long, wooden shelves jammed with accessories. Every floor had rows of shelves on five different levels from the floor to the ceiling. There were razors, scissors, tweezers, cigarette lighters, brushes, combs, watches, flashlights, irons, sunglasses, strops, toothbrushes, mirrors (a few with Gary Cooper's picture on the back), pencils of all sizes and colors, pens, family photos and scrapbooks, soap, hair clippers, darning cotton, chessmen, false teeth, Chinese checkers, and a "counter" of junk jewelry. I stepped on a full squeeze-tube of Ipana toothpaste and jumped as if it had been a snake. On another floor there were belts, corsets, pajamas. Ties hung on racks suspended from the ceiling. Everything was separated in neat stacks. Everything was sorted and counted.

I read over a signed tally sheet, officially stamped by the Gestapo—an account of stocks on hand for one day: 55,000 pairs of men's socks, 38,057 women's slips, 19,831 children's suitcases, 18,352 pairs of men's long underwear. . . . On each of the four floors there was a department store bargain basement full of clothes and articles—cold cream, umbrellas, nail files (by the hundred thousands), an orange-colored deck tennis ring, china dolls that cried when you bent them over. From the fourth floor we walked along a passage into the top balcony of the auditorium. This was the Gestapo sorting room: little items were strewn about in the balcony's back rows. The orchestra was full of empty suitcases. The stage was full of shoes.

Later, in Lublin, I talked to Polish families, and heard some of the substantiating firsthand testimony before the joint Soviet-Polish Investigating Committee. One of the witnesses was a dark, little *Obersturmführer* named Theodore Schölen. He was a Nazi party member, an SS man, whom the Red Army had grabbed when it captured Lublin. He said, "At first sight of the crematorium I was ashamed." Then he added, "But I got accustomed to it. . . ." I asked him who bore the chief responsibility for Maidanek. He replied, "Berlin," and then repeated, "We always acted on orders from Berlin." Someone asked him if it had occurred to him that he would be tried for his share in the crimes. Schölen's mouth sagged open and his eyes blinked in astonishment. "That's absurd," he said. "I only carried out orders. As for a trial, I've done nothing, absolutely nothing. I'm blameless." There were others like Schölen, all blameless and smelling of burned flesh. I don't remember much of it. After Maidanek I wanted a bath. I do remember talking to one mother who told me that on November 3, 1943, the stench was so strong, even in Lublin, that she had to get off the street, close all her windows and sit with a handkerchief pressed over her nose.

"The loudspeakers from the camp kept screeching Strauss waltzes," she said. "The 'Beautiful Blue Danube' can never be beautiful to us again." She paused and repeated the words so many Poles and Russians had said that day: "I hope you Americans will not be soft with the Germans."

9.

The story of Maidanek was printed in American newspapers and magazines. But millions of Americans have never heard of it, and many who have do not believe it. In the Soviet Union it ran in all the papers for three and four days, full-page accounts. The Russians, having suffered under German occupation, believe it. Since then, other mass atrocities have been found and exposed. Some of them are even worse than Maidanek. At Tremblyanka in Poland, an estimated 2,764,000 Jews were annihilated. At Birkenau and Auschwitz, also in Poland, more millions were exterminated. Jews were gassed. Or killed by phenol injections in the heart. Non-Jews were just shot. At Birkenau the Nazis carried on biological experiments, using human beings instead of mice or guinea pigs. They tried out sterilization by X ray, and artificial insemination of women. When "patients" failed to respond properly, they were discarded. As at Maidanek, the "life chain" was kept intact. Victims worked until they dropped, were then killed, then cremated, and then their ashes were used as fertilizer.

Already people are saying that these reports are untrue or exaggerated. American soldiers in western Europe have found evidences of Nazi bestiality but nothing on the scale that the Russians have reported, nothing like what I have seen. We forget that the Germans followed two very different procedures. In the western countries where they sought the collaboration of the upper classes and sections of the government, they behaved relatively well. Thus Paris was left almost untouched.

But in the east, the Hitler concept was different. For years he had ranted that nothing in Slav culture was worth preserving, that the Slavs had no rights. Here Hitler knew he would find few Quislings. What he wanted was territory and the wealth of that territory. The people in it would be mere slaves. To break them to his will, to really exploit the Ukraine—and he hoped even the Urals, Hitler had to smash the people, wipe them out, leaving only the broken and intimidated who would work for him.

We must not be misled by those who say that these atrocities were committed by wild, undisciplined troops. This is a myth. The German Army was well disciplined. It carried out specific orders. The Nazis' own testimony at Kharkov and at Maidanek substantiates this fact. The Russians will never be fooled by any

kind of logic, any kind of sympathy which would lighten the
penalty for those who committed the crime, those who ordered it,
and those who planned the ideological concept on which the
orders were based.

Ehrenburg at his most sarcastic, wrote in *Red Star*:

> I can see Germany after her defeat. She will lie languid and
> weak in a chemise tied with pink ribbons. She will murmur
> about brotherhood, beg for help, for Canadian cereal, Chicago
> pork, for consumers' goods and credits, for indulgence and
> amnesty. Is it possible that this "invalid" will not be dragged
> from her bed? Remember that the mattress she is lying on is
> stuffed with women's hair from Sobibur, Maidanek and Trem-
> blyanka.
>
> No, common justice must triumph, and it will triumph. . . .
> There is no room on this earth for child slayers.

While the Russians want justice, they just as definitely do not
want revenge. There may be individual acts of violence, as there
are in any army, but it will not be organized, and it will not be
countenanced by Soviet authorities.

> We will not kill children—as everyone knows; we are human
> beings [Ehrenburg writes]. We will not asphyxiate people with
> gases or bury them alive or cut off girls' breasts. We will not
> yield to the instinct of revenge. But we want to know that all
> the prisoners are going to be punished. We want to know that
> Smolensk, Warsaw, Rouen and Belgrade are rebuilt before the
> Germans are allowed to rebuild Lubeck or Cologne. . . . Silence,
> cold hatred and contempt—that must govern our attitude to-
> ward Germany. We want them to be tried. They will be tried.
> Our country, our people, are a guarantee of that.

Book 10

The World from Moscow

IT IS a mistake to think that all Russians think only what they are told to think. They do not have freedom of speech or freedom of the press in the sense that we do in the United States. That is a matter of record. But until decisions are made at party or government councils, Russians—especially Russian Communists—like to take sides and argue. You can debate with chance acquaintances for hours over vodka and ice cream as I did one night last September at the Hotel Moskva's restaurant; you can often have a healthy discussion with some of the younger members of the Foreign Office on trips to liberated areas or to the front; sometimes you can even beard a commissar or vice-commissar at a diplomatic reception and more rarely by appointment in his office; you can listen while a plain-spoken American like Eric Johnston takes issue with a party leader at the Central Committee's *dacha* in a Siberian city, you can hear Russians everywhere discussing the latest issue of their leading journal on foreign affairs—*War and the Working Class*—or griping because they can't get a copy.

It is true that American and British correspondents are not permitted to move around as freely as they would like, that many sources of information are closed to them. But it is impossible to spend any length of time in the Soviet Union without forming some impressions of what the Russians think about the outside world.

This is based on what I have read in the Soviet press, what officials have told me, what I have heard the people saying. The opinions expressed, therefore, are not necessarily my own. Nor, so far as I know, are they the official opinions of the Kremlin or the Soviet Foreign Office. But I believe they are not inaccurate recordings of that always nebulous, often dangerous catchall called "public opinion."

The Kremlin and the people want peace and will fight for it. The Russians have been fighting for peace on the battlefields, they believe they fought for it at Dumbarton Oaks and that they are fighting for it diplomatically in Lublin, London, Bucharest, Rome, Paris, Chungking, Washington and in Moscow. To Russia peace means security. To attain this security Russians think and act in terms of a simple four-point program: first, render Germany powerless for at least fifty years; second, make sure that governments of border states are friendly; third, remain on friendly terms with all countries of the world whose governments are friendly; fourth, co-operate with the United States and Great Britain in the policing of the world through an organization of United Nations as outlined at Dumbarton Oaks.

Theoretically several points in this program overlap. But not to the Russian mind, conditioned by twenty-five years of crisis, twenty-five years of fear and suspicion of the outside world. The Russians have never forgotten Allied intervention attempts[*] against the weak Soviet regime in the early 'twenties which Churchill called "the march of fourteen states"; they have not forgotten that Munich was a green light for Hitler to drive east against them; some have not forgotten the long wait for the second front. The Russians, therefore, are moving with caution, with concern.

The majority of influential Soviet leaders including Stalin believe that at this stage in world development the Soviet Union *can* live in peace with the rest of the world and avoid major conflicts. They want desperately for this to be true. But—that old fear haunts them—they have been burned before by the capitalist powers. Nevertheless, they realize that the key plank in their security platform is No. 4—acting cohesively with Britain and the United States. If this doesn't work out, if the Soviets suspect a new "sellout," or any attempt by Britain and America to "gang up" on Russia, the Soviets may retreat once again into isolationism or even internationalism of the Comintern variety.

It will take many meetings of minds, many Moscow, Teheran

---

[*] Although the latest *History of the Red Army* published in Moscow does not specifically include the United States and Britain in recounting the struggle against capitalist intervention.

and Yalta conferences before all the Russian fears and suspicions can be smoothed away. These fears and suspicions are not bogeymen built up in an "oriental" mind. To the Russians they are as real as Mussolini's rape of Ethiopia, as frightening as Hitler's massacre of the Jews. Here are some of these fears which keep worrying the Russians in their attempt to work smoothly with the United States and Britain for victory and a better peacetime world:

2.

The fear that the overwhelming anti-Soviet press in America will continue to distort the Soviet Union's true aims and policies, making understanding and friendship almost impossible.

Soviet officials and the Russian people believe that most of the American press is continually machine-gunning Russian thinking. Sometimes they admit that the firing is caused by earnest differences over important issues, other times by sheer irresponsibility. In February, 1944, the United Press cabled a supposed Teheran incident—that at Churchill's birthday party Stalin hit Timoshenko over the head with a bottle because he was making indiscreet remarks. This story was widely published in the United States. It was an obvious fabrication and easily checked since Timoshenko was not even present on the occasion described. In this instance the Soviet Foreign Office demanded and received a retraction and an apology from the United Press.

Russians do not appreciate our concept of "freedom of the press" even though some of them have painfully begun to grasp it. "How is it possible for your newspapers to keep attacking Russia if they sincerely desire to be allied and friendly with Russia?" the Russians keep asking Americans. You tell them that criticism is often helpful, that most United States papers have violently attacked Franklin Roosevelt, and yet we have elected him as our President more often than any other man.

Even the small number of worldly-wise Russians who understand our point of view on freedom of the press protest our "damned if they do and damned if they don't" attitude toward the Soviet Union and international Communism. We didn't like the Comintern. The Soviets, for reasons of their own as well as ours, abolished it. "But now," complain the Russians, "your organs go on publishing scurrilous attacks just as if we had not abolished the Comintern or as if we had done it only superficially and were still secretly using it. Do you trust us or not?"

The Russians blame the hysteria of the U. S. press for America's terrified speculations over a Communist-dominated Europe (by which they say we mean a Communism superimposed on Europe by Moscow). Russians feel that most U. S. newspapers consistently refuse to accept at face value statements and proofs that Moscow is not fomenting revolution and not exporting Marxism but is, in fact, willing to use its influence as a stabilizing, conservative force in shattered Europe.

Discussions and articles in Russian periodicals take it for granted that there is a sound basis for Soviet-Anglo-American co-operation in the postwar world. That is their cornerstone for the future and they have much faith in it. They are bewildered by the great amount of space devoted in American journals of opinion to the topic, "Is postwar collaboration with Russia possible?"

Perhaps because their own papers are official and all-important, the Russians overestimate our press, worry too much about it. But every blast against them which is quoted in Tass dispatches is cause for concern among citizens of all strata. It is more difficult for the Russian to comprehend these attacks. Soviet newspapers often berate individuals like MacArthur, Willkie, Hearst or Bullitt, but not since the Teheran Conference has there been anything like an outright attack on either the British or American governments or any of our leading officials.

3.

The Russians say that Allied newspaper and radio commentators, particularly Americans, have a way of obtaining so-called "confidential" but actually *imaginary* information about the Soviet Union's plans for the world.

Our defense against such Russian charges is usually that not enough material is made available on Soviet "plans" and we make some complaint against the U.S. State department.

What follows does not purport to come from the Kremlin's mouth. But it is indicative of the way intelligent, well-informed Russians, most of them Communists, were thinking about various countries and "spheres" when I left Moscow last fall.

Italy. Russians say the Allied press was wrong when it attacked the motives behind the Soviet exchange of representatives with Badoglio in March, 1944. Based on information supplied by shrewd, intelligent Andrei Vishinsky, First Vice-Commissar for Foreign Affairs and a member of the Advisory Council for Italy, the U.S.S.R. believed that the King and Badoglio had a strong following in the Italian armed forces. The Russians believed it important to utilize this influence in maintaining discipline and in hastening the expulsion of the Germans. The Soviets made it clear in their press and through diplomatic channels that they had no desire to restrain the right of the Italian people to choose their own form of government at a later date. The exchange did not mean that the Soviets would back the King and Badoglio once their usefulness had waned.

The Americans and British had been wavering over the same line of action, but for a number of reasons including fear of political repercussions at home, they had delayed a decision.

Another reason for the Russian move was not publicized. Soviet officials in Italy felt that they were receiving information third-hand through British General Mason Macfarlane. The Russians were intensely interested in Italian developments—they still are and will be. Italy was the first country in which the Soviets were supposedly working on equal terms with their British allies and American friends. They wanted as much information as possible, at least as much as the others. At the risk of irritating certain people, they traded "representatives" but not diplomats with Badoglio. Russians found it hard to see why this was viewed with alarm in the American press. Conservatives decried it as unilateral action which was about to smash the Teheran agreement, and which was a forerunner of what would be continuous Russian interference in Italian affairs. Liberals yelped that it meant the solidification of the reactionary Badoglio. Now, say the Russians, it is obvious that none of these widely published claims is true. As far as the "unilateral action" was concerned, the matter was explained satisfactorily to British and American officials; they realized that it had been in a measure forced by the Allied setup in Italy which had left hungry Soviets with the third lick at the bone.

Analyzing the ensuing situation in Italy, the Russians point out that the local Communist party has effectively participated with non-Communist parties in the Bonomi government. According to Soviet sources, American and British officials have kept a careful watch and a careful check on the functioning of the Reds within the government. These Allied observers agreed that the Communists have been responsible government officials who have consistently acted as Italian patriots and not as "Russian agents." The Russians ask, "Has this fact received a fair press in America or England?"

Yugoslavia. The Russians have not forgotten how long it took many Americans to believe Russian charges against Mihailovich, how long it was before we put any trust in Tito. Now, the Russians say, the American press has been blowing up the threat of a serious "conflict" between the Soviet Union and Great Britain over Yugoslavia. The Russians think this is ridiculous, and evidently the British think so, too. The Russians like Tito. So do the British. The British were the first to recognize Tito, the first to send him a military mission, the first to send him supplies. In Yugoslavia the Soviet military mission has been working smoothly with the British and frequently asks British advice on how best to deal with the Yugoslavs.

Moscow officials state vehemently that because Tito is a Communist it does not follow that he has any intention of making Yugoslavia a Soviet puppet state. It is highly improbable, they point out, that even if Tito should keep his full powers in postwar Yugoslavia he would wish to communize his country. Yugoslavia was always a land of peasants who owned their own farms. Tito has given assurance that this will once again be the basis of the nation's economy. And Churchill, at their meeting last summer, ardently accepted these assurances.

Greece and the other Balkans. The Russians say they have no interest in Greece. They told me this long before the outbreak of "civil" war. They say, and the British concur, that there has been no contact between Moscow and the Greek EAM. The Russians believed the Greeks should be free to choose their own leaders. But they seem to have remained silent while the British helped them make that choice.

At some time in the future, within the framework of the Dumbarton Oaks concord, Russians envision the possibility of a new Little Entente in the Balkans, a Little Entente based on economic as well as military and political necessities. Even though the old Little Entente was dominated by the French, Russia has always played a vitally important role in the Balkans, and Russia will continue to do so, whether her form of government be tsarist, republican or Communist. The future role of the Soviets will be based on strategic, not territorial interest.

Poland. Last spring Marshal Stalin gave a dinner at the Kremlin for members of the Union of Polish Patriots. Seated at the Marshal's right was a famous Polish professor of mathematics, the late Leon Chwistek. Warmed up by many rounds of toasts to a free, strong and independent Poland, the aged professor became extremely garrulous. He kept expounding to Stalin on the necessity of nationalizing all Polish industries, collectivizing the large estates. Stalin smoked his pipe, drank heavily, said nothing, left the banquet at an early hour.

The next day he sent for Wanda Wasilewska, chairman of the Polish Patriots and later a vice-president of the Polish Committee of National Liberation, forerunner of the Lublin government. Stalin said, very seriously, "You'd better quiet down that mathematics professor of yours."

"Why?" asked Wasilewska.

"Last night he spent two hours trying to convert *me* to Communism for Poland," Stalin said.

Wasilewska, a humorless, intense person, asked: "Did he?"

Stalin, his eyes crinkling with good humor, replied. "He *did not.*"

The moral of this story is that the Soviets claim they have not tried to "Communize" Poland. Nor did they attempt to "take over" the government through the Polish Committee of National Liberation and later the Lublin Provisional Government. The Russians believe that the Lublin leaders are sincere Poles, sincere Polish patriots, and that their actions to date have not discredited them. The independence of this committee, informed Russians maintain, is best illustrated by the argument which went on over the plan to divide up the large estates into small parcels for the peasants. The Communists on the Lublin committee, a minority, argued that the large estates should not be broken up but used for collective farming. They pointed out that the Russian Bolsheviks had made the mistake of distributing the land in tiny pieces and found it didn't work. But the Communists were outvoted by the socialists, the left-wing members of the Peasant party and others who control the committee.

Moscow's move in recognizing the Lublin Poles was dictated not only by distrust for many reactionary members of the London government, but also by the necessity of having someone available to administer portions of liberated Poland immediately. It was a job the Red Army didn't want due to the long-standing enmity between Russians and Poles; and they feared that there would have been cries from the outside world that the Soviets were coming to Poland as "conquerors" when they wanted to be "liberators."

Whatever agreement, if any, is reached on the future of Poland and the Polish government, Russians have insisted right along that it must be based on these fundamentals: that Poland is destined to be a small nation like Czechoslovakia and as such must forget its imperialist aspirations and turn to developing a very backward nation internally; that Polish landlords cannot ever hope to reclaim territory in Belorussia and the Ukraine beyond the Curzon line, although possibly the Soviets might cede Lwow to a genuinely friendly Poland; that a new democratic constitution and a new democratic government must be voted upon by the people after Poland's liberation; that Polish-Russian relations can only work smoothly if all Polish officials inside or outside of the country cease thinking and talking about a third world war in which Poland will be able to regain its "lost" territories in Russia. They also believe any democratic Polish regime will find it necessary to make internal land reforms to satisfy the peasant and help him achieve greater economic security.

Most Russians think that Poland can and should have Silesia, East Prussia and Pomerania—not only to compensate and strengthen Poland but to weaken Germany.

Most Russians implicitly believe that Marshal Stalin's often expressed desire for a "free, strong and independent" Poland means exactly what it says. They strongly resent the way in which the American press consistently accepted London's side of the Polish controversy and doubted Moscow's. "If this is the way a free press behaves," one Russian said to me after the publication of a particularly explosive anti-Soviet article in a prominent American magazine, "deliver us from it!"

Aside from the short-lived rumor of a separate British-German peace, few stories upset the Russians as much as a dispatch printed in Moscow newspapers last summer quoting accounts in the U.S. press of an exhibit which *émigré* Poles were sponsoring in Rome. This exhibit included maps showing Polish expansionist plans which called for the retaking by Poland of large slices of Soviet territory. Another map showed Polish plans for a new small-state *cordon sanitaire* against the U.S.S.R. after the war. That such plans should have been publicly promulgated by exiled Poles did not surprise or shock the Russians; what upset them was the thought that Rome had been liberated by Allied troops, that Rome was still under British-American martial law—and that permission for such anti-Soviet propaganda had been given by our authorities.

4.

Russians fear that we will not cease our brickbatting at what the Soviet Union considers its internal affairs while at the same time we resent any comment they make on our internal affairs.

When a Russian newspaper commentator intimated that he thought Roosevelt's foreign policy was more "internationalist" than Dewey's, many Americans became alarmed about Soviet "interference" in our internal affairs. But day after day American journals feel free to attack Stalin, to demand that Russia surrender territory which it considers its own, or to tell the Soviets how they should treat religious minorities. The Soviets on their part say they have been restraining their right to criticize any weakness in our system except in so far as its weakness seems to affect the United Nations' war or peace efforts. For example, since the war there has been nothing in the Soviet press about our own special minority problem—the Negroes. When I tried to file a story listing a number of questions asked me by Soviet citizens, the Russian censors would not let me mention queries about lynchings in the South because they thought that the German radio might use it as an indication of disunity among the Allies.

Last September a Soviet official, discussing "freedoms" with me, asked me if I knew that Latvian nationalists were being financed by Americans in a campaign to wrench Latvia away from the U.S.S.R. I hadn't, but the Soviet official knew all the details. I asked him what *his* government would do about it, if anything. He shrugged his shoulders. "Nothing," he replied, "but it brings up the old question regarding freedom—*freedom for what?* We abolished the Comintern. We have no connections with any party in America. But you permit such things as this scurrilous, lying attack to be financed, printed and mailed in America." I explained that this was a private matter and that the Comintern, through the Communist party of the U.S.S.R., had been a Moscow-dominated organization.

"You are quibbling," said the official. "After all the Latvian Minister Bilmanis is still recognized by your State Department.

Without this official status of his in Washington he could not hope to raise money for his anti-Soviet slanders."

Other Russians have cited the fact that we have permitted a Lithuanian relief group to organize and collect money in the United States. This group, which is strongly anti-Soviet, has no practical means whatsoever of distributing its relief in Lithuania, which is a Soviet republic. It refuses to deal with Soviet distribution officials. And, Russians state, it quietly spreads anti-Soviet propaganda. The Soviet government has never lodged any official protest. "Would you have as much forbearance if the shoe was on the other foot?" I have been asked.

The Russians do not consider that the Baltic question is open to any discussion whatsoever. Their story is that the Soviet government only recognized the independence of the Baltic States (formerly part of tsarist Russia) in 1920 because Soviet Russia had been weakened by civil war and still faced foreign intervention. They point out that the United States and Great Britain recognized the independence of the Baltics a year or two *after* the Soviets. The Russians claim that our recognition was delayed because it was still hoped that the Soviet regime would be overthrown. They say that "The United States and England recognized the rights of tsarist Russia or any other Russian government in the Baltic States but not the right of Soviet Russia." Then when it became apparent that the Soviets were becoming consolidated and chances of its overthrow were dimmer, the great powers including the United States and Britain recognized the Baltic republics hoping they would serve as jumping-off points for future intrigues against the Soviet Union.

Any attempt to re-establish the Baltic States' independence is closely linked in the Russian mind with "reactionary plans" for establishing anti-Soviet "blocs and federations." While the United States and Great Britain are *not* currently advocating the independence of the Baltics, the Russians do not forget that we permit representatives of Estonia, Latvia and Lithuania in Washington, give them official status, allow them to intrigue against the Soviet Union. If we are really allies, Russians argue, can such things go on?

If it isn't the Baltics, it's Poland. Sir Bernard Pares once said that there are more Trotskyites in the U.S.A. than there are in the U.S.S.R. It is also true, according to the Russians, that there are more anti-democratic Poles in England and the United States than there are in Poland. The Soviet government knows concretely, for example, that the exiled London Poles and organizations which they control or influence have spent millions of dollars yearly on what amounts to anti-Soviet propaganda. In many cases this propaganda has been almost word for word the same as the most vicious Goebbels variety.

Influential Americans have urged the Soviet government to open an official Soviet information bureau in the United States. They point out that many of the half-truths printed about the U.S.S.R. and Soviet officials is due to lack of any checkable, substantial material emanating from the Soviet Union. It is also pointed out that the very newspapers which freely publish stories put out by anti-Soviet groups would probably be willing to give as much space to counter-information from the Soviets. But the Soviets have refrained from starting such an information service (although the British, for example, have a large, well-organized propaganda and information office) for fear that they would be attacked for trying to flood America with Communist propaganda and thus worsen Soviet-American relations on an official level.

5.

Russians fear that we will go right ahead voicing objections to Soviet foreign policy because it tends to favor and strengthen the Soviet Union.

This sounds like a vague indictment, but I have heard many Russians make it. This "fear" is closely tied up with the previous ones, but it recurs so frequently in Russian thinking on the subject of foreign affairs that it is worth a few words. The Russians say that some Americans not only wanted Russia to abandon the Comintern but at the same time to forfeit any right to a strong affirmative foreign policy. Some say this attitude has in the past derived from our own lack of a constructive policy and that as a result our thinkers have taken the lazy alternative of sniping at everybody else's policies, especially Russia's.

A Moscow editor told me, "If the Soviet Union signs a peace pact with Czechoslovakia you scream with indignation that Russia is strengthening itself. If Russia exchanges envoys with Italy you yell that Russia is being 'tough and realistic,' implying we are putting something over on our allies." Russians say we seem unable to face the fact that the Soviet Union is emerging from this war as *the* great European power, and as *the* great European power it is going to get many concessions based on power politics which the weak, prewar Soviet state couldn't get based on the Comintern.

For example, the Russians believe that in addition to the United Nations Organization, they have as much right to promote a regional system of eastern European nations composed of co-operative and well-disposed independent governments as the United States has to develop its Pan-American policy.

And they point with pride to their relations with Czechoslovakia for the past decade. A Red Army officer who had been stationed in Prague before the war asked me: "Doesn't this show that a small, independent nation can live independently and peacefully as an ally of the Soviet Union?"

6.

Russians fear that a large body of Americans will favor a soft, unrealistic peace for Germany and that we will disagree on Germany's future.

There is currently no more widespread fear among all the Russians than that victory will bring about a "strategy of mercy" in our treatment of Germany and German war criminals. At the outset it must be repeated once again that many foreigners have misinterpreted the Russian attitude toward Germany. What they want, they say, is justice, not revenge. They have no intention of flogging, raping, burning, murdering innocent women and children, razing German historical museums and seats of culture (if there are any left intact). But their idea of justice is based on full punishment for those who committed crimes, for those who ordered the crimes to be committed, for those responsible for the planning of these crimes. Their idea of a just peace calls for such harsh restrictions on the Germany of the future that it can never again start a major holocaust in Europe.

Russians wonder whether Americans will feel as strongly as they do. On occasion Russian newspapers recall the results of the last war and blame American and British "softness" for allowing Germany to keep her war industries. The more politically aware don't call it "softness," but rather a deliberate attempt over the years to build Germany up as a bulwark against Red Russia. The bulwark, one vice-commissar told me "became a monster which not only attacked us but the very people who built him.

But we are not interested in such poetic justice—not in the past, the present or the future."

Moscow was terribly upset by reports of American fraternization with the Germans when we first invaded the Reich. They think that perhaps we have a messiah complex, that our pity will be stirred by pictures of forlorn mothers and crying babies, that we will want to let the Germans pick up all their unexploded toys of war and play with them again. They know that our cities have not been bombed, strafed and razed by Germans, that our churches have not been turned into brothels, that our civilians haven't been forced into concentration camps by the millions.

They are afraid we will split hairs over who is guilty and who is not guilty of Germany's unparalleled war crimes. They say we let the Kaiser and Hindenburg and Ludendorff escape without proper trials after the last war. Some Russians even whisper that if Hitler and some of his gang escape to Spain or Argentina, the United States may not help to get them out and punish them. But responsible Soviet leaders have faith that we would go after the Nazis anywhere.

The whole subject of postwar Germany is viewed with some trepidation. Russians have asked me what will happen if the land is divided in the Soviet-controlled area while the landlords are taken into the government in the American area? Will Americans and British attempt to build up Catholic support while the Russians do not encourage the church? Will Russian discipline be severe while British-American discipline is over-tolerant? While these unanswerable questions do come up in Russian minds, they are willing to let their military and political leaders settle them with our leaders.

Underlying Russian fears about differences in Germany is the old scare of the capitalist encirclement, the old suspicion that a new attempt may be made to use Germany as a "bulwark" against the Soviet Union. This time, Russians say, they are strong enough so that they would not stand aside, would not tolerate such an attempt.

7.

Russians fear that powerful international monied interests will attempt to rescue, rebuild and use German industry for their own interests.

The Kremlin is still very much afraid that American and British cartel interests are making secret deals in Switzerland and Portugal to preserve their connections in Germany for postwar monopolies. Last spring the official Moscow radio said this on an international broadcast:

> Some American companies have concluded agreements providing for the immediate renewal after the war of interrupted cartel relations with German companies. . . . Economic appeasers are at work behind the scenes . . . their intentions are absolutely clear. They are defending the interests of a small group of international monopolists who are making super-profits out of war supplies. They are already searching for ways and means of creating a high price structure after the war under the guise of the "reconstruction of Europe's economy" by the effort of the old international cartels. They want German monopolies to participate in this.

These international cartel interests are associated in Russian minds with the "soft peace" feelers, are linked up with plans for once more utilizing German industry as a springboard against the socialist state. Last winter *Red Star* warned: "Germany will again become the center of the international cartels as before the war, if an agreement is not achieved among the Allies to liquidate German monopolies."

Undoubtedly this is one of the agreements which England and America will make with the Soviet officials if they have not already done so.

8.

Russians fear that postwar reactionary governments in the United States and Great Britain might someday form secret coalition against the Soviet Union.

Here it must be repeated again that despite their warmth of feeling toward England and the United States, some Russians have not forgotten (what they call) the nonrecognition days of Herbert Hoover, the "Go East, Adolf" days of Chamberlain, the anti-Soviet conspiracies of Churchill. Currently Soviet fears of a possible return to these days are crystallized in the demands of Russia's delegation at Dumbarton Oaks that the permanent members of the United Nations Council—Russia, Britain, United States, China and France—should have the right to vote action by the League even if one of the Big Five is a party to the aggression under discussion.

Members of the Soviet Foreign Office point out that the League of Nations, dominated by Britain and France, forced the Soviet Union out of its councils for years. They argue that the League could never seem to achieve unanimity of action to move against Japan's aggression in Asia but it moved quickly, decisively and unanimously against the Soviet Union at the time of its first war against Finland when Russia was squeezed out of the League. They recall that during this 1939-1940 period the English and the French were even preparing to send expeditionary forces to "Little Finland" to help Baron Mannerheim against the Soviets.

The fear of capitalist encirclement and capitalist intervention is still real to the Soviets. It is the counterpart to our fear of Bolshevism. The Soviets have a pact with Britain. They respect it. They would like such an alliance with the United States, but none has been forthcoming. Although they are allied with Britain, the Soviets do not feel they can count on one of the other permanent members of the council to veto proposed action against Russia. They believe that England and the United States could almost always count on each other's veto. They believe, too, that China because of American military aid now and our postwar aid in rehabilitation would nearly always vote with the United States. The position of France was held impossible to determine at least until after the first general peacetime elections. Since I left Moscow a new pact has been signed between the Russians and the French; De Gaulle's visit to Moscow and his government's support of Soviet policy in Poland may have made the Russians feel that France, as a member of the United Nations Council would be just as friendly toward the U.S.S.R. as toward England or America. Perhaps this increasing confidence that French and Russian security are intimately correlated may induce the Russians to shift their position in regard to the voting mechanics for branding the aggressor.

Since the Baltic States still have "recognized" diplomats in Washington and London, the Soviet Union does not want to be put into the position in which ex-officials of the Baltic States or Poland might appeal to the new League through the United States for territory. James Reston of the New York *Times* aptly summed up the Soviet viewpoint on this last year when he wrote that Russia's "attitude is that we should not ask her to give up the Baltic States any more than she should ask us to give Texas land back to Mexico."

Some Russians worry about the possibility of postwar reactionary governments in England and America not only in connection

with the new League, but in terms of postwar trade. Stalin asked
Eric Johnston if he thought the Soviet Union would still be able to
obtain long-term credits from us if the Republicans returned to
power. Johnston tried to reassure the Marshal.

But the doubt remains. To a certain extent it must be in the
minds of Stalin and Molotov every time they talk to Winston
Churchill or Franklin Roosevelt. They wonder how far ahead they
can commit their governments and how future elections will
affect these commitments?

9.

*Russians fear that our sentimental, missionary attitude toward
China plus our dread of Communism will prevent us from taking
tough, realistic steps to help China out of its present miserable bog.*

The Russians do not share our enthusiasm for China nor do
they have our faith in the Kuomintang leaders.

One reason is that in their relations with China they do not
have our long record of spiritual and economic intervention.
Soviet newspapers and magazines publish very little information
about modern China. Comment is chiefly on Chiang Kai-shek's
failure to achieve a united front with the Yenan Communists
against Japan. The Chinese Ambassador in Moscow and two
Chinese news agency correspondents are treated with utmost
courtesy by Soviet officials. But the average Russian's attitude
toward China is like Stalin's attitude on the Pope—as illustrated
in the following Teheran anecdote.

When Churchill asked Stalin about the possibilities of a *rapprochement* with the Pope, Stalin reportedly frowned and replied,
"The Pope? How many divisions has he?"

Thus in the case of China, Russian skepticism is based on that
nation's current war effort. When defenders of China's position
plead the low level of development in that sprawling country and
point out that a good part of it has been occupied by the enemy,
the Russians cite the example of Marshal Tito. They say, "Look
what Tito did with three hundred thousand irregulars in what
was once a *fully* occupied country. What has Chiang done with
his three million?"

Russian support for the Chinese Communists is theoretical
support at best. They call them "margarine" Communists. They
believe the Chinese Communists should and must make certain
compromises to co-operate successfully with Chungking. They are

convinced that certain Chinese war lords have striven to prevent this unification and have thereby been delivering China into the hands of the Japanese. They believe that Chiang personally must be held responsible for "blockading" Chinese Communist armies in the north, impairing the strength of their resistance against the Japanese and also keeping thousands of picked Chungking troops from the Jap front.

Despite the general lack of confidence in the Chinese government, Soviet leaders are willing to go along with Britain and the United States in agreeing to China's potential importance in the postwar world. They are not yet ready to mix into Pacific affairs themselves, and they are letting us play our cards pretty much as we desire. On one of his missions to Chungking last fall, Presidential Envoy Donald Nelson stopped off in Moscow for a quiet chat with Foreign Commissar Molotov. Before talking to Chungking officials Nelson wanted to ascertain the Soviet attitude. Molotov laid it on the line. The Soviets, he said, will not interfere in China. They have not and will not back the Chinese Communists. They want more than anything else to see China unified on a democratic basis, and they will use their prestige and influence in assisting Washington and London to bring about such a solution.

10.

Some Russians fear that the Vatican might become an increasingly active center for anti-Soviet propaganda and that some Americans would resent Moscow's attempts to defend itself.

As Willkie, Eric Johnston, Donald Nelson and other prominent Americans have discovered, Stalin keeps pretty well abreast of the American press. He knows that the majority of Americans would feel even friendlier toward the Soviet Union if freedom of religion were clearly established. He knows that to insure a continually friendly Poland, for example, that the Soviet Union must win the respect or at least the neutrality of devout Polish Catholics. What Stalin doesn't know is how to deal with the Vatican. Like many Russians he fears the Vatican as the only imposing power which might stand out against the Soviet Union in its attempt to live on friendly terms with the world.

When Father Orlemanski, the Springfield, Massachusetts priest, came to Moscow to investigate conditions in the Polish Army, Stalin seized the opportunity to meet him and to use him as a carrier pigeon. He gave Orlemanski a letter which stated, in effect, that he saw no reason why the Soviet Union and the Vatican could not co-operate. Having done that, Stalin felt the next move was up to the Vatican. So far there has been no favorable move on the Vatican's part.

The Soviet press keeps sniping at the Pope as a long-time friend of Fascism and as a proponent of "soft peace" terms for Germany. *Pravda,* commenting on the Pontiff's 1944 Christmas message, charged that the Pope is against recognition of the people's will and that his policy is "aimed at the protection of Hitlerite Germany and its delivery from responsibility for crimes."

It would be ridiculous to say that the Kremlin has liked, does or will like the Vatican. The clause of the Stalin Constitution of 1936 which guarantees freedom of religion (and anti-religion) is now in effect throughout the Soviet Union and there has been a certain wartime resurgence of religious interest. But the leaders of the Soviet Union are Communists and as Communists they are Marxists and as Marxists they are not religious. Now they feel themselves sufficiently secure and powerful so that most religions no longer are a danger to the Soviet regime.

The Russians know that they will be able to keep the Russian Orthodox Church and many other creeds from meddling in lay matters. They have no assurance that the Roman Catholic church directly, or through organizations friendly to it, will refrain from interfering in the internal affairs of the Soviet Union. They cite Catholic support for the *émigré* officials of the Baltic States, Catholic support for the worst anti-Soviet elements of the Polish *émigrés,* Catholic support for Franco, for local Fascist movements in South America.

11.

Russians fear that we who have not rooted them up in Spain may allow the seeds of Fascism to sprout further in Latin America.

Last winter Churchill made a speech in which he had "kind words" for Franco. These pro-Franco remarks were not printed in the Soviet press version of his talk. A Foreign Office aide admitted that the cut had been made "in the interests of Allied unity" because many Russian readers would deeply resent and "misinterpret" Mr. Churchill's statement. Every Russian knows the history of "neutral" Franco's famous "Blue Division" which fought against the Red Army with the Germans. Many think these divisions had the Pope's blessing. Russians have not forgotten that England and America permitted Franco to seize power in Spain. A Komsomol in Moscow told me that she had always respected the United States until "Americans doped themselves so they could sleep through the horrible nightmare of Spain." Russians think perhaps we have learned a lesson, a lesson brought home to us at Normandy, at Anzio, at Cassino, at Aachen, at Bastogne.

However, Soviet officials still worry about "the sympathetic ear" which United States officials have given to Franco's "mouthings." They say the United States is still shipping chemicals, oil, cotton, to Spain, that Spain is still shipping food and munitions to Germany. If the average Russian does not worry too much about Franco's future, it is because they cannot picture a postwar Europe in which a Franco-ruled Fascist Spain could long exist side by side with a resurgent democratic France, a newborn democratic Italy or even a conservatively democratic England. They hope that even America will use her prestige and influence to end forever the menace of the "evil weed" which we once encouraged.

Once Fascism withers in Spain, Russians can see no other oasis where its bleeding roots could suck fresh nourishment except in the Vatican or in Latin America, specifically Argentina. They regard Latin America as our sphere not only of influence but of responsibility. It is even more difficult for them to understand the goings-on in Argentina during a world war against Fascism than it is for most Americans. What they do understand they do not like. A few of the more outspoken blame us for being too indulgent with Argentine Fascist elements. Except on an official level, Russians do not know the reasons for our Argentine policy, but rightly or wrongly they suspect not our State Department but large British and United States companies which Russians think have great investments in Argentina.

12.

Russian officials fear that if the Soviet Union allows the American and British concept of democracy to prevail in the rest of the world, we will not always back up the theory in practice.

There was never any hint of this fear in the Soviet press until the time of British armed intervention in Greece. But it has nevertheless been a very real fear to Russian leaders. In the last analysis, they realize that it is perhaps the most important single factor which could lead to a new major conflict in Europe. It is a shifting fear that comes and goes, but it is one that is in the back of Russian minds and it will come out sometime during a prolonged discussion of the future of Europe.

To understand this "fear" in its proper context, it must be assumed (and Russians do make this assumption) that at conferences in Moscow, Teheran and the Crimea, the Soviet Union agreed that democracy, as we know it, will be the pattern for the reconstituted nations of Europe. The Soviet Union has repeatedly emphasized that its main interest is to insure that these democracies have "friendly" governments. They say they mean just this and only this. For they believe that any true democracy—which comes from below and not above—will be friendly to the Soviet Union without any outside coercion.

Russian leaders do not now favor Communist regimes even in areas where their prestige and influence is so strong that Communist domination could be established without too much trouble. Russia wants a stable Europe, not one torn by internal disorders even if such strife led to temporarily successful Communist revolutions. But Russians wonder what will happen at some future time if the Communists of a European country, uncontrolled by Moscow, should come into power by democratic means, i.e., by the ballot. At present this is a purely hypothetical question, but Russians have been quick to spot thunderclouds appearing in the Allied press. They say we have indirectly blamed Russia for the fact that Communist parties in Italy and France have been gaining strength.

When a Russian puts it right up to you it is not easy to assure him that a future or present American or British government would stand quietly aside if, let us say, a coalition or outright majority in the French Assembly made a Communist or a Communist-dominated government possible in Paris.

Obviously it's a problem which the Russians as well as our own State Department and the British Foreign Office have not wished to tackle until now. Until the Greek dilemma, it has had no relevance to the immediate military situation. But it is the fundamental issue of tomorrow in Russian minds.

13.

No view of the world from Moscow would be complete without an expression of Russia's attitude toward Japan. The average

Russian hates the Japanese almost as passionately as Americans do. The Soviet government has attempted to maintain a scrupulously correct approach toward Japan until the time is ripe. To the Russians, more than to civilians and warriors of any other nation, this war has been a world war and a political war. They have been taught that militarism and Fascism anywhere in the world breed militarism and Fascism and war elsewhere. They know that this threat cannot be wiped out until the Japanese are destroyed forever as a great power.

When I have asked Russians why they are not fighting the Japanese (especially in the months before June 6 when they asked me about the second front) they looked at me with guiltless surprise. "Why we fought the Japanese back in 1939 long before you did! You didn't help us then. You didn't try to stop Japanese aggression then. We will certainly help smash them, but we must beat Germany first."

The government propaganda machine is slowly preparing the Russian people. Russian school children who read accounts of the 1905 Russo-Japanese war in new Soviet history books are strongly anti-Jap in their opinions. A new book called *Port Arthur* has been published stressing Russian claims to that Far Eastern port. Russian students learn that of all the interventionist powers during the early days of the civil war, Japan was the most vicious and the most successful. Soviet journals now emphasize that Japan has lost the war, and the Soviet official attitude to Jap diplomats has been getting harder and icier. The January 1, 1945, issue of *War and the Working Class* reviewing a new Japanese book, *Origin of the Pacific War*, declared that the author's attempt to blame the conflict on American aggression was "as far from the truth as the sky is from the ground." Such a defense of the United States is not surprising, but the review in the Russian magazine stresses that "It is impossible to overlook the chapter devoted to Japanese intervention in the Soviet Far East, entitled 'Siberian Expedition,' where tricks of falsification hide the truth that Japanese imperialism stubbornly persisted for four long years in pillaging and robbing Soviet Far Eastern Territories."

The Russians feel they have a score to settle with the Japs, and they may be able to do it after the collapse of Germany. If they don't do it now it is because their forces in the East, while large, could not immediately check the Japs who have huge, well-equipped armies in Manchuria. The chief Soviet Far Eastern port of Vladivostok is extremely vulnerable to Japanese air, sea and land power and its present garrison could not long hold out. If Jap bombers attacked the vital Trans-Siberian rail line in force, the major means of moving men and supplies to the Far East would be cut off. Granting of air bases to the United States would also present tough problems in supply, as we would have to fly in high-grade gasoline and oil.

What will the Russians want from a Pacific settlement as the result of their helping to beat Japan? They expect a share of the responsibility of safeguarding the peace. And I have heard these points mentioned: the return of Dalny and Port Arthur; complete sovereignty over all of Sakhalin Island; some of Japan's shipping; Japanese labor forces to rebuild any Soviet cities which might be destroyed in the fighting. The Soviets have also expressed interest in being one of the partners with China and the United States in any trusteeship arrangement for a future independent Korean republic.

14.

I have been back in the United States long enough now to know the questions people ask, to know some of their gravest doubts about Russia. I sincerely feel that Americans cannot hope to understand the Soviet Union unless they are first honestly willing to consider these basic assumptions:

The Russians have a greater stake in a long peace and a stable Europe than any other nation. They sincerely want to co-operate with us in maintaining peace.

The tide of history may sweep many nations of the world onto the left bank, politically, but the waves that carry them there will not be blown up by golden winds from Moscow.

The Russians have no desires for large slices of new territories. They are endowed with more than enough undeveloped resources to keep them peacefully occupied for the next hundred years. But, on the other hand, we cannot expect that the Soviet Union will be the first major power to win a war and lose territory. By this, I mean the Baltic States, and the parts of Poland and Rumania reincorporated into the Soviet Union in 1939.

The Russians say it is sheer wishful thinking to dispute the fact that the essential work of peace keeping must rest upon four or five strong military nations, or that the essential work of world

social, economic and judicial organization must be jointly undertaken by all nations.

The Russians believe that if there are factors which can obstruct
continued Anglo-American-Soviet co-operation, most of these factors can be found in the United States and England—not in the
U.S.S.R.

Book II

What's in It for Us?

ERIC JOHNSTON told Soviet trade officials at a banquet given by Mikoyan, "We in America have a proverb which says that your only true friend is the one who knows the worst about you and still likes you." Then he went on to emphasize the basic differences between the U.S. and the U.S.S.R. In fact, he said that in economics we were more different from Russia than any other country. But he wound up by saying that this difference need not be a barrier to good relations.

The Russians liked this speech. They printed the most important sections of it. I think they did more than that. They studied it, and made sure that others read and studied it. Wherever I traveled in the U.S.S.R. I found that the local inhabitants had a surprising familiarity with Johnston's ideas. The Soviet officials found things in this speech which they have been wanting to say —and Johnston said it for them.

No country in the world is envied as much as America. The Russians know that the United States provided the blueprint for their own industrial development; we sent them engineers and technicians, too. They envy our culture—our fountain pens and our shoe stores, our cans of fruit and our cigarette lighters; these things, to them, are American culture. They love our movies. They think we live like Rockefellers. They think we fight well, almost as well as Russians. They are exceedingly grateful for our material aid during the war; for millions of Russian families American supplies may have been the difference between getting by and starving.

More and more Russian citizens have been going abroad—as diplomats, as businessmen, as students, as soldiers. The capitalist world has dazzled them. It's a great tribute to their own idealism and love of country that more of them haven't decided to stay in

351

England or the United States or Mexico. We have things they only dream about. But most Russians are living for the better day that's coming, and a few years more or less do not matter so much.

Yet I found many Russians who hoped that after the war the Soviet government would become more like England and America. They hoped this because they want peace and security and they know it depends on being friendly with England and America, especially America. They admired our planes and our shoes when they saw them and marveled how we could fight a war and still have supplies to send across the seas to allies. Perhaps some of them even wished they had such an economic system.

So that when Johnston underlined the fact that our two systems were very different—and yet we could co-operate, that made Soviet officials happy. It made the Russian people happy, too. Because— and let's not kid ourselves—the vast majority of them like their own way of doing things pretty well, and maybe they wouldn't care to change it for anybody.

We like our way of running things, and I think the Russians understand pretty well that we won't tolerate outside interference. The average Russian is not interested in world revolution, and as I've already said, I don't think Stalin is going to "export" revolution, either. He'd much rather export fur and import our heavy machinery.

I have written my impressions of the Russians. When I came back to the United States I met a Russian girl who has been here since 1941. She has traveled all over our country. She has met the same kind of people here that I met in her country. Naturally she was terribly anxious to hear my impressions of Russia. Then I asked her what she thought of the United States. The question surprised her. Americans always asked her about the Soviet Union and never bothered to find out what she thought of things here. We just naturally take it for granted that a Russian would be bowled over.

And so the girl had to think for a few minutes. She had no ready answer. She told me she was thrilled at first. It seemed more wonderful than she could have imagined. Her impulse was to stay here forever. She liked Americans, they liked her.

But after three years, she wanted to go home. Not alone for sentimental or patriotic reasons, she said. I took some notes as she tried to express herself about why she preferred her own country and her own people even if it meant a harder way of life. She began by talking about how we were different. "Americans are naïve. About everything," she said. "They are the most generous people in the world. But this generosity is superficial, it is on the surface. Because living is so easy. When they give, they give from largess. When we in Russia give, we give a piece of the heart, part of the blood of life.

"The Russian is more of an individual. That is because life is very hard. He is on his own. Every day he is faced with important decisions about what to eat, whether to eat, how to work, whether to sleep or whether to keep fighting. He must, in the last analysis, make these decisions himself.

"I lived my whole life under the Soviets. Many times there have been things I wanted to say but I could not say them and I did not understand why. Freedom of speech you call it. But is that the main barometer of happiness? Here you can say anything. You can call Roosevelt anything you want. Does that really make you happier?"

She paused, not really expecting me to answer. Then continued in her uncertain English, "We have something I do not find, I cannot find here, not anywhere. A sense of achievement made from our own strength. The sense that we did it together. The sense that no one is going to make a profit from our labor except ourselves. The sense that when Mrs. Ostrovsky in Moscow gets a gold compact a Mrs. Ostrovsky in Sverdlovsk or Komsomolsk or Erivan is going to get one too, if she has earned it."

This talk surprised me. The girl is not a Soviet official. She is not a Communist. She is the wife of an American, and she could undoubtedly stay in the United States if she wanted to do so. Maybe she will, eventually. But I had just returned from Russia, feeling that I certainly wanted to live here and not there. So it was surprising to meet a Russian with my feeling, in reverse.

Despite the chasm between our two political and economic systems, I think Russians are more like Americans in character and temperament than any other foreigners. This comparison has been frequently repeated, but it bears repetition in any discussion of future relations between our two countries. We both talk big, plan big. We live in lands of opportunity. In the United States every laborer thinks of his future as a "middle-class" future; in the U.S.R.R. every laborer looks to the day when he will study and become an engineer and get better food, housing, and other privileges. We are both multi-national countries. We are machine-minded and city-minded. The urban population of Russia more than doubled between 1931 and 1941, and in one generation 25,000,000 Soviet peasants became mechanics, welders, pilots, chauffeurs, gunners.

We are pioneer peoples. We love to explore. We are hospitable, friendly. We are self-reliant and proud and we have our own sense of humor. We are versatile, energetic, self-sacrificing—although perhaps the Russians have more experience at that. We like sports. We like to watch them, and to compete in them. We have great fondness for gadgets, for speed, for progress.

Despite the sharp difference in our economic methodology, most Americans and most Russians are united in their belief that everyone is born with the right of equal opportunity. There is much more equal opportunity in the Soviet Union than most Americans realize—and no discrimination because of race or color. Conversely Russians do not always know about the checks and balance of our system which tend to equalize opportunity—inheritance taxes, for example.

In both countries there's no kick coming when another man lives better and has more privileges and comforts—if he earns it. And nowhere else in the world have women been given so much independence as in the U.S. and the U.S.S.R.

Love of family cannot be left off the list of similarities. For the family in Russia has weathered the early Bolshevik storm, and its roots are still firm and deep among the people.

As nations we have common paths to follow. A girl reporter for Tass asked Eric Johnston one day in Omsk, "What is in common between the U.S. and the U.S.S.R.?"

"Many things," he answered. "Desire for long-term peace, improvement of living standards, further development of our own countries, no conflicting territorial interests—that is, land which one country wants from another." He added that he believed, too, that the volume of trade between us would increase after the war "undoubtedly several times."

2.

Last summer Foreign Trade Commissar Mikoyan said that Russia wished to purchase "many billions of dollars" worth of goods from the United States after the war. Stalin asked Eric

Johnston how much the Soviet Union would have to buy from us to keep our men fully employed.

The Russians cannot buy billions from us unless they get long-term credits and unless we increase our imports from them. Before the war we never bought more than 30 million dollars worth from the U.S.S.R. in any given year. The Russians believe that we can easily triple or even quadruple this figure. They hope we will make it ten or twenty times greater. They point out that they have things to sell which we need—furs, manganese, flax, tungsten, copper, chrome, platinum, wood pulp, oil, novelties and handicrafts.

The credits which Russia needs for large-scale orders that will speed her rehabilitation are for ten to twenty-five years. I have traveled 20,000 miles in the Soviet Union. I have seen what they have done, and I think the country and the people are a good, sound investment. They have proved that they can produce in war. They will do even more in peace.

Soviet purchasing agents are in America negotiating for equipment to rebuild the Donbas coal mines, the docks of the Black Sea, the grain elevators of the Ukraine. They are ordering electrical equipment, refinery machinery, radio tube manufacturing facilities, steel rails and heavy locomotives, some nonferrous metal mining machinery and crushing equipment, heavy tractors, as well as whole steel and chemical plants.

The Russians want to buy equipment to make things, not the things themselves. In the case of construction materials, they are not ordering prefabricated houses but equipment to make the houses.

A Soviet Vice-Commissar of Foreign Trade told me that his office was planning a giant exhibition in Moscow which would enable Russian citizens to see displays of the latest in American machine tools, oil drillers, bulldozers, kitchen and plumbing equipment, prefabricated houses, and the most modern plastic consumer goods.

Some observers foresee a clash between Russia and ourselves over markets. But Russia has a big enough market of its own to satisfy. In many fields their techniques are still very far behind ours—food processing and canning, pharmaceuticals, steel mill equipment and precision tools, to name just a few.

American manufacturers lose nothing, they figure, by selling complete steel or chemical or rubber plants to the Russians. By the time the Russians set them up and get them going, the United States will have new factories that will make the ones we sold outmoded. They know they are losing some of their potential market by selling a complete plant, but they are shrewd enough to compensate for part of this loss by boosting the sale price.

Stalin reiterated recently that the Soviet Union "has never engaged in the fight for foreign markets. We have a policy of exporting only those goods which have a direct bearing on imports. For instance, raw materials to pay for heavy machinery.

"Soviet production of raw materials for export to the U.S.," he asserted, "will adapt itself to what the U.S. requires. We can furnish any quantity you wish, if we can get the equipment to produce it. That is the reason we are interested in long-term credits. We can get along without them, but it will be slower."

No matter how much we import from Russia or export to them it is obvious that the Russian market will not be the panacea for our own postwar trade problems. In Moscow and in Washington I have heard five billion dollars as an optimistic estimate of our annual postwar market in Russia. This will serve as a very handy cushion for the first three to five years after the war, particularly in heavy machine tools.

The important part about our postwar trade is that we must have peace with England and Russia or our business will be 100 percent in supplying the "merchants of death." If America and the Soviet Union begin a race for military supremacy, there will be no market anywhere for anything but cannon and cannon fodder. If there is no sound peace between Russia and America, Europe will not want to rebuild. If we are making fists at Moscow, while Moscow is readying a haymaker against Washington, the Balkans won't want American credits or American engineers.

American business fondly dreams of China as a vast potential market after Japan's defeat. But even China will be a shaky investment if there are war clouds over the Kremlin and the White House.

3.

For the next generation, and perhaps much longer, the bulk of the world's military and industrial power will be possessed by two nations, the U.S.A. and the U.S.S.R. This concentration of power can lead to good or evil; it can be used to keep the peace, to build up a world-wide standard of living beyond our current dreams;

or it can lead to war, to tearing down once again everything so many have died to preserve.

I am convinced that the last thing in the world that the Russians want, any of them, is a war with the United States. I am also convinced that we can no longer afford the drawing room or editorial room pleasure of asking ourselves, "Can we get along with Russia?" or "Should we try to get along with Russia?" The hope of the world is peace. Without effective collaboration between the U.S.A. and the U.S.S.R. a peace of long duration is just another giddy word on a politician's tongue, just a monosyllable that Tin-Pan Alley rhymes with fleece.

We must and can get along with the Soviet Union.

There are plenty of things the Russians will have to learn about us before the gears grind smoothly. They are sometimes brash, sometimes too brusque, sometimes downright un-co-operative in the business of getting along or of international politics or anything else you want to call it. But we can be equally irritating to them. We have a way of reacting to their crude methods not only with disapproval but with unrestrained horror, with name calling, with dire predictions. We have got to realize that there are going to be plenty of mistakes made and that Russia is going to make her share. We can help our relations with Russia by not having a public temper tantrum every time the Soviets do something which we consider wrong. And we would like more restraint in *Pravda*, when the Russians attack us.

We are sure to have plenty of personal problems with returned soldiers who have been at war too long. Sometimes they will be over-shy and cautious, non-talkative; other times they will assert themselves out of all proportion to the occasion. The Soviets have been at war too long; they've been fighting for more than a quarter of a century against all kinds of odds, against all kinds of enemies. Gradually, I think, they are feeling their own strength, and with it a measure of security.

What's required of us as a people and a government is succinctly expressed by Sumner Welles, former Under Secretary of State, in his book *The Time for Decision*: ". . . It's no exaggeration to say that Russia's future course depends very largely on whether the U.S. can persuade the Russian people and their government that their permanent and truest interest lies in cooperating with us in the creation and maintenance of a democratic and effective world organization."

This persuasion process does not mean appeasement. It means more patience, more understanding, more thought and a more consistently aboveboard policy of our own so that Russia will know where we are heading and why. They have a right to know our policy on Franco; we knew theirs on Poland, even if we didn't like it.

I think, too, they have earned much more trust than many Americans have been prepared to give them. They have earned it on the battlefield withstanding four-fifths of the German Army; they earned it with their lives and their blood more surely than Finland ever earned it by paying regular cash installments on a debt.

Before I left Moscow I had a long talk with one of the men in the Soviet Foreign Office who knows as much about England and America and about Russia's postwar security plans as any one in Moscow. I told him that in Poland the Germans had been pushing the propaganda line that the next world war would be between the Soviet Union and the United States. The Germans claimed that the Atlantic Charter was evidence of this since it pledged to exterminate the dictatorships and the Soviet Union was admittedly a dictatorship. I asked him what he thought about this.

He smiled at me in a kindly, almost fatherly fashion. "I am not worried about *German* propaganda. But this is not a new thought. We have heard that many high-ranking American officers think the same thing and say it, off-the-record."

"Do you think this will be?"

"Not in my lifetime," he said, "and I hope not in yours."

Later in our conversation he indicated that the Soviet Union would like a twenty-five-year alliance with the United States somewhat like the ones it now has with Britain and France. At one point I asked if Russia would favor close staff co-operation and interchange of military information with the Allies after the war, and I was reminded: "We have a military pact with Great Britain. In peace we will naturally maintain our mutual security. Conferences for the interchange of information would come within that framework."

There is no easy formula for getting along with Russia. It's something that has to be worked on hard by both parties all the time, like a successful marriage. We must look beyond labels; we must re-examine old prejudices. The Russians must do the same thing.

We are going to have to put as much united effort, thought and fight into building a peace machine as we did into building a war machine. The only alternative is a certain third world war.

More than a year before he died, Wendell Willkie had a conversation about world affairs with Samuel Grafton, columnist for the New York *Post*. Grafton quoted Willkie as follows:

> I tell you that if a man is not, deep in his belly, in favor of closest possible relations with Britain and Russia, then it does not matter what else he is. Such a man will be anti-Labor, even if he praises labor twenty-four hours a day. He will be anti-Labor because he will be working for a constricted America, a less prosperous America. For the very same reason the very same man will also be anti-business, in the deepest sense, even though he may consider himself a servant of business, even though he falls on his knees before business. He will be anti-business because he will be working for a smaller America, a less important America. This is the touchstone to a man's entire position in politics today. Only occasionally does it happen that one issue arises which is so controlling that every other issue is subsidiary to it, and this is it. But it is not enough for a man merely to repeat the right words about world collaboration. He has to be on fire with it. He has to feel, in his belly, that this is the door which will open outward to an expansion of American activity and prosperity. You cannot be wrong on this issue and right on any other.

This statement, is I think, the final answer to the question in the title of this chapter, "What's in It for Us?"

In a word, *everything*.

Index

361